RIGHTFUL RELATIONS WITH DISTANT STRANGERS

This book provides a philosophical critique of legal relations between the EU and 'distant strangers' neither located within, nor citizens of, its Member States. Starting with the EU's commitment in Articles 3(5) and 21 TEU to advance democracy, human rights, and the rule of law in 'all its relations with the wider world', Ganesh examines in detail the salient EU and international legal materials and thereafter critiques them in the light of a theory of just global legal relations derived from Kant's philosophy of right. In so doing, Ganesh departs from comparable Kantian scholarship on the EU by centring the discussion not around the essay *Toward Perpetual Peace*, but around the *Doctrine of Right*, Kant's final and comprehensive statement of his general theory of law.

The book thus sheds light on areas of EU law (EU external relations law, standing to bring judicial review), public international law (jurisdiction, global public goods) and human rights (human rights jurisdiction) and also critiques the widespread identification of the EU as a Kantian federation of peace.

Volume 12 in the series Law and Practical Reason

Law and Practical Reason

The intention of this series is that it should encompass monographs and collections of essays that address the fundamental issues in legal philosophy. The foci are conceptual and normative in character, not empirical. Studies addressing the idea of law as a species of practical reason are especially welcome. Recognising that there is no occasion sharply to distinguish analytic and systematic work in the field from historico-critical research, the editors also welcome studies in the history of legal philosophy. Contributions to the series, inevitably crossing disciplinary lines, will be of interest to students and professionals in moral, political, and legal philosophy.

Recent titles in the series

Volume 6: Law and Authority under the Guise of the Good
Veronica Rodriguez-Blanco

Volume 7: Shared Authority
Dimitrios Kyritsis

Volume 8: Private Law and the Value of Choice
Emmanuel Voyiakis

Volume 9: Freedom and Force: Essays on Kant's Legal Philosophy
Edited by *Sari Kisilevsky and Martin J Stone*

Volume 10: The Nature and Value of Vagueness in the Law
Hrafn Asgeirsson

Volume 11: Law's Humility: Enlarging the Scope of Jurisprudential Disagreement
Triantafyllos Gkouvas

Volume 12: Rightful Relations with Distant Strangers: Kant, the EU, and the Wider World
Aravind Ganesh

Rightful Relations with Distant Strangers

Kant, the EU, and the Wider World

by
Aravind Ganesh

•HART•
OXFORD • LONDON • NEW YORK • NEW DELHI • SYDNEY

HART PUBLISHING

Bloomsbury Publishing Plc

Kemp House, Chawley Park, Cumnor Hill, Oxford, OX2 9PH, UK

1385 Broadway, New York, NY 10018, USA

29 Earlsfort Terrace, Dublin 2, Ireland

HART PUBLISHING, the Hart/Stag logo, BLOOMSBURY and the Diana logo are trademarks of Bloomsbury Publishing Plc

First published in Great Britain 2021

A catalogue record for this book is available from the British Library.

Library of Congress Cataloging-in-Publication data

Names: Ganesh, Aravind R., author.

Title: Rightful relations with distant strangers : Kant, the EU, and the wider world / by Aravind Ganesh.

Description: Oxford, UK ; New York, NY : Hart Publishing, an imprint of Bloomsbury Publishing, 2021. | Series: Law and practical reason ; volume 12 | Includes bibliographical references and index.

Identifiers: LCCN 2020051771 (print) | LCCN 2020051772 (ebook) | ISBN 9781509941315 (hardback) | ISBN 9781509946754 (paperback) | ISBN 9781509941339 (pdf) | ISBN 9781509941322 (Epub)

Subjects: LCSH: European Union countries—Foreign relations—Law and legislation. | International law—European Union countries—Philosophy. | Law—European Union countries—Philosophy.

Classification: LCC KJE5105 .G36 2021 (print) | LCC KJE5105 (ebook) | DDC 341.242/2—dc23

LC record available at https://lccn.loc.gov/2020051771

LC ebook record available at https://lccn.loc.gov/2020051772

ISBN: HB: 978-1-50994-131-5
ePDF: 978-1-50994-133-9
ePub: 978-1-50994-132-2

Typeset by Compuscript Ltd, Shannon

Acknowledgements

As I type these words from an overgrown garden on a clear summer evening in plague-stricken Oxford, it dawns upon me that this book belongs everywhere and nowhere. Although it has been with me in some form or another for over a decade, its most recognisable ancestor was a doctoral thesis that began in Geneva, took shape in Tel Aviv, was written primarily in Luxembourg, and defended at the VU Amsterdam Faculty of Law in June 2019. And so, I owe my first debt of gratitude to Ester Herlin-Karnell, my supervisor. To have had the opportunity to pursue a doctorate was itself an incredible luxury, but to have been able to do it under the conscientious guidance (which continues even today) of the person who inspired it, is to be blessed indeed. The next is owed to Geoffrey Gordon, my second reader, who stuck with me despite having no obligation to do so. His comments and insights were as helpful as they were incisive, and vastly improved my text and thoughts.

The research for this book was possible only because of a position as a research fellow at the Max Planck Institute Luxembourg for Procedural Law. As director of the Institute and my departmental head, Hélène Ruiz Fabri was unstintingly supportive, as well as patient with early attempts to express my ideas. The Institute was an incredibly stimulating setting for my doctoral research, and afforded me such an unexpected quantum of independence that not once did I experience the stress and worry that commonly afflicts doctoral students. I am immensely grateful to Hélène, to the Max Planck Luxembourg, and to my colleagues who – in addition to their salient virtues as legal scholars, librarians, editors, administrators and canines – were truly excellent company. In particular, I thank Henok Asmelash, Ivan Cavdarević, Michel Erpelding, Alessandra Donati, Flint, Edouard Fromageau, Stephanie Law, Allan Molundo, Parvathi Menon, Janek Nowak, André Nuñes Chaïb, Dalia Palombo, Nathalie Perrin, Derek Stemple, Edoardo Stoppioni, Arlyne Vandeventer and Alain Zamaria. Thanks also to Lucie Casadei, Heleen De Geest, Alexandra Piletić, Julia Sauter, Luc Schiltz, the Siry tribe, Lisa Urban and the Bouneweger Stuff – all sources of much-needed inspiration.

Next, I am grateful to Eyal Benvenisti, without whose intellectual and practical support this book project would not have gotten off the ground. The seven months I spent in Tel Aviv at his invitation with the support of the GlobalTrust Research Project were unforgettable for many, many reasons. As such, I would like to thank him, the Buchmann Faculty of Law, Tel Aviv University, my fellow participants on the 'Sovereigns as Trustees of Humanity' seminar (Natalie Davidson, Sergio Dellavalle, Miriam Feinberg, Olga Frishman, Benoît Mayer, Natalie Oman, Mikko Rajavuori, Surabhi Ranganathan, Rebecca Schmidt,

Sivan Shlomo Agon, Mirjam Streng and Lorenzo Zucca), as well as my Tel Aviv friends Natalie Ashuel, Gaya Cohen, Ben Cooke and Emanuela Hernandéz. I should in particular like to remember Jason Hoth, who told me of an evening that he would like to read this book when it was finished. Whether this was said sincerely or out of politeness is, alas, a question to which I will now never know the answer. Crucially, thanks are due to Ayelet Banai, who, when told that I was interested in Kant, gave me the singularly useful advice to read the work of someone called Arthur Ripstein.

This brings us to Arthur, whose first correspondence with me was an out-of-office reply stating that my email had been filed for future reading, but that if the matter was urgent I really ought to speak to someone other than a philosopher. Mere moments afterwards, I received a gracious email sharing with me the draft manuscripts I had requested. I am indebted to him for introducing me to Kant's philosophy of right, and for coming to Amsterdam four years later to examine my thesis. Speaking of my examiners, I am grateful to Alice Pinheiro Walla, Enzo Rossi, Cedric Ryngaert, Wouter Veraart, as well as to Mattias Kumm and Peter Niesen, who submitted additional reports as part of the process for awarding the '*cum laude*' distinction. Their comments, insights and encouragement, given both in their reports and subsequently, were of invaluable help in turning the PhD thesis into a manuscript. Lastly, I thank Jamuna Ganesh and Harald Zitzlaff for their moral support, as well as David Vrijlandt and Eva Lani for stepping in at the last minute to act as ceremonial assistants – 'paranymphs' – at my defence. In their orisons be all my sins remembered.

I currently occupy the position of Vice-Chancellor's Research Fellow at Oxford Brookes University. I am deeply grateful to Lucy Vickers for her assistance with the publication process, as well as to my colleagues at the Oxford Brookes School of Law. Thanks are also due to George Pavlakos, Kate Whetter, Rosemarie Mearns and Victoria Broom, as well as to the anonymous reviewers whose advice I have endeavoured to incorporate. Earlier versions of some of the arguments of this book appeared in 'The European Union's Human Rights Obligations Towards Distant Strangers' (2016) 37 *Michigan Journal of International Law* 475; 'Unilateral Jurisdiction to Provide Global Public Goods: A Republican Account' (2017) 42 *Brooklyn Journal of International Law* 571; and 'Distant Strangers and Standing in *Polisario*' in Hélène Ruiz Fabri (ed), *International Law and Litigation* (Baden-Baden, Nomos, 2019). While they have been extensively rewritten, I am grateful for permission to use these materials in this book.

Finally, there are my parents Latha and Ratnam, my brother Bharath, and my grandmothers Padma (who passed away before this book could see light) and Saraswati. These I could never thank enough, even if I were to devote several lifetimes to the task.

AG
Oxford, November 2020

Table of Contents

Acknowledgements .... *v*
List of Abbreviations .... *xi*
Table of Cases .... *xiii*
Table of International Treaties and Instruments .... *xxv*
Table of Legislation and Official Documents .... *xxxi*

1. Introduction 1
I. Force, Freedom and Formality: Kant's Philosophy of Right 3
II. Methodology: Immanent Critique and Private Law Analogies 13
III. Outline of the Book 17
IV. Conclusion 21

2. Territorial Extension: Power and Authority in the Wider World 22
I. The Post-Lisbon Articles 23
A. Between Multilateralism and Evangelism 25
II. Bartels and the 'Compliance' Interpretation 28
A. Human Rights Jurisdiction 31
B. Jurisdiction under General International Law 34
C. Standing 36
III. Legal Effects and the Spatial Scope of EU Law 36
A. Defending *Air Transport*: Emerging Explanations and Forgotten Precedents 39
B. *Fluctuat nec mergitur*: The *Lotus* Case in CJEU Jurisprudence 41
IV. Power and Authority: A Subtle Difference 44
A. The Nature of Territorial Extension 46
V. Conclusion 52

3. The 'Missionary' Principle: A False Start 53
I. The Sovereign Trusteeship of Humanity 56
II. Harms and Wrongs 63
A. Public Actors and Human Rights Jurisdiction 65
B. The Failure of the Argument from Well-Being 67
III. Blurred Frontiers: Values and Constitutional Objectives 69
A. Policy Consistency/Coherence in the Light of EU Constitutional Objectives 69
B. The Missionary Principle and Territorial Extension 72
IV. Conclusion: Dignity as Independence 77

4. Kant's International Legal Order and the Forms of Private Law 82
I. Private Right: The Building Blocks of Kant's General Theory of Law 83
A. The Division of Torts: Damage and Injury 86
B. The Three Defects in the State of Nature 91
C. Legislating on Property and Personality 96
II. Public Right: The Fiduciary State 97
A. The Separate, Public Person of the State 97
B. Human Rights and the Fiduciary State 100
III. International Law: Property and Personality 103
A. Territory: Property or Body? 105
B. No Property, Only Personality 109
IV. Conclusion 114

5. Extraterritorial Jurisdiction to Provide Global Public Goods 121
I. Ripstein's Roads 122
A. Expanding the Concept: Other Public Goods 128
B. Limitations upon the Right to Provide Public Goods 131
II. Global Public Goods 132
A. The Right to Regulate Global Public Goods 132
B. The Irrelevance of Harm 139
C. Public Purpose and Necessity 144
III. Appraising the EU 146
IV. Conclusion 152

6. Extraterritorial Human Rights Obligations 154
I. Human Rights as Public Fiduciary Rights 156
A. 'Moral' Theories of Human Rights Law 156
B. Human Rights as Legal and Directed all the Way Down 160
C. Human Rights as Rights and as Philanthropy 166
II. Authority and Human Rights Jurisdiction 167
A. Capability 169
B. Control 175
C. Arendt's Loophole 182
III. Territorial Extension and Human Rights Jurisdiction 185
IV. Conclusion 188

7. Closing the Courthouse Door: The Standing of Distant Strangers 190
I. Standing in EU Law 192
A. The Requirement of Legal Effects 193
B. Direct and Individual Concern under Article 263 TFEU 195
II. The EU-Morocco Agreements: Trustees *de son tort* of Humanity 198

III. *Polisario* and *Western Sahara Campaign* 206
A. Case T-512/12 *Front Polisario v Council* – The General Court Decision 207
B. Case C-104/16 *Council v Front Polisario* – Before the ECJ 211
C. Case C-266/16 *Western Sahara Campaign* – The Preliminary Reference 216
IV. Conclusion 221

8. General Conclusion 224
I. Are the EU's Unilateral Assertions of Authority over Distant Strangers Defensible? 224
II. Does the EU Owe Obligations towards Distant Strangers over whom it Claims Authority? 226
III. If So, does the EU Fulfil them? 227

Bibliography *230*
Index *245*

List of Abbreviations

ARS	Articles on the Responsibility of States
ARIO	Articles on the Responsibility of International Organizations
CJEU	Court of Justice of the European Union
CLJ	Cambridge Law Journal
CML Rev	Common Market Law Review
D	Digest of Justinian
DR	Doctrine of Right
ECHR	European Convention on Human Rights
EU	European Union
G	Institutes of Gaius
GATT	General Agreement on Tariffs and Trade
ICCPR	International Covenant on Civil and Political Rights
ICESCR	International Covenant on Economic, Social and Cultural Rights
ILC	International Law Commission
J	Institutes of Justinian
LQR	Law Quarterly Reports
MLR	Modern Law Review
OJLS	Oxford Journal of Legal Studies
PP	Toward Perpetual Peace
PPM	Process and Production Method
RGDIP	Revue générale de droit international public
TEC	Treaty on the European Communities
TEU	Treaty on European Union

TFEU	Treaty on the Functioning of the European Union
UDHR	Universal Declaration of Human Rights
UK	United Kingdom
UN	United Nations
UNCLOS	United Nations Convention on the Law of the Sea
US	United States
VCLT	Vienna Convention on the Law of Treaties
WTO	World Trade Organization

Table of Cases

Arbitrations

Iron Rhine Arbitration (Belgium v Netherlands) (2005)
XXVII RIAA 35 .... 62, 137

Island of Palmas Arbitration (or Miangas) (US v Netherlands)
(1928) II (1949) RIAA 829 .... 58, 107

Lake Lanoux Arbitration, (France v Spain) (1957) XII
(1963) RIAA 281 .... 62, 137–38

Rainbow Warrior (New Zealand v France) (1990) XX RIAA 217 113

Trail Smelter Arbitration (US v Canada) (1941) 3 RIAA 1905 .... 33, 54, 139, 140

European Court of Human Rights

Al-Saadoon and Mufdhi v United Kingdom, Admissibility
App no 61498/08; (2009) 49 EHRR SE 95 185

Al-Skeini and ors v United Kingdom, Merits and just satisfaction [2011] ECHR 1093; (2011) 53 EHRR 18 ....66, 169–70, 182–85

Banković and ors v Belgium and ors, Admissibility
ECHR 2001-XII; [2001] ECHR 890 .... 32–33, 66, 169, 176–77, 184, 186–88

Behrami and Behrami v France, Saramati v France, Germany and Norway, Admissibility App no 71412/01; App no 78166/01; (2007) 45 EHRR SE 10 179

Ben El Mahi v Denmark, Admissibility App no 5853/06;
2006 ECHR XV (11 December 2006) 185–87

Bosphorus Hava Yolları Turizm ve Ticaret Anonim Şirketi v Ireland, Admissibility App no 45036/98 (30 June 2005) 151

Catan v Moldova and Russian Federation, Merits and just satisfaction [2012] ECHR 1827; (2013) 57 EHRR 4 .... 177, 180–82

Fadeyeva v Russian Federation, Merits and just satisfaction
[2005] ECHR 376; (2007) 45 EHRR 10 130

von Hannover v Germany, Association of German Magazine Publishers (intervening) and Hubert Burda Media GmbH & Company KG (intervening), Merits ECHR 2004-VI;
[2004] ECHR 294 185

Hassan v United Kingdom, Merits [2014] ECHR 1162 183

Ilaşcu and ors and Romania (intervening) v Moldova and Russian Federation, Admissibility ECHR 2004-VII; [2004] ECHR 318 179–82
Ireland v United Kingdom, Merits and just satisfaction A/25; [1978] ECHR 1 164
Isaak v Turkey, Admissibility App no 4458798 (28 September 2006) 170, 177
Issa and ors v Turkey, Merits [2004] ECHR 629; (2004) 41 EHRR 567 170
Jaloud v Netherlands, Merits and just satisfaction [2014] ECHR 1292 .... 177–79, 183
Kovačić and ors v Slovenia, Admissibility App no 4457498, App no 4513398, App no 4831699 (9 October 2003) 185–87
Kovačić and ors v Slovenia, Struck out of the List App no 4457498, App no 4513398, App no 4831699 (6 November 2006) 187
Lawless v Ireland (No 3) A/3; [1961] ECHR 2; (1961) 1 EHRR 15 101
Loizidou and Cyprus (intervening) v Turkey, Merits ECHR 1996-VI; [1996] ECHR 70 33
López Ostra v Spain, Merits and just satisfaction A/303-C; [1994] ECHR 46; (1995) 20 EHRR 277 130
Medvedyev and ors v France, Merits and just satisfaction [2010] ECHR 384; (2010) 51 EHRR 39 185
Öcalan v Turkey, Merits and just satisfaction ECHR 2005-IV; (2005) 41 EHRR 45 185
Pad and ors v Turkey, Admissibility App no 60167/00 (28 June 2007) 170, 177
Tătar and Tătar v Romania, Merits and just satisfaction App no 67021/01 (27 January 2009) 130
White v Sweden, Merits [2006] ECHR 793; (2008) 46 EHRR 3 185

European Union

European Court of Justice

Joined Cases 89/85, 104/85, 114/85, 116/85, 117/85 & 125/85 to 129/85 *Ahlström Osakeyhtiö and others v Commission (Wood Pulp I)* [1988] ECR 5193 49–50
Case C-366/10 *Air Transport Association of America and ors v Secretary of State for Energy and Climate Change* [2011] ECR I-13755 .... 28, 53, 221
C-617/10 *Åklagaren v Åkerberg Fransson* ECLI:EU:C:2013:105 (26 February 2013) 155
Case 26/62 *NV Algemene Transport- en Expeditie Onderneming van Gend & Loos v Nederlandse administratie der belastingen* [1963] ECR 1 .... 56, 117

Case C-286/90 *Anklagemyndigheden v Poulsen and Diva Navigation* [1992] ECR I-06019..........39
Case C-214/94 *Boukhalfa v Germany* [1996] ECR I-2253..........50
Case C-309/89 *Codorníu SA v Council* [1994] ECR I-1853..........196
Case 22/70 *Commission v Council (ERTA)* [1971] ECR 273..........23, 116, 193
Case C-25/94 *Commission v Council (FAO)* [1996] ECR I-1469..........75
Case C-459/03 *Commission v Ireland* [2006] ECR I-4635..........151
Case C-258/89 *Commission v Spain* [1991] ECR I-3977..........75
Case C-246/07 *Commission v Sweden (PFOS)* ECLI:EU:C:2010:203 (20 April 2010)..........71
Case C-6/04 *Commission v UK* [2005] ECR I-1111..........75
Case 6/64 *Costa v ENEL* [1964] ECR 585..........116–17
Case C-104/16 P *Council v Front Polisario* ECLI:EU:C:2016:973 (21 December 2016)..........191, 200, 212–14, 227
Case 34/86 *Council v Parliament* [1986] ECR 2155..........194
Case C-166/07 *Council v Parliament (International Fund for Ireland)* [2009] ECR I-7135..........69
Case C-112/80 *Dürbeck* [1981] ECR 1095..........69
Case C-405/92 *Etablissements Armand Mondiet SA v Armement Islais SARL* [1993] ECR I-6133..........75
Joined Cases C 464/13 and C 465/13 *Europäische Schule München v Oberto and O'Leary* ECLI:EU:C:2015:163 (11 March 2015)..........213
Case C-592/14 *European Federation for Cosmetic Ingredients v Secretary of State for Business, Innovation and Skills* ECLI:EU:C:2016:703 (21 September 2016)..........40
Case 6/72 *Europemballage and Continental Can v Commission* [1973] ECR 215..........69
Case 8/55 *Fédération Charbonnière de Belgique v High Authority* [1954] ECR 292..........23
Case C-386/08 *Firma Brita GmbH v Hauptzollamt Hamburg-Hafen* [2010] ECR I-1289..........199
Case C-482/18 *Google Ireland Limited v Nemzeti Adó-és Vámhivatal Kiemelt Adó-és Vámigazgatósága* ECLI:EU:C:2020:141 (3 March 2020)..........44
Case 135/81 *Groupement des Agences de voyages v Commission* [1982] ECR 3800..........209
Case 60/81 *IBM v Commission* [1981] ECR 2639..........193
Case C-413/14 *Intel v Commission* ECLI:EU:C:2017:632 (6 September 2017)..........49
Case C-583/11 *Inuit Tapiriit Kanatami v Parliament and Council* ECLI:EU:C:2013:625 (3 October 2013)..........193, 197–98
Joined Cases C-402/05, C-415/05 *Kadi v Council and Commission* [2008] ECR I-6351..........30, 214

Case C-571/10 *Kamberaj v Istituto per l'Edilizia sociale della Provincia autonoma di Bolzano* ECLI:EU:C:2012:233 (26 April 2012)....................155
Case 15/63 *Lassalle v Parliament* [1963] ECR 50..209
Case C-137/00 *Milk Marque and National Farmers' Union* [2003] ECR I-7975 69–70
Joined Cases 3,4 and 6/76 *Officier van Justitie v Kramer* [1976] ECR 1279...75
Opinion 2/94 [1996] ECR I...149
Opinion 2/13 ECLI:EU:C:2014:2454 (18 December 2014) 149–51, 155
Case C-263/14 *Parliament v Council* ECLI:EU:C:2016:435 (14 June 2016)...30
Case 294/83 *Parti écologiste 'Les Verts' v Parliament* [1986] ECR 1339...196
Joined Cases C-78/16, C-79/16 *Pesce and Others* ECLI:EU:C:2016:428 (9 June 2016)..124, 132
Case C-72/15 *PJSC Rosneft Oil Company v Her Majesty's Treasury*, ECLI:EU:C:2017:236 (28 March 2017)..194
Case 25/62 *Plaumann v Commission* [1963] ECR 95 .... 196, 198, 209–10
Case C-268/94 *Portugal v Council* [1996] ECR I....................................69, 167
Case C-347/10 *Salemink* ECLI:EU:C:2012:17 (17 January 2012) 73
Case C-101/12 *Schaible v Land Baden-Württemberg* ECLI:EU:C:2013:661 (17 October 2013) 132
Case 18/74 *Syndicat Général du Personnel des Organismes européens v Commission* [1974] ECR 933..209
Case C-50/00 *Unión de Pequeños Agricultores v Council* [2002] ECR I-6681 197
Case 175/73 *Union syndicale-Amalgamated European Public Service Union and others v Council* [1974] ECR 917 209
Case C-266/16 *Western Sahara Campaign UK, The Queen v Commissioners for Her Majesty's Revenue and Customs, Secretary of State for Environment, Food and Rural Affairs* ECLI:EU:C:2018:118 (27 February 2018) 191, 218–19, 227
Case C-424/13 *Zuchtvieh-Export GmbH v Stadt Kempten* ECLI:EU:C:2015:259 (23 April 2015)...40

General Court

Case T-212/02 *Commune de Champagne v Council* [2007] ECR II-2023 .... 36–37, 49–50, 167, 187–88, 198–202, 221
Case T-694/14 *European Renewable Energies Federation (EREF) v Commission* ECLI:EU:T:2015:915 (23 November 2015)........... 196
Case T-512/12 *Front Polisario v Council* ECLI:EU:T:2015:953 (10 December 2015) 72, 166, 191, 207–11

Case T-180/14 *Front Polisario v Council (Polisario II)* ECLI:EU:T:2018:496 (19 July 2018) 192, 219–20, 222
Case T-102/96 *Gencor v Lonrho* [1999] ECR II-753 49
Case T-286/09 *Intel v Commission* ECLI:EU:T:2014:547 (12 June 2014) 49
Case T-18/10 *Inuit Tapiriit Kanatami v Parliament and Council* [2011] ECR II-05599 197
Case T-177/01 *Jégo-Quéré v Commission* [2002] ECR II-2365 197
Case T-85/09 *Kadi v European Commission* [2010] ECR II-5177 30
Case T-253/04 *Kongra-Gel v Council* [2008] ECR II-46..................................36
Case T-262/10 *Microban v Commission* [2011] ECR II-7697 196
Case T-229/02 *PKK v Council* [2008] ECR II-45 ....36, 209
Joined Cases T-108/07, T-354/08 *Spira v Commission* ECLI:EU:T:2013:367 (11 January 2013) 36

Opinions of Advocates General (AG)

Case 89/85, 104/85, 114/85, 116/85, 117/85 and 125/85 to 129/85 *Ahlström Osakeyhtiö and others v Commission (Wood Pulp)* ECLI:EU:C:1988:258 (25 May 1988), Opinion of AG Darmon 43
Case C-366/10 *Air Transport Association of America and ors v Secretary of State for Energy and Climate Change* ECLI:EU:C:2011:637 (6 October 2011), Opinion of AG Kokott.....29, 37, 42
Case C-73/08 *Bressol and Chaverot v Gouvernement de la Communauté française* [2010] ECR I-2735, Opinion of AG Sharpston..2
Case C-491/01 *British American Tobacco (Investments) Ltd and Imperial Tobacco* [2002] ECR I-11461, Opinion of AG Geelhoed.. 197
Case C-104/16 P *Council v Front Polisario* ECLI:EU:C:2016:677 (13 September 2016), Opinion of AG Wathelet 191, 200, 213
Case C-358/89 *Extramet v Council (Admissibility)* [1991] ECR I-2507, Opinion of AG Jacobs 197
Case C-482/18 *Google Ireland Limited v Nemzeti Adó-és Vámhivatal Kiemelt Adó-és Vámigazgatósága* ECLI:EU:C:2019:728 (12 September 2019), Opinion of AG Kokott 43
Case C-583/11 *Inuit Tapiriit Kanatami v Parliament and Council* ECLI:EU:C:2013:21 (17 January 2013), Opinion of AG Kokott 194, 196–98
Opinion 2/15 (EU-Singapore FTA) ECLI:EU:C:2016:992 (21 December 2016), Opinion of AG Sharpston 167

Case C-130/10 *Parliament v Council* ECLI:EU:C:2012:50 (31 January 2012), Opinion of Advocate General Bot 29
Case C-658/11 *Parliament v Council (Somali Pirates)* ECLI:EU:C:2014:41 (30 January 2014), Opinion of AG Bot 29
Case C-268/94 *Portugal v Council* [1996] ECR I, Opinion of AG La Pergola 167
Case C-347/10 *Salemink* ECLI:EU:C:2011:562 (8 September 2011), Opinion of AG Cruz Villalón 74
Case C-507/13 *UK v Parliament and Council* ECLI:EU:C:2014:2394 (20 November 2014), Opinion of AG Jääskinen, ... 43
Case C-50/00 *Unión de Pequeños Agricultores v Council* [2002] ECR I-6681, Opinion of AG Jacobs 197
Case C-266/16 *Western Sahara Campaign UK, The Queen v Commissioners for Her Majesty's Revenue and Customs, Secretary of State for Environment, Food and Rural Affairs* ECLI:EU:C:2018:1 (10 January 2018), Opinion of AG Wathelet 148, 191, 216–18

Other Materials

Case C-507/13 *United Kingdom v Parliament and Council* (20 September 2013), Application of United Kingdom 43

Inter-American Court of Human Rights

Case of the Pueblo Bello Massacre v Colombia, del Carmen Álvarez Blanco and ors v Colombia, Merits, reparations and costs [2006] IHRL 1524 180
Judicial Guarantees in States of Emergency (Arts 27(2), 25 and 8 American Convention on Human Rights) IACHR Series A No 9; IHRR 3443 (IACHR 1987) 102

International Court of Justice

Decisions

Application of the Convention on the Prevention and Punishment of the Crime of Genocide (Bosnia and Herzegovina v Serbia and Montenegro) (Judgment) [2007] ICJ Rep 43... 202
Armed Activities on the Territory of the Congo (Democratic Republic of the Congo v Uganda) (Merits) [2005] ICJ Rep 168............................ 204
Arrest Warrant of 11 April 2000 (Democratic Republic of Congo v Belgium) (Judgment, merits, preliminary objections) [2002] ICJ Rep 35 42

Barcelona Traction, Light and Power Co Ltd (Belgium v Spain) (Judgment, merits, second phase) [1970] ICJ Rep 3 54
Certain Activities carried out by Nicaragua in the Border Area; Construction of a Road in Costa Rica along the San Juan River (Costa Rica v Nicaragua) (Judgment) [2015] ICJ Rep 665 141
Corfu Channel (UK v Albania) (Judgment) [1949] ICJ Rep 4 .... 33, 54, 139
Dispute Regarding Navigational and Related Rights (Costa Rica v Nicaragua) (Merits) [2009] ICJ Rep 213 .... 62, 137–38
Frontier Dispute (Burkina Faso v Mali) (Merits) [1986] ICJ Rep 554 107–09
Military and Paramilitary Activities in and Against Nicaragua (Nicaragua v United States) (Merits) [1986] ICJ Rep 14 .... 35, 48, 67
Pulp Mills on the River Uruguay (Argentina v Uruguay) (Judgment) [2010] ICJ Rep 14 .... 140, 142
Right of Passage over Indian Territory (Portugal v India) (Judgment, merits) [1960] ICJ Rep 6 .... 62, 137
Sovereignty over Pedra Branca/Pulau Batu Puteh, Middle Rocks and South Ledge (Malaysia v Singapore) (Judgment, merits) [2008] ICJ Rep 12 107

Advisory Opinions

Legal Consequences of the Construction of a Wall in the Occupied Palestinian Territory (Advisory Opinion) [2004] ICJ Rep 136 (9th July 2004) 34
Legal Consequences for States of the Continued Presence of South Africa in Namibia (South West Africa) (Advisory Opinion) [1971] ICJ Rep 16 .... 33, 206
Legality of the Threat or Use of Nuclear Weapons (Advisory Opinion) [1996] ICJ Rep 226 .... 139, 162
Reparation for Injuries Suffered in the Service of the United Nations (Advisory Opinion) [1949] ICJ Rep 174 115
Western Sahara (Advisory Opinion) [1975] ICJ Rep 12 .... 190, 206

Other Materials

'Application Instituting Proceedings, Timor-Leste v Australia (17 December 2013)' (2013), www.icj-cij.org/files/case-related/156/17962.pdf 111
'Articles on Responsibility of States for Internationally Wrongful Acts, Adopted by the Commission at Its Fifty-Third Session in 2001' (International Law Commission 2001) UN Doc A/56/10, 43, UN Doc A/RES/56/83, Annex, UN Doc A/CN.4/L.602/Rev.1, GAOR 56th Session Supp 10, 43 .... 32, 113, 201–02
'Counter-Memorial of Australia, Timor-Leste v Australia (28 July 2014)' (2014), www.icj-cij.org/files/case-related/156/18702.pdf 112

'Timor-Leste v Australia, Verbatim Record (20 January 2014, 10:00 AM)' (2014), www.icj-cij.org/files/case-related/156/156-20140120-ORA-01-00-BI.pdf 111
'Timor-Leste v Australia, Verbatim Record (21 January 2014, 10:00 AM)' (2014), www.icj-cij.org/files/case-related/156/156-20140121-ORA-01-00-BI.pdf 112

International Criminal Tribunal for the Former Yugoslavia

Krajina, Prosecutor v Brđanin (Radoslav) (Judgment) ICTY-99-36-T, [2004] ICL 121 (1 September 2004) 164
Prijedor, Prosecutor v Tadić (Duško) aka 'Dule' (Decision on the Defence motion for interlocutory appeal on jurisdiction) ICTY-94-1-AR72, (1996) ILM 32 (2 October 1995) 58
Tuta and Štela, Prosecutor v Naletilić (Mladen) and Martinović (Vinko) (Trial judgment) [2003] ICTY-98-34-T (31 March 2003) 204

International Tribunal for the Law of the Sea

Responsibilities and Obligations of States Sponsoring Persons and Entities with Respect to Activities in the Area (Advisory Opinion of 1 February 2011) ITLOS Reports 2011, 10 142

Permanent Court of International Justice

The Case of SS Lotus, France v Turkey, Judgment, Judgment No 9 [1927] PCIJ (series A) No 10 (7 September 1927) 41, 56

World Trade Organization

Appellate Body

United States – Import Prohibition of Certain Shrimp and Shrimp Products (12 October 1998) WT/DS58/AB/R, Doc No 98-3899; DSR 1998:VII, 2755 .... 46–47, 49–51

Panel

United States – Measures Affecting Alcoholic and Malt Beverages (7 February 1992) Doc DS23/R-39S/206 47

United States – Restrictions on the Imports of Tuna (not adopted) (16 Aug 1991) Doc DS21/R 47
United States – Restrictions on the Imports of Tuna (not adopted) (20 May 1994) Doc DS29/R 47
United States – Standards for Reformulated and Conventional Gasoline (20 May 1996) WT/DS2/AB/R, Doc No 96-1597; DSR 1996:I, 3 47
United States – Taxes on Automobiles (not adopted) (30 September 1994) Doc DS31/R 47

UN Committee on Economic, Social and Cultural Rights

'General Comment No 12: The Right to Adequate Food (Art 11)' (1999) UN Doc E/C 12/1999/5 ..... 31, 164
'General Comment No 14: The Right to the Highest Attainable Standard of Health (Art 12)' (2000) UN Doc E/C 12/2000/4 31
'General Comment No 15: The Right to Water (Arts 11 and 12)' (2002) UN Doc E/C 12/2002/11 32
'Maastricht Guidelines on Violations of Economic, Social and Cultural Rights' (1998) 20 Human Rights Quarterly 691; (2000) UN Doc E/C.12/2000/13 171

UN Human Rights Committee

Celiberti de Casariego v Uruguay (1981) Communication No 56/1979; UN Doc CCPR/C/13/D/56/1979; UN Doc CCPR/C/OP/1, 92 170
'General Comment No 31: The Nature of the General Legal Obligation Imposed on States Parties to the Covenant' (2004) UN Doc CCPR/C/21/Rev.1/Add.13 170
Lichtensztejn v Uruguay (Merits) (1983) UN Doc CCPR/C/18/D/77/1980 170
López Burgos v Uruguay (1981) UN Doc CCPR/C/13/D/52/1979; UN Doc A3640, Annex XIX 170

Australia

Farah Constructions Pty Ltd v Say-Dee Pty Ltd [2007] HCA 22 (High Court) 202
H Jones & Co Pty Ltd v Kingborough Corporation (1950) 82 CLR 282 (High Court) 128
The Age Co Ltd v Elliott (2006) 14 VR 375 (Court of Appeal, Victoria) 143
Uren v John Fairfax & Sons Pty Ltd (1966) 117 CLR 118 (High Court) 143

Canada

Air Canada v M & L Travel Ltd (1993) 3 SCR 787 (Supreme Court) 202
Frame v Smith (1987) 2 SCR 99 (Supreme Court) 86
Hill v Church of Scientology of Toronto (1995) 2 SCR 1130 (Supreme Court) 143
Malette v Shulman (1990) 72 2d 417 (Court of Appeal, Ontario) 64
Norberg v Wynrib (1992) 1992 SCR 2 (Supreme Court) 86

Egypt

President of the Republic et al v Ali Ayyoub et al [2017] Supreme Administrative Court of Egypt Judgment, on appeal No 74236/62 J S 108

France

Baget c Rosenweigh (1833) I Sirey 458 (Cassation, Chambre Réunies) 114

Germany

Gauweiler v Federal Parliament and Federal Government, Final judgment [2009] Constitutional Court (FRG) 2 BvE 2/08,2 BvE 5/08, 2 BvR 1010/08, 2 BvR 1022/08, 2 BvR 1259/08, 2 BvR 182/09, 123 BVerfGE 267 59

Israel

Public Committee against Torture in Israel v The Government of Israel (Targeted Killings) [2005] HCJ 769/02 (Supreme Court of Israel, sitting as the High Court of Justice) 66

Italy

Arafat and Salah, Re (1988) 7 Ital YB Intl L 295 (Italy, Supreme Court of Cassation, 1st Criminal Section) 208

South Africa

Khumalo v Holomisa (2002) (5) SA 401 (Constitutional Court) 143
Mostert Snr and another v State (2010) 2 SA 482
(Supreme Court of Appeal) 127–28
Van Niekerk & Union Government (Minister of Lands) v Carter
(1917) 359 AD (Supreme Court of Appeal) 126

United Kingdom

England

A and others v Secretary of State for the Home Department; X and another v Secretary of State for the Home Department
[2004] UKHL 56 (HL) 101
Al-Skeini and ors, R (on the application of) v Secretary of State for Defence [2005] EWCA (Civ) 1609 (CA) 171
Anonymous decision (1535) fo 27 YB Mich 27 Hen VIII 125
Ashby v White (1703) 87 Eng Rep 808 (KB) 114
Ashby v White (1703) 91 Eng Rep 665 (HL) 114
Barnes v Addy (1874) 9 LR Ch App 244 (CA) 201
Belt v Lawes [1882] LJ QB 359 (CA) 143
Coggs v Bernard (1703) 2 Ld Raym 909; 92 ER 107 (KB) 86
Dubai Aluminium Company Ltd v Salaam [2002] UKHL 48 (HL) 202
Dudley v Dudley (1705) 24 ER 118 (Ch) 61
Earl of Oxford's Case (1615) 21 ER 485 (Ch) 61
Entick v Carrington (1765) 19 St Tr 1030; 95 ER 807 (KB) 63
Entick v Carrington (1765) 19 Howell's St Tr 1029 (KB) 89
Horwood v Millar's Timber and Trading Co Ltd (1917) 1 KB 305 (CA) 123
Hunter v Canary Wharf Ltd [1997] UKHL 14 (1997) 1 AC 655 (HL) 130
Iveson v Moore (1699) 91 ER 486 (KB) 125
Jameel v The Wall Street Journal Europe Sprl [2006]
UKHL 44 (2007) 1 AC 359 (HL) 143
Khorasandjian v Bush [1993] QB 727 (CA) 130
Lepre v Lepre (1963) 2 WLR 735 38
Mara v Browne [1896] 1 Ch 199 (CA) 203
Merest v Harvey (1814) 5 Taunt 442, 128 ER 761 (Common Pleas) 88
Ministry of Defence v Ashman (1993) 25 HLR 514 (CA) 88
R v Bentham [2005] UKHL 18 (HL) 90
R (on the application of Middleton) v West Somerset Coroner
[2004] UKHL 10 (HL) 160
Rose v Miles (1815) 105 ER 773 (KB) 125

Royal Brunei Airlines v Tan [1995] UKPC 4 (Privy Council) 202
Tate & Lyle Industries Ltd v Greater London Council [1983] 2 AC 509 (HL) 125
Taylor v Whitehead (1781) 99 ER 475 (KB) 124

Scotland

Magistrates of Linlithgow v Elphinstone (1768) 3 Kames Decisions 331 (SC) 128

United States

Federal Decisions

El Shifa Pharmaceutical Industries Company and Idris v United States 378 F3d 1346 (Fed Cir 2004) 66
Lochner v New York 198 US 45 (1905) 93
Massachusetts v Mellon 262 US 447 (1923) 68
Morrison v National Australia Bank 561 US 247 (2010) 39
The Apollon 22 US (9 Wheat) 362 (1824) 75
United States v Aluminum Co of America 148 F2d 416 (2d Cir 1945) 35
Van Brocklin v Tennessee 117 US 151 (1886) 110
Wedding v Mayler 192 US 573 (1904) 51
Woodson v North Carolina 428 US 280 (1976) 165

State Decisions

City of Chicago v American Cyanamid Co 823 NE 2d 126 (IL 2005) 125
City of Milwaukee v State 193 Wis 423 (WI 1927) 127
Curran v Bosze 566 NE2d 1319 (IL 1990) 64
Edwards v Lee's Administrator 96 SW 2d 1028; 265 Ky 418 (KY 1936) 88
McFall v Shimp 10 Pa C 3d 90 (PA 1978) 64
State v Lead Industries Association 951 A2d 428 (RI 1936) 125

Table of International Treaties and Instruments

Bilateral Treaties and Instruments

Euro-Mediterranean Agreement establishing an association agreement between the European Communities and their Member States, of the one part, and the Kingdom of Morocco, of the other part (EU-Morocco) [1996] OJ L70/2 191

Agreement on Scientific and Technological Cooperation, of 4 April 2002 on the conclusion of Seven Agreements with the Swiss Confederation in the sectors free movement of persons, air and land transport, public procurement, scientific and technological cooperation, mutual recognition in relation to conformity assessment, and trade in agricultural products (EU-Switzerland) [2002] OJ L114/132 199

Fisheries Partnership Agreement between the European Communities and the Kingdom of Morocco (EU-Morocco) [2006] OJ L141/4 191

Preamble 221

Article 2(a) 192, 216, 218

Article 2(a) 192, 216, 218

Article 3 216

Article 6 216

Article 11 .... 192, 218

Air Transport Agreement between the European Community and the United States of America [2007] OJ L134/4 ('Open Skies' Agreement) 48

Article 11 48

Protocol between the European Union and the Kingdom of Morocco setting out the fishing opportunities and financial contribution provided for in the Fisheries Partnership Agreement between the European Union and the Kingdom of Morocco [2013] OJ L328/2 191

EU Treaties and Instruments

Schuman Declaration (1980) 13 Bull EC 14 (9 May 1950) 3, 26

Treaty establishing the European Economic Community (Treaty of Rome) (adopted 25 March 1957, entered into force 1 January 1958) 298 UNTS 11
Article 230 .... 195–96, 199
Article 288 194
Article 292 151
Article 299 .... 36, 50, 199
Consolidated Treaty on European Union (Treaty of Maastricht) (1992) [2006] OJ C321E/5 50
Charter of Fundamental Rights of the European Union [2000] OJ C364/1 124
Article 17(1) 124
Treaty of Nice amending the Treaty on European Union, the Treaties establishing the European Communities and certain related acts (adopted 26 February 2001, entered into force 1 February 2003) [2001] OJ C80/1 50
Declaration on the Future of the European Union (Laeken Declaration) (2001) 12 EU Bull 19 (15 December 2001) 25
Draft Treaty Establishing a Constitution for Europe [2004] OJ C310/401
Article I-3(4) 25
Article III-365(4) 195
Treaty of Lisbon amending the Treaty on European Union and the Treaty establishing the European Community (adopted 13 December 2007, entered into force 1 December 2009) [2007] OJ C306/1 26
Treaty on European Union (as amended by the Treaty of Lisbon) (adopted 9 May 2008, entered into force 1 December 2009) [2008] OJ C115/13, [2012] OJ C326/1 22
Article 1(3) 71
Article 2 27
Article 3(5) .... i, 23, 25, 27, 30, 39, 43, 52, 55, 69, 118–19, 166, 206, 210, 216–18, 221–24, 227
Article 4(3) 70–71
Article 6 210
Article 6(1) 155
Article 6(2) 149
Article 6(3) 155
Article 11(3) 70
Article 21 .... 24, 27, 29, 166, 210
Article 21(1) 24, 27, 29–30, 218
Article 21(2) 24, 29–30
Article 21(2)(a) 55

Article 21(2)(b) 29–30, 159, 218
Article 21(3) 18, 24–25, 29–30, 69–71
Article 23 .... 29–30, 218
Article 24(1) 149
Article 40 149
Article 47 .... 71, 116
Article 335 116
Treaty on the Functioning of the European Union (adopted 13 December 2007, entered into force 1 December 2009) [2008] OJ C115/47, [2010] OJ C83/47, [2012] OJ C326/47 22
Article 7 .... 70, 72
Article 67 210
Article 191 25
Article 191(2) 38, 131
Article 205 .... 25, 210, 218
Article 207 .... 25, 65
Article 208 .... 25, 65
Article 208(1) 65, 70
Article 263 .... 36, 193–198, 206, 221–222, 227
Article 263(2) 193
Article 263(4) 198, 208, 220
Article 267 .... 192–195, 222, 227
Article 275 149
Article 277 .... 194, 198
Article 289 197
Article 289(1) 197
Article 340 194
Article 349 70
Article 355 .... 36, 50, 56, 199

UN Instruments

UNGA Res 2131 (XX): Declaration on the Inadmissibility of Intervention in the Domestic Affairs of States and the Protection of their Independence and Sovereignty (1965) UN Doc A/RES/2131(XX) 34
UNGA Res 2229 (XXI) on the question of Ifni and Spanish Sahara (1966) UN Doc A/RES/2229(XXI) 206
UNGA Res 2625 (XXV): Declaration on Principles of International Law concerning Friendly Relations and Cooperation among States in accordance with the Charter of the United Nations (1970) UN Doc A/RES/2625(XXV) 34

UNGA Res 3452 (XXX): Declaration on the Protection of All Persons from being Subjected to Torture and Other Cruel, Inhuman or Degrading Treatment or Punishment (1975) UN Doc A/RES/3452(XXX) 164
Article 1 164
UNGA Res 34/37 on the Question of Western Sahara (1979) UN Doc A/RES/34/37 207
Article 5 207
Article 7 207
UNGA Res 35/19 on the Question of Western Sahara (1980) UN Doc A/RES/35/19 207
Article 3 207
Report of the Secretary General, 'Report of 1 February 2016, Information from Non-Self-Governing Territories Transmitted under Art 73 (e) of the Charter of the United Nations' (2016) UN Doc A/71/68, annex 207

Other Materials

Corell H, 'Letter Dated 29 January 2002 from the Under-Secretary-General for Legal Affairs, the Legal Counsel, Addressed to the President of the Security Council' 204

International Law Commission

ILC, United Nations Yearbook of the International Law Commission 2 (2000) 113
ILC, Articles on Prevention of Transboundary Harm from Hazardous Activities: Text adopted by the Commission at its fifty-third session, in 2001 (Final Outcome) (2001) UN Doc A/56/10, 370 139–140
Article 3 140
ILC, Articles on Responsibility of States for Internationally Wrongful Acts, Adopted by the Commission at Its Fifty-Third Session in 2001 (2001) UN Doc A/56/10, 43 .... 32, 113, 201
Article 14 201
Article 16 .... 32, 201–02
Article 17 32
Article 18 32
Article 31(2) 113
ILC, Articles on the Responsibility of International Organizations, Adopted by the Drafting Committee in 2011 (Final Outcome) (2011) UN Doc A/CN.4/L.778 201
Article 14 .... 32, 201
Article 15 32
Article 16 32

Multilateral Treaties and Instruments

Hague (IV) Regulations respecting the Laws and Customs of War on Land (adopted 18 October 1907, entered into force 26 January 1910) 205 CTS 277 204
Article 42.......... 204, 208
Article 43.......... 204
Article 55.......... 218
Universal Declaration of Human Rights 1948 (adopted 10 December 1948) UNGA Res 217 A(III) (UDHR).......... 58, 65–66, 184
Article 29.......... 161
Convention for the Protection of Human Rights and Fundamental Freedoms (adopted 4 November 1950, entered into force 3 September 1953) 213 UNTS 222 (ECHR).......... 20, 31, 149–51, 155, 175, 180, 226
Article 1 .... 32, 66, 167, 168–69, 177, 184, 186
Article 8 130
International Covenant on Civil and Political Rights (adopted 16 December 1966, entered into force 23 March 1976) 999 UNTS 171 (ICCPR).......... 2, 170
International Covenant on Economic, Social and Cultural Rights (adopted 16 December 1966, entered into force 3 January 1976) 993 UNTS 3, CTS 1976/46, S Exec Doc D, 95-2 (1978), GAOR 21st Session Supp 16, 49, UN Doc A/6316, UN Doc A/RES/21/2200.......... 2, 34–35
Vienna Convention on the Law of Treaties (adopted 23 may 1969, entered into force 27 January 1980) 1155 UNTS 331 199
Article 29.......... 214
Article 31.......... 213
Article 34.......... 199
Article 38.......... 199
Article 53.......... 148
Stockholm Declaration of the United Nations Conference on the Human Environment (adopted 16 June 1972) UN Doc A/CONF48/14/Rev1, 3, UN Doc A/CONF48/PC/6.......... 139–40
Principle 21 139
Agreement Governing the Activities of States on the Moon and Other Celestial Bodies (adopted 5 December 1979, entered into force 11 July 1984) 1363 UNTS 3 1979.......... 111
Article 5(1) 111
Article 5(2) 111
Convention on the Law of the Sea (adopted 10 December 1982, entered into force 16 November 1994) 1833 UNTS 3 111
Annex III, Article 1 111

Framework Convention on Climate Change (adopted 9 May 1992, entered into force 21 March 1994) 1771 UNTS 107 54
Preamble 54
Rio Declaration on Environment and Development (adopted 14 June 1992) UN Doc A/CONF151/5/Rev1; UN Doc A/CONF151/26/Rev1 Vol1, Annex I 139
Principle 2 139
Agreement relating to the implementation of Part XI of the United Nations Convention on the Law of the Sea of 10 December 1982 (adopted 28 July 1994, entered into force 16 November 1994, 28 July 1996) 1836 UNTS 3 111
Annex 111
Kyoto Protocol to the United Nations Framework Convention on Climate Change (adopted 11 December 1997, entered into force 16 February 2005) 2303 UNTS 162 27
Article 12 27
Convention on Jurisdictional Immunities of States and their Property (adopted 2 December 2004, entered into force 17 January 2005) UN Doc A/RES/59/38, Annex, UN Doc 111
Article 1 111

Table of Legislation and Official Documents

Canada

Standing Senate Committee on Human Rights, 'Promises to Keep – Implementing Canada's Human Rights Obligations' (Senate, Parliament of Canada, 2001), https://sencanada.ca/content/sen/committee/371/huma/rep/rep02dec01-e.htm 32

European Union

Council Regulation 3094/86/EEC of 7 October 1986 laying down certain technical measures for the conservation of fishery resources [1986] OJ L288/1 39
Council Directive 92/43/EEC on the conservation of natural habitats and of wild fauna and flora [1992] OJ L206/7 75
Euratom, Council and Commission Decision 2002/309/EC as regards the Agreement on Scientific and Technological Cooperation, of 4 April 2002 on the conclusion of seven Agreements with the Swiss Confederation [2002] OJ L114/1 199
Parliament and Council Regulation 1726/2003/EC amending Regulation 417/2002/EC on the accelerated phasing-in of double-hull or equivalent design requirements for single-hull oil tankers [2003] OJ L249/1 60
Parliament and Council Directive 2003/87/EC of 13 October 2003 establishing a scheme for greenhouse gas emission allowance trading within the Community and amending Council Directive 96/61/EC [2003] OJ L275/32 ....145, 221, 225
Article 16(3) 49, 68
Article 16(5)–(12) 49
Council Regulation 764/2006/EC of 22 May 2006 on the conclusion of the Fisheries Partnership Agreement between the European Community and the Kingdom of Morocco Fisheries Partnership Agreement between the European Communities and the Kingdom of Morocco [2006] OJ L141/1
Recital 1 216

Parliament and Council Directive 2008/101/EC of 19 November 2008 amending Directive 2003/87/EC so as to include aviation activities in the scheme for greenhouse gas emission allowance trading within the Community [2009] OJ L8/3 .... 28, 37, 39–40, 46, 49, 51, 55, 68
Parliament and Council Regulation 391/2009/EC of 23 April 2009 on common rules and standards for ship inspection and survey organisations [2009] OJ L131/11 48
Parliament and Council Regulation 1223/2009/EC of 30 November 2009 on cosmetic products (recast) [2009] OJ L342/59 40
Council Decision 2012/497/EU of 8 March 2012 on the conclusion of an Agreement in the form of an Exchange of Letters between the European Union and the Kingdom of Morocco concerning reciprocal liberalisation measures on agricultural products, processed agricultural products, fish and fishery products, the replacement of Protocols 1, 2 and 3 and their Annexes and amendments to the Euro-Mediterranean Agreement establishing an association between the European Communities and their Member States, of the one part, and the Kingdom of Morocco, of the other part [2012] OJ L241/2 191
Parliament and Council Directive 2013/36/EU of 26 June 2013 on access to the activity of credit institutions and the prudential supervision of credit institutions and investment firms, amending Directive 2002/87/EC and repealing Directives 2006/48/EC and 2006/49/EC Text with EEA relevance [2013] OJ L176/338 43
Council Decision 2013/785/EU of 16 December 2013 on the conclusion, on behalf of the European Union, of the Protocol between the European Union and the Kingdom of Morocco setting out the fishing opportunities and financial contribution provided for in the Fisheries Partnership Agreement between the European Union and the Kingdom of Morocco [2013] OJ L349/1 220
Commission Implementing Decision 2015/789/EU of 18 May 2015, as regards measures to prevent the introduction into and the spread within the Union of Xylella fastidiosa [2015] OJ L125/36 124
Parliament and Council Regulation 2016/679/EU of 27 April 2016 on the protection of natural persons with regard to the processing of personal data and on the free movement of such data, and repealing Directive 95/46/EC [2016] OJ L119/1 148

Other Materials

Rules of Procedure of the Court of First Instance of the European Communities [1991] OJ L136/1
Rule 44(5) 208

Secretariat of the European Convention, 'Final Report of the Discussion Circle on the Court of Justice of 25 March 2003' (2003) CONV 636/03 198
Secretariat of the European Convention, 'Cover Note from the Praesidium to the Convention of 12 May 2003' (2003) CONV 734/03 198
Commission and High Representative of the European Union for Foreign Affairs and Security Policy, 'Communication on Human Rights and Democracy at the Heart of EU External Action – Towards a More Effective Approach' (2011) COM (2011) 886 final 30
Commission, Proposal for a Regulation of the European Parliament and of the Council amending Directive 2003/87/EC to continue current limitations of scope for aviation activities and to prepare to implement a global market-based measure from 2021 (2017) COM(2017) 54 final 53

France

French Civil Code
Section 1382 114
Section 1383 114

Germany

German Civil Code
Section 249(1) 89
Section 906 130

Roman Law

D. 4.9.1 pr – 1 (Ulpian 14, *On the Edict*) 86
D. 9.2.13.8 (Ulpian 18, *On the Edict*) 90
D.43.13.1.2–3 (Ulpian 68,*On the Edict*) 126
D.9.2.49.1 (Ulpian 9, *Disputations*) 124
D. 47.10.1.2 (Ulpian 56, *On the Edict*) 86
G.1.8 84
J. Inst. 1.2.12 84

Singapore

Transboundary Haze Pollution Act 2014
Sections 4–8 53
Section 8(2) 144

Other Materials

Parliament Deb Vol. 94, Sess. 1, Sitting No. 30, (Jan 9, 2017) 2017 112

Spain

'Letter Dated 26 February 1976 from the Permanent Representative of Spain to the UN Secretary-General' 207

United States

Public Law 101–162 (codified at 16 USC 1537) (21 November 1989)
Section 609 46

Other Materials

Restatement (Second) of Torts (1979)
Section 821B, cmt g 125
Restatement (Third) of Foreign Relations Law of the United States (1987)
Section 403(2)(c) 35
Section403(2)(g) 35
Section 403(2)(h) 35

Other Materials

US Department of Justice, Office of Legal Counsel, 'Memorandum for Alberto R Gonzales Regarding Standards of Conduct for Interrogation under 18 USC §§ 2340–2340A' (2002), www.justice.gov/sites/default/files/olc/legacy/2010/08/05/memo-gonzales-aug2002.pdf 164

1

Introduction

THIS BOOK OUTLINES a theory of rightful relations with distant strangers; that is to say, of morally defensible legal relations between a political community and persons who are not its members. Rather than develop it in the abstract, it does so by reference to an existing body of positive law concerning legal relations between the European Union on the one hand, and persons who are neither citizens of its Member States nor located in their territories on the other. Thus, while the philosophical inspiration behind this book lies in the legal and political writings of Immanuel Kant, the germ of the legal discussion lies in several articles scattered about in the constitutive documents of the European Union that commit the EU to advance certain objectives in all its 'relations with the wider world'. Broadly, these objectives comprise: (1) the advancement of human rights, democracy, and the rule of international law; and (2) the provision of a range of policy goals, often grouped under the rubric of 'global public goods'.

A survey of the law arising from these provisions reveals that they have often been pressed into service to consolidate and provide new grounding for the EU's long tradition of asserting jurisdiction over distant strangers – that is, 'extraterritorially' – in numerous regulatory fields. This gives rise to three linked questions:

(1) Are such unilateral assertions of authority over distant strangers defensible?
(2) Does the EU then owe any obligations towards the distant strangers for whom it purports to make law?
(3) If so, does it fulfil them?

To illustrate the kinds of questions examined here, consider the following scenario of an imaginary 'merger application':

> *Two supermarket chains operating in the EU seek to combine. The Commission, as the competent regulator, determines that the merger will not have any negative effects upon consumer welfare within the EU – for instance, by increasing prices or reducing product choice – such as would ordinarily justify a regulative intervention under EU competition law.*
>
> *However, it also finds that the merger will very likely result in the creation of an entity with monopsony or 'buyer' power over downstream markets for coffee, tea, and other commodities, all of which are produced in developing countries. This post-merger monopsony power may be so considerable as to undermine the ability*

> *of the foreign farmers producing those commodities to earn enough income, and consequently to afford adequate housing, food, healthcare and education for their children.*[1]
>
> *Ruritania is one of the developing countries whose farmers are likely to be affected in this way. Despite the deleterious effects upon its farmers, however, the Ruritanian Government nevertheless champions the merger, because it espouses a general economic policy of substituting agricultural production with heavy industry. The Ruritanian merger authority has already approved the merger. Ruritania is not a party to any human rights treaties, nor does it recognise protections for such rights in its domestic law.*

Commission officials tasked with deciding on this merger application face a simple and stark choice: to approve the merger 'as is', or to regulate it. A moment's thought reveals that this is a *legal* question admitting no room for 'policy discretion'. Any decision to regulate the merger, even to impose a single pre-condition, must see off administrative challenges on the part of the supermarkets and, equally importantly, a claim of a right on the part of Ruritania to administer its economy as its sees fit. Conversely, any decision to approve the merger must overcome a claim of potential obligations owed to Ruritanian farmers concerning rights to housing, food and education. Such claims may arise, say, under the International Covenant on Economic, Social, and Cultural Rights (ICESCR), an instrument which, for reasons that need not detain us, bears some constitutional significance within the EU legal order.[2] But, if Ruritanian farmers could invoke that instrument against the EU to challenge the merger, might they not similarly challenge the practice of awarding subsidies to European farmers under the Common Agricultural Policy, which, by all appearances, undercuts their income and drives them into poverty far more systematically?

Answers to these questions cannot be supplied merely by examining EU legal and policy materials, the technical rules of EU competition law, or other highly specific directives and regulations. They also implicate human rights law and public international law, because the Commission's decision as to whether or

[1] The hypothetical is not as far-fetched as one might imagine. For discussions of the very real phenomenon of global agribusiness concentration, see *World Development Report 2008: Agriculture for Development* (Washington, World Bank, 2007) 135–37; O De Schutter, 'UN Special Rapporteur on the Right to Food, Addressing Concentration in Food Supply Chains: The Role of Competition Law in Tackling the Abuse of Buyer Power' Briefing Note 3 (31 December 2010), www.srfood.org/images/stories/pdf/otherdocuments/20101201_briefing-note-03_en.pdf; ME Stucke, 'Looking at the Monopsony in the Mirror' (2012) 62 *Emory Law Journal* 1509; T Feunteun, 'Cartels and the Right to Food: An Analysis of States' Duties and Options' (2015) 18 *Journal of International Economic Law* 341.

[2] See Case C-73/08 *Bressol and Chaverot v Gouvernement de la Communauté française* ECLI:EU:C:2009:396, Opinion of AG Sharpston, para 136:

> The Court has held that the International Covenant on Civil and Political Rights (ICCPR) is one of the international instruments for the protection of human rights of which it takes account in applying the general principles of Community law. It seems to me that the same should hold good for the ICESCR which, like the ICCPR, binds each individual Member State.

not to approve the merger must draw from and be assessed against both the law on the extraterritorial application of human rights obligations and of general jurisdiction under international law. As we shall see, however, these areas are themselves by no means settled but are in fact arenas of heated controversy. As such, the questions examined in this book lie at the cutting edge not just of EU law, but also of human rights law and international law. Accordingly, despite the apparent granularity of the issues raised by the hypothetical merger, this book cannot be limited to an analysis of positive law, or even to an account of the rationalities behind the EU's exercises of power and influence,[3] although these are no doubt crucial stops along the way. Instead, my goal in this book is by necessity far more abstract and normative: it is to provide a critique of the EU's legal relations with the wider world in the light of a normative theory of global justice.

I. FORCE, FREEDOM AND FORMALITY: KANT'S PHILOSOPHY OF RIGHT

In this connection, a name that comes naturally to mind is that of Immanuel Kant. The widespread notion of the EU as 'some kind of Kantian cosmopolitan construction'[4] is related to its origin myth of having been founded as a peace project by six European nations seeking to end not just regular internecine war between them, but for the sake of world peace generally. For this reason more than any other, the EU has often been theorised in light of the essay *Toward Perpetual Peace: A Philosophical Sketch* (1795), in which Kant proposes a model treaty setting up a 'pacific league' of European political communities for the purpose of maintaining a stable peace between them, which in the fullness of time comes to envelop the entire world.[5] Something of this programme is reflected in the Schuman Declaration – the EU's equivalent of the American Declaration of Independence – which declaims that 'World peace cannot be safeguarded without the making of creative efforts proportionate to the dangers which threaten it. The contribution which an organised and living Europe can bring to civilisation is indispensable to the maintenance of peaceful relations.'

[3] See, eg, J Lawrence, *Governmentality in EU External Trade and Environment Policy: Between Rights and Market* (Abingdon, Routledge, 2018); A Bradford, *The Brussels Effect: How the European Union Rules the World* (New York, Oxford University Press, 2020).

[4] D Harvey, *Cosmopolitanism and the Geographies of Freedom* (New York, Columbia University Press, 2009) 83. Harvey cites Beck and Habermas as the primary sources of this impression. See also GW Brown, 'The European Union and Kant's Idea of Cosmopolitan Right: Why the EU Is Not Cosmopolitan' (2014) 20 *European Journal of International Relations* 671, 672.

[5] I Kant, 'Toward Perpetual Peace' [hereinafter '*PP*'] in MJ Gregor (ed & tr), *Practical Philosophy: The Cambridge Edition of the Works of Immanuel Kant*, 9th edn (Cambridge, Cambridge University Press, 2006) 327 (8:356).

Instances of this general idea often appear in popular discourse. For instance, in a 2012 newspaper column the popular science author Steven Pinker observed, in between musings about vegetarianism and extreme sportsmen, that the decision to award the Nobel Peace Prize to the EU was entirely appropriate because its basic tenets of 'democracy, free trade and an international community should discourage leaders from dragging their countries into war'; a 'rationale' Pinker believes 'came right out of Immanuel Kant's 1795 essay "Perpetual Peace" …'.[6] Another example is the notorious essay by Robert Kagan written following the declaration of the second Gulf War, in which he surmised that while the United States remained 'mired in history, exercising power in the anarchic Hobbesian world where international laws and rules are unreliable and where true security and the defence and promotion of a liberal order still depend on the possession and use of military might',[7] Europeans had instead deceived themselves into believing that they had 'stepped out of the Hobbesian world of anarchy into the Kantian world of perpetual peace …'.[8]

There is, of course, a considerable amount of serious academic scholarship exploring Kantian themes concerning the EU, of which perhaps the most prominent voice is Jürgen Habermas.[9] However, that literature has largely focussed upon problems of cultural and political integration 'internal' to the EU. Moreover, with a few recent exceptions,[10] it has tended to revolve primarily around the *Perpetual Peace*, with occasional references to other of Kant's shorter essays. Third, where the literature deals with the EU's 'external' relations with the wider world, it has tended to proceed from Kant's ethical theory to identify the broad 'norms', 'values' or 'virtues' the EU ought to manifest in its foreign relations.[11]

This book differs from the above literature in all the enumerated respects. First and foremost, it is not primarily concerned with matters 'internal' to the European Union. This is not to say that such questions will not intrude upon

[6] S Pinker, 'This Week's Big Questions: The End of Men, Vegetarianism and Is Felix Baumgartner a Showoff?' *The Independent* (19 October 2012), www.independent.co.uk/voices/comment/this-weeks-big-questions-the-end-of-men-vegetarianism-and-is-baumgartner-a-show-off-8218849.html.

[7] R Kagan, *Of Paradise and Power: America and Europe in the New World Order* (New York, Alfred A Knopf, 2003) 3.

[8] *Ibid* 57.

[9] See, eg, J Habermas, 'Kant's Idea of Perpetual Peace: With the Benefit of 200 Years' Hindsight' in C Cronin and P De Greiff (eds & trs), *The Inclusion of the Other: Studies in Political Theory* (Cambridge-Malden, Polity Press, 1998); J Habermas, 'The Crisis of the European Union in Light of a Constitutionalization of International Law: An Essay on the Constitution for Europe' in C Cronin (tr), *The Crisis of the European Union: A Response* (Cambridge-Malden, Polity Press, 2012).

[10] See P Eleftheriadis, *A Union of Peoples* (Oxford, Oxford University Press, 2020).

[11] See, eg, I Manners, 'Normative Power Europe: A Contradiction in Terms?' (2002) 40 *Journal of Common Market Studies* 235; I Manners, 'The Constitutive Nature of Values, Images and Principles in the European Union' in S Lucarelli and I Manners (eds), *Values and Principles in European Union Foreign Policy* (Abingdon, Routledge, 2006); and the collection of essays discussing the EU's 'constitutional virtues' in Part III of J Dickson and P Eleftheriadis (eds), *Philosophical Foundations of European Union Law* (Oxford, Oxford University Press, 2012).

the discussion from time to time. As and when this happens, however, they do so as matters of secondary importance. Second, my main source of inspiration is not the *Perpetual Peace*, which by no means expressed Kant's final thoughts about law, but the *Metaphysical First Principles of the Doctrine of Right*, which constitutes the first part of Kant's final statement on practical philosophy – the *Metaphysics of Morals* (1797). The second part of the *Metaphysics of Morals* is made up of the *Metaphysical First Principles of the Doctrine of Virtue*, which deals with ethics. The focus upon the *Perpetual Peace* at the expense of the *Doctrine of Right* is understandable, given that the latter was largely ignored even by professional Kant scholars until relatively recently, for reasons ranging from the impenetrability of Kant's language and conceptual apparatus,[12] the likelihood that mistakes occurred in the publishing process making it appear unsystematic and badly organised,[13] to the charge that the text dates from a stage of Kant's life marred by the 'decrease of his mental faculties, which finally led into senile imbecility …'.[14] The traditional attitude of wholesale neglect and dismissal was perhaps most notoriously expressed by Hannah Arendt, who remarked that:

> As far as the *Doctrine of Right* (or of Law) is concerned – which you will find only in the book edited by Reiss and which, if you read it, you will probably find rather boring and pedantic – it is difficult not to agree with Schopenhauer, who said about it: 'It is as if it were not the work of this great man, but the product of an ordinary common man [*gewöhnlicher Erdensohn*].' … if we want to study the philosophy of law in general, we certainly shall not turn to Kant but to Pufendorff or Grotius or Montesquieu.[15]

Over the past two decades, however, the *Doctrine of Right* has witnessed a tremendous resurgence in interest due to the work of scholars such as Katrin Flikschuh, Sharon Byrd and Joachim Hruschka,[16] but most significantly as the result of the Canadian legal philosopher Arthur Ripstein's ground-breaking explication of that text.[17] One of my aims, then, is to bring to bear Ripstein's

[12] Kant's most popular English translator in the 20th century once remarked of the *Doctrine of Right* that 'Kant has never been accused of underestimating his readers, but he seldom treats them so harshly'. M Gregor, 'Kant's Theory of Property' (1988) 41 *Review of Metaphysics* 757, 787.

[13] B Ludwig, '"The Right of a State" in Immanuel Kant's Doctrine of Right' (1990) 28 *Journal of the History of Philosophy* 403, 403–409.

[14] H Arendt, *Lectures on Kant's Political Philosophy* (Chicago, University of Chicago Press, 1982) 9.

[15] *Ibid* 7–8. The excised part of the passage represented by the ellipses reads 'The concept of law is of great importance in Kant's practical philosophy, where man is understood as a legislative being …'

[16] For representative works, see K Flikschuh, *Kant and Modern Political Philosophy* (Cambridge, Cambridge University Press, 2000); and BS Byrd and J Hruschka, *Kant's Doctrine of Right: A Commentary* (Cambridge, Cambridge University Press, 2012).

[17] A Ripstein, *Force and Freedom: Kant's Legal and Political Philosophy* (Cambridge, Harvard University Press 2009).

'rediscovery' of the *Doctrine of Right* to EU legal and political discourse.[18] In doing so, I treat Kant as if he were a contemporary commentator on current affairs, rather than as an interesting figure in the history of philosophy.

Thirdly, and most significantly, I do not treat legal relations as functions, applications or explications of 'deeper' moral or ethical values. Perhaps the most important result of the rediscovery of the *Doctrine of Right* has been the articulation of a normative legal philosophy which, although firmly grounded in the tradition of natural rights, nevertheless recognises such a thoroughgoing separation between law and ultimate moral ends, that a debate exists as to whether it might in fact constitute a variant of legal positivism.[19] To be sure, on the commonly held definition of legal positivism as the view that 'what is law and what is not is a matter of social fact',[20] Kant is no positivist. He mocks such views in the *Doctrine of Right*: after likening them to 'the wooden head in Phaedrus's fable', Kant declares that an 'empirical' theory of this sort 'may be beautiful but unfortunately it has no brain'.[21] Nevertheless, Kant's general theory of law bears two of the hallmarks normally associated with legal positivism: namely, that law must be 'posited' by authority, and that there is an 'adamantine'[22] barrier between law and ethics.

These statements may come as a surprise to non-specialist readers, whose image of Kant's legal philosophy likely involves a sort of a 'teleological application'[23] of the basic moral principle known as the Categorical Imperative. Examples of this impression may be found in John Rawls, who argued that 'Kant's account of the Categorical Imperative applies to the personal maxims of sincere and conscientious individuals in everyday life', and that Kant thus 'proceeds from the particular, even personal case of everyday life; he assumed that this process carried out correctly would eventually yield a coherent and sufficiently complete system of principles, including principles of social justice'.[24]

[18] Pavlos Eleftheriadis and Richard Bellamy have been trailblazers in this field. See P Eleftheriadis, 'The Moral Distinctiveness of the European Union' (2011) 9 *International Journal of Constitutional Law* 695; R Bellamy, 'A European Republic of Sovereign States: Sovereignty, Republicanism and the European Union' (2017) 16 *European Journal of Political Theory* 188.

[19] See J Waldron, 'Kant's Legal Positivism' (1996) 109 *Harvard Law Review* 1535. Waldron characterises Kant as a positivist on the basis of Kant's exhortation that rights are impossible without political institutions entitled to make and enforce law. For critiques of Waldron, see MJ Stone, 'Kant's Apparent Positivism' in S Kisilevsky and MJ Stone (eds), *Freedom and Force: Essays on Kant's Legal Philosophy* (Oxford, Hart Publishing, 2017); R Alexy, 'Kant's Non-Positivistic Concept of Law' (2019) 24 *Kantian Review* 497.

[20] J Raz, 'Legal Positivism and the Sources of Law' in *The Authority of Law* (Oxford, Oxford University Press, 1979) 38.

[21] I Kant, 'The Doctrine of Right' [hereinafter '*DR*'] in MJ Gregor (ed & tr), *Practical Philosophy: The Cambridge Edition of the Works of Immanuel Kant*, 9th edn (Cambridge, Cambridge University Press, 2006) 6:380, 387.

[22] EJ Weinrib, 'Poverty and Property in Kant's System of Rights' (2002) 78 *Notre Dame Law Review* 795, 799.

[23] Ripstein (n 17) 11–13.

[24] J Rawls, 'Kantian Constructivism in Moral Theory' (1980) 77 *Journal of Philosophy* 515, 552–53.

The same thought is expressed differently by Habermas, who, in contrast to Rawls's expansionary imagery, states that Kant

> starts with the basic concept of the moral law and obtains juridical laws from it by way of *limitation* .... This construction is guided by the Platonic intuition that the legal order imitates the nominal order of a 'kingdom of ends' and at the same time embodies it in the phenomenal world.[25]

While these themes of expansion and limitation have their place, such conceptions of Kantian legal philosophy can be better described as having more in common with 'Neo-Kantianism', so named because its proponents purport to derive political philosophy straight out of the *Groundwork of the Metaphysics of Morals* (1785).[26] These are of course worthy of attention in their own right, but they bear little resemblance to Kant's actual philosophy of right,[27] which designates central roles for the concepts of property and force, both of which are incapable of being grounded upon or derived from the Categorical Imperative. Moreover, while Kant designates the Categorical Imperative (defined as 'Autonomy of the Will') as the 'supreme principle of morality' in the *Groundwork*,[28] the *Doctrine of Right* is instead organised around a different idea of the 'Universal Principle of Right', which holds that 'Any action is *right* if it can coexist with everyone's freedom in accordance with a universal law, or if on its maxim the freedom of choice of each can coexist with everyone's freedom in accordance with a universal law.'[29] Although both of these principles use the language of universalisation, a crucial difference lies in the thing being universalised. While the Categorical Imperative is concerned with 'Autonomy of the *Will*', the Universal Principle of Right is concerned instead with 'choice' (*Willkür*) – a broader notion that 'can indeed be *affected* but not *determined* by impulses and is therefore of itself ... not pure but can still be determined to actions by pure will'.[30] Importantly, the Universal Principle of Right is described as a 'postulate that is incapable of further proof';[31] that is to say, it is incapable of being derived from the Categorical Imperative.

[25] J Habermas, William Rehg (tr), *Between Facts and Norms: Contributions to a Discourse Theory of Law and Democracy* (Cambridge, MIT Press 1996) 105–106.

[26] Paul Anselm Feuerbach, an early exponent of the school, effectively pre-empted Kant during his lifetime by publishing a philosophy of law a year before the *DR* came out in print. PJA von Feuerbach, *Kritik des natürlichen Rechts als Propädeutik zu einer Wissenschaft der natürlichen Recht* (Altona, Verlagsgesellschaft, 1796).

[27] Kant scholars prefer this usage to 'philosophy of law' first because it resembles the title Kant chose, and second because it is appropriately ambiguous as to the connotations of law, 'right' as correctness, and 'right' as entitlement encompassed by the German *Recht*.

[28] I Kant, *Kant: Groundwork of the Metaphysics of Morals*, MJ Gregor (ed & tr) (Cambridge, Cambridge University Press, 1998) 47 (4:440).

[29] *DR* 6:230, 387.

[30] *DR* 6:213, 375. See also Habermas (n 25) 105; TW Pogge, 'Is Kant's *Rechtslehre* a Comprehensive Liberalism?' in M Timmons (ed), *Kant's Metaphysics of Morals: Interpretative Essays* (Oxford, Oxford University Press, 2002) 137 (describing an individual's choice as a 'domain of her control').

[31] *DR* 6:231, 388.

Such considerations have led some to argue that Kant's philosophy of 'right' can form no part of his general moral philosophy, such that the validity of the former is independent of and to be developed entirely without reference to the latter.[32] This, however, contradicts numerous statements insisting on an ineliminable connection between the two domains in the Introduction to the *Metaphysics of Morals*, such as those where Kant defines laws of morality in contradistinction to scientific laws as comprising both juridical laws and ethical laws,[33] or when he speaks of an ethical duty to comply with the law out of respect for it alone such that all duties of right 'indirectly' become duties of virtue.[34] Even more obviously, the philosophy of right is not just included in the *Metaphysics of Morals*; it makes up the very *first* part.[35] Accordingly, if Kant's philosophy of right is no mere 'application' or 'derivation' of the Categorical Imperative, neither can it be entirely unconnected to it.

The key to grasping the distinction between juridical and ethical lawgiving lies in drawing a deeper distinction between the 'internal' and 'external' dimensions of an action:

> As directed merely to external actions and their conformity to law they are called *juridical* laws; but if they also require that they (the laws) themselves be the determining grounds of actions, they are *ethical* laws, and then one says that conformity with juridical laws is the *legality* of an action and conformity with ethical laws is its *morality*.[36]

Internal motivations are central in assessing whether a particular act is 'all-things-considered' good. Acts do not fulfil the Categorical Imperative unless they are done purely for the sake of the substantive moral end: a shopkeeper fulfils no duties of virtue if he refrains from cheating his customers only because he believes dishonesty will prove unprofitable in the long run. His honesty would remain morally worthless even if he was moved out of an entirely creditable desire to avoid feelings of shame arising from behaving dishonestly. This is because the only motivation that counts towards the fulfilment of a duty of virtue, is the sense of moral duty in itself. The dignity of an autonomous will lies entirely in self-legislation; it is not a 'value' that can be promoted or curtailed by anything as empirical or contingent as external compulsion.[37] This, however, means that a system of laws 'applying' the Categorical Imperative – by coercing, inducing, or otherwise 'nudging' individuals into acting in accordance

[32] Pogge (n 30) 153–58; M Willaschek, 'Why the *Doctrine of Right* Does Not Belong in the *Metaphysics of Morals*: On Some Basic Distinctions in Kant's Moral Philosophy' (1997) 5 *Jahrbuch für Recht und Ethik* 205.

[33] *DR* 6:214, 375–76.

[34] *DR* 6:221, 385.

[35] Ripstein (n 17) 356.

[36] *DR* 6:214, 375.

[37] M Willaschek, 'Right and Coercion: Can Kant's Conception of Right Be Derived from His Moral Theory?' (2009) 17 *International Journal of Philosophical Studies* 49, 60.

with it – would get nowhere in fulfilling its dictates, and would thus destroy the very idea of a free will altogether.

In contrast, the question of whether an act is *rightful* involves nothing more than asking whether it is compatible with a like 'external' freedom on the part of all other persons. Although the self-interested shopkeeper is a contemptible wretch as far as virtue is concerned, he has done quite enough to fulfil his legal obligations. Indeed, he would be in perfect compliance with his *legal* obligations even if he comported himself less than virtuously, say by being unfriendly or miserly towards his customers. In this way, when inquiring into rightfulness 'no account at all is taken of the *matter* of choice'; that is to say, its substance or content. Instead, '[a]ll that is in question is the *form* …'.[38] Put differently, Kant's philosophy of right is concerned with means rather than ends: 'anyone can be free so long as I do not impair his freedom by my *external action*, even though I am quite indifferent to his freedom or would like in my heart to infringe upon it'.[39] However deeply it might implicate general moral philosophy, the question of whether the end sought to be achieved by a choice is morally praiseworthy or abhorrent is ultimately not one for legal philosophy. Instead, all that matters is whether that choice can be reconciled with all other persons setting ends for themselves under a universal law.

External freedom thus relies upon a conception of freedom fundamentally different from that which animates Kant's moral philosophy. While the latter is concerned with *autonomy* or self-legislation liberated from one's contingent desires and motivations, the freedom implicated in Kant's philosophy of right is 'independence from being constrained by another's choice',[40] which is simply the idea that no person is merely at the mercy of another. Both senses of freedom, however, are distinguished from the prevalent 'liberal' concept of freedom as the absence of constraint, and both are also coldly indifferent to considerations of utility, interests or welfare.[41] A slave may have a kindly master who provides for her every need and lets her go anywhere she likes. She nevertheless lacks freedom simply because she is formally a *thing* wholly subject to the master's choice. Regardless of how well-kept and unhindered she may be, it matters that she is not a free *subject* of political institutions, but an *object* without rights under the law. If she should be attacked by another, she would not be able to bring a claim in her own name, but would have to rely upon her master or on the kindness of free passersby. In this way, whatever freedom she possesses is no

[38] *DR* 6:230, 387.
[39] *Ibid.*
[40] *DR* 6:237, 393.
[41] Although couched in Kantian language and concepts, John Rawls's theory of justice ultimately assimilates Kant into some variety of contemporary liberalism by means of incorporating consequentialist and utilitarian ideas regarding the allocation of benefits and burdens. Flikschuh (n 16) Ch 1; Ripstein (n 17) 20–21, 27. For an example of a conflation of Kantian freedom with the libertarian notion of being left alone, see N Rao, 'Three Concepts of Dignity in Constitutional Law' (2011) 86 *Notre Dame Law Review* 183, 199–207.

different from that of an unchained dog. In contrast, independence is a positive status; the possession of a civil guarantee that no one may deal with you with impunity as a thing at their disposal. Such a notion of freedom may properly be termed 'republican', both because it requires the setting up of political institutions, and because it recalls the concept of being *sui iuris* that underlies the law of the Roman republic.[42]

Freedom and the legal form are linked together by *force*. The motivation required by virtue must come from within; that for a duty of right can come from without. Accordingly, whereas the defining feature of a duty of virtue is that its fulfilment can never be enforced by another, legal obligations can be fulfilled through external coercion. As such, the lawyer's basic inquiry is not the moral philosopher's question of 'how people *ought* to treat each other', but 'the distinctly political question of how they may legitimately be *forced* to treat each other'.[43] Thus, the task of Kant's philosophy of right is to reconcile the choices of a multiplicity of individuals under a universal law. *Choice*, as we have already seen, envisages the willing of a range of maxims more expansive than that allowed under the Categorical Imperative. At the same time, however, this expanded set of maxims one can potentially act upon must be limited to ensure a like range of possible maxims on the part of all others.[44] Coercion makes its entrance at this point, along with the correlative juridical concepts of right and obligation. In any interpersonal interaction, a person has an obligation not to act inconsistently with another person's right. If the former so acts, she may be coerced into rectifying the inconsistency by providing a remedy to be specified by political institutions acting on behalf of everyone. As such, right is always and everywhere 'connected with an authorization to use coercion'.[45]

In identifying coercion as the fundamental problem of all law, Kant comes to some agreement with the most prominent anti-positivist of the twentieth century, Ronald Dworkin.

> Day in day out we send people to jail, or take money away from them, or make them do things they do not want to do, under coercion of force, and we justify all this by

[42] See P Pettit, *Republicanism: A Theory of Freedom and Government* (Oxford, Oxford University Press, 1997) Ch 1 (setting out the intellectual history of the concept of freedom, and arguing that the prevalent mode of thinking of freedom in the Anglophone world was in republican terms of non-domination, until the 19th century, when the Hobbesian idea of freedom as non-interference was resurrected and popularised under the influence of Jeremy Bentham); H Arendt, 'Foundation I: Constitutio Libertatis' in *On Revolution* (London, Penguin Press, 1963) (claiming that American revolutionary language, though couched in themes of recovery of ancient liberties or limited government familiar to English political tradition, fundamentally differed from that tradition by constituting an entirely new type of governmental power consecrating freedom); Q Skinner, *Liberty Before Liberalism* (Cambridge, Cambridge University Press, 1998) (detailing the proliferation of 'neo-roman' political theorists during the English Civil War and Revolution, and their stamping out following Cromwell's establishment of a protectorate and the restoration).

[43] A Ripstein, 'Authority and Coercion' (2004) 32 *Philosophy & Public Affairs* 2, 6.

[44] Ripstein (n 17) 387 ('... the principles of right, including public and private right, constrain the means available for agents to use, and *thereby* constrain the maxims on which they may act').

[45] *DR* 6:231, 388.

> speaking of such persons as having broken the law or having failed to meet their legal obligations, or having interfered with other people's legal rights ... We may feel confident that what we are doing is proper, but until we can identify the principles we are following we cannot be sure that they are sufficient, or whether we are applying them consistently.[46]

To wit, Dworkin's project was to 'construct a conception of law – an account of the grounds needed to support a claim of right enforceable on demand in that way – by finding a justification of those practices in a larger integrated network of political value'.[47] Dworkin thus placed law within a 'tree structure' of morality: ethics is the stem that branches out into personal morality, which then branches out yet again into political morality in communities that possess political institutions. Law is the 'highest' branch on the tree; it is that part of political morality that can be enforced without the need for further deliberation by the political community.[48]

Kant's strategy has to be different. He can neither appeal to ultimate ends nor identify legal rights as crystallised, concretised, or otherwise particularly tumescent principles of political morality, because the causal link to the Categorical Imperative was broken at the very first step when the leap was made from 'will' to 'choice'. If the Categorical Imperative as the supreme principle of morality is out of the picture, then neither can sub-principles of political morality have any place. Instead, Kant turns to something else to order and coordinate the use of force: Newtonian physics.

> Resistance that counteracts the hindering of an effect promotes this effect and is consistent with it. Now whatever is wrong is a hindrance to freedom in accordance with universal laws. But coercion is a hindrance or resistance to freedom. Therefore, if a certain use of freedom is itself a hindrance to freedom in accordance with universal laws (ie wrong), coercion that is opposed to this (as a hindering of a hindrance to freedom) is consistent with freedom in accordance with universal laws, that is, it is right.[49]

Thus, Kant arranges rights and obligations within a system of reciprocally limited independence in distinctly mechanical terms modelled upon the motion of particles. The system of the *Doctrine of Right* may be thought of as a complex multi-level, multi-player 'game'[50] where persons are cast as billiard balls rolling around a finite table, with the salient difference that they get to choose whether to roll around or stop.[51] The first iteration of force – someone else pushing you

[46] R Dworkin, 'The Model of Rules I' in *Taking Rights Seriously* (Cambridge, Harvard University Press, 1978) 15.

[47] R Dworkin, *Justice for Hedgehogs* (Cambridge, Harvard University Press, 2011) 405.

[48] *Ibid* 405–407.

[49] *DR* 6:231, 388.

[50] Pogge (n 30) 145–50.

[51] This image is also suggested by Willaschek's notion of 'spheres of freedom'. Willaschek (n 32) 225.

to move, or forcing you to come to a stop – is incompatible with freedom, and therefore 'wrong'. The second iteration of force, deployed to 'correct' the prior wrongful use, is consistent with reciprocal independence, and therefore 'right'. As such, the coordination of force in interpersonal legal relations is set out 'by analogy with presenting the possibility of bodies moving freely under the law of the *equality of action and reaction*'.[52] As unusual as it might seem, essentially the same thought was expressed (albeit in more 'optical' terms) by Peter Birks, the greatest English private lawyer of the twentieth century, when he described a remedial obligation as simply 'the same thing as the right, looked at from the other end'.[53]

Thus, the forms of legal relations do not apply, derive from, express, give effect to, or otherwise participate in ultimate moral ends at all. Their task is simply to specify 'with mathematical exactitude'[54] all the possible trajectories in which embodied rational beings may roll around or come to a stop compatible with a like ability of all other rational embodied beings to roll around or come to a stop *in entirely unmoralised fashion*. This irrelevance of virtue with respect to questions of legality is perhaps best reflected in the passage in the *Perpetual Peace* where Kant rejects the then common idea that republican government required for its existence a citizenry imbued with civic virtue, but claims instead that the 'problem of establishing a state … is *soluble* even for a nation of devils (if only they have understanding)' because that problem is fundamentally not about 'the moral improvement of human beings but only the mechanism of nature …'.[55] As such, juridical norm-giving possesses what Sorin Baiasu calls 'inclusive disjunction': it 'will have legality whether we act on the norm with an ethical or with a non-ethical motive'.[56] In other words, as long as we are engaged solely in explicating the law, we do not actually have to know *anything* about ethics.

And so we come to a picture of the relationship between law and morality very different from Dworkin's tree. First, the starting point for Kant's concept of law is not to be found in principles of political morality, or even in 'public' legal norms such as constitutional or human rights. Instead, it lies in the *private* law juridical categories of delict, contract and quasi-obligation, because these are the basic forms in which persons may interact freely with one another regardless of the internal maxims motivating their acts. Public law is developed 'bottom-up' out of these private law categories; it contains 'no further or other duties of human beings than can be conceived' at private law.[57] Second,

[52] *DR* 6:233, 389.

[53] P Birks, 'Definition and Division: A Meditation on *Institutes* 3.13' in P Birks (ed), *The Classification of Obligations*, vol 1 (Oxford, Clarendon Press, 1997) 24.

[54] *DR* 6:233, 390.

[55] *PP* 8:366, 335.

[56] S Baiasu, 'Right's Complex Relation to Ethics in Kant: The Limits of Independentism' (2016) 107 *Kant-Studien* 2, 32.

[57] *DR* 6:306, 451.

instead of being an application of or derivation from ultimate moral ends, law is conceptually prior to these ends. The claim that a theory of law has to be worked out without reference to the Categorical Imperative does not mean that the latter 'is completely out of play', but that 'if it can come into play, it can do so only from a position behind the Universal Principle of Right'.[58] This is why the *Doctrine of Right* comes before the *Doctrine of Virtue*. One must first work out how any person *qua* rational billiard ball can roll around or come to a stop in a manner compatible with a like ability of all other persons *qua* rational billiard balls under a universal law. Only after completing this level can we move on to figuring out whether any particular decision to roll around or stop is good or bad.

To sum up, while Kant agrees with the positivists that law is to be worked out without reference to ultimate moral ends, he disagrees with them in insisting that there is nevertheless a necessary connection between law and morality. Unlike non-positivists like Dworkin, however, he denies that law 'depends' upon morality. Rather, it is morality that depends upon law.[59] Right must come before virtue: if you are not free, your choices are not yours to be praised or blamed for.

II. METHODOLOGY: IMMANENT CRITIQUE AND PRIVATE LAW ANALOGIES

By and large, current global justice scholarship generally proceeds from a conception of human dignity chiefly as a matter of having or enjoying some minimal standard of well-being, paradigmatically, by being supplied with things necessary for the satisfaction of interests and needs required for human flourishing.[60] Thus conceived, global justice unsurprisingly becomes a matter of

[58] Alexy (n 19) 500.

[59] Kant means something different from Tony Honoré's claim that 'for moral thinking to guide the conduct of people living in communities and belonging to political entities, as we all do, it needs to be filled out by various means, including formal institutions'. T Honoré, 'The Dependence of Morality On Law' (1993) 13 *OJLS* 1, 2. Honoré suggests that the dependence upon law is a feature of the morality peculiar to civilised conditions, and that outside such conditions, a different morality might prevail, which does not depend upon law in the same way. In contrast, Kant takes the more extreme position in that morality is radically incomplete outside of a rightful condition, such that it cannot even be 'thought'.

[60] See, eg, S Caney, 'Cosmopolitan Justice, Rights and Global Climate Change' (2006) 19 *Canadian Journal of Law and Jurisprudence* 255, 259 ('it is difficult to think of how one could derive a system of rights that took no account of persons' interests'). Compare Shue's famous definition of basic rights as '(1) the rational basis for a justified demand (2) that the actual enjoyment of a substance be (3) socially guaranteed against standard threats'. H Shue, *Basic Rights: Subsistence, Affluence, and U.S. Foreign Policy*, 2nd edn (Princeton New Jersey, Princeton University Press, 1996) 1. See also H Shue, 'Mediating Duties' (1988) 98 *Ethics* 687, 687 ('universal human rights' relate to 'the conviction that every person ought to be guaranteed a few basics by other people when helpless to secure them for herself').

allocating just or fair distributions of holdings, resources or values. As Jakob Huber argues, such approaches presume a neutral 'god's-eye perspective from which goods are allocated'.[61] The problem is not just that this 'Archimedean "view from nowhere"' does not exist, but that discovering it would transform human beings into passive recipients of largesse rather than agents in charge of their own lives.[62] In contrast, the Kantian commitments to formality, freedom and force start from the idea of reflexivity in interactions between persons; that is, from the notion of one person having rights or committing wrongs against another.

Accordingly, my argument does not proceed from the list of EU 'values' normally given pride of place in the scholarship on the EU external relations law or foreign policy.[63] The single organising principle guiding the analysis is the idea of one person not being a thing at the arbitrary choice of another. The substantive 'norms' or 'values' enumerated in the various treaty provisions to be examined subsequently can neither justify assertions of extraterritorial jurisdiction over distant strangers by themselves, nor can they be invoked without more by those distant strangers to ground claims of extraterritorial human rights obligations owed to them. Instead, the EU's rights of extraterritorial jurisdiction over distant strangers are wholly explicated in terms of rights of the EU and its subjects not to be dominated by the arbitrary will of others. Contrariwise, the human rights claims of distant strangers against the EU derive from their right not to be dominated by the arbitrary choices of the EU as a political institution. This is not to say that the EU may conduct itself viciously or imprudently in its relations with the wider world. Such questions would be entirely appropriate, essential even, in an all-things-considered moral evaluation of the EU's foreign policy.[64] In an evaluation of its *legality*, however, they play a merely secondary, and far more circumscribed role.[65] Put differently, international relations must

[61] J Huber, 'Theorising from the Global Standpoint: Kant and Grotius on Original Common Possession of the Earth' (2017) 25 *European Journal of Philosophy* 231, 243.

[62] *Ibid* 235.

[63] See, eg, I Hadjiyianni, 'The Court of Justice of the European Union as a Transnational Actor through Judicial Review of the Territorial Scope of EU Environmental Law' (2019) 21 *Cambridge Yearbook of European Legal Studies* 128, 137 (arguing that judicial review of EU extraterritorial measures should follow an approach that is 'in line with EU external action values and objectives, which provide the normative foundation for conducting the EU's external relations'); and generally U Khaliq, *Ethical Dimensions of the Foreign Policy of the European Union: A Legal Appraisal* (Cambridge, Cambridge University Press, 2008).

[64] In this spirit, Ester Herlin-Karnell argues that the legitimacy of the EU's 'role as a promoter of global values' depends upon its 'ability to uphold its values internally'. E Herlin-Karnell, 'EU Values and the Shaping of the International Legal Order' in D Kochenov and F Amtenbrink (eds), *The European Union's Shaping of the International Legal Order* (Cambridge, Cambridge University Press, 2014) 106.

[65] See J Larik, *Foreign Policy Objectives in European Constitutional Law* (Oxford, Oxford University Press, 2016) 31–50 (examining German, French, and Indian constitutional jurisprudence on '*Staatszielbestimmungen*', '*objectifs de valeur constitutionelle*' and 'directive principles' and finding them largely non-justiciable).

bend its knee before international law because as a discipline, international law is independent of, and conceptually prior to international relations.[66] Accordingly, this book does not enumerate for EU policymakers the various considerations which should be taken into account and explain how to weigh or balance them. Instead, it seeks to tell them what the *rules* are. We must first assess whether an EU extraterritorial measure is rightful before addressing the question of whether it is prudent or praiseworthy.

Another feature that tends to distinguish Kantian scholarship concerns its general method of proceeding. As Allen Wood notes,

> Analytical philosophers often aim at producing moral principles that may be very complex in structure, full of subclauses and qualifications, because these principles enable them to capture 'our moral intuitions' and the precisely worded epicyclic subclauses enable us to deal cleverly with threatened counterexamples of various kinds.[67]

My approach cannot be like this, because, as established in the previous section, I maintain that our moral intuitions are radically incomplete without political institutions. An alternative would be to identify some fundamentally and axiomatically valid *a priori* premises, construct a comprehensive system of rights out of this premise, and then posit this system as an ideal 'external' standard against which the EU's conduct is evaluated. Such a 'transcendental' methodology would be beyond my poor ability, as well as uninteresting to most lawyers. Instead, I have opted for a kind of 'immanent' critique that starts by setting out the relevant aspects of EU law and social practices, identifies contradictions within them, followed by a demonstration of how Kant's philosophy of right resolves them, which finally, leads to further critical demands upon yet other aspects of EU law and social practice. Some clarifications regarding immanent critique: the normative theory against which the relevant EU legal and political practices are criticised is not 'internal' to those practices in the sense meant by political realists, because it is not derived out of an interpretive understanding of the practice of EU law and politics itself.[68] If anything, very many of the EU legal practices considered here are fundamentally inimical to the Kantian normative framework, which turns out to champion a deeply old-fashioned, statist conception of sovereignty. Neither, however, is it 'moralist', in the sense of identifying limits to legal and political practices by reference to *ethical* ideals either interpolated from without or derived from within through some Herculean interpretation of all the relevant legal materials. The point is not that such ethical ideals do not exist, it is that they cannot in and of themselves justify the coercion of others.

[66] *PP* 8:381, 347; 8:385, 351.

[67] A Wood, 'The Supreme Principle of Morality' in P Guyer (ed), *The Cambridge Companion to Kant and Modern Philosophy* (Cambridge, Cambridge University Press, 2006) 346.

[68] E Rossi and M Sleat, 'Realism in Normative Political Theory' (2014) 9 *Philosophy Compass* 689, 690.

Thirdly, my argument is deeply constitutionalist in spirit; it envisages a single comprehensive global institutional framework for the use of public power under the rule of law. Such an approach is of course not without its dangers. Counselling against it. Nico Krisch claims that various forms of 'postnational constitutionalism' fail to offer 'continuity' at the international level, because mere 'power-limiting constitutionalism' is too thin to 'redeem the full promise of the domestic constitutionalist tradition', while 'foundational constitutionalism' of the type advocated in this book would 'require massive social and institutional change' such as would 'not only have utopian overtones … [but would also] sit uneasily with major – and likely persistent – features of European and global societies'.[69] Krisch is entirely correct on this last point. Nevertheless, utopias remain relevant if not unavoidable because they supply constitutive and regulative principles that govern imperfect and defective things according to the same principles that apply to their ideal versions.[70] Moreover, the kind of continuity envisaged here between domestic and international law does not entail the wholesale replication of domestic politics or institutions at the international level via a global democracy or world state. In fact, it is implacably opposed to it.

Finally, like Kant, I have adopted the methodology of explicating doctrines of public law through 'analogies' to concepts of private law. While this is an ancient tradition in international law scholarship, it is somewhat novel for EU law, such that the reader may find herself perplexed at being often brought very far away from customary discussions of EU law and public international law. These detours into private law are not just forgivable, but necessary. Forgivable, because they are no less impenetrable than the 'fuzzy neologisms'[71] through which much EU legal discourse is conducted. Indeed, for a legally trained reader, the private law analogies ought to be much more familiar than technical terms imported from economics and political science. Necessary, because the use of private law analogies to explicate international law has emerged from a period in the academic wilderness to a significant resurgence in the past decade, with several important contributions adopting that methodology to address topics central to this book.[72]

[69] N Krisch, *Beyond Constitutionalism: The Pluralist Structure of Postnational Law* (Oxford, Oxford University Press, 2010) 67.

[70] Eleftheriadis (n 18) 709 (arguing that 'the legitimacy of both internal political institutions and international institutions of cooperation among states [is] a matter of a single system of justice … the legitimacy of nonstate institutions and the authority of nonstate laws is … not to be justified through something outside the state, but – strictly speaking – through the same argument that justified domestic institutions').

[71] T Isiksel, 'On Europe's Functional Constitutionalism: Towards a Constitutional Theory of Specialized International Regimes' (2012) 19 *Constellations* 102, 102.

[72] See ch 3 of this volume.

III. OUTLINE OF THE BOOK

This book has eight chapters. After this introductory first chapter, chapter two sets the scene by examining certain provisions in the EU treaties committing the EU to a certain posture in its relations with 'the wider world', and exploring several examples of EU 'extraterritorial' regulation in fields commonly described as involving global public goods. It then recounts and refutes an influential interpretation of these provisions by Lorand Bartels, which starts from the premise that they mandate 'compliance' with international law by the EU in all its actions. On the understanding of 'compliance' as meaning that the EU should not and does not create legal effects extraterritorially, Bartels ends by largely denying any 'extraterritorial' human rights duties, particularly 'positive' obligations to 'protect'.[73] While very much of Bartels's 'compliance' reading is insightful and correct, the chapter demonstrates from relevant case law that the notion of 'international law' to be 'complied with' is a peculiar one knowing no geographical boundaries to prescriptive jurisdiction – that is, to a political institution's authority to prescribe rules binding upon conduct. Moreover, it is argued that such extraterritorial measures operate on a rationality of 'territorial extension', whereby conduct taking place outside the territory of the Member States is treated as having taken place inside the EU internal market and regulated accordingly. As such, the chapter demonstrates that such EU measures produce not just factual effects overseas, but *legal* effects. In other words, the EU does not simply 'affect' distant strangers; it very often *governs* them. Such claims of authority over distant strangers require both legal and moral justification, none of which can be supplied from within EU law itself. For this, we must turn to public international law and political theory.

With this in mind, chapter three then examines a bevy of international legal scholars who justify such extraterritorial measures on the basis that they provide 'global public goods', that expression being understood in terms borrowed from the economic sciences as utility-enhancing things desired or needed by all, but which tend to be undersupplied due to their being non-rivalrous in consumption and non-excludable in terms of benefits. According to this commonplace definition, the structural features of non-excludability and non-rivalrousness mean that individual actors have no incentive to supply them, but instead every reason to free ride on the efforts of others. The chapter focuses upon Eyal Benvenisti's rich and fascinating ideas about the 'Sovereign Trusteeship of Humanity', which draw upon Grotius, Locke and Mill to argue that sovereignty should be redefined as a form of trusteeship held for the benefit of humanity in general.[74]

[73] L Bartels, 'The EU's Human Rights Obligations in Relation to Policies with Extraterritorial Effects' (2014) 25 *European Journal of International Law* 1071.

[74] E Benvenisti, 'Sovereigns as Trustees of Humanity: On the Accountability of States to Foreign Stakeholders' (2013) 107 *American Journal of International Law* 295.

Although Benvenisti's conviction that sovereigns are fiduciaries is correct and valuable, the flaw in the argument is that it conflates harms with wrongs. The fact that a globalised world presents us with incomparably more opportunities to affect each other's welfare does not automatically mean that we acquire legal obligations towards each other. The opposite is also true: the mere fact that measures may advance global interests or values does not in and of itself justify coercive extraterritorial assertions of authority over distant strangers. Rather, the question of *how* a political community goes about advancing those values is crucial in determining whether it is permissible, or whether it amounts to imperial overreach. In this regard, the chapter discusses (1) the uselessness of the Article 21(3) TEU language of policy coherence and consistency based on values for generating determinate rights and obligations; and (2) the relationship between 'messianism' and certain deeply imperial tendencies found in EU jurisprudence.

In contrast to the theories examined in chapter three, chapter four sets out an alternative based upon Kant's republican vision of international order. The specific aspects of importance in Kant's legal theory are:

(1) the fiduciary nature of the relationship between sovereigns and their subjects;
(2) the right of all sovereign states to use coercion to ensure that they are not subject to the will of another; and
(3) that 'harms' cannot be central in ascertaining the international rights of sovereigns.

It is in this chapter that Kant's legal philosophy and private law analogies feature most heavily. Drawing from the core elements of Kant's legal and political philosophy, as well as from the categories of the Roman private law from which Kant takes inspiration, I argue that dignity conceived as freedom from domination gives rise to three kinds of essentially private legal rights – tortious, contractual and fiduciary – all of which are unrealisable without a particular configuration of political institutions invested with authority, ideally the *state*. States are persons constituted to have no purpose other than to assure subjects of their freedom, which makes them essentially *public* fiduciaries of their subjects. These obligations give rise to *rights* that apply not only domestically against subjects, but internationally against all other persons – state and non-state – for no state is to be frustrated by the arbitrary will of any other person in the fulfilment of its sole purpose. Importantly, violations of these rights – international wrongs – are not predicated upon harms or losses. They are structurally akin not to damage-based wrongs like negligence or private nuisance, but to injury-based wrongs like battery, trespass and defamation, where harm is irrelevant. The fact that the EU is not a Kantian republican democracy, and indeed in many respects the very antithesis of one, does not mean that it is barred from exercising the rights of a democratic republican state in its external relations.

Neither, however, can it be exempted from the obligations such a state ordinarily owes to those over whom it claims authority.

Chapter five then sets out an alternative, republican theory of extraterritorial jurisdiction to provide global public goods. The chapter departs from conventional economic definitions of public goods and instead defines them as those goods, services and facilities that must be provided *publicly* within any political community for its members to remain free equals not systematically dominated by others. As public fiduciaries, states are not only *obligated* to provide public goods, they are also equipped with *rights* to compel persons into cooperating with the system of public provision, and to seek remedies against those responsible for frustrating such provision. These rights extend to individual distant strangers located outside state territory, who threaten the state's provision of public goods by, say, polluting, cartelising, etc. Given that international wrongs have the nature of injury, they cannot be predicated upon harms. The chapter then argues that harm-based justifications of extraterritorial jurisdiction – paradigmatically, the 'no-harm' principle of environmental law and the 'effects doctrine' found in antitrust law – are incoherent, and demonstrates a dawning appreciation of this in emerging legal practice. As such, it turns out that the European Court of Justice's (ECJ) steadfast refusal to rely upon harm-based theories such as the 'effects doctrine' to justify EU extraterritorial competition regulation, or the 'no harm principle' to justify extraterritorial environmental measures, is *largely* defensible. The stumbling-block rendering the legitimacy of such measures defective is the ECJ's equally steadfast aversion to submitting questions over the legality of EU measures to the jurisdiction of an international court or tribunal.

Chapter six turns to the question of the EU's extraterritorial human rights obligations. In the same way private law contains a set of legal principles to prevent private trustee-beneficiary relations from degenerating into exploitation, public law contains a set of legal principles preventing relations from political authorities and subjects from degenerating into domination. These are human rights. It espouses a view of human rights as legal claims made by subjects against political authorities for breach of their *public* fiduciary obligations. They are political rights (not natural rights), claimed by individuals as a matter of constitutional law (not international law), primarily against those public persons (not private persons) in a relation of authority (not mere power or influence) over them. It is then shown that these theoretical claims both explain and account for human rights as they actually operate in legal practice. Drawing from the case law of the Strasbourg Court, whose jurisprudence on extraterritorial 'human rights jurisdiction' is the most extensive and well-developed of any human rights court, the chapter argues that the threshold criterion for the imposition of extraterritorial human rights obligations arising under the Convention is not an ability to bring about factual changes in a distant stranger's state of material welfare, but a claim of *authority* over those distant strangers; that is, an entitlement to alter their *legal* rights and obligations. To this end, the chapter criticises theories of human rights jurisdiction put forward by Yuval Shany,[75] Marko Milanovic[76] and Lea Raible,[77] and instead veers closer to Samantha Besson's account.[78] Finally, it demonstrates that according to the logic of established European Convention on Human Rights (ECHR) jurisprudence, the technique of 'territorial extension' regularly resorted to by the EU must give rise to extraterritorial human rights jurisdiction. Moreover, the human rights obligations that arise in this way are not limited to just so-called 'negative' obligations of respect – that is, to refrain from actively violating rights; but extend to 'positive' obligations to 'protect' and 'fulfil' – that is, to prevent third parties from causing human rights violations, and to establish mechanisms for the vindication of those rights.

Chapter seven then returns to matters internal to EU law, or more precisely, to matters concerning its defective internal constitution. It argues first that the ECJ interprets rules of procedure concerning access to EU courts in a manner that effectively insulates the EU from fulfilling its obligations of fiduciary accountability towards the distant strangers over whom it asserts authority. Worse, it employs the rhetoric about fidelity to international law for the entirely self-serving purpose of foreclosing any and all accusations of international wrongfulness. All this is demonstrated in the context of recent litigation over the Western Sahara, which involved several different challenges interposed by an indigenous Sahrawi liberation movement and a UK-based non-governmental organisation (NGO) against EU measures adopting international agreements between the EU and Morocco – the occupying power in the Western Sahara – which would have produced legal effects upon that territory. To this end, the chapter analyses the various stages of the relevant case law and ultimately concludes that there are severe problems with the standard claim that the EU is a constitutional order. The upshot of these cases is that distant strangers are treated not as dignity-bearing subjects, but as objects that may neither claim rights nor be owed obligations. Chapter eight summarises and concludes.

[75] Y Shany, 'Taking Universality Seriously: A Functional Approach to Extraterritoriality in International Human Rights Law' (2013) 7 *Law & Ethics of Human Rights* 49.

[76] M Milanovic, *Extraterritorial Application of Human Rights Treaties: Law, Principles, and Policy* (Oxford, Oxford University Press, 2011).

[77] L Raible, 'Title to Territory and Jurisdiction in International Human Rights Law: Three Models for a Fraught Relationship' (2018) 31 *Leiden Journal of International Law* 315.

[78] S Besson, 'The Extraterritoriality of the European Convention on Human Rights: Why Human Rights Depend on Jurisdiction and What Jurisdiction Amounts To' (2012) 25 *Leiden Journal of International Law* 857.

IV. CONCLUSION

Some final observations. First, in earlier work, I described the Kantian, republican conception of freedom animating this book as 'autonomy'.[79] I now realise that this is liable to give rise to confusion because it suggests ethical or internal freedom, or worse, the Millian-Razian idea of a special discretionary core of 'protected interests' required to be shielded against external interference. The Kantian concept of a human being's basic juridical status trades neither upon ethics nor upon the notion of core and peripheral interests but consists entirely and merely in independence; in not being a thing at the mercy of another. Second, the private law materials referred to are intended only as illustrations, not as authorities. The reader absolutely must not come away thinking that the Scottish and South African cases on riparian rights cited in chapter four constitute binding or even persuasive authorities before EU or international courts. Instead, these references are meant only to demonstrate a point about how various communities have thought about the morality of coercive interpersonal interactions. To reiterate, this book is a normative critique, not an exposition of doctrine. Third, references to Kant's works are made in customary fashion according to the pagination of Kant's collected writings compiled by the Berlin-Brandenburg Academy of Sciences, also known as the *Akademie* edition. For the reader's convenience, citations also refer to the page number of Mary Gregor's popular translation. For example, '*DR* 6:230, 387' means a citation to the *Doctrine of Right* found on page 230, Volume 6 of the *Akademie* edition, as reprinted at page 387 of Gregor's translation. Fourth, and finally, a note on abbreviations. As the judicial arm of the EU, the Court of Justice of the European Union comprises two separate courts: the Court of Justice (the higher instance) and the General Court (the lower instance). The overall institution is abbreviated as CJEU, and the Court of Justice as ECJ. I have left the General Court unabbreviated.

[79] A Ganesh, 'The European Union's Human Rights Obligations Towards Distant Strangers' (2016) 37 *Michigan Journal of International Law* 475.

2

Territorial Extension: Power and Authority in the Wider World

THIS CHAPTER INTRODUCES the central provisions of the EU treaties regulating the EU's relations with the wider world, considers salient examples of EU 'extraterritorial' legislation, and examines the rationales by which they have been justified in the Court of Justice of the European Union's (CJEU) jurisprudence. In contrast to other chapters, this one involves extensive discussion of EU and international doctrinal materials, because some careful parsing of the measures and treaty provisions is necessary to figure out what precisely the EU 'does' in the wider world. At the end of this exercise, it will hopefully be clear that EU extraterritorial measures very often create not just factual effects upon distant strangers, but *legal* effects. The EU does not simply 'affect' distant strangers in the sense of creating, removing or modifying their options. Instead, it often purports to 'govern' them; that is, to determine their legal rights and obligations. The question that then arises is how, if at all, this is defensible. This, simply stated, is the *problématique* that occupies the rest of the book.

We begin with certain provisions in the EU's foundational documents – the Treaty on European Union (TEU) and the Treaty on the Functioning of the European Union (TFEU) – which require the EU to advance democracy, human rights and the rule of law, as well as a list of 'global public goods' in all its relations with the wider world. This is followed by a discussion of an important article by Lorand Bartels that constitutes one of the very few attempts to address the implications of the provisions in terms of legal rights and obligations.[1] While my project is ultimately broader than Bartels's, the key issues in which he frames his inquiry – compliance with international law, general jurisdiction, human rights obligations and standing – resonate throughout its entirety.[2] While I agree with very much of Bartels's legal analysis, I depart from it in one

[1] L Bartels, 'The EU's Human Rights Obligations in Relation to Policies with Extraterritorial Effects' (2014) 25 *European Journal of International Law* 1071. My attempt at a rights-based analysis of these same provisions was written as a response to Bartels. A Ganesh, 'The European Union's Human Rights Obligations Towards Distant Strangers' (2016) 37 *Michigan Journal of International Law* 475.

[2] One might even call this book a 'reverse-engineering' of Bartels's article.

fundamental respect. I argue that the EU very often legislates in a way that recognises no geographical boundaries to its authority to legislate rules binding upon conduct; that is, its 'prescriptive jurisdiction'. While many view this as an entirely new and heterodox departure from the ordinary rules of jurisdiction, I contend that it has some extremely venerable precedents in international law. This then sets the scene for chapter three, which discusses several variants of the predominant approach of justifying such exercises of extraterritorial jurisdiction normatively in terms of advancing or protecting global 'interests' or 'values'.

I. THE POST-LISBON ARTICLES

The foundational treaties of the EU were amended by the Lisbon Treaty to include several provisions concerning its relations with the wider world. While similar provisions are not unknown in national constitutions, the articles are nonetheless fascinating in that they make the EU treaties 'amongst the most verbose constitutional documents with regard to foreign policy objectives'.[3] As a preliminary matter, it must be noted that the rules of treaty interpretation in international law do not apply to EU treaties, which have from the very beginning been subjected to 'dynamic', 'purposive' or 'teleological' methods of interpretation.[4] The first provision of interest – and the one in which the connection between the themes of global public goods and extraterritorial human rights is most apparent – is Article 3(5) TEU:

> In its relations with the wider world, the Union shall uphold and promote its values and interests and contribute to the protection of its citizens. It shall contribute to peace, security, the sustainable development of the Earth, solidarity and mutual respect among peoples, free and fair trade, eradication of poverty and the protection of human rights, in particular the rights of the child, as well as to the strict observance and the development of international law, including respect for the principles of the United Nations Charter.

[3] J Larik, *Foreign Policy Objectives in European Constitutional Law* (Oxford, Oxford University Press, 2016) 67. Joris Larik finds similar though more circumscribed provisions in the constitutional documents of the EU's Member States, as well as in those of 11 other non-EU Member States. In contrast, Bruno De Witte observes a 'clear contrast between the traditional scarcity of relevant provisions … in *national* constitutions, and the overabundance of [similar] norms in *EU* primary law'. B De Witte, 'Too Much Constitutional Law in the European Union's Foreign Relations?' in M Cremona and B De Witte (eds), *EU Foreign Relations Law: Constitutional Fundamentals* (Oxford, Hart Publishing, 2008) 7.

[4] See Case 8/55 *Fédération Charbonnière de Belgique v High Authority* [1954–56] ECR 292, 299; Case 22/70 *Commission v Council (ERTA)* [1971] ECR 273, paras 28–29; J Klabbers, *An Introduction to International Institutional Law* (Cambridge, Cambridge University Press, 2002) 68–80; and M Poiares Maduro, 'Interpreting European Law: Judicial Adjudication in a Context of Constitutional Pluralism' (2007) 1 *European Journal of Legal Studies* 137.

Situated in the 'Common Provisions' of Title I of the TEU, the provision applies generally across all areas of EU policy.

The second major provision of note is Article 21 TEU, which is placed in the first chapter of Title V on the 'General Provisions on the Union's External Action and Specific Provisions on the Common Foreign and Security Policy'. Because of its location, some have argued that Article 21 TEU pertains specifically to issues of foreign policy, or, in the parlance of EU lawyers, 'EU external relations'. As we shall see, this is neither warranted by the text of Article 21 TEU nor have the courts of the EU interpreted it as such. The first paragraph of Article 21(1) TEU provides that

> The Union's action on the international scene shall be guided by the principles which have inspired its own creation, development and enlargement, and which it seeks to advance in the wider world: democracy, the rule of law, the universality and indivisibility of human rights and fundamental freedoms, respect for human dignity, the principles of equality and solidarity, and respect for the principles of the United Nations Charter and international law.

The second paragraph goes on to provide that the 'Union shall seek to develop relations and build partnerships with third countries, and international, regional or global organisations' and 'promote multilateral solutions to common problems …' After this, Article 21(2) TEU provides that the EU 'shall define and pursue common policies and actions', and 'work for a high degree of cooperation in all fields of international relations' in order to:

a) safeguard its values, fundamental interests, security, independence and integrity;
b) consolidate and support democracy, the rule of law, human rights and the principles of international law;
c) preserve peace, prevent conflicts and strengthen international security, in accordance with the purposes and principles of the United Nations Charter …;
d) foster the sustainable economic, social and environmental development of developing countries, with the primary aim of eradicating poverty;
e) encourage the integration of all countries into the world economy, including through the progressive abolition of restrictions on international trade;
f) help develop international measures to preserve and improve the quality of the environment and the sustainable management of global natural resources, in order to ensure sustainable development;
g) assist populations, countries and regions confronting natural or man-made disasters; and
h) promote an international system based on stronger multilateral cooperation and good global governance.

Lastly, the first paragraph of Article 21(3) TEU provides – again using the descriptor 'shall' – that the EU 'respect the principles and pursue the objectives set out in paragraphs 1 and 2 in the development and implementation of the different areas of the Union's external action ..., and of the external aspects of its other policies'. The second paragraph continues:

> The Union shall ensure consistency between the different areas of its external action and between these and its other policies. The Council and the Commission, assisted by the High Representative of the Union for Foreign Affairs and Security Policy, shall ensure that consistency and shall cooperate to that effect.

The phrase 'external aspects of its other policies' as it appears in the first paragraph of Article 21(3) TEU does pertain solely to questions of external relations. Specifically, it refers to such matters as the 'external dimension' of competition law; that is, chapters on EU competition rules in bilateral agreements between the EU and third countries.[5] The phrase 'between the different areas of its external action and between these and its other policies' in the second paragraph, however, indicates a blurring of the line between domestic and foreign policy. It introduces a principle of consistency or coherence applicable across external policy and the EU's 'other', that is, *internal* policies.

The above provisions in the TEU are supplemented by others in the TFEU, mainly in Part V on EU External Action. Article 205 TFEU, which serves as the *chapeau* for Part V TFEU, requires that EU external action be 'guided by the principles, pursue the objectives and be conducted in accordance with the general provisions laid down in Chapter 1 of Title V [TEU]'. The same applies to Article 207 TFEU on the Common Commercial Policy, and Article 208 TFEU on development cooperation. Another relevant provision is Article 191 TFEU, which provides in its first subsection that 'Union policy on the environment shall contribute to the pursuit of' a list of environmental objectives, including 'promoting measures at the international level to deal with regional or worldwide environmental problems, and in particular combating climate change'.

A. Between Multilateralism and Evangelism

The text of Article 3(5) TEU was taken from that of Article I-3(4) of the proposed 'Constitutional Treaty' that was ultimately rejected by the French and Dutch electorate in the national referenda in 2005. The Constitutional Treaty had been drafted following the 'Convention on the Future of Europe' – an event that was supposed to have been the EU's answer to the Philadelphia Constitutional Convention of 1787. That Convention was itself launched in 2001 by the Laeken Declaration, which declaims in the following terms:

> What is Europe's role in this changed world? Does Europe not, now that it is finally unified, have a leading role to play in a new world order, that of a power able both to

[5] See A-M Bossche, 'EU Competition Law in 3D' in I Govaere et al, *The European Union in the World: Essays in Honour of Marc Maresceau* (Leiden-Boston, Martinus Nijhoff, 2014) 372–78.

> play a stabilising role worldwide and to point the way ahead for many countries and peoples? …
>
> Now that the Cold War is over and we are living in a globalised, yet also highly fragmented world, Europe needs to shoulder its responsibilities in the governance of globalisation …. A power seeking to set globalisation within a moral framework, in other words to anchor it in solidarity and sustainable development.

Such 'missionary'[6] or 'evangelical'[7] sentiments were by no means simply a product of post-Cold War bravado. They can be found as early as the Schuman Declaration of 1950, which expressed a hope that with the 'increased resources' made available by the establishment of peace between the Member States, 'Europe will be able to pursue the achievement of one of its essential tasks, namely, the development of the African Continent'.[8]

Given this context, there have arisen considerable bodies of legal and political science scholarship offering descriptive and empirical analyses of the EU's performance as an 'standard setter' or 'norm exporter' in various regulatory fields,[9] expositions of the EU's competence to enter into international treaties and the attribution of responsibilities arising under them to the EU,[10] and the law surrounding 'human rights conditionality' clauses in trade or investment agreements with third states.[11] This literature builds upon and complements similar legal and political science scholarship pre-dating the Lisbon Treaty.[12]

[6] M Broberg, 'Don't Mess with the Missionary Man! On the Principle of Coherence, the Missionary Principle and the European Union's Development Policy' in PJ Cardwell (ed), *EU External Relations Law and Policy in the Post-Lisbon Era* (The Hague, TMC Asser Press, 2011); E Herlin-Karnell, 'EU Values and the Shaping of the International Legal Order' in D Kochenov and F Amtenbrink (eds), *The European Union's Shaping of the International Legal Order* (Cambridge, Cambridge University Press, 2014) 90–92.

[7] L Ankersmit, J Lawrence and G Davies, 'Diverging EU and WTO Perspectives on Extraterritorial Process Regulation' (2012) 21 *Minnesota Journal of International Law* 14, 40, 56.

[8] Schuman Declaration 1950.

[9] See, eg, E Fahey, *The Global Reach of EU Law* (Abingdon, Routledge, 2016) 3, 5–6; I Hadjiyianni, *The EU as a Global Regulator for Environmental Protection: A Legitimacy Perspective* (Oxford, Hart Publishing, 2019) Ch 1; A Bradford, *The Brussels Effect: How the European Union Rules the World* (New York, Oxford University Press, 2020).

[10] See, eg, the collected essays in M Evans and P Koutrakos, *The International Responsibility of the European Union: European and International Perspectives* (Oxford, Hart Publishing, 2013); and A Delgado Casteleiro, *The International Responsibility of the European Union: From Competence to Normative Control* (Cambridge, Cambridge University Press, 2016).

[11] See, eg, M Broberg, 'What Is the Direction for the EU's Development Cooperation after Lisbon? A Legal Examination' (2011) 16 *European Foreign Affairs Review* 539; L Bartels, 'A Model Human Rights Clause for the EU's International Trade Agreements' (Berlin-Aachen, German Institute for Human Rights & MISEREOR, 2014); V Kube, *EU Human Rights, International Investment Law and Participation: Operationalizing the EU Foreign Policy Objective to Global Human Rights Protection* (Cham, Springer, 2019).

[12] The legal scholarship includes E Fierro, *European Union's Approach to Human Rights Conditionality in Practice* (Leiden-Boston, Martinus Nijhoff, 2003); A Williams, *EU Human Rights Policies: A Study in Irony* (Oxford, Oxford University Press, 2005); L Bartels, *Human Rights Conditionality in the EU's International Agreements* (Oxford, Oxford University Press, 2005); U Khaliq, *Ethical Dimensions of the Foreign Policy of the European Union: A Legal Appraisal* (Cambridge, Cambridge University Press, 2008).

Alongside these largely descriptive analyses there exists a normative literature which trades for the most part in the theme of spreading 'values'.[13] This is understandable given that Article 3(5) TEU speaks of the EU's task in the wider world as one of upholding and promoting '*its* values'; that is, those enumerated in Article 2 TEU as 'respect for human dignity, freedom, democracy, equality, the rule of law and respect for human rights'.

Amidst this embarrassment of riches, however, we find relative silence surrounding some far more basic questions. Could these provisions possibly entitle a distant stranger to require something of the EU as a matter of *right* personal to her? Conversely, is the EU ever entitled to require something of a distant stranger as a matter of personal *obligation*?

To be sure, one reason for the silence might be that early commentators considered such claims most unlikely. For instance, a piece written around the time the Lisbon Treaty first came into force considered the provisions as merely aspirational verbiage 'redolent of motherhood and apple pie',[14] while another earlier text commented that the

> substantive mandate as expressed in Article 3(5) TEU [was] to be achieved by developing relations and building partnerships with third countries and international organisations which share the Union's principles and values, and promoting multilateral solutions to common problems (Article 21(1) TEU).[15]

Shortly after these statements were published, however, a series of events took place that spectacularly exploded the idea that the provisions were no more than toothless exhortations to international cooperation.

Following the failure of efforts in the International Civil Aviation Organization to set up a comprehensive regulatory regime for offsetting and reducing aircraft emissions pursuant to the Kyoto Protocol[16] despite negotiations lasting over 15 years,[17] the EU unilaterally enacted the EU Emissions Trading Scheme

[13] In the field of political science, Ian Manners cites the EU's surprising success in advocating the abolition of capital punishment worldwide to portray the EU as possessing the 'soft' power to redefine 'what passes as "normal" in world politics', which is 'ultimately, the greatest power of all'. I Manners, 'Normative Power Europe: A Contradiction in Terms?' (2002) 40 *Journal of Common Market Studies* 235, 253.

[14] A Dashwood et al, *Wyatt and Dashwood's European Union Law*, 6th edn (Oxford, Hart Publishing, 2011) 903.

[15] M Cremona, 'Coherence through Law: What Difference Will the Treaty of Lisbon Make?' (2008) 3 *Hamburg Review of Social Sciences* 11, 35. See also M Emerson et al, *Upgrading the EU's Role as Global Actor* (Brussels, Centre for European Policy Studies, 2011) 16–18. Emerson et al describe the 'high principles' of Article 21 TEU as evidencing – rhetorically at least – a 'liberal institutionalist' approach to international relations, whose main project was 'taming great powers with international norms and multilateral processes, and going beyond the primacy of interstate relations towards the domestication of international affairs.

[16] Kyoto Protocol to the United Nations Framework Convention on Climate Change (adopted 11th Dec 1997, entered into force 16th Feb 2005) 2303 UNTS 162, UN Reg No A-30822, Art 12.

[17] For a useful summary of these developments, see J Scott and L Rajamani, 'EU Climate Change Unilateralism' (2012) 23 *European Journal of International Law* 469, 470–74.

in Directive 2008/101 (the 'Emissions Trading Directive'),[18] which required air carriers to offset the carbon emissions of all aircraft entering or leaving airports in the EU regardless of the country of registration, and even if those emissions were made over the high seas or the airspace of foreign countries. The legality of the scheme was challenged before the EU's courts by a consortium of American airline operators. In December 2011, the European Court of Justice (ECJ) handed down the Decision in *Air Transport Association of America* (*Air Transport*),[19] in which it upheld the legality of the Emissions Trading Directive by reference to the provisions listed above. Following that ruling, the literature suddenly ceased to speak about multilateralism but instead began to rhapsodise about the EU's heroic role in global governance,[20] its unique ability to shape the international legal order,[21] and the exciting hope that EU unilateralism might lead to *more* multilateral cooperation in international affairs.[22]

II. BARTELS AND THE 'COMPLIANCE' INTERPRETATION

In an important article published in 2014, Bartels staked a path between these two poles to claim that the provisions (1) render the human rights norms internally applicable in the EU into norms it must 'respect' in the conduct of the EU's external action,[23] and (2) that they mandate 'compliance' with international law by turning international human rights 'norms' into norms of EU law binding upon EU institutions and actions.[24] Bartels uses the word 'respect' in the technical language of international human rights lawyers as denoting obligations not actively to cause harm; that is, to 'avoid measures that could prevent the enjoyment of the right'.[25] Such merely 'negative' obligations are customarily

[18] Parliament and Council Directive 2008/101/EC of 19 November 2008 amending Directive 2003/87/EC so as to include aviation activities in the scheme for greenhouse gas emission allowance trading within the Community [2009] OJ L8/3 101.

[19] Case C-366/10 *Air Transport Association of America and ors v Secretary of State for Energy and Climate Change* [2011] ECR I-13755, para 10.

[20] See, eg, B van Vooren, S Blockmans and J Wouters, *The EU's Role in Global Governance: The Legal Dimension* (Oxford, Oxford University Press, 2013). See also the Special Issue of the German Law Journal, Volume 13, Issue no 11 published in November 2012: 'Deciphering Regulatory and Constitutional Competence between EU Environmental Law and Global Governance'.

[21] See the collection of essays in D Kochenov and F Amtenbrink, *The European Union's Shaping of the International Legal Order* (Cambridge, Cambridge University Press, 2014).

[22] Joanne Scott and Lavanya Rajamani observe that the EU's 'ambitious strategy of contingent unilateralism … seeks to use the EU's market share as a means to stimulate climate action, globally and on the part of individual states'. Scott and Rajamani (n 17) 493.

[23] Bartels (n 1) 1074–75.

[24] Bartels (n 1) 1078–87.

[25] A Clapham, *Human Rights: A Very Short Introduction*, 2nd edn (Oxford, Oxford University Press, 2015) 130.

contrasted against proactive obligations to 'protect' and 'fulfil' human rights.[26] On this basis, he concludes that 'negative' obligations to respect human rights apply universally, while positive obligations to protect and fulfil are limited to EU territory. Accordingly, for Bartels, the provisions regulate the EU's *own* conduct, rather than that of the third parties who might be enabled to do certain things as a result of EU legislation or policy.

One objection should be dispatched at this point. In a short response to Bartels, Enzo Cannizzaro argued that Article 21 TEU was limited to policies falling under the Common Foreign and Security Policy (CFSP) pillar – the specialised regime within EU external relations for dealing with matters of defence and diplomacy – on the basis that 'Article 23 [TEU] assigns the pursuit of the political objectives laid down by Article 21(1) and (2) to the primary competence of the CFSP'.[27] Lorand Bartels responded in a rejoinder that the text of Article 23 TEU – which states that the conduct of the CFSP 'shall be guided by the principles, shall pursue the objectives of, and be conducted in accordance with' the general provisions on EU external relations (such as Article 21 TEU) – cannot sensibly be read to mean the CFSP is the *only* means by which the Article 21 TEU objectives are to be pursued.[28] Bartels was subsequently vindicated in *Parliament v Council (Tanzania Pirate Transfer Agreement)* by both the Advocate General and the ECJ. In the Opinion, Advocate General Kokott submitted that Articles 21(1), 21(2)(b) and 21(3) TEU properly interpreted provide that the 'rule of law and protection of human rights are, in general, among the principles governing the Union's external action which are to be observed and implemented not only, but also within the framework of the CFSP …'[29] The ECJ followed her advice, holding that 'compliance

[26] See *ibid* ('… the obligation to protect requires states to take measures that prevent third parties from interfering with the right … [and] the obligation to fulfil requires states to take positive measures that enable individuals and groups to enjoy the right …'). The typology of duties to respect, protect and fulfil was formulated by Henry Shue and entered international human rights discourse through Asbjørn Eide, at the time a member of the UN Sub-Commission on the Promotion and Protection of Human Rights. See H Shue, *Basic Rights: Subsistence, Affluence, and U.S. Foreign Policy*, 2nd edn (Princeton, Princeton University Press, 1996) Ch 2; A Eide, 'The International Human Rights System' in A Eide and W Barth Eide (eds), *Food as a Human Right* (Tokyo, United Nations University, 1984) 154.

[27] E Cannizzaro, 'The EU's Human Rights Obligations in Relation to Policies with Extraterritorial Effects: A Reply to Lorand Bartels' (2014) 25 *European Journal of International Law* 1093, 1098.

[28] L Bartels, 'The EU's Human Rights Obligations in Relation to Policies with Extraterritorial Effects: Rejoinder to Enzo Cannizzaro' (*EJIL: Talk!*, 23 January 2015), www.ejiltalk.org/rejoinder-to-enzo-cannizzaro.

[29] Case C-366/10 *Air Transport Association of America and ors v Secretary of State for Energy and Climate Change* ECLI:EU:C:2011:637 (6th October 2011), Opinion of AG Kokott, para 72. Advocate General Bot has also opined on several occasions that the provisions of Article 21(2) TEU bind all EU external action, including the CFSP. Case C-658/11 *European Parliament v Council of the European Union (Somali Pirates)* ECLI:EU:C:2014:41 (30 January 2014), Opinion of AG Bot, paras 85–90; Case C-130/10 *European Parliament v Council of the European Union* ECLI:EU:C:2012:50 (31st January 2012), Opinion of AG Bot, paras 62–64.

[with the principles set out in Article 21(1), Article 21(2)(b) and (3) TEU, and Article 23 TEU] is required of all actions of the European Union, including those in the area of the CFSP …'[30]

The first limb of Bartels's theory is a claim internal to EU law: it is that the provisions impose duties under EU law, for instance, by prohibiting the EU from imposing sanctions upon a third country if it would cause mass starvation there, or from entering into an agreement with another country to spy on that country's citizens in violation of its human rights obligations towards them. Regarding positive obligations, however, Bartels finds the provisions to be 'much more muted';[31] they give rise solely to duties to cooperate internationally through intergovernmental channels, civil society engagement, and other non-prescriptive means. Because the provisions do not specify any particular manner by which the EU is to achieve these ends, Bartels considers them legally unenforceable.[32]

In contrast, the second limb of Bartels's argument concerns international law: it is a claim that in addition to the above-mentioned obligations arising under EU law, 'the EU is also required to respect international human rights obligations to the extent these are binding on the EU under treaties or customary international law'.[33] This theme of compliance is implicit in numerous EU official and judicial pronouncements: for instance, a December 2011 Joint Communication by the Commission and CFSP High Representative (henceforth 'Joint Communication') states that 'EU external action has to comply with the rights contained in the EU Charter of Fundamental Rights which became binding EU law under the Lisbon Treaty, as well as with the rights guaranteed by the European Convention on Human Rights'.[34] The General Court in *Kadi II* also somewhat impertinently hinted at it when it cited Articles 3(5), 21(1) and 21(2) TEU in the course of observing that 'some' had expressed 'certain doubts'[35] about the *Kadi I*[36] judgment, in which the ECJ famously defied a UN Security Council resolution ordering the freezing of bank accounts belonging to individuals suspected of financing terrorism.

However, the most important source of doctrinal support for Bartels's interpretation is a passage in the *Air Transport* Decision where the ECJ observed that '[u]nder Article 3(5) TEU, the European Union is to contribute to the strict observance and the development of international law'. From this, it followed

[30] Case C-263/14 *European Parliament v Council of the European Union* ECLI:EU:C:2016:435 (14 June 2016), para 47.

[31] Bartels (n 1) 1074.

[32] Bartels (n 1) 1075.

[33] Bartels (n 1) 1078.

[34] Commission and High Representative of the European Union for Foreign Affairs and Security Policy, 'Communication on Human Rights and Democracy at the Heart of EU External Action – Towards a More Effective Approach' COM (2011) 886 final, 7.

[35] Case T-85/09 *Kadi v European Commission* [2010] ECR II-5177, para 115.

[36] Joined Cases C-402/05 and C-415/05 *Kadi v Council of the European Union and Commission of the European Communities* [2008] ECR I-6351.

that 'when it adopts an act, [the EU] is bound to observe international law in its entirety, including customary international law, which is binding upon the institutions of the European Union'.[37]

If, so the argument goes, the provisions are primarily about mandating compliance with international law and international human rights law, it must follow that there can be no positive *obligations* to protect or fulfil human rights from violation by third parties extraterritorially, because neither international human rights law nor international law *requires* them. Bartels sets out several reasons, which I develop only slightly.

A. Human Rights Jurisdiction

The first is the concept of 'state jurisdiction' or 'human rights jurisdiction' featuring in most human rights treaties. Such provisions are generally not interpreted merely as procedural hurdles imposed for housekeeping purposes, but as substantive 'thresholds' that an applicant must cross before the state concerned can be said to have obligations towards them under the treaty.[38] One view contends that the term 'human rights jurisdiction' is simply shorthand for 'the existence of a factual link between the State and the person',[39] such that the threshold is crossed by demonstrating that the state created some sufficiently intense, substantial or foreseeable factual effect upon the interests, needs, or welfare of the putative rights-bearer. For instance, such a theory has been advocated in several 'General Comments' of the Committee on Economic, Social and Cultural Rights (CESCR).[40] However, despite the promiscuity with which human rights activists cite instruments like CESCR General Comments,

[37] *Air Transport Association* (n 19) para 101. See also para 123.

[38] See M Milanovic, *Extraterritorial Application of Human Rights Treaties: Law, Principles, and Policy* (Oxford, Oxford University Press, 2011) 19 ('The notion of 'jurisdiction' in human rights treaties refers to the jurisdiction of a *state*, not to the jurisdiction of a *court*, even though this latter use of the word is otherwise the most frequent.'); S Besson, 'The Extraterritoriality of the European Convention on Human Rights: Why Human Rights Depend on Jurisdiction and What Jurisdiction Amounts To' (2012) 25 *Leiden Journal of International Law* 857, 861. ('Jurisdiction qua normative relationship between subjects and authorities actually captures the core of what human rights are about qua normative relationships between right-holders and institutions as duty-bearers. It is no wonder, therefore, that the ECHR has made the relationship of jurisdiction a pivotal notion to understanding who the right-holders, but also the duty bearers, of ECHR rights are.')

[39] M Scheinin, 'Just Another Word? Jurisdiction in the Roadmaps of State Responsibility and Human Rights' in M Langford et al (eds), *Global Justice, State Duties: The Extraterritorial Scope of Economic, Social, and Cultural Rights in International Law* (Cambridge, Cambridge University Press, 2012) 226.

[40] See, eg, Committee on Economic, Social and Cultural Rights, 'General Comment No 12: The Right to Adequate Food (Art 11),' UN Doc E/C 12/1999/5, para 36 ('In implementing this commitment [to take joint and separate action to achieve the full realization of the right to adequate food], States parties should take steps to respect the enjoyment of the right to food in other countries, to protect that right, to facilitate access to food and to provide the necessary aid when required.'); Committee on Economic, Social and Cultural Rights, 'General Comment No 14: The Right to the Highest Attainable Standard of Health (Article 12),' UN Doc E/C 12/2000/4, para 39 ('States parties

the consensus is that they are not legally binding,[41] which in turn means that they cannot count as sources of international law the EU must comply with.[42] Moreover, the Strasbourg Court, about whose judgments there is no question of bindingness, emphatically rejected such a theory in the *Banković* Decision, when it described it as

> tantamount to arguing that anyone adversely affected by an act imputable to a Contracting State, wherever in the world that act may have been committed or its actions felt, is thereby brought within the jurisdiction of that State for the purpose of Article 1 of the Convention.[43]

However else *Banković* may have been qualified or reversed, the rejection of a human rights 'effects doctrine' remains good law. As shall be demonstrated in chapter six, it is also normatively unassailable.

On a related note, Bartels usefully observes that harmful effects arising from the actions of private non-state actors also do not give rise to human rights jurisdiction, because those acts cannot be attributed to states or international organisations unless they knowingly aided or abetted those actors,[44] directed or controlled them,[45] or coerced them to that end.[46] Certainly, a different view is expressed in the set of rules proposed by a group of distinguished human

have to respect the enjoyment of the right to health in other countries, and to prevent third parties from violating the right in other countries, if they are able to influence these third parties by way of legal or political means, in accordance with the Charter of the United Nations and applicable international law.'); Committee on Economic, Social and Cultural Rights, 'General Comment No 15: The Right to Water (Arts 11 and 12),' UN Doc E/C 12/2002/11, para 31. ('International cooperation requires States parties to refrain from actions that interfere, directly or indirectly, with the enjoyment of the right to water in other countries. Any activities undertaken within the State party's jurisdiction should not deprive another country of the ability to realize the right to water for persons in its jurisdiction.')

[41] See, eg, Parliament of Canada, Standing Senate Committee on Human Rights, 'Promises to Keep: Implementing Canada's Human Rights Obligations' (2001), www.sencanada.ca/content/sen/committee/371/huma/rep/rep02dec01-e.htm ('... the views and decisions of these treaty-monitoring bodies are not binding on Canada, either under international or domestic law'); Ministry of Foreign Affairs, Norway, 'Focus on Human Dignity: A Plan of Action for Human Rights' (1999) Report No 21 to the Storting, Ch 4.3.2 (Box 4.2). ('While the recommendations and criticism of the monitoring committees are not legally binding, the Norwegian authorities attach great importance to them and they constitute important guidelines in the continuous efforts to ensure the conscientious implementation of the human rights conventions.') For a comprehensive, if somewhat dated, survey of the legal authority of human rights treaty body pronouncements, see R van Alebeek and A Nollkaemper, 'The Legal Status of Decisions by Human Rights Treaty Bodies in National Law' in G Ulfstein and H Keller (eds), *UN Human Rights Treaty Bodies: Law and Legitimacy* (Cambridge, Cambridge University Press, 2012).

[42] Bartels (n 1) 1087.

[43] *Banković and ors v Belgium and ors*, Admissibility [2001] ECHR 890, para 75.

[44] See International Law Commission, 'Draft Articles on Responsibility of States for Internationally Wrongful Acts, Adopted by the Commission at Its Fifty-Third Session in 2001' (2001) UN Doc A/56/10, 43, art 16 [hereinafter *ARS*]; International Law Commission, 'Articles on the Responsibility of International Organizations, Adopted by the Drafting Committee in 2011 (Final Outcome)' (2011) UN Doc A/CN.4/L.778, art 14 [hereinafter *ARIO*].

[45] See *ARS* art 17; *ARIO* art 15.

[46] See *ARS* art 18; *ARIO* art 16.

rights scholars known as the *Commentary to the Maastricht Principles*. That non-binding instrument takes the *Trail Smelter*[47] and *Corfu Channel*[48] principle that states have a general duty not to cause harm outside their territory, and extends the idea of internationally wrongful 'harm' to include abusive conduct by domiciliary multinational corporations overseas.[49] For this to make sense, however, that harm must amount to a human rights violation, which in turn presumes a human rights 'relationship' between the putative overseas right-holder and the state party duty-bearer.[50] That, however, is precisely the question at hand. Because it begs that question, the *Maastricht Commentary* ultimately results in precisely the human rights 'effects' doctrine rejected in *Banković*.

Bartels's article is, at its core, a sustained rejection of the view that human rights jurisdiction and therefore obligations result from the production of factual effects. States have no obligation under human rights law towards the individuals they affect. Instead, they bear responsibility for effects only upon individuals to whom they are obligated under human rights law.[51] But if human rights obligations are not functions of 'effects', how else are we to explain them? As indicated by his use of the word 'extraterritorial' to describe exceptional, problematic instances of human rights jurisdiction, it appears, for Bartels at least, to have something to do with *territory*. This association is not uncommon; the earliest expression of the idea of human rights jurisdiction was a statement in the *Namibia* Advisory Opinion, where the International Court of Justice observed that by

> occupying [Namibia] without title, South Africa incurs international responsibilities arising from a continuing violation of an international obligation. It also remains accountable for any violations of its international obligations, or of *the rights of the people of Namibia … Physical control of a territory, and not sovereignty or legitimacy of title, is the basis of State liability* for acts affecting other States (emphasis added).[52]

[47] *Trail Smelter Arbitration, United States v Canada* (1941) 3 RIAA 1905, 1965 ('under the principles of international law … no State has the right to use or permit the use of its territory in such a manner as to cause injury by fumes in or to the territory of another or the properties or persons therein …').

[48] *Corfu Channel, United Kingdom v Albania*, Judgment [1949] ICJ Rep 4, 22 (grounding Albania's obligation to inform British ships about the presence of mines on 'every State's obligation not to allow knowingly its territory to be used for acts contrary to the rights of other States').

[49] See commentary to Principle 3, para 9 in O De Schutter et al, 'Commentary to the Maastricht Principles on Extraterritorial Obligations of States in the Area of Economic, Social and Cultural Rights' (2012) 34 *Human Rights Quarterly* 1084, 1095–96 (because 'customary international law prohibits a state from allowing its territory to be used to cause damage on the territory of another state … [there is now] a duty for the state to respect and protect human rights extraterritorially'); *Loizidou v Turkey* (1996) ECHR 70, para 62 (state party may be responsible for a violation of international human rights treaty obligations where 'acts of their authorities, whether performed within or outside national boundaries … produce effects outside their own territory').

[50] Bartels (n 1) 1082.

[51] See Bartels (n 1) 1077–78, 1082–83.

[52] *Legal Consequences for States of the Continued Presence of South Africa in Namibia (South West Africa)*, Advisory Opinion [1971] ICJ Rep 16, para 118. See R Wilde, 'Human Rights Beyond

Indeed, the territorial association has even led to jurisdictional limitations being implied into treaties not expressly providing for them.[53] To be sure, Marko Milanovic, the most prominent scholar of the extraterritorial application of human rights treaties, argues in his widely-cited monograph that such a 'spatial' model is inadequate, and incorporates 'personal' elements to his theory of human rights jurisdiction.[54] Nevertheless, territorial control – 'boots on the ground'[55] – remains central to his model as well.[56] Accordingly, so the argument goes, the EU cannot owe any human rights obligations towards persons located outside territory controlled by its Member States, even if EU measures were to affect them significantly.

B. Jurisdiction under General International Law

From this association of human rights jurisdiction with territorial delimitation, it follows that measures to protect human rights 'extraterritorially' may be *prohibited*, rather than just not required. The EU would not just have no obligation, but no *competence* to enact extraterritorial legislation protecting the human rights of distant strangers, if doing so would constitute interference in the sovereignty of other states; that is, in their ability to control what goes on within their territory. Recall our hypothetical problem from the last chapter, where the Commission had to decide whether to regulate a proposed merger on the basis of the Ruritanian farmers' human rights, thereby frustrating the Ruritanian Government's industrialisation plans. Such an intervention might run afoul of the principle of non-intervention enshrined in Article 2(7) UN Charter and expressed in the UN General Assembly declarations on Inadmissibility of Intervention in the Internal Affairs of States (1965)[57] and Friendly Relations (1970).[58] In *Nicaragua*, the International Court of Justice (ICJ) invoked these

Borders at the World Court: The Significance of the International Court of Justice's Jurisprudence on the Extraterritorial Application of International Human Rights Law Treaties' (2013) 12 *Chinese Journal of International Law* 639, 661–62.

[53] In the *Wall* Opinion, the ICJ explained the lack of a jurisdictional stipulation in the International Covenant on Economic, Social, and Cultural Rights (ICESCR) as arising from 'the fact that this Covenant guarantees rights which are essentially territorial …' *Legal Consequences of the Construction of a Wall in the Occupied Palestinian Territory*, Advisory Opinion [2004] ICJ Rep 136, paras 111–13.

[54] See Milanovic (n 38) 127–208.

[55] Besson (n 38) 868.

[56] See ch 6, section II.B.

[57] United Nations General Assembly Resolution 2131 (XX): Declaration on the Inadmissibility of Intervention in the Domestic Affairs of States and the Protection of their Independence and Sovereignty, UN Doc A/RES/2131(XX), GAOR 20th Session Supp 14, 11 (1965).

[58] United Nations General Assembly Resolution 2625 (XXV): Declaration on Principles of International Law concerning Friendly Relations and Cooperation among States in accordance with the Charter of the United Nations, UN Doc A/RES/2625(XXV), GAOR 25th Session Supp 28, 121, UN Doc A/8028 (1970).

instruments to hold that the principle of non-intervention 'forbids all States or groups of States to intervene directly or indirectly in the internal or external affairs of other States', explaining that a 'prohibited intervention must accordingly be one bearing on matters in which *each State is permitted ... to decide freely* ... Intervention is wrongful when it uses methods of coercion *in regard to such choices, which must remain free ones*'.[59] Mere verbal condemnation of Ruritanian policy might restrict Ruritania's scope of action, but does not take away Ruritania's ability to make choices.[60] What would though, is if the Commission were to unilaterally sign it up to the International Covenant on Economic, Social and Cultural Rights (ICESCR), by regulating the merger for the benefit of Ruritanians.

International law generally requires all state action to have a jurisdictional basis in at least one of the grounds routinely described as territoriality, nationality, universality or the protective principle. Other than massive humanitarian disasters causing hordes of refugees to pour into the EU, it is difficult to imagine how the universality, passive personality or protective principles could justify jurisdiction over violations of human rights overseas. This leaves territoriality and nationality. Regarding the former, there is the 'effects doctrine' – a variant of objective territorial jurisdiction – seminally expressed in the *Alcoa* case, where Judge Learned Hand held that it was 'settled law ... that any State may impose liabilities, even upon persons not within its allegiance, for conduct outside its borders which has consequences within its borders which the State reprehends ...'.[61] This offers no help for the Ruritanian farmers because the reprehended consequences are felt outside the EU's borders. As for nationality jurisdiction, the classic exposition in the US Third Restatement of Foreign Relations Law provides that even where some link such as nationality obtains, 'a state may not exercise jurisdiction to prescribe law with respect to a person or activity having connections with another state when the exercise of such jurisdiction is unreasonable'.[62] Among the factors required to be taken into account in assessing 'reasonableness' are: 'the importance of regulation to the regulating state';[63] 'the extent to which another state may have an interest in regulating the activity';[64] and 'the likelihood of conflict with regulation by another state'.[65] Again, no help for the Ruritanians.

[59] *Military and Paramilitary Activities in and Against Nicaragua, Nicaragua v United States*, Merits [1986] ICJ Rep 14, para 205.

[60] *Ibid*, paras 244–45.

[61] *United States v Aluminum Co of America (Alcoa)* 148 F2d 416, 443 (2d Cir, 1945).

[62] *Restatement (Third) of Foreign Relations Law of the United States* (1987) s 403(2)(g).

[63] *Ibid* s 403(2)(c).

[64] *Ibid* s 403(2)(g).

[65] *Ibid* s 403(2)(h). See C Ryngaert, *Jurisdiction in International Law*, 2nd edn (Oxford, Oxford University Press, 2015) 146 (supporting the Third Restatement's 'rule of reason' approach to jurisdiction, 'since, as long as concurrent jurisdiction exists, in the field of both criminal and civil/economic law, there should be a method of designating the State which has, objectively, the best case for exercising jurisdiction'). See generally *ibid* Ch 5.

C. Standing

Bartels raises a final, devastating point of EU procedural law that seems to demolish even the few limited duties of respect arising under his compliance reading. Article 263 TFEU provides that individual standing to bring judicial review arises only against EU acts (1) addressed to the applicant or of *direct and individual concern* to them, and (2) against regulatory acts of *direct concern* to the applicant and not entailing implementing measures. Crucially, it limits judicial review to legislative acts or acts 'intended to produce *legal* effects vis-à-vis third parties' (emphasis added). *Factual* effects are not enough. In *Commune de Champagne*, the General Court invoked the principle of sovereign equality in Article 2(1) UN Charter and cited the then Article 299 TEC (now Article 355 TFEU) – which limits the application of the EC Treaty to the territory of the European Community – to hold that 'an act of an institution adopted pursuant to the Treaty, as a unilateral act of the Community, cannot create rights and obligations outside the territory thus defined'.[66] If correct, this would mean that distant strangers could never meet the standing requirements to review an EU act on the basis of violations of their human rights extraterritorially.[67] Instead, distant strangers will have to repose their hopes in EU institutions or Member States who as 'privileged applicants' are unfettered by normal standing requirements,[68] but are unlikely to undertake litigation on behalf of distant strangers.[69]

III. LEGAL EFFECTS AND THE SPATIAL SCOPE OF EU LAW

To reiterate, I agree with very much of Bartels's framework. However, I ultimately arrive at the opposite conclusion in chapter six. As a matter of the internal rationale of its relations with distant strangers, the EU can indeed come to owe 'positive' human rights obligations towards distant strangers. The route to this destination begins, however, in the seemingly peripheral observation Bartels makes in the course of discussing the 'procedural' question of standing to bring judicial review before EU courts – that the EU does not create legal effects outside the borders of its Member States. As indicated by the reasoning

[66] Case T-212/02 *Commune de Champagne v Council* [2007] ECR II-2023, paras 89–90. See also Joined Cases T-108/07 and T-354/08 *Spira v Commission* ECLI:EU:T:2013:367 (11 July 2013), para 123 (Commission requests for information do not create legal rights and duties outside the EU.)

[67] There have been several cases where Kurdish nationalist movements were held to have standing to challenge acts of the EU placing them on lists of terrorist organisations. See, eg, Case T-253/04 *Kongra-Gel v Council* [2008] ECR II-46; Case T-229/02 *PKK v Council* [2008] ECR II-45. Because these were taken pursuant to UN Security Council resolutions, I consider them not fully 'unilateral'.

[68] See Bartels (n 1) 1088, fn 89.

[69] Bartels (n 1) 1089.

in *Commune de Champagne*, this is related to being in 'compliance' with international law. The following section demonstrates there is much more to the notion of compliance than this.

Consider the reasoning of *Air Transport*, the main pillar of Bartels's compliance theory. The Court began by asserting the priority of international agreements over EU secondary legislation, that the EU was bound by norms of customary international law such as the freedom of the high seas and of airspace belonging to the territorial state underneath, and the general obligation of the EU to exercise its competences in light of the international legal requirements.[70] It then proceeded to state that actions of EU institutions could be reviewed against customary international law only in cases of 'manifest error' – a rather high bar.[71] This, however, turned out to be unnecessary: the Court ultimately found the extraterritorial imposition of emissions offsetting requirements to be in full accordance with treaty and customary international law.

The ECJ nowhere relied upon the nationality or protective principles, nor could it have: no security interests were involved, and the whole point of the Directive was to subject *foreign* airline operators to the same burdens borne by European operators. Territoriality was, therefore, the sole reed that could have supported the Emissions Trading Directive, and the Court invoked it in a singularly peculiar fashion. Jurisdiction was not premised upon the effects doctrine, despite being urged to do so by the Advocate General.[72] While the judgment does remark that aeroplane emissions 'contribute to the pollution of the air, sea or land territory of the Member States',[73] this appears almost as an afterthought. This is not for no reason: if effects upon the local environment alone could justify the assertion of jurisdiction, there would be no need for the planes to land in the territory – the relevant Member State authorities could simply calculate each airline operator's global emissions and bill them for it, regardless of where they were emitted.[74]

Instead, the Court held that the imposition of charges upon foreign aeroplanes for emissions made over the high seas or third states offended neither the customary rules of territorial jurisdiction nor the sovereignty of other states over their airspace, because these charges were only collected *after* the aeroplanes entered EU Member State territory, at which point they became subject to the 'unlimited' jurisdiction of the EU and the relevant Member State.[75] Once the aeroplanes had entered the airspace of the EU Member States, the EU could

[70] *Air Transport Association* (n 19) paras 50, 101, 123.
[71] *Air Transport Association* (n 19) para 110.
[72] *Air Transport Association*, Opinion of AG Kokott (n 29) para 154.
[73] *Air Transport Association* (n 19) para 129.
[74] G De Baere and C Ryngaert, 'The ECJ's Judgment in Air Transport Association of America and the International Legal Context of the EU's Climate Change Policy' (2013) 18 *European Foreign Affairs Review* 389, 401. See also L Bartels, 'The WTO Legality of the Application of the EU's Emission Trading System to Aviation' (2012) 23 *European Journal of International Law* 429, 459.
[75] *Air Transport Association* (n 19) paras 124–26.

validly charge to offset emissions made outside that airspace, simply because, in the Court's view, the treaties had given it the competence to specify the terms upon which commercial trade could be carried on within EU territory, which could include a high level of protection for the environment.[76] As such, the only necessary ground for establishing jurisdiction over the aircraft was *presence* on EU territory. Besides, the Decision was phrased not so much in terms of avoiding reprehended effects, but as a question of advancing important policy goals; namely, the 'environmental protection objectives which it has set for itself, in particular where those objectives follow on from an international agreement to which the European Union is a signatory …'.[77]

In this respect, the reasoning in *Air Transport* resembles what FA Mann termed the '*application* of legislation to a matter' whereby a state maintains it is not in any way regulating matters extraterritorially, but merely pronouncing upon the effect of foreign conduct domestically. In his classic text on jurisdiction in international law, Mann considered a hypothetical example of a statute prohibiting marriages between persons below 16 years of age, and intended to apply to the entire world irrespective of nationality, domicile or residence. That such a statute constituted an illegal excess of jurisdiction was, in Mann's view, 'doubtless'.[78] For this reason, Eyal Benvenisti concludes that the 'explicit reasoning of the judgment is not convincing', and that in so far as it 'does not recognize any limits to the prescriptive jurisdiction of the European states [it] is incompatible with basic principles of international law on state jurisdiction'.[79]

Indeed, in an earlier piece, Bartels developed Mann's focus on legislative intention to advocate the following test for whether a measure was extraterritorial and therefore illegal:

> The first step is to define legislation as 'extraterritorial' according to the *legal* connection between the legislation and the extraterritorial subject-matter; the second is to ask whether this amounts to a 'denial of opportunities normally open to the person against whom enforcement is directed'.[80]

[76] *Air Transport Association* (n 19) para 128, citing Art 191(2) TFEU.

[77] *Air Transport Association* (n 19) para 128, citing Art 191(2) TFEU. The international agreement in question here is the Framework Convention and the Kyoto Protocol.

[78] FA Mann, *The Doctrine of Jurisdiction in International Law* (The Hague, AW Sijthoff, 1964) 11. See *ibid* 12, discussing *Lepre v Lepre* [1963] 2 WLR 735 (disregarding for excess of jurisdiction a Maltese decree voiding all marriages by Roman Catholic Maltese citizens not conducted in accordance with the Catholic rites).

[79] E Benvenisti, 'Legislating for Humanity: May States Compel Foreigners to Promote Global Welfare?' in R Liivoja and J Petman (eds), *International Law-making: Essays in Honour of Jan Klabbers* (Abingdon, Routledge, 2014) 13–14.

[80] L Bartels, 'Article XX of GATT and the Problem of Extraterritorial Jurisdiction: The Case of Trade Measures for the Protection of Human Rights' (2002) 36 *Journal of World Trade* 353, 381. Bartels's notion of 'legal connection' does not appear to mean the same thing as causation of legal effects. *Ibid* ('… a measure defined by something located or occurring abroad should be considered just as extraterritorial as a measure specifically mandating or forbidding conduct abroad.').

What Bartels means by 'legal connection' is that the measure is 'directed' at, or '*made applicable* to conduct abroad in a relevant sense'.[81] On this definition, the Emissions Trading Directive is emphatically extraterritorial: it was *directed* at foreign airline operators to impose burdens upon them equivalent to those faced by their European counterparts, and, had it come into effect, would have resulted in a reduction of the opportunities they had enjoyed before. As such, we appear to have discovered a delicious irony: the primary authority Bartels relies upon for interpreting Article 3(5) TEU as mandating compliance with international law itself appears in flagrant violation of its jurisdictional rules – at least on Bartels's own extremely respectable interpretation of them.[82]

A. Defending *Air Transport*: Emerging Explanations and Forgotten Precedents

Despite not finding its explicit reasoning convincing, Benvenisti nevertheless discerns in *Air Transport* the outlines of an emerging theory of jurisdiction which allows 'relatively strong actors to promote global public goods unilaterally',[83] albeit one that can 'only be read between the lines and with great effort'.[84] Similarly, in their commentary on the *Air Transport* Decision, Geert De Baere and Cedric Ryngaert focus upon the citation made in passing to *Poulsen and Diva Navigation* – where the ECJ upheld the application of EU fishing regulations in the high seas through a similarly expansive claim of prescriptive jurisdiction[85] – to suggest that the ECJ in *Air Transport* was in effect proposing a 'novel ground of jurisdiction' aiming at the preservation 'of global public goods that are insufficiently protected by international solutions …'.[86]

De Baere and Ryngaert subject their conception of expanded jurisdictional competence to the proviso that 'the global public goods which they protect are laid down in international instruments with a global reach …, and provided that a territorial link with the regulator can be discerned'.[87] There are, however, several examples of extraterritorial EU measures advancing goods, values, or

[81] *Ibid* 382.

[82] For approaches similar to Bartels, see Scalia J in *Morrison v National Australia Bank* 561 US 247, 264–65 (2010) (having regard to the 'focus' or the 'solicitude' of a particular statute in assessing whether it had an extraterritorial purpose); and B Cooreman, 'Addressing Environmental Concerns through Trade: A Case for Extraterritoriality?' (2016) 65 *ICLQ* 229, 235–39 (distinguishing between 'inward' and 'outward' looking trade restrictions with environmental objectives on the basis of the 'location of the concern').

[83] Benvenisti (n 79) 16.

[84] Benvenisti (n 79) 13.

[85] Case C-286/90 *Anklagemyndigheden v Poulsen and Diva Navigation* [1992] ECR I-06019, paras 28–29, 34. The legislation involved was Council Regulation 3094/86/EEC of 7 October 1986 laying down certain technical measures for the conservation of fishery resources [1986] OJ L288/1.

[86] De Baere and Ryngaert (n 74) 401.

[87] De Baere and Ryngaert (n 74) 401.

other ends unilaterally 'before the relevant international standards have entered into force, when the international standards are in a form that is not binding, and when they have been ratified by only a small number of states'.[88] Indeed, quite a few extraterritorial EU measures regulate matters upon which other states have taken the diametrically opposite position, and the clearest examples of these tend to come from animal welfare regulation. In *European Federation for Cosmetic Ingredients*, the ECJ confirmed that Member States could, pursuant to EU animal testing regulations, create criminal liability within their domestic legal orders simply for relying upon information obtained from animal testing conducted in China and Japan, where such testing was positively *required* by those jurisdictions.[89] Similarly, in *Zuchtvieh*, the ECJ considered a preliminary reference from Bavaria on the question of whether Regulation 1/2005 prohibited a transport company being granted an export permit, where that company planned to truck cattle to Azerbaijan over a 7,000 km journey lasting nine days, during which there would only be two 24-hour stops. Although the claimants were unable to prove it, there was a possibility that this requirement would conflict with legislation in the countries the cattle were being transported through.[90] Nevertheless, the ECJ held that compliance with the regulation was required before Member State authorities could authorise the transportation of animals over long journeys commencing on the territory of the European Union and continuing outside it.[91]

In contrast to the above scholars who defend such expansive assertions of jurisdiction based on the substantive policies pursued, Joanne Scott looks to the form and structure of the measures to claim that *Air Transport* expresses a new theory of jurisdiction which she terms 'territorial extension'. On her definition, a measure is extraterritorial and illegal if it 'imposes obligations on persons who do not enjoy a relevant territorial connection with the regulating state'.[92] In contrast, territorial extension is permissible and obtains when 'application (depends) upon the existence of a relevant territorial connection, where the relevant regulatory determination will be shaped as a matter of law, by conduct or circumstances abroad'.[93] She argues that the EU only rarely acts

[88] J Scott, 'Extraterritoriality and Territorial Extension in EU Law' (2014) 62 *American Journal of Comparative Law* 87, 112; N Krisch, 'The Decay of Consent: International Law in an Age of Global Public Goods' (2014) 108 *American Journal of International Law* 1, 19–20 (viewing the EU's inclusion of international flights in the Emissions Trading Directive as involving 'a redefinition of the jurisdictional limits on extraterritorial action, or at least a "territorial extension" in response to transboundary challenges') (citations omitted).

[89] Case C-592/14 *European Federation for Cosmetic Ingredients v Secretary of State for Business, Innovation and Skills* ECLI:EU:C:2016:703 (21 September 2016) paras 39–40. The secondary legislation concerned was Parliament and Council Regulation 1223/2009/EC of 30 November 2009 on cosmetic products (recast) [2009] OJ L342/59.

[90] Case C-424/13 *Zuchtvieh-Export GmbH v Stadt Kempten* ECLI:EU:C:2015:259 (23 April 2015) paras 30, 53.

[91] *Ibid* para 56.

[92] Scott (n 88) 89.

[93] Scott (n 88) 90.

'extraterritorially' on her definition, but that it often resorts to territorial extension, finding examples in the domains of climate change, environment, maritime transport, air transport, financial services and competition, some of which will be examined shortly.[94]

B. *Fluctuat nec mergitur*: The *Lotus* Case in CJEU Jurisprudence

While Benvenisti, De Baere, Ryngaert and Scott all consider the theory of jurisdiction enunciated in *Air Transport* to be something new, it is in fact highly reminiscent of, if not in perfect accordance with, the one expressed in *Lotus* – the first and perhaps still only sustained exploration of that subject by an international court.[95] As legally-trained readers may recall from their earliest lectures on public international law, the Permanent Court of International Justice (PCIJ) held in that case that Turkey was entitled to exercise criminal jurisdiction over a French national, whose piloting of a French steamship resulted in a collision in the high seas with a Turkish vessel and the deaths of eight Turkish nationals. The technical reason given for the decision was that a vessel constituted part of the territory of its flag state under the then applicable law.[96] The long-standing significance of that decision, however, lies in the fact that the PCIJ laid out for the first time the distinction between enforcement and prescriptive jurisdiction. The relevant remarks are contained in a passage which, although technically *obiter*, have nevertheless become canonical:

> Now the first and foremost restriction imposed by international law upon a State is that – failing the existence of a permissive rule to the contrary – *it may not exercise its power in any form in the territory of another State*. In this sense jurisdiction is certainly territorial; it cannot be exercised by a State outside its territory *except by virtue of a permissive rule derived from international custom or from a convention.*
>
> *It does not, however, follow that international law prohibits a State from exercising jurisdiction in its own territory, in respect of any case which relates to acts which have taken place abroad, and in which it cannot rely on some permissive rule of international law*. Such a view would only be tenable if international law contained a general prohibition to States to extend the application of their laws and the jurisdiction of their courts to persons, property and acts outside the territory, and if, as an exception to this general prohibition, it allowed States to do so in certain specific cases. *But this is certainly not the case under international law as it stands at present.* Far from laying down a general prohibition to the effect that States may not extend the application of their laws and the jurisdiction of their courts to persons, property and acts outside their territory, *it leaves them in this respect a wide measure of*

[94] Scott (n 88) 95–96.

[95] *The Case of SS Lotus, France v Turkey, Judgment*, Judgment No 9 [1927] PCIJ (series A) No 10 (7 September 1927).

[96] *Ibid* 25. The facts are recited at *ibid* 10–12.

> *discretion which is only limited in certain cases by prohibitive rules*; as regards other cases, every State remains free to adopt the principles which it regards as best and most suitable.[97]

All the ingredients of *Air Transport* – that states may not exercise their power on the territory of other states absent a permissive rule, that they may legislate for persons, property and acts outside of their territory if they can call upon some other validating norm, and, that they have wide discretion regarding such extraterritorial legislation absent clear prohibitive rules – are present in the above two paragraphs. One may wonder, then, why *Lotus* was not explicitly cited as an authority in *Air Transport*.[98] One possible reason is the almost universal consensus among contemporary international legal scholars that there is something deeply amiss with it.[99] In his classic text, Mann describes the *Lotus* principle as 'a most unfortunate and retrograde theory … (which) cannot claim to be good law'.[100] Similarly, in what is the most authoritative contemporary monograph on the law of jurisdiction, Ryngaert argues that current practice, particularly in comparative criminal law, stands as a 'scathing indictment' of 'the *Lotus*-like jurisdictional merry-go-round with States doing whatever they like …'.[101] Instead, under 'the customary international law of jurisdiction …, extraterritorial prescriptive jurisdiction is arguably prohibited in the absence of a permissive rule'.[102]

There is, however, some reason to believe that this general antipathy towards *Lotus* is not shared by the judges of the CJEU, or at least the ECJ. Of course one cannot expect it to be admitted openly given the intense controversy surrounding it – hence Benvenisti's remark about having to read between the lines. This is particularly so given that ECJ judgments are written by committee in

[97] *Ibid* 18–19 (emphasis added).

[98] Advocate General Kokott makes a fleeting reference to *Lotus* on the subject of whether an aircraft may be deemed as part of the territory of the flag state. *Air Transport Association*, Opinion of AG Kokott (n 29) fn 126.

[99] See, eg, J Crawford, *Brownlie's Principles of Public International Law* (Oxford, Oxford University Press, 2012) 40 (describing *Lotus* as an instance of when 'some discretion is called for in handling decisions' of the ICJ and its predecessors and detailing the rejection of its jurisdictional theory by the International Law Commission (ILC) in 1958 and 1982); R Higgins, *Problems and Process: International Law and How We Use It* (Oxford, Clarendon Press, 1995) 77 ('Although I am not unsympathetic to the exercise of extraterritorial jurisdiction over certain conduct, I do feel that one cannot one cannot read too much into a mere dictum of the Permanent Court.'); AV Lowe, 'Blocking Extraterritorial Jurisdiction: The British Protection of Trading Interests Act, 1980' (1981) 75 *American Journal of International Law* 257, 263 ('It seems likely that the Court in the *Lotus* case only intended the presumption to apply in cases such as that before it … If it intended more than this, it was probably wrong.'). More recent international decisions read *Lotus* merely as stating a presumption of the legality of jurisdictional assertions. See *Arrest Warrant of 11 April 2000, Democratic Republic of Congo v Belgium*, Judgment, Separate Opinion of Judge Guillaume [2002] ICJ 35 (14 February 2002), para 4.

[100] Mann (n 78) 35.

[101] Ryngaert (n 65) 34.

[102] Ryngaert (n 65) 35.

a distinctly oracular fashion. However, some indication as to the dispositions of the judges might be obtained from the advisory opinions of the Advocates General, each of which is fundamentally a campaign to convince a majority of the bench. In this light, consider the Opinion in *UK v Parliament and Council*, in which the United Kingdom sought the annulment of the cap on bankers' bonuses imposed by Directive (EU) 2013/36,[103] and which went as far as the Advocate General's Opinion. The case would have been of awesome significance had it gone to judgment, but the UK withdrew its application before this happened. In its application, the UK urged an essentially Bartelsian compliance reading of Article 3(5) TEU, arguing that to 'the extent that [the Directive] is required to be applied to employees of institutions outside the EEA, it infringes Article 3(5) TEU and the principle of territoriality found in customary international law'.[104] In response, Advocate General Jääskinen opined that the UK 'would simply be wrong if it sought to claim that only territorial jurisdiction to legislate is permitted under international law', because customary international law [does] not contain a general prohibition on extending legislative jurisdiction of a State ('jurisdiction to prescribe') beyond its own territory.[105] To this end, he cited the Opinion in *Wood Pulp*, where Advocate General Darmon had earlier observed that despite doubts as to whether the *Lotus* was 'still sailing', that judgment could nevertheless be relied upon in the determination of a state's or international organisation's prescriptive jurisdiction, 'in contradistinction with the jurisdiction to enforce its power in any form in the territory of another State'.[106] Advocate General Jääskinen then dismissed the rest of the UK's argument, declaring that 'there can be no violation of Article 3(5) TEU because no such principle of international law against extraterritoriality … exists'.[107]

Finally, *Lotus* made a fleeting appearance in the recent important Decision in *Google Ireland*, which concerned whether Hungary could validly impose tax liabilities upon an Irish corporation not resident in Hungary but providing web services in the Hungarian language. Advocate General Kokott cited it in her Opinion as authority for the assertion that 'international law leaves States a wide measure of discretion which is only limited in certain cases for rules which relate to acts outside their territory'.[108] On this basis, she then argued that

[103] Parliament and Council Directive 2013/36/EU of 26 June 2013 on access to the activity of credit institutions and the prudential supervision of credit institutions and investment firms, amending Directive 2002/87/EC and repealing Directives 2006/48/EC and 2006/49/EC Text with EEA relevance [2013] OJ L176/338.

[104] Case C-507/13 *United Kingdom v Parliament and Council*, Application of United Kingdom (20 September 2013) 6th plea.

[105] Case C-507/13 *United Kingdom v Parliament and Council* ECLI:EU:C:2014:2394 (20 November 2014), Opinion of AG Jääskinen, paras 37–38.

[106] *Ibid*, para 37. See also Case 89/85, 104/85, 114/85, 116/85, 117/85 and 125/85 to 129/85 *Ahlström Osakeyhtiö and others v Commission (Wood Pulp)* ECLI:EU:C:1988:258 (25 May 1988), Opinion of AG Darmon, paras 27–30.

[107] *UK v Parliament and Council*, Opinion of AG Jääskinen (n 105), para 41.

[108] Case C-482/18 *Google Ireland Limited v Nemzeti Adó-és Vámhivatal Kiemelt Adó-és Vámigazgatósága* ECLI:EU:C:2019:728 (12 September 2019), Opinion of AG Kokott, para 44, fn 15.

extraterritorial taxation was objectionable in international law only if imposed upon 'persons or transactions in the world to which it has no connection at all',[109] and that the simple use of a country's language could constitute sufficient connection, even if speakers of that language were also to be found elsewhere.[110] She explained this position as being because '[n]o one can deny that language forms an important part of national identity and is thus strongly connected with a State and its territory'.[111] What if a country's language has come to be spoken throughout the world, like English? Advocate General Kokott felt 'no need' to address that problem.[112] The ECJ avoided the question of Hungary's jurisdictional rights under international law and disposed of the case in terms of EU fundamental freedoms and proportionate restrictions.[113]

Thus, in the final reckoning, it appears that the compliance reading is indeed correct to interpret the provisions in terms of mandating compliance with international law. The catch, however, is that the conception of 'international law' to be complied with is one that contemplates almost geographically unlimited rights of prescriptive jurisdiction.

IV. POWER AND AUTHORITY: A SUBTLE DIFFERENCE

Recall the line in *Lotus* about a state 'exercising jurisdiction in its own territory, in respect of any case which relates to acts which have taken place abroad'. What does it mean for an exercise of jurisdiction to 'relate' to acts abroad? One possibility is that it induces, influences, or otherwise manipulates persons abroad into acting in some desired way. Let us call this 'power'. Alternatively, a measure may relate to acts abroad by presuming to *govern* persons there; that is, by claiming an entitlement on the part of the legislator (1) directly to tell such persons abroad to do or desist from doing certain acts, and (2) to force them to do as they are told. This I term 'authority'. To illustrate, imagine someone who approaches you at a social occasion while you are in open company, and asks you to donate to his charity. Such a person may be said to 'oblige' you into doing what she wants by leveraging the pain of social awkwardness against you. However, she cannot be said to 'obligate' you – that is, to place you under an enforceable, binding duty. You might be thought miserly and anti-social for brushing off the request – and this might not be without consequence for you – but nobody would describe you as doing *wrong*. In contrast, however, the command of a person with authority, say a parent or an official, does imply some power to bind your will, and you do wrong by refusing to comply.

[109] *Ibid*, para 45.
[110] *Ibid* 48–55. There is a Hungarian-speaking population in Romania.
[111] *Ibid* 50.
[112] *Ibid*.
[113] Case C-482/18 *Google Ireland Limited v Nemzeti Adó-és Vámhivatal Kiemelt Adó-és Vámigazgatósága* ECLI:EU:C:2020:141 (3 March 2020).

This brings us to another difference concerning the implications for your normative position in relation to your things. The charity-organiser evidently possesses some form of factual power over you, but she cannot be described as changing your normative rights and obligations. In the same way, if a gunman robs you of your watch, you certainly no longer possess it 'empirically', but you still retain your *right* to it. The gunman's factual deprivation of your watch leaves your normative relations with respect to it entirely unchanged. In contrast, the official does change your normative position by his command: you now have an obligation to hand over money where previously you had none. In this sense, a claim of authority is more than just a question of brute power; it is a claim of a 'normative power to change [your] normative relations'.[114] Or, to put it differently, the possession of authority is not simply a matter of 'having an ability to influence people'.[115] Rather, it 'is coupled with a claim that those people are bound to obey'.[116]

Authority differs from social influence or the 'soft power' wielded by private corporations, as well as from non-practical forms of authority such as the 'epistemic' authority of pundits. Although there may be significant overlaps between these two categories, the pronouncements, standards and recommendations of the former cannot in and of themselves amount to examples of practical, much less political authority.[117] Compliance with standards set by informal or private organisations can only be for prudential reasons: one may lose access to certain markets or professions if one declines to comply.[118] One is 'obliged'

[114] SJ Shapiro, 'Authority' in J Coleman and SJ Shapiro (eds), *The Oxford Handbook of Jurisprudence and Philosophy of Law* (Oxford, Oxford University Press, 2004) 398.

[115] J Raz, 'Authority and Justification' in *Authority* (New York, New York University Press, 1990) 118.

[116] *Ibid.*

[117] N Roughan, *Authorities: Conflicts, Cooperation, and Transnational Legal Theory* (Oxford, Oxford University Press, 2013) 20. *cf* the concept of *auctoritas*, which Roman public law accorded the Senate, and which rendered its pronouncements something 'more than advice and less than a command, an advice which one may not safely ignore'. H Arendt, 'What Is Authority?' in H Arendt, *Between Past and Future: Six Exercises in Political Thought* (New York, Viking Press, 1961) 92–93; citing T Mommsen, *Römisches Staatsrecht*, vol 3 (Berlin, S Hirzel, 1888) 1034.

[118] In recent writings, Nico Krisch rejects traditional identifications of authority with command and obedience – he calls it 'solid authority' – in favour of a more 'liquid' conception that accommodates deference. This, he argues 'has the potential to broaden our view significantly' and 'to diagnose a greater extent of authority' in international relations than before. N Krisch, 'Liquid Authority in Global Governance' (2017) 9 *International Theory* 237, 242. On Krisch's view, this is desirable because it both 'captures a broader part of consequential practices in global governance … [and] also paves the way for asking harder questions about, and developing more calibrated approaches to, questions of law, legitimacy and accountability in this context'. N Krisch, 'Authority, Solid and Liquid, in Postnational Governance' in R Cotterell and M Del Mar (eds), *Authority in Transnational Legal Theory: Theorising Across Disciplines* (Cheltenham, Edward Elgar Publishing, 2016) 27. While Krisch is certainly correct to call for the asking of hard questions regarding legitimacy in international and transnational affairs, it is submitted that this may be encouraged just as well by describing these relationships in terms of 'power', which is equally in need of normative justification. In fact, the strategy of conflating relationships of obedience and deference under a single idea of 'liquid authority' runs the risk of impeding the task of asking and answering the hard questions, because these relations require very different normative justifications.

rather than 'obligated' to follow those standards. As for epistemic authority, there may be very good prudential reasons to follow a pundit's advice – she has received advanced training in subjects about which you are wholly uninformed – but the proper response to such imperatives is deference, which implies choice, and in turn a non-hierarchical relationship between the maker of the statement and the recipient.[119] In contrast, subjects of practical authorities – children *vis-à-vis* their parents, and citizens *vis-à-vis* the State – are expected not simply to defer, but to obey.[120] Exercises of influence, manipulation or outright coercion do not imagine that the target has a moral duty to obey. In contrast, obedience is the first demand of political authority.[121]

A. The Nature of Territorial Extension

With this broad distinction in mind, it may be taken as given that the EU wields considerable power in the wider world, simply by being the world's largest trading bloc, at least at the time of writing. A well-known discussion of this phenomenon is Anu Bradford's thesis of a 'Brussels Effect' in international corporate regulation, according to which the EU sets global standards in a fashion that results in races to the top rather than to the bottom.[122] My thesis, however, is that there is something more at hand.

Contrast the Emissions Trading Directive introduced above with another environmental measure with extraterritorial implications: the prohibition enacted under the US Endangered Species Act against the importation of shrimp caught in the high seas using nets that tended to snare endangered turtles.[123] In the *Shrimp/Turtle* World Trade Organization (WTO) dispute,[124] the Appellate Body declared it incompatible with the General Agreement on Trade and Tariffs (GATT), not because such a measure was in and of itself contrary to the GATT,

[119] In order to illustrate this idea, Roughan chooses the more problematic example of advice given by a physician. Roughan (n 117) 20 ('... my doctor knows far more about medicine than I do, but decisions about my treatment are ultimately mine to make, not hers'). While she is correct that doctors and other epistemic authorities such as financial advisers do not actually change your normative position, other factors relating to their personal relationship of trust and confidence with you mean that they are held to the same legal obligations towards you as those who directly make decisions for you. See ch 4 of this volume, text to nn 18–20.

[120] Roughan (n 117) 109.

[121] Raz (n 115) 116 ('The exercise of coercive or any other form of power is no exercise of authority unless it includes an appeal to compliance by the persons subject to the authority.'); and generally Roughan (n 117) Ch 2.

[122] Bradford (n 9) 52–53. See also G Greenleaf, 'The Influence of European Data Privacy Standards Outside Europe: Implications for Globalization of Convention 108' (2012) 2 *International Data Protection Law* 68, 76 (suggesting 'a strong inference that European privacy standards have been, either directly, or indirectly, influential [as an impetus for adopting internet data privacy laws] in all of these [twenty-nine] Latin American, Asian, African, and Australasian countries').

[123] Public Law 101–162, s 609 (codified at 16 USC 1537) (21 November 1989).

[124] *United States – Import Prohibition of Certain Shrimp and Shrimp Products*, Appellate Body (adopted 12 October 1998) WT/DS58/AB/R (hereinafter *Shrimp/Turtle*).

but because there had been insufficient consultation with other WTO Members before it was enacted.[125] In due course, *Shrimp/Turtle* became the poster-child for discussions in trade law regarding 'Process and Production Methods' (PPM) measures, where one state restricts or places conditions upon trade in its markets of foreign goods, not based on their tangible physical characteristics, but because of the intangible question of how they were produced overseas, for instance through environmentally unsustainable, or exploitative methods.[126] Such measures *prima facie* raise an issue of extraterritoriality because by focusing on the manufacturing process, they appear to be 'directed' at production in the exporting state rather than the effects of products in the importing state.[127] For this reason, Bartels argues that PPM measures – he calls them 'ecological trade measures' – are extraterritorial, while tariffs and subsidies are in contrast territorial.[128]

Due to their common purpose, commentators such as Benvenisti, Ryngaert and Scott have all discussed *Air Transport* and *Shrimp/Turtle* in the same breath, with Ryngaert and Scott specifically asserting that support for the supposedly new technique of 'territorial extension' is offered by *Shrimp/Turtle*.[129] There is, however, a subtle but crucial difference. The measure in *Shrimp/Turtle* pursued its objectives by placing conditions upon the entry of the product into the jurisdiction: by banning it, taxing it, excluding it from public procurement schemes, etc. It therefore never actually *commanded* any specific conduct outside the regulating state. All it did was regulate conduct within the borders in a manner that incentivised, induced or manipulated individuals outside into acting in the way desired by the regulating jurisdiction. Although the regulating jurisdiction certainly wielded *power* over the producer extraterritorially, it did so by exercising its *authority* – that is, its entitlement to create legal rights and duties – only inside its borders. It was as if the regulator was affecting to say: '*By all means carry on using turtle-unfriendly nets on the high seas if you think yourself tough enough to survive not having access to our markets.*' The same logic animates the 'effects doctrine' in US antitrust law:

> *You can do whatever you want outside the borders. But, if you so much as cause a single direct, substantial, and reasonably foreseeable effect within the borders, then our regulation bites. If you can avoid this, you are perfectly entitled to your pound of flesh.*

[125] See *ibid*, paras 121, 133, 159.

[126] See, eg, *United States – Restrictions on the Imports of Tuna*, Panel Report (16 August 1991 (not adopted)), GATT Doc DS21/R; *United States – Measures Affecting Alcoholic and Malt Beverages*, Panel Report (adopted 7 February 1992), GATT Doc DS23/R-39S/206; *United States – Restrictions on the Imports of Tuna*, Panel Report (20 May 1994 (not adopted)), GATT Doc DS29/R; *United States – Taxes on Automobiles*, Panel Report (30 September 1994 (not adopted)) GATT Doc DS31/R; *United States – Standards for Reformulated and Conventional Gasoline*, Panel Report (adopted 20 May 1996) WT/DS2/AB/R.

[127] See Bartels (n 80) 381–86; Ankersmit, Lawrence and Davies (n 7) 14.

[128] Bartels (n 80) 382.

[129] See Benvenisti (n 79) 13–14; Scott (n 88) 115–16; Ryngaert (n 65) 97–98.

Strictly speaking, in both of these examples, you are only 'obliged' – never 'obligated' – to amend your overseas conduct. In fact, they cannot even be said to *coerce* you, for the regulating state has no obligation to open its markets to you.[130] Obligations under a trade agreement are owed to other states party to the agreement, not to you. Thus, such measures do not, as it were, take anything 'away' from you, but merely change the world in a way that you might not prefer. The fact that they restrict your 'opportunities' is neither here nor there unless you have a *right* to those opportunities. If not, then having them is simply your good fortune.

Territorial extension, at least as exemplified by *Air Transport*,[131] seems different. The EU Emissions Trading Scheme did not simply incentivise, induce, or manipulate the foreign airlines into offsetting their overseas carbon emissions – it directly *commanded* it. Certainly, airline operators could have avoided its application by choosing not to enter the EU. However, that is where the similarities end. The Emissions Trading Scheme was not an exclusionary barrier like a tariff; it applied to foreign aeroplanes *leaving* the EU as well. This question was specifically litigated in *Air Transport*. The applicants had argued that the scheme was an exclusionary fuel tax in violation of the Open Skies Agreement.[132] The ECJ rejected this argument, holding plausibly that the scheme by its nature was not a tax, duty, fee or charge imposed on the fuel load, but a 'market-based measure' which left airline operators with carbon allowances, which, if used prudently, might even have earned the operators a profit.[133]

The non-'exclusionary' logic of the Emissions Trading Scheme can be demonstrated more simply. The primary sanction for non-compliance with the Emissions Trading Scheme was not exclusion. Non-compliant aeroplanes landing in the EU Member States would have been permitted to land and take off as per normal, and the competent Member State authorities would simply

[130] See *Military and Paramilitary Activities in and Against Nicaragua* (n 59) para 138 ('A State is not bound to continue particular trade relations longer than it sees fit to do so, in the absence of a treaty commitment or other specific legal obligation.') and *ibid*, para 253 ('Trade is not a duty of a State under general international law but may only be a duty imposed by a treaty.') (Judge Oda, dissenting).

[131] Scott includes PPM-like exclusionary measures within her understanding of territorial extension. See Scott (n 88) 101–102, 111–13, citing the 'Class Societies Regulation', or Parliament and Council Regulation (EC) No 391/2009 of 23 April 2009 on common rules and standards for ship inspection and survey organisations [2009] OJ L131/11. The Class Societies Regulation regulates organisations engaged in ensuring the safety of maritime transport by providing certificates attesting to a particular vessel's seaworthiness and general compliance with relevant international maritime safety and marine pollution conventions. Such bodies are permitted to operate in the EU only if granted recognition by the EU and authorised by a Member State. The EU's grant of recognition is conditional upon *worldwide* compliance with EU standards on ship safety and environmental protection, which exceed those set out in international instruments such as the Code on Recognized Organizations promulgated by the International Maritime Organization.

[132] *Air Transport Association* (n 19) para 21; Air Transport Agreement between the European Community and the United States of America ('Open Skies' Agreement) [2007] OJ L134/4, Art 11.

[133] *Air Transport Association* (n 19) paras 142–45.

have imposed upon the operator a fine of €100 per non-surrendered allowance, coupled with an injunction to make up for the shortfall in the following year.[134] Exclusion would have kicked in only secondarily if the operator refused to pay those fines.[135] In comparison, the measure in *Shrimp/Turtle* never at any point presumed to sanction foreign ships simply for using turtle-unfriendly nets on the high seas. Any secondary sanctions imposed, say, for selling prohibited shrimp within the US, simply reiterate the primary norm of exclusion. In short, the rationale behind the measure in *Shrimp/Turtle* was to 'induce' conduct overseas by threatening exclusion from the market. In contrast, the Emissions Trading Directive in *Air Transport* treated overseas conduct 'as if' it had taken place within the domestic internal market, and on this basis *included* it within the scope of the EU's legislative competence. As such, the Emissions Trading Scheme was not extraterritorially 'binding' but also coercive.

Other clear examples of this basic logic may be found in CJEU jurisprudence on extraterritorial competition regulation. Unlike the General Court,[136] the ECJ has *never* relied upon the effects doctrine.[137] The seminal case is *Wood Pulp I*, which involved an international cartel coordinating the prices of wood pulp being sold into the EU. Just like *Air Transport*, the Court rejected pleas by both the Commission and the Advocate General for the adoption of the effects doctrine, holding instead that the 'decisive factor … is the place where the [anti-competitive agreement] is implemented'.[138] The conduct constituting such 'implementation' was the making of quarterly price announcements within the EU. Now, if *Commune de Champagne* was correct and the EU's ability to create legal effects really stopped at its Member States' borders, the appropriate

[134] Parliament and Council Directive 2003/87/EC of 13 October 2003 establishing a scheme for greenhouse gas emission allowance trading within the Community and amending Council Directive 96/61/EC [2003] OJ L275/32, Art 16(3).

[135] *Ibid*, Arts 16(5)–(12).

[136] See Case T-102/96 *Gencor v Lonrho* [1999] ECR II-753, para 90.

[137] The closest the ECJ has come to this was in *Intel v Commission*, in which it heard an appeal from a Decision by the General Court which found that the Commission had validly asserted jurisdiction over the foreign applicant on the basis of the substantial, immediate and foreseeable effect its conduct was liable to have within the internal market. See Case T-286/09 *Intel v Commission* ECLI:EU:T:2014:547 (12 June 2014), para 296. The ECJ did not overrule this holding, but it did not exactly adopt it either. Instead, it held that although the General Court's 'qualified effects' doctrine of jurisdiction differed in rationale from the ECJ's own 'implementation' theory of jurisdiction, the effects of the two theories were the same, and so no appeal could be allowed. See Case C-413/14 *Intel v Commission* ECLI:EU:C:2017:632 (6 September 2017), paras 43–45.

[138] Joined Cases 89/85, 104/85, 114/85, 116/85, 117/85 & 125/85 to 129/85 *Ahlström Osakeyhtiö and others v Commission (Wood Pulp I)* [1988] ECR 5193, para 16. See generally *ibid*, paras 11–18 (finding that although the sources of wood pulp were located outside the EU, the fact that the undertakings concerned competed for custom within it meant they were engaging in competition within the EU, such that the application of EU competition regulation to them was a valid exercise of jurisdiction under the territoriality principle). Note that the prohibition against anticompetitive agreements requires such agreements to have as its object or effect the restriction of competition within the common market. However, market effects enter into the picture as a condition for merger regulation, not as the basis for jurisdiction. *Ibid*, para 2.

response in *Wood Pulp I* would have been to regulate the quarterly price announcements occurring inside EU territory, not the cartel activity outside. Instead, we find that the activity of announcing prices is of no concern to the EU regulator, merely the *presence* established for implementing such activity. Such presence, euphemistically called 'implementation', is enough to *govern* behaviour all over the world.[139]

Effectively, this means that the rule in *Commune de Champagne* cannot be correct. It is in fact directly contradicted by prior and higher ECJ jurisprudence. In *Boukhalfa*, the ECJ faced the question of whether EU prohibitions against nationality discrimination could apply to a Belgian national employed as a member of the local staff at the German embassy in Algiers, under a contract concluded under Algerian law. The ECJ rejected Germany's argument that the then Article 227 TEC[140] limited the application of the EU Treaties to the territory of the Member States, holding instead that that 'article does not … preclude Community rules from having effects outside the territory of the Community'.[141] The effects concerned in that case were clearly legal effects.[142] Properly interpreted, that provision and its heirs in Articles 25 TEU and 355 TFEU do not place geographical limits upon the normativity of EU law. Instead, they specify the High Contracting Parties that are bound by it.[143]

These considerations reveal that the crucial distinguishing mark of the EU's mode of asserting extraterritorial jurisdiction lies in the creation of *legal* effects extraterritorially. The terms of a *Shrimp/Turtle*-style measure only 'govern' conduct within the territory, even if the objective of that command is to 'affect' behaviour outside it. In contrast, under territorial extension, those terms govern the entire world directly. We must therefore reject both Scott's claim that

[139] In an early and perceptive discussion of comparative US and EU 'paradigms' of jurisdiction to adjudicate private disputes, Michaels argues that

> in the domestic U.S. paradigm, the role of boundaries is one of *delimitation*. The power of a court goes to the state's boundaries, not beyond them … By contrast, the role of state boundaries in the international European paradigm is one of *allocation*: the locus of an event or a party defines the place that has jurisdiction in a multilateral fashion.

R Michaels, 'Two Paradigms of Jurisdiction' (2005–06) 27 *Michigan Journal of International Law* 1003, 1058. Jurisdiction to settle private disputes is widely considered to be an aspect of prescriptive jurisdiction.

[140] This was the same provision interpreted by the General Court in *Commune de Champagne*. 'Article 227 TEC' is the numbering in the Treaty of Maastricht (1992) and the Treaty of Rome (1957), while 'Article 299 TEC' is its numbering in the Treaty of Nice (2001).

[141] Case C-214/94 *Ingrid Boukhalfa v Germany* [1996] ECR I-2253, para 14.

[142] See *ibid*, para 15 ('[T]he Court has consistently held that provisions of Community law may apply to professional activities pursued outside Community territory as long as the employment relationship retains a sufficiently close link with the Community.').

[143] V Moreno-Lax and C Costello, 'The Extraterritorial Application of the EU Charter of Fundamental Rights: From Territoriality to Facticity, the Effectiveness Model' in S Peers et al, *The EU Charter of Fundamental Rights* (Oxford, Bloomsbury Publishing, 2014) 1664.

'territorial extension' is distinct from 'extraterritoriality', as well as Bartels's argument that extraterritoriality is a question of whether a measure is 'directed' at, or 'made applicable to conduct abroad'. The problem with Scott's claim is the assumption that the place of enforcement is the crucial factor in determining whether a measure is extraterritorial. Instead, it is *prescription* that matters, because that is what modifies your legal position.[144] Enforcement is merely the final act in the piece: by the time a rule is being enforced against you, your legal position should already have been determined. If not, then you have much bigger problems on your hands than just excess of jurisdiction. In contrast, the problem with Bartels's argument is that it is not the intention behind the measure, but its formal structure that matters. There is really no difference between the 'focus' or 'solicitude' of agricultural subsidies on the one hand, and tariffs defined by conduct or events overseas on the other. Both are equally carefully calibrated by teams of trade economists to erode the comparative advantage of foreign firms. This is why the report in *Shrimp/Turtle* was phrased not in terms of an excess of jurisdiction, but in terms of a possible violation of a bargain between states to keep their domestic markets open to traders from each other except in certain instances; that is, as a breach of contract.[145]

Put simply, the only test for whether a measure is extraterritorial is to ask 'where are you when you are being told what to do?' If the answer is 'overseas', then it is extraterritorial. If not, not. This reading of the phrase 'extraterritorial jurisdiction' takes seriously both the words 'extraterritorial' and 'jurisdiction': the second word in the phrase means 'speaking law'.[146] By this standard, the Emissions Trading Directive, as well as a great deal of the EU's competition and financial regulation, is emphatically extraterritorial. The EU does not just wield *power* over distant strangers in its relations with the wider world – it often claims *authority* over them, and has done so for a very long time.

[144] See Mann (n 78) 14 (while 'the mere exercise of prescriptive jurisdiction, without any attempt at enforcement, will not normally have to pass the test of international law … it is not difficult to visualize circumstances in which the exercise of legislative jurisdiction plainly implies the likelihood of enforcement that foreign States are entitled to challenge its presence on the statute book').

[145] *United States – Import Prohibition of Certain Shrimp and Shrimp Products* (n 124) para 159. ('The task of interpreting and applying the chapeau is, hence, essentially the delicate one of locating and marking out a line of equilibrium between the right of a Member to invoke an exception under Article XX and the rights of other Members … so that neither of the competing rights will cancel out the other and thereby distort and nullify or impair the balance of rights and obligations constructed by the Members themselves in that Agreement.') See Cooreman (n 82) 230 (observing that the Appellate Body 'avoided answering whether there is an "implied jurisdictional limitation" in Article XX GATT – i.e. whether WTO Members can only act to protect a concern within their jurisdiction …').

[146] Mann (n 78) 13 ('Jurisdiction is concerned with the State's right of *regulation* or, in the incomparably pithy language of Mr. Justice Holmes, with the right "to apply the law to the acts of men"'), citing *Wedding v Mayler* 192 US 573, 479 (1904).

V. CONCLUSION

This chapter has argued that the EU does not just exercise 'power' in its relations with the wider world, but has often claimed a geographically unbounded *authority* to prescribe rules binding upon distant strangers. It does not just create factual effects over distant strangers in a manner that merely affects them. Instead, it often creates *legal* effects over them – it governs them. If so, this raises the possibility that the ECJ's deployment of Article 3(5) TEU is self-contradictory, in that its delineation of the EU's jurisdictional rights does not just depart from the 'strict observance of international law,' but is, in fact, absolutely antithetical to it. In this regard, Andrea Gattini remarks of the *Air Transport* Decision that it effectively arrogates to the EU 'the role of legislator, fee collector, and lastly exclusive beneficiary of the revenues [of the Emissions Trading Scheme], for the sake of the entire world'.[147] In Gattini's view, such a claim smacks of imperial hubris; it can be 'understood only if one posits himself [*sic*] on a universal plane, in a supposed *civitas mundi*'.[148]

Nonetheless, as we have seen, the jurisdictional theory in *Air Transport* is not without powerful support in *Lotus*, a foundational Decision which, though much maligned and traduced, has never actually been overruled. This raises the possibility that the entire project of international law is itself inescapably imperial, and in turn whether objections to imperialism and hegemony are just 'simplistic worries'[149] in light of the prolonged failure of multilateral political efforts to address global concerns such as climate change, terrorism, financial crime and other 'global public bads'. The next chapter picks up this thread in examining the claim that extraterritorial jurisdiction is legitimate when asserted in pursuit of providing 'global public goods'. It explores some recent attempts developing this claim to find that they fail deeply.

[147] A Gattini, 'Between Splendid Isolation and Tentative Imperialism: The EU's Extension of Its Emission Trading Scheme to International Aviation and the ECJ's Judgment in the *ATA* Case' (2012) 61 *ICLQ* 977, 983.

[148] *Ibid* 982–83.

[149] Benvenisti (n 79) 4.

3

The 'Missionary' Principle: A False Start

MULTILATERAL EFFORTS TO provide 'global public goods' – a term used capaciously to refer to numerous policy areas requiring cross-border cooperation – often progress very slowly if at all. Even then, all it takes is a few uncooperative players to ruin everything. For example, in the time this book was written, the world witnessed both the conclusion of the 2015 Paris Climate Accord by 195 countries to reduce greenhouse gas emissions and its effective scuppering following the United States' withdrawal in 2017. Faced with such challenges, individual states and political communities of jurisdiction have sometimes acted 'unilaterally' – as if to force the wider world into a form of 'mandatory' cooperation. Such measures are by no means the preserve of global economic or military powers: in 2014, the tiny island republic of Singapore legislated to create civil and criminal liability for corporations engaging in the fire-clearing of Indonesian forests, resulting in the chronic air pollution of Singapore.[1]

Unsurprisingly, however, they are fraught with legal and political controversy. Following the *Air Transport* Decision,[2] 23 countries threatened retaliation such as international litigation, review or repudiation of air transport service agreements with the EU. The Commission subsequently shelved emissions offsetting requirements on international flights, and in 2017 proposed to impose them only on flights within the European Economic Area.[3] Notwithstanding this question of political viability, several scholars have attempted to argue that as far as international legal validity is concerned, unilateral measures like the EU Emissions Trading Scheme are entirely unobjectionable in so far as they: (1) address 'harms' which cannot be contained within any one state; and/or (2) advance universal 'values,' 'common concerns' or 'community interests'

[1] Transboundary Haze Pollution Act 2014 (Singapore) ss 4–8.

[2] Case C-366/10 *Air Transport Association of America and ors v Secretary of State for Energy and Climate Change* [2011] ECR I-13755.

[3] Commission, 'Proposal for a Regulation of the European Parliament and of the Council amending Directive 2003/87/EC to continue current limitations of scope for aviation activities and to prepare to implement a global market-based measure from 2021' COM(2017) 54 final.

purportedly 'shared by all individuals, irrespective of their nationality'.[4] The roots of the first argument lie in the *Trail Smelter* and *Corfu Channel*[5] cases discussed in the previous chapter, while those of the second may be traced to *Barcelona Traction*, where the International Court of Justice (ICJ) observed *obiter* that certain international obligations are owed to the 'international community as a whole', rendering the fulfilment of those obligations 'the common concern of all States', which, therefore 'have a legal interest in their protection'.[6] The central premise underlying both of these approaches is an understanding of the point and purpose of law as advancing 'well-being'; expressed variously as the fulfilment of 'basic interests' such as security, subsistence or pursuit of 'values' supposedly essential for human flourishing.[7] For this reason, both strands of discourse tend to deploy the concept of 'public goods' as it is commonly defined in the economic sciences.[8] That is to say, environmental protection, the prevention of terrorism, competitive markets, and other similar things are designated as 'global public goods' because they enhance utility for all, but tend to be 'undersupplied' due to certain structural features of non-rivalrousness and non-excludablility.[9] This, in turn, leaves particular

[4] NL Dobson and C Ryngaert, 'Provocative Climate Protection: EU "Extraterritorial" Regulation of Maritime Emissions' (2017) 66 *ICLQ* 295, 300. See also J Brunnée, 'The Global Climate Regime: Wither Common Concern?' in A Seibert-Fohr et al (eds), *Coexistence, Cooperation and Solidarity: Liber Amicorum Rüdiger Wolfrum*, vol 1 (Leiden, Brill, 2011) 723. ('The concept of common concern of humankind is applicable to environmental concerns that arise beyond the jurisdiction of states as well as those that arise within states. Importantly, it is not areas or resources that are common concerns, but certain environmental processes or protective actions.')

[5] *Trail Smelter Arbitration, United States v Canada* (1941) 3 RIAA 1905; *Corfu Channel, United Kingdom v Albania*, Judgment [1949] ICJ Rep 4.

[6] *Barcelona Traction, Light and Power Co Ltd (Belgium v Spain)*, Judgment, merits, second phase [1970] ICJ Rep 3, para 33. While the *Barcelona Traction* comments seem to refer to obligations, the preamble to the United Nations Framework Convention on Climate Change (UNFCC) instead employs that phrase with respect to events: 'change in the Earth's climate and its adverse effects are a common concern of humankind'. UN Framework Convention on Climate Change, 1771 UNTS 107, (1992) 31 ILM 849.

[7] See, eg, I Kaul, 'Global Public Goods: Explaining Their Underprovision' (2012) 15 *Journal of International Economic Law* 729, 732–33 (distinguishing between 'Publicness in utility and publicness in consumption' and arguing that 'In which way and to what extent a public good, notably a [global public good], affects the welfare and well-being of different population groups depends not only on the overall provision level of the good but also on how it is shaped'); E Morgera, 'Bilateralism at the Service of Community Interests? Non-Judicial Enforcement of Global Public Goods in the Context of Global Environmental Law' (2012) 23 *European Journal of International Law* 743, 746 ('Common but differentiated responsibility encapsulates the need for concerted action by all states to contribute to the 'general global welfare' based on mutual responsibility and solidarity as the basis for a sense of community and global partnership.').

[8] For the canonical texts, see PA Samuelson, 'The Pure Theory of Public Expenditure' (1954) 36 *Review of Economics and Statistics* 387 and M Olson, *The Logic of Collective Action: Public Goods and the Theory of Groups*, 2nd edn (Cambridge, Harvard University Press, 1965).

[9] See, eg, I Kaul, I Grunberg and MA Stern, 'Defining Global Public Goods' in I Kaul, I Grunberg and MA Stern (eds), *Global Public Goods: International Cooperation in the 21st Century* (Oxford, Oxford University Press, 1999) 2–9; Morgera (n 7) 748; D Bodansky, 'What's in a Concept? Global Public Goods, International Law, and Legitimacy' (2012) 23 *European Journal of International Law* 651, 652–53; F Cafaggi, 'Transnational Private Regulation and the Production of Global Public Goods and Private "Bads"' (2012) 23 *European Journal of International Law* 695, 695–96.

individuals and states with no incentive to supply them, but rather to 'free ride' on the efforts of others.[10] As Nico Krisch puts it, the central problem emphasised by the designation of 'public goods' is of distribution: 'More than anything, using the label *public goods* in this context points to the difficulties of maintaining adequate availability or production.'[11]

As we may recall from the previous chapter, such themes of advancing and promoting 'interests' and 'values' feature prominently in Articles 3(5) and 21(2)(a) of the Treaty on European Union (TEU), which has led some scholars to describe them as expressing a 'missionary principle'. In this vein, the *Air Transport* Decision has been interpreted as confirmation of an emerging international legal consensus that 'when international agreements are not forthcoming, because some nations drag their feet ... individual States or regional groupings such as the EU should be allowed to "go it alone"' and assert jurisdiction unilaterally, and extraterritorially.[12] In this chapter, I argue that such defences of unilateralism are deeply problematic. Although such considerations are proper and even essential in political decisions, in so far as *law* is concerned, talk of advancing values or aligning interests at best fails to offer guidance because they provide few standards by which EU action in the wider world can be criticised, much less controlled. At worst, where used to justify measures coercive of distant strangers, they are indefensibly imperial. These claims are demonstrated both from within EU law as well as more broadly from a normative critique of public international law.

Concerning the latter, we examine Eyal Benvenisti's bold and fascinating concept of the 'Sovereign Trusteeship of Humanity',[13] which draws upon Grotius, Locke and John Stuart Mill to provide a broadly liberal normative framework for the duties and powers of sovereigns to advance the welfare of distant strangers.[14]

cf PC Mavroidis, 'Free Lunches? WTO as Public Good, and the WTO's View of Public Goods' (2012) 23 *European Journal of International Law* 731, 731. By mentioning that he 'assumes the commonplace definition', Mavroidis suggests that there may be others.

[10] G Shaffer, 'International Law and Global Public Goods in a Legal Pluralist World' (2012) 23 *European Journal of International Law* 669, 674 (the 'major challenge for the production of many (but not all) global public goods ... is collective action and free-riding'). See also Kaul (n 7) 730–36.

[11] N Krisch, 'The Decay of Consent: International Law in an Age of Global Public Goods' (2014) 108 *American Journal of International Law* 1, 3. For a still relatively rare example of a legal scholar who rejects this conventional approach, see D Augenstein, 'To Whom It May Concern: International Human Rights Law and Global Public Goods' (2016) 23 *Indiana Journal of Global Legal Studies* 225.

[12] G De Baere and C Ryngaert, 'The ECJ's Judgment in Air Transport Association of America and the International Legal Context of the EU's Climate Change Policy' (2013) 18 *European Foreign Affairs Review* 389, 401. Similarly, Nico Krisch views the EU's inclusion of international flights in the Emissions Trading Directive as involving 'a redefinition of the jurisdictional limits on extraterritorial action, or at least a "territorial extension" in response to transboundary challenges' (citations omitted). Krisch (n 11) 19–20.

[13] E Benvenisti, 'Sovereigns as Trustees of Humanity: On the Accountability of States to Foreign Stakeholders' (2013) 107 *American Journal of International Law* 295.

[14] I hesitate to include Locke in this list as a 'liberal', because his concept of freedom is more or less the same republican notion as Kant's. See J Locke, 'Second Treatise of Government' in P Laslett (ed),

Benvenisti casts his discussion in the language of 'state' and 'sovereignty', which might seem inappropriate for discussing a polity such as the EU, whose constitutive documents studiously avoid the word 'sovereign' or any variation of it.[15] This initial impression is misleading for several reasons: First, Benvenisti's theory is an attempt to reconcile sovereignty with globalisation, and the way he seeks to do this is by transforming the traditional conception of sovereignty as an absolute, indivisible power into one that accommodates the notion familiar to EU law of the 'pooling' of sovereign functions.[16] Moreover, in developing his argument, Benvenisti relies upon numerous EU measures and makes no distinction between them and measures taken by conventional territorial states. Finally, in his 2014 General Course at the Academy of International Law, Benvenisti developed the basic themes of his article into a theoretical framework not just for states but for all 'global governance bodies', and observed specifically that the 'argument for applying the trusteeship concept for the global context begins with the same insight – that every sovereign State or any other body it created or it permitted to act is an agent'.[17] For these reasons, an examination of Benvenisti's sovereign trusteeship concept is not just relevant to any theory of the EU's right to assert extraterritorial jurisdiction over distant strangers, but essential to it.

I. THE SOVEREIGN TRUSTEESHIP OF HUMANITY

Benvenisti begins by criticising 'positivist' conceptions of international law – such as that animating the *Lotus* Decision – that envision sovereign states as powers unlimited by law which can be bound by international law only with their consent or at their convenience.[18] The standard reason given for

Locke: Two Treatises of Government, Student Edition (first published 1690) (Cambridge, Cambridge University Press, 1988) 269 (s 4, Ch 2). Moreover, it is not so much Locke's theory of freedom but his theory of property that I disagree with. Nevertheless, I defend my decision not to class him as a Republican because he 'would have been horrified to be described as' one. Q Skinner, 'Freedom as the Absence of Arbitrary Power' in C Laborde and J Maynor (eds), *Republicanism and Political Theory* (Malden-Oxford, Blackwell, 2009) 84.

15 The only mention is in Article 355 Treaty on the Functioning of the European Union (TFEU), precluding application of the treaties on the UK 'Sovereign' Base Areas of Akrotiri and Dhekelia in Cyprus.

16 Case 26/62 *NV Algemene Transport- en Expeditie Onderneming van Gend & Loos v Nederlandse administratie der belastingen* [1963] ECR 1, 2 (defining 'the Community [as constituting] a new legal order of international law for the benefit of which the States have limited their sovereign rights, albeit within limited fields, and the subjects of which comprise not only Member States but also their nationals'); S Douglas-Scott, *Constitutional Law of the European Union* (London, Longman, 2002) 10–11.

17 E Benvenisti, *The Law of Global Governance* (Leiden, Brill-Nijhoff, 2014) 134. See also *ibid* 98–99, 130–31 (describing the obligations of accountability of the UN Mission in Kosovo (UNMIK) in fiduciary terms).

18 Benvenisti (n 13) 296. *The Case of SS Lotus, France v Turkey, Judgment*, Judgment No 9 [1927] PCIJ (series A) No 10 (7 September 1927).

according them this paramount status is the possession of popular legitimacy, often expressed through representative institutions.[19] As his demolition tool, Benvenisti deploys an arresting metaphor: the global condominium. Although sovereignty in previous ages may have seemed 'akin to owning a large estate separated from other properties by rivers or deserts', Benvenisti claims that in our present condition it is more like 'owning a small apartment in one densely packed high-rise that is home to two hundred separate families'.[20] Formerly distant populations now affect and are affected by measures taken by one another's governments, such that there is increasingly less congruence between the persons setting policies and those affected by them.[21] Thus, for Benvenisti, the traditional assumption that states speak for their peoples is rapidly being revealed as false.[22]

At the same time, Benvenisti is also deeply sceptical that such losses in accountability can be recovered by removing policymaking functions to international levels, for reasons to which I am entirely sympathetic. He criticises theories eschewing the Westphalian state model as well as those strands of global constitutionalism calling for drastic changes to international institutional structures, and singles out the global administrative law school for having not much to say on moral or normative matters.[23] Moreover, Benvenisti adduces in evidence numerous domestic and international examples to demonstrate that flights to 'international governance' invariably allow powerful actors to shut out weaker ones from international policymaking, as well as strengthen unaccountable private lobbies and executive branches at the expense of domestic legislatures.[24] In short, Benvenisti declines 'to endorse the demise of sovereignty', but claims instead that it is in dire need of reform. Specifically, it is 'through *other-regardingness*, [that] sovereigns can indirectly promise global welfare as well as global justice'.[25]

[19] See T Hobbes, R Tuck (ed) *Hobbes: Leviathan: Revised Student Edition* (first published 1651) (Cambridge, Cambridge University Press, 1996) 88:

> … yet in all times, Kings, and Persons of Soveraigne authority, because of their Independency, are in continuall jealousies, and in the state and posture of Gladiators; having their weapons pointing, and their eyes fixed on one another; that is, their Forts, Garrisons, and Guns upon the Frontiers of their Kingdomes; and continuall Spyes upon their neighbours; which is a posture of War. But because they uphold thereby, the Industry of their Subjects; there does not follow from it, that misery, which accompanies the Liberty of particular men.

See also JL Goldsmith and EA Posner, *The Limits of International Law* (Oxford, Oxford University Press, 2005), and Jens David Ohlin, *The Assault on International Law* (Oxford, Oxford University Press, 2015) (criticising Goldsmith and Posner but also explicating international law from 'enlightened self-interest' along the lines of David Gauthier).

[20] Benvenisti (n 13) 295; Benvenisti (n 17) 122–23.

[21] Benvenisti (n 13) 295, 297–98, 303; Benvenisti (n 17) 122.

[22] Benvenisti (n 13) 297–98.

[23] Benvenisti (n 13) 298–300.

[24] Benvenisti (n 17) 73–102.

[25] Benvenisti (n 13) 300.

Benvenisti then sets out a series of four moral intuitions – he calls them 'normative bases'[26] – grounding his programme for a system of duties of altruism to outsiders. The first is that sovereign states are *necessary* because they remain the only viable means at our disposal for achieving personal and communal self-determination.[27] On the one hand, a world without borders would deny the world's distinct communities the ability to live out their unique cultures and values, while on the other, governments would become unworkable if they ranged over populations not held together by 'common sympathies' – that is, language, religion, ethnicity, or other communal bonds.[28] Second, all human beings possess 'equal moral worth' entitling them to human rights, which Benvenisti conceives in terms of well-being, again in reliance upon Mill.[29] On this rationale, the world's governments are instituted to ensure the general welfare of human beings, and each, therefore, bears the burden of *legally* justifying its exclusion of non-members.[30] This then implies an international legal order devoted to human rights, which 'allocates' responsibilities for ensuring the same between governments depending on their ability to promote the interests grounding those rights.[31] In this connection, Benvenisti cites the *Island of Palmas* arbitration, in which the arbitrator Max Huber held that the concept of sovereignty 'serves to divide between nations the space upon which human activities are employed, in order to assure them at all points the minimum of protection of which international law is the guardian …'.[32] From this, Benvenisti argues that

> given that the global legal order has its foundations in human rights, sovereigns can and should be viewed as organs of a global system that allocates competences and responsibilities for promoting the rights of human beings and their interest in sustainable utilization of global resources.[33]

Crucially, Benvenisti submits that this legal order was actually created at an identifiable point in history: the 1948 Universal Declaration of Human Rights (UDHR).[34]

[26] Benvenisti (n 13) 301.

[27] Benvenisti (n 13) 302–303.

[28] Benvenisti (n 13) 306, citing JS Mill, *Considerations on Representative Government* (London, Parker, son, and Bourn, 1861) 303.

[29] Benvenisti (n 13) 306–307.

[30] Benvenisti (n 13) 307–308.

[31] Benvenisti (n 13) 308. See also Benvenisti (n 17) 138–40.

[32] *Island of Palmas Case (or Miangas) (United States v Netherlands)* (1928) 2 (1949) RIAA 829, 839.

[33] Benvenisti (n 13) 307 (internal citations omitted).

[34] Benvenisti (n 13) 307, citing *Prijedor, Prosecutor v Tadić (Duško) aka 'Dule'* (Decision on the Defence motion for interlocutory appeal on jurisdiction) ICTY-94-1-AR72, (1996) 35 ILM 32 (2 October 1995), para 97:

> … the impetuous development and propagation in the international community of human rights doctrines, particularly after the adoption of the Universal Declaration of Human Rights in 1948, has brought about significant changes in international law, notably in the approach

Third, Benvenisti envisions sovereigns as exercising *ownership* over discrete portions of the globe:

> As much as it is an extension of the personal right to autonomy, sovereignty is also the extension of the private claim for ownership. Both ownership and sovereignty are claims for intervention in the state of nature by carving out valuable space for exclusive use.[35]

Just as the exclusion of distant strangers from the benefits of government requires legal justification, so too must their exclusion from property.[36] In this regard, Benvenisti recalls some well-known tropes from the social contract theories of Hugo Grotius and John Locke. First, he cites the passage in the *Law of War and Peace* in which Grotius likens the original acquisition of property to occupying a seat in a public theatre: even though the theatre is originally a public place, 'it is correct to say that the seat which a man has taken belongs to him', as long as the persons involved depart as little as possible from natural equity.[37] Benvenisti similarly invokes Locke's 'proviso' whereby rights in property may be acquired in a state of nature only if, among other things, one ensures that there is 'enough and as good, left in common' for others after each act of enclosure.[38] Note that in the *Second Treatise of Government*, the proviso operates only until the creation of money as a permanent store of wealth.[39] As such, Benvenisti's use of the proviso might be described as unorthodox in that he recasts it into grounds for limiting established property rights. This, however, is not without support from other prominent Locke and property scholars.[40] Finally, in his Hague Academy General Course, Benvenisti introduces a fourth normative ground: the interdependence of individual sovereigns.[41] Building on his vision of sovereigns as enveloped in a deeper legal order, he argues that sovereignty is not an inherent quality of states but a 'freedom that is organized by international law and committed to it'.[42]

At its core, Benvenisti's basic moral claim is that as bearers of unique and awesome powers, sovereigns must have regard and owe an account to those

> to problems besetting the world community. A State-sovereignty-oriented approach has been gradually supplanted by a human-being-oriented approach. Gradually the maxim of Roman law *hominum causa omne jus constitutum est* (all law is created for the benefit of human beings) has gained a firm foothold in the international community …

[35] Benvenisti (n 13) 308.

[36] Benvenisti (n 13) 308–309.

[37] H Grotius, FW Kelsey (tr), J Brown Scott (ed), *De Jure Belli Ac Pacis [On the Law of War and Peace]* (first published 1625) (Oxford, Oxford University Press, 1925) 193.

[38] Locke (n 14) 288 (s 27, Ch 5). Benvenisti cites to the later s 33 instead. Benvenisti (n 13) 311, fn 87.

[39] Locke (n 14) 299–302 (ss 46–50, Ch 5).

[40] See J Waldron, 'Enough and as Good Left for Others' (1979) 29 *Philosophical Quarterly* 319 (arguing that the proviso applies not to original acquisition, but to life in the civil condition).

[41] Benvenisti (n 17) 143–45.

[42] Benvenisti (n 17) 144, citing *Gauweiler v Federal Parliament and Federal Government*, Final judgment [2009] Constitutional Court (FRG) 2 BvE 2/08,2 BvE 5/08, 2 BvR 1010/08, 2 BvR 1022/08, 2 BvR 1259/08, 2 BvR 182/09, 123 BVerfGE 267, para 223 (internal citations omitted).

whom they affect, whether by action or omission. In this spirit, Benvenisti identifies four 'trusteeship' obligations to distant strangers:

1) To 'take into account' or give 'due respect' in the making of domestic policy to the interests of distant strangers whose interests may be affected.[43]
2) To allow potentially affected distant strangers to participate and voice opinions in domestic policymaking processes.[44]
3) To accommodate foreign interests when such accommodation would not result in any loss.[45]
4) To accommodate foreign interests where not doing so would be catastrophic.[46]

These trusteeship principles not only ground obligations on the part of sovereigns to outsiders, but also empower them with *rights*:

> The trusteeship concept offers a clear endorsement to democracies that wish to unilaterally promote global welfare .... As trustees of humanity, national decision-makers must regard themselves as partaking in a collective effort to promote global welfare .... In fact, the sovereign-as-trustee concept even obliges states to pursue such policies. The fact that some states fail to cooperate should not hinder those who wish to act in pursuit of improving global standards, provided that they take into account the interests of others when devising policies ...[47]

Benvenisti specifically cites the EU Emissions Trading Scheme, as well as Regulation 1726/2003 (requiring all oil tankers visiting EU ports to have a 'double-hull' to prevent oil spills worldwide) as paradigmatic examples of such 'legislation for humanity'.[48] As we saw in chapter two, he criticises the reasoning in *Air Transport* as unconvincing. Nevertheless, he submits that his model of sovereign trusteeship might supply a better rationale for the decision[49]

[43] Benvenisti (n 13) 314–18. See also Benvenisti (n 17) 163. ('Even before the instrumental benefits that accrue from an open and inclusive decision-making process, the intrinsic argument applies: decision-makers that affect the lives of others must respect and ensure the individual rights of those they affect.')

[44] Benvenisti (n 13) 318–20. See also Benvenisti (n 17) 162–68.

[45] Benvenisti (n 13) 320–25.

[46] Benvenisti (n 13) 325–26.

[47] E Benvenisti, 'Legislating for Humanity: May States Compel Foreigners to Promote Global Welfare?' in R Liivoja and J Petman (eds), *International Law-making: Essays in Honour of Jan Klabbers* (Abingdon, Routledge, 2014) 12. Note that Benvenisti appears to resile somewhat from this position in a later article, where he claims that 'the version of trusteeship of humanity advocated in this [article] does not justify more powers over foreign stakeholders. In fact, it calls for just the opposite'. E Benvenisti, 'Upholding Democracy Amid the Challenges of New Technology: What Role for the Law of Global Governance?' (2018) 29 *European Journal of International Law* 9, 53.

[48] Benvenisti (n 47) 3, citing Regulation (EC) No 1726/2003 amending Regulation (EC) No 417/2002 on the accelerated phasing-in of double-hull or equivalent design requirements for single-hull oil tankers [2003] OJ L249/1. See also Benvenisti (n 17) 73–74.

[49] Benvenisti (n 47) 16 (observing that the European Court of Justice (ECJ) 'failed to articulate a convincing legal basis' in the *Air Transport* Decision, but that his 'legislation for humanity' might 'provide such a political underpinning').

because the European Court of Justice (ECJ) went 'to great length to emphasize that the European directives imposing the emission trading obligations … remained open to multilateral agreements and to adaptation to third countries' "equivalent measures"'.[50]

In terms of generating rights and obligations to provide global public goods, most of the heavy lifting is done by the third obligation to accommodate harmless interests – Benvenisti relies upon it to ground obligations to supply life-saving drugs, allow compulsory licensing of pharmaceutical products, and share disease samples.[51] The basic rationale is that exclusion must be justified, and to illustrate it, Benvenisti once again invokes some classic Grotiana:

> If any person should prevent any other from taking fire from his fire or light from his torch, I should accuse him of violating the law of human society … Why then, when it can be done without any prejudice to his own interests, will not one person share with another things which are useful to the recipient, and no loss to the giver?[52]

This quotation is taken from the sixth chapter of the *Free Seas* where Grotius defends the freedom of the high seas in terms of non-excludability and non-rivalrousness:

> all that has been so constituted by nature that although serving some one person it still suffices for the common use of all persons, is today and ought in perpetuity to remain in the same condition as when it was first created by nature.[53]

Importantly, Benvenisti reads the torch passage as a defence of *equity* – that is, as an argument for preventing individuals from standing upon their strict legal rights if to do so would be ethically disgraceful or unconscionable.[54] In this connection, he recalls an equitable precept in Jewish law condemning the unbending insistence upon 'what's mine is mine and what's yours is yours' as the 'manner of Sodom'.[55] Benvenisti's rule of equity not only obligates; it also empowers. In the same way a maker of a harmless request has a claim-right to the satisfaction of her request, a state may enact extraterritorial measures if 'costless' to others, which presumably obtains if the costs are outweighed by the benefits resulting therefrom: 'The fact that some states fail to cooperate should not hinder those who wish to act in pursuit of improving global standards, provided that they take into account the interests of others when devising

[50] Benvenisti (n 47) 14.

[51] Benvenisti (n 13) 324–25.

[52] H Grotius, R von Deman Magoffin (tr), J Brown Scott (ed), *Mare Liberum [The Freedom of the Seas]* (first published 1609) (New York, Oxford University Press, 1916) 38.

[53] *Ibid* 27.

[54] See, eg, *Earl of Oxford's Case* (1615) 21 ER 485 (Ch) 486 (the purpose of equity is to 'mollify the Extremity of the law'); *Dudley v Dudley* (1705) 24 ER 118 (Ch) 119 ('… equity is no part of the law, but a moral virtue which qualifies, moderates and reform the rigour, hardness and edge of the law').

[55] Benvenisti (n 13) 321, citing A Kirschenbaum, *Equity in Jewish Law: Halakhic Aspirationism in Jewish Civil Law* (Hoboken, KTAV Publishing, 1991) 187–91.

policies …'[56] Crucially, however, Benvenisti requires that his proposed obligation of harmless accommodation be limited by a criterion of 'restricted Pareto optimality' forbidding states from offering themselves up to foreign interests in exchange for side payments.[57] To substantiate his claim that the obligation of harmless accommodation is either already law or is in the process of becoming law, Benvenisti refers to the following cases: *Right of Passage over Indian Territory*,[58] the *Iron Rhine Railway Arbitration*,[59] *Dispute Regarding Navigational and Related Rights*,[60] and the *Lake Lanoux Arbitration*.[61] We will revisit them in chapter five.

In short, sovereign trusteeship:

1) proceeds from interests;
2) conceives of states and similar entities exercising sovereign powers as tools employed by the international order to advance human well-being; and
3) considers ethical standards as capable of displacing legal rules.

Cedric Ryngaert draws upon all three of these premises to develop a similar, 'equity-based' theory of unilateral measures to provide global public goods in which the strict legal rights of States are tempered by considerations of 'reasonableness'.[62] Ryngaert deflects the predictable charge of vagueness in appropriate Chancery style by formulating a list of maxims:

- 'reasonableness' in terms of the distribution of costs and benefits between the sovereign enacting the measure and the sovereign imposed upon;[63]
- 'dual illegality' between sovereigns;[64]
- 'democratic participation' by potentially affected persons;[65]

[56] Benvenisti (n 47) 12. Benvenisti does say, however, that this equitable right is not necessarily enforceable. See section II.B. below.

[57] Benvenisti (n 13) 320–21.

[58] *Right of Passage over Indian Territory (Portugal v India)* (Judgment, merits) [1960] ICJ Rep 6.

[59] *Iron Rhine Arbitration (Belgium v Netherlands)* (2005) 27 RIAA 35.

[60] *Dispute Regarding Navigational and Related Rights (Costa Rica v Nicaragua)* (Merits) [2009] ICJ Rep 213.

[61] *Lake Lanoux Arbitration (France v Spain)* (1957) 12 (1963) RIAA 281.

[62] C Ryngaert, *Unilateral Jurisdiction and Global Values* (The Hague, Eleven International Publishing, 2015) 124–30. Ryngaert has recently updated his ideas with reference to my arguments expressed elsewhere. See C Ryngaert, *Selfless Intervention: The Exercise of Jurisdiction in the Common Interest* (Oxford, Oxford University Press, 2020) 97–98.

[63] Ryngaert, *Unilateral Jurisdiction, ibid* 111–18. See also Ryngaert, *Selfless Intervention, ibid* 97–102.

[64] Ryngaert, *Unilateral Jurisdiction, ibid* 118–21; Ryngaert, *Selfless Intervention, ibid* 102–103.

[65] Ryngaert, *Unilateral Jurisdiction, ibid* 121–33; Ryngaert, *Selfless Intervention, ibid* 101–108. See also I Kaul and RU Mendoza, 'Advancing the Concept of Public Goods' in I Kaul et al (eds), *Providing Global Public Goods: Managing Globalization* (Oxford, Oxford University Press, 2003) 91 (proposing a principle of 'equivalence of publicness' that requires 'matching the circle of stakeholders in a particular public good with the circle of participants in negotiations on its provision …').

- 'equivalence' or non-duplication of measures across sovereigns;[66] and
- compensation offered by the State taking the unilateral measure to the State whose interests are affected.[67]

Ryngaert's last maxim is incompatible with Benvenisti's restricted Pareto optimality condition.

II. HARMS AND WRONGS

Consider Benvenisti's third proposed legal obligation to accommodate interests if they impose no costs. While Benvenisti recognises that States differ in some fundamental way from private persons,[68] his rationale from property ownership suggests that the obligation of costless accommodation might also apply to private persons, who, after all, are known to own property. Doing this, however, reveals certain problems. Imagine that a total stranger enters your house in the middle of the night. He neither steals nor damages anything but simply stands by your bedside to watch you as you sleep. From time to time he strokes your hair, but so softly that it does not disturb you. All of this is 'costless' to you. Nevertheless, most legal systems not only would not require you to accommodate your nocturnal visitor, but would actively provide you causes of action against him. For instance, a common law decision of seminal civil and constitutional significance pronounces that 'no man can set foot upon his neighbour's close without his leave; if he does he is a trespasser, though he does no damage at all …'[69] Similarly, it does not matter that his stroking your hair did not disturb you: battery is actionable even if entirely painless.[70]

At this point, a Grotian might object that the obligation of harmless accommodation applies only in the case of non-rivalrous, non-excludable things like fire and the high seas; that is, a thing that is 'so constituted by nature that although serving some one person it still suffices for the common use of all other persons'.[71] The problem is that non-rivalrousness is a quality that attaches not to things, but to *uses* of things. The high seas, for instance, are non-rivalrous with respect to navigation; not so as regards fishing.[72] Your nocturnal visitor's

[66] Ryngaert, *Unilateral Jurisdiction, ibid* 133–35; Ryngaert, *Selfless Intervention, ibid* 125–30.

[67] Ryngaert, *Unilateral Jurisdiction, ibid* 135–40; Ryngaert, *Selfless Intervention, ibid* 132–35.

[68] Benvenisti (n 13) 306.

[69] *Entick v Carrington* (1765) 95 ER 807 (KB) 817.

[70] See, eg, MA Franklin, Injuries and Remedies: Cases and Materials on Tort Law and Alternatives, 2nd edn (Mineola, Foundation Press, 1979) 606 ('those who suffer the indignity of having his coat lapels grabbed or of being spat on may recover').

[71] Grotius (n 52) 27.

[72] William Welwod makes exactly this point in his polemic against Grotius, stating that 'if the uses of the seas may be in any respect forbidden and stayed it should be chiefly for the fishing, as by which the fishes may be said to be exhaust and wasted, which daily experience these twenty years past and more hath declared to be overtrue'. W Welwod, 'Of the Community and Propriety

specific designs are non-rivalrous in this way: his 'use' of your house and hair 'leaves it no less yours than it was before …'.[73] Why then should you not be expected to tolerate them? In fact, it turns out that rivalrousness of benefits is immaterial. You would have your action in trespass even if the nocturnal visitor positively *increased* your material welfare, say, by doing your laundry before leaving.[74] An action in false imprisonment lies even if the plaintiff is kept in luxurious surroundings.[75] The same principle applies to unwanted touchings: one can wrong another by saving their life.[76]

Second, the fact that it might be inequitable, unreasonable or otherwise ethically disgraceful to proceed against a harmless nocturnal visitor does not modify your right to your cause of action, much less deprive you of it. The most powerful demonstrations of this probably come from those heart-breaking cases involving terminally ill plaintiffs, whose only hope of evading a painful death lies in a close relative consenting to a relatively harmless medical procedure, say, a bone marrow transplant. A legal obligation not to withhold consent in such cases might follow not just from Benvenisti's proposed obligation to accommodate costless interests, but also from his fourth proposed obligation to avert catastrophes. Instead, courts often decline to make such orders, despite being more than ready to declare the defendants to be 'morally indefensible'.[77] This reasoning is not limited to omissions. Suppose you start a business that drives another's into bankruptcy, resulting in him and his elderly grandmother being evicted from their cottage in the middle of a snowstorm on Christmas Eve. As unquestionably bad as it is, you have not *wronged* either of them. It is also possible to harm others – grievously – without wronging them in the slightest.

Such thought experiments might seem far removed from the questions of international law and global public goods of concern to Benvenisti's theory of

of the Seas (1613)' in H Grotius, R Hakluyt (tr), D Armitage (ed) and R Hakluyt (tr), *The Free Sea* (Indianapolis, Liberty Fund, 2004) 73–74.

[73] Grotius (n 52) 38.

[74] See S Warren, '"Cleaning Fairy", Allegedly Breaks Into Random Home, Tidies Up' *The Huffington Post* (31 May 2012).

[75] Baroness Hale has remarked that the 'fact that my living arrangements are comfortable, and indeed make my life as enjoyable as it could possibly be, should make no difference [to a finding of a violation of the human right to liberty]. A gilded cage is still a cage'. *P v Cheshire West and Chester Council* [2014] 1 AC 896 (HL), para 46.

[76] In a famous case from Ontario, a doctor was held liable in battery and required to pay the plaintiff C$ 20,000 in damages for administering the plaintiff an emergency blood transfusion after being made aware that she was a Jehovah's Witness. *Malette v Shulman* (1990) 72 OR 2d 417.

[77] In a case from Pennsylvania, a plaintiff who was dying of leukaemia sought an order enjoining a close relative to donate his bone marrow. The defendant was also the only possible donor, and the medical procedure was entirely harmless, albeit painful. The Court held it had no power at equity to issue the injunction. *McFall v Shimp* 10 Pa D & C 3d 90 (PA 1978) 91–92. See also *Curran v Bosze* 566 NE2d 1319 (IL 1990) (refusing to order the defendant, the mother and legal guardian of twins, of whom the plaintiff was the father, to submit the twins for medical tests to see if they were suitable as bone marrow donors for another of the plaintiff's children, a 12-year-old dying of leukaemia).

sovereign trusteeship, but they in fact undermine its very core. The fact that globalisation presents us with incomparably more opportunities to inflict harms upon each other does not in and of itself mean that we thereby also acquire *obligations* toward one other, much less violate them.[78] Of course, it would be very well if our political communities took account of the effects of their actions upon outsiders, but this is a matter of beneficence, prudence or 'enlightened self-interest',[79] not of *legal* obligation.

A. Public Actors and Human Rights Jurisdiction

Perhaps a rescue may be found in Benvenisti's notion of the UDHR as a global original contract that constituted an international order devoted to advancing 'human rights' understood in terms of well-being. This device would allow Benvenisti to nullify the objections above by distinguishing between private persons and sovereigns and imposing extraordinary obligations of altruism only upon the latter. Recall that Benvenisti understands the UDHR as 'allocating' human rights obligations among the various sovereign states according to their ability to advance well-being. On this conception of the human rights practice, the provisions on 'human rights jurisdiction' contained in most human rights treaties ought to track each state's ability to *affect* the interests of human beings all over the world, or at least those basic interests such as security, subsistence and/or sociability said to form the substance of each human right. As we shall see in chapter six, this is the view taken by Marko Milanovic, the author of the most widely cited monograph on that topic.

As already mentioned in the previous chapter, precisely that approach has been rejected by the European Court of Human Rights. It is always within a

[78] M Kumm, 'The Cosmopolitan Turn in Constitutionalism: An Integrated Conception of Public Law' (2013) 20 *Indiana Journal of Global Legal Studies* 605, 624. ('Interdependence alone is not itself sufficient to establish the duty of a national community to take into account the effects of their actions on outsiders.')

[79] In an examination of US and EU rulemaking processes, Ayelet Berman argues that to the extent they impose consultations with potentially affected foreigners, they do so primarily 'as a tool for opening markets, improving competition and achieving economic growth', and that as such, '(o)penness to foreign interests is best explained by their "enlightened self-interest"'. Concerning the EU, however, she also discerns a sense of moral obligation towards people of developing countries not dissimilar to Benvenisti's sovereign trusteeship. A Berman, 'Taking Foreign Interests into Account: Rulemaking in the US and EU' (2017) 15 *International Journal of Constitutional Law* 235, 254. In contrast, Bartels argues that while 'the EU institutions – in particular the European Commission – appear willing to take into account development objectives in their policymaking … it does so on an *ad hoc* basis, at the wrong time, at best using inappropriate methodologies'. L Bartels, 'Policy Coherence for Development Under Article 208 of the Treaty on the Functioning of the European Union-Towards a Complaints Mechanism' (2016) *Cambridge Legal Studies Research Paper Series* 1, 7–8. He claims further that there is 'significant evidence that the impact assessments that are undertaken do not in fact take into account development objectives, as they are required to do' under Article 208(1) TFEU, and that when they are undertaken, it is 'frequently at a point when they are too late, practically speaking, to have any effect upon the regulatory process'. *Ibid* 9.

state's ability not to bomb someone, so one obvious way in which states may advance the well-being of distant strangers would be by not dropping bombs on them. Nonetheless, if a state party to the European Convention on Human Rights (ECHR) were to launch drone strikes today upon wedding parties in a land far away, an application by the family members of those killed would almost certainly be declared inadmissible for lack of human rights jurisdiction.[80] The dismissal would be ordered not on the reasoning in *Banković*, most of which has been abandoned after deserved criticism.[81] Instead, it would follow according to the reasoning of *Al-Skeini*, which definitively settled the test for 'state jurisdiction' under Article 1 ECHR, a state has 'human rights jurisdiction' only if (1) it exercises 'effective control' over the territory, or (2) its agents exercise '*authority* and control' over individuals.[82] A fighter pilot dropping bombs from a great height exerts neither effective control over the territory nor 'authority and control' over the individuals down below.[83] As such,

> *Bankovic* is … still perfectly correct in its result. While the ability to kill is 'authority and control' over the individual if the state has public powers, killing is not authority and control if the state is merely firing missiles from an aircraft. Under this reasoning, drone operations in Yemen or wherever would be just as excluded from the purview of human rights treaties as under *Bankovic*.[84]

Thus, human rights practice contradicts Benvenisti's assumption that a state's human rights obligations track its capacity to affect an individual's material interests, say, in existence. Even if one reads Benvenisti as making only the weaker claim that the UDHR *should* be interpreted as imposing legal obligations on states to advance human flourishing where feasible, the fact remains that the settled jurisprudence of the world's pre-eminent human rights court – and pre-eminent particularly on matters of extraterritorial application – totally rejects that position. Instead, it appears that you can purposely be dealt the most appalling harms without having even the beginnings of a human rights

[80] See *Banković and ors v Belgium and ors*, Admissibility (2001) ECHR 890, para 75 (application brought by relatives of civilians killed by NATO during bombing of Belgrade dismissed for lack of jurisdiction.) Other jurisdictions take a broadly similar position. See *El Shifa Pharmaceutical Industries Company and Idris v United States* 378 F3d 1346 (DC Cir, 2004) (plaintiff's factory in Sudan destroyed by US bomb strike. Claim for compensation under Takings Clause dismissed as nonjusticiable political question). The Supreme Court of Israel has considered *obiter* that in 'appropriate cases it is appropriate [*sic*] to pay compensation as a result of harm caused to an innocent civilian'. *Public Committee against Torture in Israel v The Government of Israel (Targeted Killings* case) Judgment, HCJ 769/02 (11 December 2005) (Supreme Court of Israel sitting as the High Court of Justice) para 40. This, however, was offered as a recommendation under international humanitarian law, not as an obligation under human rights law.

[81] This is explored in detail in ch 6, section II.A.

[82] *Al-Skeini and ors v United Kingdom, Merits and just satisfaction* (2011) 53 EHRR 18, paras 133–40.

[83] See M Milanovic, 'Al-Skeini and Al-Jedda in Strasbourg' (2012) 23 *European Journal of International Law* 121, 132 (acknowledging that '*Al-Skeini* leaves unchanged the outcome of *Bankovic*').

[84] *Ibid* 130 (internal citations omitted).

claim. The attempt to abolish the difference between harms and wrongs by invoking the positive legal practice of human rights fails because that practice itself makes that distinction.

B. The Failure of the Argument from Well-Being

As Kumm puts it, 'the more effective provision of public goods globally is not itself an argument against denying states the authority to determine for themselves whether and how to address issues relating to the provision of public goods'.[85] While international law provides

> means to reap the benefits of better cooperation and coordination between interdependent actors ... this assertion merely provides a functional argument for states to sign up for certain kinds of international cooperative endeavours. It does not, without further argument, undermine the claim that it is within the state's authority to decide on how to address concerns surrounding the provision of public goods.[86]

Precisely such considerations are reflected by the principle of non-intervention in Article 2(7) of the United Nations Charter, which the ICJ interpreted in *Military and Paramilitary Activities in and against Nicaragua* to mean that '[i]ntervention is wrongful when it uses methods of coercion *in regard to such choices, which must remain free ones*'.[87]

It is impossible for one state or political community to *bind* others by its unilateral decisions, even if the various costs and benefits were calibrated perfectly following extensive consultation. Suppose Cagliostro unilaterally extended Ruritanians rights not just to participate in its legislative hearings, but to vote and stand in its general elections. Despite this sweeping gesture, Cagliostro would not be entitled to prescribe a single jot or tittle of regulation over Ruritania's oilfields. Nor would it have any right to enact extraterritorial laws for Ruritanians simply because, contrary to a human rights treaty binding upon both parties, Ruritania habitually issued parking tickets in a manner contrary to the right against self-incrimination.[88] Ryngaert is alive to this concern, for instance in his observation that when 'exercising unilateral jurisdiction in the perceived

[85] M Kumm, 'Sovereignty and the Right to Be Left Alone: Subsidiarity, Justice-Sensitive Externalities, and the Proper Domain of the Consent Requirement in International Law' (2016) 79 *Law and Contemporary Problems* 239, 244.

[86] *Ibid.*

[87] *Military and Paramilitary Activities in and Against Nicaragua, Nicaragua v United States*, Merits [1986] ICJ Rep 14, para 205.

[88] U Khaliq, *Ethical Dimensions of the Foreign Policy of the European Union: A Legal Appraisal* (Cambridge, Cambridge University Press, 2008) 39. ('It does not automatically follow, however, that because a state has ratified an international treaty protecting such rights that other states have a right to comment or take other action in response to its violations of that treaty. This is especially the case as almost all such conventions have their own specific enforcement mechanisms.')

global interest, it appears indeed inevitable that states will apply *their* notions of global justice to foreign territories and persons'.[89] It is for this reason that American private international law, in contrast to Ryngaert's proposed 'dual illegality' rule, recognises a 'public law taboo' against the application of foreign criminal, regulatory or administrative law.[90]

These problems of unilateralism are compounded by the high levels of discretion admitted by these strategies. Ryngaert concedes that invocations of 'jurisdictional reasonableness' as pioneered in US antitrust law have, 'not surprisingly – come under severe criticism for failing to provide legal certainty'.[91] For this reason, rather than offering a pragmatic solution to problems of global coordination, a 'reasonableness' approach to unilateral jurisdiction might actually be the perfect recipe for discord. Benvenisti for his part remarks that the 'obligation to weigh the interests of foreign stakeholders does not *necessarily* imply an obligation to succumb to those interests, and does not even require full legal responsibility for ultimately preferring domestic interests in balancing various opposing claims'.[92] Instead, all it requires is that the regulator give 'due respect to those foreign and global interests'.[93] One cannot expect an abstract theory to provide definite answers in all imaginable concrete instances, but there must nevertheless be some discernible *principle* by which a policymaker can tell when she ought to 'succumb', or what sort of respect is 'due'. These blurred lines are also to be found around Benvenisti's conception of a sovereign's *rights* of unilateral jurisdiction: 'foreigners – including foreign states – affected by such unilateral policies *must consider complying with them* due to their own duty to take others' interests into account and to promote global welfare'.[94] This formulation does not quite capture the gravity of the situation: the EU Emissions Trading Directive did not simply invite foreign airline operators to 'consider' offsetting their emissions. It *required* them to do so, on pain of a fine of €100 per non-surrendered allowance, coupled with an order to make up for the shortfall in the following year.[95]

There is, however, one final respect in which the *Air Transport* Decision, and in fact all of the ECJ's extraterritoriality jurisprudence, is fundamentally irreconcilable with Benvenisti's sovereign trusteeship or with Ryngaert's theory

[89] Ryngaert, *Unilateral Jurisdiction* (n 62) 114.

[90] *Massachusetts v Mellon* 262 US 447, 481 (1923) ('the courts of no country will execute the penal laws of another'). See also AF Lowenfeld, 'Public Law in the International Arena: Conflict of Laws, International Law and Some Suggestions for Their Interaction' (1980) 163 *Recueil des cours* 311, 322–26.

[91] Ryngaert, *Unilateral Jurisdiction* (n 62) 113.

[92] Benvenisti (n 13) 314.

[93] *Ibid*. See also Benvenisti (n 17) 136, 230.

[94] See Benvenisti (n 47) 12 (emphasis added).

[95] Parliament and Council Directive 2003/87/EC of 13 October 2003 establishing a scheme for greenhouse gas emission allowance trading within the Community and amending Council Directive 96/61/EC [2003] OJ L275/32, Art 16(3).

of unilateral jurisdiction. As demonstrated in chapter two, the ECJ has not once relied upon the 'effects doctrine' or any other harm-based theory in upholding an extraterritorial measure. Accordingly, its theory of extraterritorial jurisdiction cannot be explained as a matter of 'balancing' or other empirical assessment of interests or costs of the various stakeholders involved.

III. BLURRED FRONTIERS: VALUES AND CONSTITUTIONAL OBJECTIVES

These same problems of lack of guidance and unilateralism obtain in the EU legal discourse regarding the advancement and promotion of its values and interests in the wider world. The former is demonstrated by the jurisprudence surrounding the justiciability of the objectives in Article 3(5) TEU, as well as on the concepts of policy consistency and coherence as provided in Article 21(3) TEU. The latter obtains when extraterritorial measures are justified upon their content, rather than their form. What matters is not the 'value' or 'interest' the EU aims to advance in the wider world, but the way it goes about it.

A. Policy Consistency/Coherence in the Light of EU Constitutional Objectives

In principle, the 'basic objectives of the Treaty' now enumerated in Article 3 TEU have long been supposed to possess 'obligatory force',[96] such that they are required to be considered in the formulation of policies, internal and external.[97] However, as regards the ability of litigants before EU courts to control acts of the EU by reference to them – that is, their justiciability – a very different position has equally long been taken. In *Dürbeck*, the ECJ held that the

> aim to contribute, in the common interest, to the harmonious development of world trade, the progressive abolition of restrictions on international trade and the lowering of customs barriers', cannot be interpreted as prohibiting the [EU] from enacting, upon pain of committing an infringement of the Treaty, any measure liable to affect trade with non-member countries.[98]

Similarly, in *Milk Marque*, the Court held that while the 'no single aim may be pursued in isolation in such a way as to make the achievement of the others impossible', one may be allowed 'temporary priority in order to satisfy the

[96] Case 6/72 *Europemballage and Continental Can v Commission* [1973] ECR 215, para 25. The CJEU also described the 'pursuit' of the objectives as 'indispensable'. *Ibid*, para 23.

[97] See Case C-268/94 *Portugal v Council* [1996] ECR I-6177, para 5; Case C-166/07 *Council v Parliament (International Fund for Ireland)* [2009] ECR I-7135, para 7.

[98] Case C-112/80 *Dürbeck* [1981] ECR 1095, para 44.

demands of the economic or other conditions in light of which their decisions are made'.[99]

This essential non-justiciability is not affected by the principle of consistency as expressed in the second paragraph of Article 21(3) TEU, which, to recall the previous chapter, requires 'consistency' or 'coherence' between external and internal policies.[100] Other relevant provisions include Article 7 TFEU, which provides that 'The Union shall ensure consistency between its policies and activities, taking all of its objectives into account and in accordance with the principle of conferral of powers', as well as less explicitly in other provisions such as Article 208(1) TFEU, which requires the EU to 'take account of the objectives of development cooperation in the policies that it implements which are likely to affect developing countries'. A similar principle of coherence and/or consistency also applies in other areas of EU law, primarily in the so-called 'duty of loyalty' owed by the Member States to the Union under Article 4(3) TEU – a principle of federalism by which the CJEU examines questions of 'vertical' consistency between actions of individual Member States and policies of the EU.[101]

The first difficulty lies in the use of both 'consistency' and 'coherence' in the treaties,[102] which has lead numerous authors down an approach of careful textual parsing, a task complicated by the multiplicity of language versions, all of them authentic.[103] The dominant school[104] holds that the terms have specific meanings, whereby 'consistency' pertains to the mere 'absence of contradictions, whereas coherence refers to positive connections'.[105] Although much ink has been spilt on these fine distinctions, EU lawyers nevertheless still find them somewhat elusive. Unsurprisingly, the most extensive body of law

[99] Case C-137/00 *Milk Marque and National Farmers' Union* [2003] ECR I-7975, para 91.

[100] E Herlin-Karnell, 'EU Values and the Shaping of the International Legal Order' in D Kochenov and F Amtenbrink (eds), *The European Union's Shaping of the International Legal Order* (Cambridge, Cambridge University Press, 2014) 97 (observing that the Lisbon Treaty '[singles] out consistency as the guiding principle for EU action abroad and at home', and 'consistency of EU action is as important internally as externally'). See also M Cremona, 'Coherence in European Union Foreign Relations Law' in P Koutrakos (ed), *European Foreign Policy: Legal and Political Perspectives* (Cheltenham, Edward Elgar, 2011) 77.

[101] J Larik, *Foreign Policy Objectives in European Constitutional Law* (Oxford, Oxford University Press, 2016) 218–28.

[102] Article 11(3) TEU; Article 349 TFEU.

[103] C Tietje, 'The Concept of Coherence in the Treaty on European Union and the Common Foreign and Security Policy' (1997) 2 *European Foreign Affairs Review* 211, 211–12. While the English version of Article 21(3) TEU speaks of 'consistency', the same provision is rendered as *Kohärenz* in the German version, as *coherence* in the French, and as *coherencia* in the Spanish.

[104] L den Hertog and S Stroß, 'Coherence in EU External Relations: Concepts and Legal Rooting of an Ambiguous Term' (2013) 18 *European Foreign Affairs Review* 373, 375.

[105] Tietje (n 103) 212. See also G De Baere, *Constitutional Principles of EU External Relations* (Oxford, Oxford University Press, 2008) 251; C Hillion, 'Tous Pour Un, Un Pour Tous! Coherence in the External Relations of the European Union' in M Cremona, *Developments in EU External Relations Law* (Oxford, Oxford University Press, 2008) 12; P Gauttier, 'Horizontal Coherence and the External Competences of the European Union' (2004) 10 *European Law Journal* 23, 40–41.

dealing with policy consistency and/or coherence tends to be the Article 4(3) TEU jurisprudence on 'vertical' consistency between Member State actions and EU policies.[106] While this topic is technically outside the scope of this book, it is noteworthy that in their critique of this jurisprudence, Ester Herlin-Karnell and Theodore Konstantinidis conclude that it is neither 'value-driven, nor does it forge a constitutional interpretative tool in the Dworkinian sense of consistency as integrity' but instead appears to move 'towards a "constitutional diktat" based on the methodical application of coercive constitutional principles to justify EU competence and ensure the maximum effectiveness of EU law …'[107] As a result, it appears little more than an 'adherence to a line of judgment and a certain mode of conduct which is historically crafted by definition and which is not attached to a clear political goal'.[108]

As regards the principle of policy consistency and/or coherence between internal and external actions, there is a consensus that neither concept is 'well substantiated [as a] constitutional principle of EU law'.[109] The imperative in Article 21(3) TEU was inserted not to provide justiciable standards by which to criticise particular policy measures, but to address certain institutional tensions that plagued the pre-Lisbon 'pillar' arrangement of the Union, which envisaged a strict separation of the Common Foreign and Security Policy (CFSP) from the then European Communities. As Piet Eeckhout explains, 'the constitutional emphasis on consistency is something of a subterfuge, an attempt to cover up inter-institutional strife, to throw a constitutional blanket on the struggles between the Council and the Commission, not to mention the Parliament'.[110] The pillar structure was abolished by the Lisbon Treaty, which provides that there is but one Union[111] endowed with legal personality.[112] Nevertheless, certain traces of the separation between the CFSP and the rest of the EU remain, particularly in the form of the special rules and procedures that apply to the former.[113] In short, Article 21(3) TEU consistency/coherence pertains to essentially administrative questions about whether a measure is properly taken under the CFSP

[106] Larik (n 101) 161. ('The case law of the Court of Justice reveals that it is often Member States that are condemned for having acted when this duty obliged them to "refrain from any measure which could jeopardise the attainment of the Union's objectives", not least in the area of external relations.') (Internal citations omitted.)

[107] E Herlin-Karnell and T Konstadinides, 'The Rise and Expressions of Consistency in EU Law: Legal and Strategic Implications for European Integration' (2013) 15 *Cambridge Yearbook of European Legal Studies* 139, 152, citing Case C-246/07 *Commission v Sweden (PFOS)* ECLI:EU:C:2010:203 (20 April 2010) (holding that in proposing the addition of a certain chemical substance to Annex A to the Stockholm Convention on Persistent Organic Pollutants, Sweden had failed to fulfil its obligation of loyalty under Art 4(3) TEU).

[108] Herlin-Karnell and Konstadinides, *ibid* 153.

[109] den Hertog and Stroß also add that the 'case law of the [CJEU] explicitly dealing with the principle is scarce and lacks concretization …' den Hertog and Stroß (n 104) 378.

[110] P Eeckhout, *EU External Relations Law*, 2nd edn (Oxford, Oxford University Press, 2011) 187.

[111] Article 1(3) TEU.

[112] Article 47 TEU.

[113] Eeckhout (n 110) 168–72.

or elsewhere.[114] They do not, as it were, provide legal standards for challenging particular measures as incompatible with the EU's professed 'values', or for undermining other measures advancing those values in the wider world.

This was demonstrated in relation to the specific object of this study – the rights and obligations of the European Union with respect to distant strangers – by the General Court's Decision in *Polisario*.[115] The applicant in that case was the indigenous national liberation movement in the Western Sahara, currently occupied by Morocco, which sought to challenge an 'Association Agreement' between the EU and Morocco whose terms appeared to apply in the Western Sahara territory. The applicant argued in its fourth plea that an EU legislative instrument implementing the Agreement was vitiated by illegality due to a failure to comply with the requirement of consistency laid down in Article 7 TFEU. In particular, it pointed to apparent inconsistencies: (1) between the EU's professed respect for principles of sovereignty and self-determination on the one hand, and its political and financial support for the Moroccan occupation on the other;[116] (2) between its criticism of human rights violations in places like Syria and its silence regarding those allegedly taking place in Morocco;[117] and (3) between its allocating substantial aid for Sahrawi refugee camps while at the same time taking pro-Moroccan measures such as the Agreement which allegedly resulted in producing more such refugees.[118] The General Court easily swatted away these arguments, and went as far as to claim that simultaneously supporting Sahrawi refugee camps and entering into dealings with Morocco concerning the territory was in fact an *example* of consistency, because it manifested a desire not 'to take sides in the dispute between the applicant and the Kingdom of Morocco, while supporting the efforts of the UN towards a just and lasting resolution of that dispute by negotiation'.[119]

The thin, 'pragmatic' concepts of consistency and coherence are unable to give much guidance, but are instead easily manipulated to reach a pre-determined result. It is impossible to know how to make different policies 'work' together without first having some idea of what 'working' even means.

B. The Missionary Principle and Territorial Extension

A more pressing concern lies in the relationship between EU discourses on the advancement of values, and certain tendencies apparent in CJEU extraterritoriality jurisprudence that might be described as 'imperial'. The literature is generally reluctant to lay this charge, even as it freely admits that there

[114] Larik (n 101) 198–200.
[115] Case T-512/12 *Front Polisario v Council* ECLI:EU:T:2015:953 (10 December 2015).
[116] *Ibid*, paras 149–50.
[117] *Ibid*, para 151.
[118] *Ibid*, para 152.
[119] *Ibid*, para 157.

is much that is unusual in the way the EU acts in the wider world. For instance, Anu Bradford takes the view that the EU cannot be accused of 'regulatory imperialism' because far from 'consciously seeking to externalize the single market … much of the EU's rule-making [instead] stems from the internal goal to protect the integrity of the single market'.[120] Bradford's assumption that imperialism requires specific intent stands somewhat askance to the famous remark that the British Empire was acquired in a fit of absence of mind,[121] and is contradicted by Jan Zielonka – a rare scholar analysing the EU in the framework of historical empires – who argues that the

> metropolis does not always have a master plan of imperial conquest. States can become empires by default because they try to bring some order to unstable neighbours or try to convert barbarians into 'good' citizens or Christians. Likewise, an empire does not need to arise via outright aggression. Some empires rose quietly or even surreptitiously through uneven modernization and social differentiation.[122]

In this light, it may be useful to examine a little-known Opinion by Advocate General Cruz Villalón in *Salemink* – issued three months before the *Air Transport* Decision – which went out of its way to present an unnecessary argument for the purpose of developing the law. As mentioned in chapter two, every opinion is a campaign aimed at convincing a majority of the bench. *Salemink* involved a Dutchman working on an oil rig in the continental shelf adjacent to the Netherlands, who had moved his primary address to Spain. Upon returning to dry land, he discovered his prolonged lack of residence in the Netherlands rendered him no longer eligible for Dutch invalidity benefits and therefore brought suit alleging a violation of his EU freedom of establishment. The issue, simply put, was whether EU fundamental freedoms applied on an oil rig located on the Dutch continental shelf.[123]

The Advocate General presented the Court with two options: (1) an 'easy' one holding under established rules of EU law that EU fundamental freedoms apply even if that work was carried out outside Member State territory if it had a sufficiently close connection to the Member State; and (2) an 'innovative'

[120] A Bradford, *The Brussels Effect: How the European Union Rules the World* (New York, Oxford University Press, 2020) 20. See also M Broberg, 'From Colonial Power to Human Rights Promoter: On the Legal Regulation of the European Union's Relations with the Developing Countries' (2013) 26 *Cambridge Review of International Affairs* 675, 685 (arguing that 'the EU's promotion of its values is not merely aimed at the ACP [African, Caribbean, and Pacific] countries', but that 'the countries that arguably have been under the strongest pressure to comply with the so-called European values are not the former colonies, but rather the EU's Eastern European neighbours, which have been required to meet the so-called Copenhagen criteria (setting the political, economic and administrative standards for EU membership applicants) when applying for accession').

[121] JR Seeley, *The Expansion of England: Two Courses of Lectures* (first published 1883) (Cambridge, Cambridge University Press, 2010) 8.

[122] J Zielonka, *Europe as Empire: The Nature of the Enlarged European Union* (Oxford, Oxford University Press, 2007) 13.

[123] Case C-347/10 *Salemink* ECLI:EU:C:2012:17 (17th January 2012).

option where the Court would take the opportunity to pronounce on whether the continental shelf counted as Member State territory, and on the scope of the Member State's EU law obligations there.[124] He proceeded to make the following arguments, which repay close examination:

> 44. As a physical space under the sovereignty of a State, the concept of territory covers territorial space as such and also airspace and maritime space. In all cases it consists of areas, recognised by international law, where each State exercises exclusive sovereignty, although these areas do not represent the full extent of the domain in which States can exercise their sovereign powers, since international law also recognises the existence of extraterritorial State powers.
>
> 45. Just as the area in which State sovereignty can be exercised does not necessarily coincide exactly with the extent of its territory, neither do the competences of a State which derive from sovereignty always exhibit the exclusivity and absolute nature which are characteristic of sovereign power. On the contrary, precisely as a result of the progressive legal regulation of the international community, the exercise of sovereignty is subject to variations in intensity, becoming less pronounced as the connection between the area of exercise and the territorial base of the State becomes weaker ....
>
> 47. If State sovereignty over territorial sea is already restricted in the way I have indicated, the characteristic powers of a sovereign State diminish progressively the further one travels, so to speak, from 'dry land', such powers becoming reduced in the case of the continental shelf, as we shall go on to see in more detail, to a collection of 'sovereign rights' intended to be used for particular purposes, and diluted to the mere exercise of certain freedoms upon reaching the high seas, where any claim to sovereignty is quite simply invalid.

The Advocate General then deduced that since EU competences are conferred by the Member States, 'EU law will apply to whatever extent the Member States exercise official authority in the areas of competence conferred on the Union', subject to limitations specified in the Treaties.[125]

In the judgment that followed, the ECJ silently but definitively chose the innovative route:

> Since a Member State has sovereignty over the continental shelf adjacent to it – albeit functional and limited sovereignty – work carried out on fixed or floating installations positioned on the continental shelf, in the context of the prospecting and/or exploitation of natural resources, is to be regarded as work carried out in the territory of that State for the purposes of applying EU law.[126]

[124] Case C-347/10 *Salemink*, Opinion of AG Cruz Villalón ECLI:EU:C:2011:562 (8th September 2011), paras 38–39, 41.

[125] *Ibid*, paras 54–55.

[126] *Ibid*, para 35.

The Court depicted the *Salemink* holding as a natural development of existing case law dating from as far back as *Kramer*,[127] and continuing through *Commission v Spain*,[128] *Mondiet*,[129] and *Commission v UK*.[130] Such a conception of the geographical scope of the application of EU law also accords with the *Air Transport* judgment, which, as demonstrated in chapter two, claims a right to prescribe rules in a territorially unbounded fashion, rather than an ability merely to influence conduct overseas.[131]

The *Salemink* passages excerpted above are striking in their portrayal of the relationship between sovereignty and territory. They represent the polar opposite of the classic description in *The Apollon*, where Story J held that

> The laws of no nation can justly extend beyond its own territories, except so far as regards its own citizens. They can have no force to control the sovereignty or rights of any other nation, within its own jurisdiction. And, however general and comprehensive the phrases used in our municipal laws may be, they must always be restricted in construction, to places and persons, upon whom the Legislature have authority and jurisdiction.[132]

Although the *Apollon* formulation does envisage the assertion of authority outside of the territory, it is nevertheless premised upon a conception of borders as *limits*, with the exceptions to them being carefully specified. In *Salemink*, however, territory is viewed as the fount of authority, which is conceived 'like radio waves from a transmitter';[133] that is to say, as a force potentially spreading all over the world but becoming weaker the further away it travels from the source.

[127] Joined Cases 3,4, and 6/76 *Officier van Justitie v Kramer* [1976] ECR 1279, para 30–33 (EU rules on the conservation of marine biological resources extend not just to the territorial waters of the Member States, but to the high seas 'in so far as the Member States have similar authority under public international law').

[128] Case C-258/89 *Commission v Spain* [1991] ECR I-3977, para 18 (EU measures regulating fishing activities of EU vessels applies on high seas 'outside the Community fishing zone').

[129] Case C-405/92 *Etablissements Armand Mondiet SA v Armement Islais SARL* [1993] ECR I 6133, para 12 ('… with regard to the high seas, the Community has the same rule-making authority in matters within its jurisdiction as that conferred under international law on the state whose flag the vessel is flying or in which it is registered'). See also Case C-25/94 *Commission v Council (FAO)* [1996] ECR I-469, para 44 ('It has also been consistently held that, as regards the high seas, the Community has the same regulatory powers, in areas falling within its authority, as are recognized under international law to the State whose flag the vessel flies or in which it is registered …').

[130] Case C-6/04 *Commission v United Kingdom* [2005] ECR I-1111, para 17 (rejecting the UK's argument that Council Directive on the conservation of natural habitats and of wild fauna and flora (Council of the European Union) 92/43/EEC [1992] OJ L206/7, or the 'Habitats Directive' applied only to UK national territory and territorial waters and not to the exclusive economic zone, holding instead that where 'the United Kingdom exercises sovereign rights in its exclusive economic zone … (i)t follows that the directive must be implemented in that exclusive economic zone').

[131] Six of the judges in *Salemink* also sat in *Air Transport*: Skouris, Tizzano, Cunha Rodriguez, Lenaerts, Bonichot and Silva de la Puerta.

[132] *The Apollon* 22 US (9 Wheat) 362, 370 (1824).

[133] MW Doyle, *Empires* (Ithaca, Cornell University Press, 1986) 24.

Put differently, the world of *Salemink* does not have borders, but *frontiers*. In this respect, consider Herfried Münkler's discussion of the basic differences between the concept of authority in a State and an Empire.

> In Staaten hat die Machtausübung überall und jederzeit auf die gleiche Weise und nach denselben Prinzipien zu erfolgen, und das um so mehr, je stärker sich der Staat zum Rechts- und Verfassungsstaat entwickelt hat. Imperiale Machtausübung ist dagegen nach einem System von Kreisen und Ellipsen geordnet, die vom Zentrum zur Peripherie auseinanderlaufen. Mit diesen Kreisen und Ellipsen verändert sich auch die Art und das Maß der Selbstbindung imperialer Macht. Im Zentrum, im eigentlichen Kernland des Imperiums, ist sie am stärksten, und hier gleicht sie dem, was für die Selbstbindung der Macht im Staaten gilt. Zur Peripherie hingegen nimmt sie immer weiter ab, ohne daß damit gegen die Funktionsprinzipien der imperialen Ordnung verstoßen würde.[134]

In their discussion of the EU as a 'Cosmopolitan Empire', Ulrich Beck and Edgar Grande adopt and develop Münkler's theory to define a state as 'a permanent political association based directly on the formal power of command over those subject to it', while an empire is a mode of exercising power that 'permanently strives for control over non-subjects'.[135] While a state 'seeks to solve its security and welfare problems by establishing fixed borders', an empire 'solves them through variable borders and external expansion'.[136]

Put simply, Beck and Grande suggest that there are essentially two ways a political community may resolve external threats or advance its goals in the wider world. First, it may shut its borders to the external world and thereby exclude the threat from entering. If it happens to be a particularly attractive destination or market, such closure may induce persons outside the borders into changing their behaviour in order to be allowed in. Alternatively, that political community may unilaterally extend its borders, thereby bringing the persons posing external threats directly under its authority. The first strategy is, in Beck

[134] H Münkler, 'Das Prinzip Empire' in U Speck and N Sznaider (eds), *Empire Amerika: Perspektiven einer neuen Weltordnung* (Munich, Deutsche Verlags-Anstalt, 2003) 112–13. Although Münkler uses the term *Macht*, he must be taken as meaning *normative* power or authority. His interest is clearly not in economic influence or military might, but political order. See *ibid* 112 ('Imperien und Staaten unterschieden sich nicht nur im Umgang mit Grenzen, sondern auch hinsichtlich der einheitlichen politischen Gestaltung des je eigenen Raumes.').

[135] U Beck and E Grande, *Cosmopolitan Europe* (Cambridge, Polity Press, 2007) 56. See also Zielonka (n 122) 2–3 ('the Union is anything but a state. It has no effective monopoly over the legitimate means of coercion. It has no clearly defined centre of authority. Its territory is not fixed. Its geographical, administrative, economic, and cultural borders diverge.'). Beck and Grande describe their understanding of 'cosmopolitanism' in the following terms: 'Cosmopolitanism combines appreciation of difference and alterity with attempts to conceive of new democratic forms of political rule beyond the nation-state'. Beck and Grande, *ibid* 12. They explicitly reject Kant's cosmopolitanism. *Ibid* 258–60. Moreover, as we shall see in the conclusion to chapter 4, their ambition to transcend the nation-state renders their project decidedly un-Kantian.

[136] Beck and Grande, *ibid* 57. See also J Zielonka, 'America and Europe: Two Contrasting or Parallel Empires?' (2011) 4 *Journal of Political Power* 337, 345.

and Grande's view, typical of a sovereign state. This 'hegemonic' approach is not unproblematic, and students of history and international relations may disagree on whether its results tend to be benevolent or oppressive. Whatever the answer to that might be, it raises a different set of problems than the second strategy, which, in claiming not just power but authority in a geographically unlimited fashion, is distinctly *imperial*.[137] In so far as this second strategy contemplates the unilateral extension of the physical space governed by a legal order, one might even call it 'territorial extension'.

IV. CONCLUSION: DIGNITY AS INDEPENDENCE

This chapter examined attempts to justify the EU's assertions of extraterritorial jurisdiction upon the advancement of human well-being – expressed variously in terms of common concerns, universal values and interests – and found them wanting in several respects. This first problem is that this approach contradicts the distinction between harms and wrongs that informs our most basic and paradigmatic legal practices. Not only may you do no wrong by retarding others' welfare, as well as wrong others without affecting their welfare; you can in fact wrong others by conferring benefits upon them as an officious intermeddler. Second, this chapter demonstrated by reference to EU jurisprudence that the values, objectives, ends or goods purportedly pursued by an extraterritorial measure cannot serve as standards against which its legality can be assessed. The EU 'missionary principle' is perhaps an aspect of what Joseph Weiler calls 'political messianism', or the tendency to substitute and replace processes of political contestation with appeals to abstract values:

> In political messianism, the justification for action and its mobilizing force derive not from process, as in classical democracy, or from result and success, but from the ideal pursued, the destiny to be achieved, the promised land waiting at the end of the road. Indeed, in messianic visions *the end always trumps the means*.[138]

Weiler's critique applies to external lawmaking as well. The ends do not justify the means: the burdens imposed upon distant strangers cannot be justified on the basis of the benevolent 'content' of extraterritorial measures. It is not the 'rightness' of its decisions that grounds the legitimacy of an institution and its decision-making procedures. Rather, 'the justness or correctness of a decision depends on the institution making the decision and/or the procedure by which the decision came about'.[139]

[137] *cf* Ryngaert, *Selfless Intervention* (n 62) 38. In his recent book, Ryngaert uses the term 'hegemon' to cover both of these distinct strategies. See text to n 143 below.

[138] JHH Weiler, 'The Political and Legal Culture of European Integration: An Exploratory Essay' (2011) 9 *International Journal of Constitutional Law* 678, 683 (emphasis added). See also *ibid* 684 ('Some old habits, such as the 'white man's burden' and the missionary tradition, die hard …').

[139] A Harel, *Why Law Matters* (Oxford, Oxford University Press, 2014) 2.

It might appear that Benvenisti and Ryngaert take care of such considerations of institutional legitimacy by proposing elaborate mechanisms for stakeholder consultation and cooperation between legal orders. However, the institutions and procedures they envisage are primarily engaged in information gathering and at best provide a 'voice' for individual groups of foreign stakeholders. They therefore lack the *associative* aspect of the legitimacy of any lawmaking institution. Instead, the mechanisms they call for effectively blur the lines between separate institutions and the persons they get to speak for, thus rendering their approaches disassociative, and therefore anti-institutional. The end result is a contradiction that resolves itself in paternalism. Recall Benvenisti's first premise that sovereignty is valuable because it remains the only viable means for peoples to live out their distinct cultures and values – a thought he expresses by borrowing Martti Koskenniemi's beautiful phrase that sovereignty articulates the 'the hope of experiencing the thrill of having one's life in one's own hands'.[140] Contrast this with his somewhat chilling remark towards the end that 'the stark question for the weaker countries is whether clinging to formal nineteenth century-type sovereignty remains in their best interest'.[141] In contrast to Benvenisti, Ryngaert starts from a position of deep scepticism about the concept of sovereignty. Emphasising the historical contingency of both sovereignty and the territorial principle of jurisdiction, Ryngaert identifies it as the greatest obstacle standing in the way of collective solutions to global problems.[142] For this reason, he writes in his recent book that his 'fundamental argument' is that 'hegemonic states, that is, internationally leading states, may, under certain circumstances, harness their power and capacities to extend their sovereignty with a view to protecting global values and common interests'.[143] Statements like these might perhaps send a shiver down the spines of those who have actually experienced the tender ministrations of hegemonic states, which is why Ryngaert then spends many pages constructing legal techniques to restrain the potential for paternalism and domination. My purpose here is not to comment on whether these rescue attempts are successful, but to suggest that they could be avoided by starting from a different premise – that ends do not justify means.

The beginnings of this alternative may be found by returning to the problem of the secret nocturnal visitor. Why do most legal systems allow you significant legal redress against him, despite his harmlessness – or even advantage – to you? One common argument is that trespassers are usually up to no good, such that even though your particular secret visitor was harmless, overall societal interests

[140] Benvenisti (n 13) 302; Benvenisti (n 17) 124; Benvenisti (n 47) 7. Citing M Koskenniemi, 'What Use for Sovereignty Today?' (2011) 1 *Asian Journal of International Law* 61, 70.
[141] Benvenisti (n 13) 328.
[142] Ryngaert, *Unilateral Jurisdiction* (n 62) 47. See generally *ibid* Ch 3.
[143] Ryngaert, *Selfless Intervention* (n 62) 38.

in individual personal security are more likely to be advanced rather than set back by a general prohibition against such conduct.[144] On this rule-utilitarian argument, however, societal interests in security could be protected just as effectively while at the same time maximising individual liberty by allowing a 'harmlessness' exception, the burden of proving which would lie with the defendant. No known legal system does this. Moreover, it appears limited to types of conduct which seem harmful by default, or unproductive of social benefit.[145] However, conduct may be actionable even if it is of a type presumptively beneficial to the individual and society, for instance, medical treatment. To account for such situations, the rule-utilitarian must either manufacture elaborate empirical speculations or resort to ever more expansive definitions of personal security resembling pique or paranoia more than any meaningful sense of harm.[146]

Another strategy would be to posit some 'protected interests' as particularly important, because they are fundamental to the enjoyment of all other interests. On this view, your visitor's trespass is actionable even in the absence of damage because your 'interest in the exclusive possession of land is a more important and inherently valuable interest than [your] interest in quiet enjoyment of land'.[147] Out of an abundance of caution, therefore, the private law provides you a remedy to 'vindicate' that interest.[148] The problem with this 'protected interest' strategy, is that it almost does away with the idea of an interest altogether. The interests grounding torts such as trespass, defamation, battery and false imprisonment seem 'basic' only in certain instances, but entirely whimsical in others. Why is your interest in the exclusive possession of land accorded 'basic' importance, rather than your interest in adequate food and housing? Even if it is conceded that possession of land for housing is a basic interest, why does that possession have to be 'exclusive'? As the secret visitor and Grotius's torch both demonstrate, it is entirely possible to enjoy the material benefits of home and many other forms of possession without excluding others, unless 'enjoyment' is defined in purely technical terms.

[144] See C Bird, 'Harm Versus Sovereignty: A Reply to Ripstein' (2007) 35 *Philosophy & Public Affairs* 179, 184 ('The thought that at any moment complete strangers might freely enter and observe these most intimately personal places will leave most of us profoundly uncomfortable, the fact that they would do no damage, harbor no ill intentions, or that we would be unaware of their presence would do little to remove that discomfort.'). See *ibid* 183, citing JS Mill, *Utilitarianism*, 7th edn (London, Longmans, Green, and Co, 1879) 81 ('The interest involved is that of security, to everyone's feelings the most vital of interests. Nearly all other earthly benefits are needed by one person, not needed by another; … but security no human being can possibly do without …').

[145] Bird, *ibid* 188 ('… there is no vital social interest in sleeping in other people's beds').

[146] See Bird, *ibid* 185 ('Our sense of personal security therefore rises and falls with our ability to rely confidently upon the law … to properly recognize both our interests and what is necessary to protect them. Viewed from this angle, the knowledge that those who are found to have invaded others' bodies or personal space can escape legal sanction by claiming that in themselves their actions caused no direct harm plausibly contributes to a sense of insecurity.').

[147] JNE Varuhas, 'The Concept of 'Vindication' in the Law of Torts: Rights, Interests and Damages' (2014) 34 *OJLS* 253, 259.

[148] *Ibid* 258 ('In this sense, vindication means to attest to, affirm and reinforce the importance and inherent value of particular *interests*.').

Interest-theorists will no doubt have more ingenious strategies to offer, but these cannot be anticipated here. Instead, I suggest a far more parsimonious and intuitive explanation for why your rights against the secret visitor are what they are. The reason why the secret visitor wrongs you by harmlessly entering your house or touching you without your consent, is because your body and your house are *yours*. Only *you* get to decide what to do with them. If others could simply use you and your property as they pleased, that would mean you had neither a life nor purposes of your own. It is irrelevant that their purposes may be ultimately beneficial to you. A human being's fundamental legal status is not about being kept happy by being supplied with things necessary for the satisfaction of interests, even the very basic ones called 'needs'. As mentioned in chapter one, the condition of a well-kept, happy slave is repugnant simply because as a matter of formal status, she is completely subject to the master's will. Instead, dignity lies in freedom understood as *independence*; that is, in not being subject to the will of another. As Kant puts it, '*Freedom* (independence from being constrained by another's choice), insofar as it can coexist with the freedom of every other in accordance with a universal law, is the only original right belonging to every man by virtue of his humanity.'[149]

Kant's entire general theory of law emerges from this single concept of independence, which is not a 'value' in the sense of a goal or a good supplied or advanced instrumentally via the law, but the organising principle structuring and shaping the forms of all legal relations.[150] As he explains in a passage known as the Universal Principle of Right, it is the fundamental moral *status* that must be respected in all interpersonal interactions involving coercion: 'an action is right if it can coexist with everyone's freedom in accordance with a universal law, or if on its maxim the freedom of choice of each can coexist with everyone's freedom in accordance with universal law'.[151] In contrast, an action constitutes a *wrong* if it hinders the actions of another person that are rightful according to the Universal Principle of Right, for the simple reason that it is incompatible with that other person's independence from the necessitating choice of others.[152] As will be explained in the next chapter, to claim that you have been wronged implies more than simply saying that your interests have been harmed, your urgent needs unmet, or your particular purposes frustrated. Rather, it is to say that in their interactions with you, someone else has acted inconsistently with your ability to set purposes *altogether*; that is, in a manner that dominates and instrumentalises you as a *thing*. Crucially, it turns out that

[149] I Kant, 'The Doctrine of Right' [hereinafter '*DR*'] in MJ Gregor (ed & tr), *Practical Philosophy: The Cambridge Edition of the Works of Immanuel Kant*, 9th edn (Cambridge, Cambridge University Press, 2006) 6:237, 393.

[150] See RB Pippin, 'Mine and Thine? The Kantian State' in P Guyer (ed), *The Cambridge Companion to Kant and Modern Philosophy* (Cambridge, Cambridge University Press, 2006) 425–28.

[151] *DR* 6:230, 387.

[152] *DR* 6:230–31, 387.

a system of persons interacting with one another compatibly with their freedom is impossible without political institutions entitled to use force to maintain each in their freedom. As such, despite my deep and pervasive objections to Benvenisti's and Ryngaert's theories of extraterritorial jurisdiction, subsequent chapters will show their intuition that sovereignty is a fiduciary office to be correct and valuable.

The next chapter develops upon these fundamental premises to set out further principles of political theory relevant to the legal topics treated in this book. These are:

- the fiduciary nature of the relationship between sovereigns and their subjects;
- the right of sovereign states to use coercion to ensure that they are not subject to the will of another; and
- that factual 'harms' cannot be central in ascertaining the international rights of sovereigns.

This then lays the foundation for chapter five, which sets out an alternative, 'republican' theory of extraterritorial jurisdiction to provide global public goods, which does genuinely proceed from the idea of having one's life in one's own hands, rather than on unilateral determinations about what interests, goods or ends are correct or valuable. Moreover, that chapter also demonstrates that the EU's unique method of asserting jurisdiction over distant strangers to providing public goods is largely defensible on Kant's legal and political theory, even if, as it turns out, the EU is itself most decidedly not.

4

Kant's International Legal Order and the Forms of Private Law

THIS CHAPTER LAYS the foundations for an alternative theoretical framework for thinking about the EU's rights and obligations concerning distant strangers. Starting from the simple idea that no person is subject to the will of another, it sets out certain salient aspects of Kant's philosophy of right, many of which are already discernible in the relevant practices in EU law, human rights and public international law, which ultimately provide the basis for showing that: (1) the methods by and purposes for which the EU asserts authority extraterritorially are largely (though not wholly) defensible; and (2) the EU acquires human rights obligations towards distant strangers to the extent that it asserts such authority over them.

As stated in chapter one, the source materials from which this book draws what it claims to be Kant's legal and political philosophy are primarily the *Doctrine of Right* and secondarily the essay *Toward Perpetual Peace*. I begin with a summary of Kant's basic forms of private right, from which he eventually crafts a general theory of constitutional, international and cosmopolitan law. The picture that emerges is of a global cosmopolitan order composed of human beings interacting with one another through their membership of independent democratic republics, each of which are themselves persons. Given that this book attempts to bridge the disciplines of Kant's philosophy of right on the one hand, and EU law and public international law on the other, a certain amount of leniency has been necessary. For instance, I have departed from Kant's obtuse terminology for his concepts, as well as been judicious in presenting their nuances. Besides, I have developed Kant's concepts in ways not immediately apparent in the texts by recourse to his obvious inspirations in Roman private law.

On that last note, the amount of space devoted to private law may seem unusual for a book purporting to deal with EU law and public international law. However, the basic forms of private law and the concept of property so thoroughly permeate Kant's philosophy of right that even as brief an overview as this simply has to engage with them. Thus, no apology is offered for straying away from more traditional concerns of EU legal scholarship. The EU will not be mentioned again until the conclusion, where it is argued that, contrary to popular belief, the EU as a political organisation is in many ways inimical to Kant's republican and statist vision of international order. This, however, does not and cannot deprive Kant's philosophy of right of its normative power in expounding the EU's rights and obligations relating to distant strangers.

I. PRIVATE RIGHT: THE BUILDING BLOCKS OF KANT'S GENERAL THEORY OF LAW

As we saw at the end of the previous chapter, Kant's entire theory of law derives from the premise that the single natural right of human beings – the Innate Right of Humanity – lies in not being subject to the will of another.[1] As demonstrated by the example of the harmless nocturnal visitor in the previous chapter, it serves as a plausible organising principle for our most basic intuitions about law. The natural right of freedom relies upon a distinction between persons and things: in the *Doctrine of Right*, Kant defines a *person* as capable of attribution and responsibility because self-legislating: he is 'a subject whose actions can be imputed to him' as a result of which he is 'subject to no other laws than those he gives to himself'.[2] In contrast, a *thing* is an 'object of free choice' to which 'nothing can be imputed'.[3] These simply restate the familiar Roman notions that a free man is *sui juris*, while things such as animals or slaves are *alieni juris*. Being treated rightly as a person consists in being treated according to one's nature as a person. A 'wrong' accordingly obtains when a person is dominated or instrumentalised as a thing. Not all instances of domination or instrumentalisation amount to wrongs, only those that are 'coercive'. What constitutes coercion is explained below in subsection A.

The 'innate' right to freedom gives rise to three kinds of 'acquired' rights:

> a right to a thing (*ius reale*), or a right against a person (*ius personale*), or a right to a person akin to a right to a thing (*ius realiter personale*), that is, possession (though not use) of another person as a thing.[4]

This crucial passage can be explicated as follows. A thing can be both used and possessed at the same time. To wit, the innate right of human beings lies in not being treated as a thing. This, however, does not mean that persons can neither be possessed nor used, but only that they cannot be possessed and used *at the same time*. Accordingly, three forms of *legal* relations of right and obligation are possible depending on combinations of possession and use between persons and things.

(1) '*A right to a thing*' is a right of a person to prevent all others from interfering with the things she is rightfully controlling in pursuit of her

[1] I Kant, 'The Doctrine of Right' [hereinafter '*DR*'] in MJ Gregor (ed & tr), *Practical Philosophy: The Cambridge Edition of the Works of Immanuel Kant*, 9th edn (Cambridge, Cambridge University Press, 2006) 6:237, 393.

[2] *Ibid* 6:223, 378.

[3] *Ibid*.

[4] *Ibid* 6:260, 412.

purposes – her 'means'. These consist of *property*, and her *person*.[5] To interfere with another's things, say, by damaging her goods, or injuring her, is a *tort*.

(2) '*A right against a person*' entitles one person to *use* another.[6] It is a right to performances; to the obligor's delivery of a good, rather than title in it.[7] For instance, your employer gets to use you in pursuit of her purposes. 'Using' you like this is perfectly compatible with right, so long as she does not also possess you. You must have signed up for the job, and you can always quit.[8] These are *contractual* relations.

(3) '*A right to a person akin to a right to a thing*' is a right of one person to *possess* another – that is, to make decisions for another. If a child, your mother can tell you to eat your dinner, and you must do it. If your attorney accepts a settlement in your name you are – in a revealing phrase – 'bound' by it. If another possesses you in this way, they cannot also use you. The decisions they make in respect of you have to be consistent with purposes you could have set for yourself, never theirs.[9] This works the other way as well: if they possess you, you get to use them. Their 'status' in relation to you is an 'external object of choice' in your possession, like a performance promised to you by contract, or a thing in your rightful control.[10] This is the structure of a *fiduciary* relation.

This classification will also be familiar to lawyers: the names of the categories are intended almost to mirror the traditional Roman classification of obligations relating to persons, things and actions.[11] Together, these basic relations

[5] A Ripstein, *Force and Freedom: Kant's Legal and Political Philosophy* (Cambridge, Harvard University Press, 2009) 66–69 (describing this category of rights as 'property', paralleled by similar rights against interferences with one's person). How one comes to be in rightful control of such things is explained below in subsection B.

[6] *Ibid* 69–70.

[7] *DR* 6:274, 424. As Ripstein puts it, such rights 'enable parties to modify their respective rights, so that one person is entitled to depend upon the specified deed of another'. Ripstein (n 5) 69.

[8] This is not to deny that oppressive employment contracts, lack of alternatives, and other considerations might render the employee's 'choice' illusory. That is certainly a problem, but it is not a problem *for the employer*. Preventing this form of domination is not the task of private law but for public law, which must enact labour regulation as well as set limits on the terms of employment contracts.

[9] Ripstein (n 5) 70–76.

[10] Kant defines the three categories of external objects of choice as: '1) a (corporeal) *thing* external to me'; 2) another's *choice* to perform a specific deed (*praestatio*); 3) another's *status* in relation to me'. *DR* 6:247, 402.

[11] G.1.8; J.1.2.12. Kant constructs his third category not as the law of actions or as a miscellaneous collection of obligations fitting neither in contract or delict. Instead, as indicated by the designation '*dinglich-persönliches Recht*', which Mary Gregor attractively translates as 'a right to a person akin to a right to a thing' (*DR* 6:260, 412). This category is a triangulation of the first two categories, whereby a right to a person is *treated as a case of* a right to a thing. Kant later takes pains to defend his departure from orthodoxy as truly a 'new phenomenon in the juristic sky', rather than 'merely a shooting star'. *DR* 6:358–59, 494.

provide the structure for all legal relations, be it private or public, or at domestic, international or cosmopolitan law. Everything that is called a *legal* right has to have one of these three forms, because these are the only ways one person can use force consistently with another's freedom.[12] Accordingly, as Kant puts it, public law contains 'no further or other duties' than can be conceived at private law.[13]

The most relevant categories for this book are the first and the third, which I script as tortious and fiduciary relations. The next section will expand upon torts. Concerning the concept of a fiduciary relation, it is important to recall the distinction between law and ethics discussed in chapter one, exemplified by Kant's remark that a nation of devils bereft of even the slightest inkling of ethics might still work out a rightful condition, so long as they have understanding. Accordingly, fiduciary obligations are not to be understood as legal instantiations of ethical duties binding upon the fiduciary's conscience.[14] Second, while Kant does recognise a place for equity in his philosophy of right, he does not depict it as form of recourse to ethical standards extraneous to law but instead treats them as legal claims lacking in crucial particulars, thus requiring judges to employ their discretion in filling them out. Such arbitrary judicial discretion would amount to domination if resorted to generally, and so equity cannot be invoked by a judge except when deciding upon (1) her *own* rights – say, whether or not to accept irregularly filed pleadings – or (2) the rights of someone on whose behalf she is authorised to speak – for instance, the sovereign in a lawsuit between the sovereign and his employees. In all other cases, equity is a 'mute divinity who cannot be heard'.[15] Third, my use of 'fiduciary relation' is not intended to suggest the notion of differentiated and limited property rights associated with trusteeship in English law, and which animates Benvenisti's theory of sovereign trusteeship. A CEO is a fiduciary of the company even though none of the corporate assets vest in her. Rather, the basic case of a fiduciary relation is where one person possesses a 'discretionary authority to set or pursue practical interests (including matters of personality, welfare or right) of another'.[16] As Paul Miller puts it, 'fiduciary power is not properly understood as connoting relative strength, ability, or influence', but is instead 'to be understood as a form of *authority*' – that is to say, the ability to 'render rightful conduct that would otherwise be wrongful'.[17] In other words, a relationship where one person 'governs' another.

[12] Kant defines 'Right [as] connected with an authorization to use coercion'. *DR* 6:231, 388.

[13] *DR* 6:306, 451.

[14] *cf* AB Laby, 'The Fiduciary Obligation as the Adoption of Ends' (2008) 56 *Buffalo Law Review* 99; M Harding, 'Manifesting Trust' (2009) 29 *OJLS* 245. Both of these scholars argue that fiduciary duties are directly derived or manifest either the fiduciary's duties of virtue or the principal's goals or ends. For an argument that fiduciary duties cannot be 'derived' from morality, see PB Miller, 'Justifying Fiduciary Duties' (2013) 58 *McGill Law Journal* 969, 995–99.

[15] *DR* 6:234–35, 390–91.

[16] PB Miller, 'A Theory of Fiduciary Liability' (2010) 56 *McGill Law Journal* 235, 278.

[17] Miller (n 14) 1012–13.

There are, however, exceptional cases of fiduciaries with no ability to change the normative position of their principals, but only a position of trust combined with systematic power and influence. Contemporary examples include professional investment advisers, physicians and other persons described as 'epistemic authorities' in chapter two, while more traditional examples are bailees with whom goods are left for safekeeping.[18] Accordingly, some formulations have fiduciary relations arising also when 'the beneficiary is peculiarly vulnerable to or at the mercy of the fiduciary holding the discretion or power'.[19] Even in these cases, however, fiduciary obligations are not justified solely upon factual effects. Vulnerability alone cannot give rise to a fiduciary relationship: a grandmaster who happens to be your opponent in a chess match is not your fiduciary. Instead, an important consideration is that such fiduciaries have assumed the *purposes* of their principals, who then systematically lack factual or legal recourse if the fiduciary departs from it.[20] This exceptional case will become briefly relevant in chapter seven.

A. The Division of Torts: Damage and Injury

I stated earlier that I would be developing Kant's ideas in ways not immediately apparent from his texts by recourse to Roman law. In this section, I argue that the category defined as torts divides into two – wrongful deprivation and wrongful use – which correspond to the categories of *damnum iniuria datum* and *iniuria* in Roman delict. As is the case with delict, the former are identified as violations solely of rights in *property*, and the latter solely with rights in *personality* – canonically enumerated as rights in body, reputation and *dignitas* (status, honour or worth).[21] Crucially, harm or loss is central to the first category,

[18] D.4.9.1 *pr*–1 (Ulpian, 14 *On the Edict*) (holding innkeepers, ship's masters and stable keepers strictly and vicariously liable to restore goods left in their safekeeping on account of their ability to collude with thieves); *Coggs v Bernard* (1703) 2 Ld Raym 909; 92 ER 107.

[19] *Frame v Smith* (1987) 2 SCR 99, para 60 (Wilson J, dissenting).

[20] Consider the landmark Decision by the Supreme Court of Canada holding physicians to be fiduciaries of their patients, which involved a doctor who had exploited his patient's dependency on painkillers to extort sexual favours from her. The patient's 'consent', however reluctant, precluded any action in tort or contract, leaving her with no remedy unless a fiduciary relationship was held to exist. *Norberg v Wynrib* (1992) 1992 SCR 2. Second, in his fascinating piece on the history of the English law of innkeeping, Reinhard Zimmermann observes that justifications of the innkeeper's unique and onerous obligations of strict liability for losses of guests' property evolved from a general societal distrust of innkeepers, to a notion that guests would be in a systematically vulnerable position if the innkeeper were to conspire with thieves to rob his guests. He puts the thought in strikingly Kantian terms: 'Hätte [der Gast] "regelmäßig den Beweis einer dem Gastwirthe zur Lastfallenden Verletzung einer der kontraktlichen Pflicht" als Ursache für den eingetretenen Schaden zu führen, *so wäre er weithin rechtlos*' (emphasis added). R Zimmermann, 'Innkeepers' Liability – Die Entwicklung Der Gastwirtshaftung in England' in A Heldrich, J Prölss and I Koller (eds), *Festschrift für Claus-Wilhelm Canaris zum 70. Geburtstag*, vol 2 (Munich, Beck, 2007) 1435.

[21] D.47.10.1.2 (Ulpian, 56 *On the Edict*).

but irrelevant to the second. Before entering into that discussion, something needs to be said about the concept of coercion.

Torts are interferences with the things you are rightfully using and/or possessing in pursuit of your purposes – that is, your *means*. The frustration of a 'mere wish'[22] – a project you would like to accomplish but do not have the means for – may inconvenience you but it does not coerce you. As Arthur Ripstein explains:

> What you can accomplish depends on what others are doing – someone else can frustrate your plans by getting the last quart of milk in the store. If they do so, they don't interfere with your independence, because they impose no limits on your ability to use your powers to set and pursue your purposes. They just change the world in ways that make your means useless for the particular purpose you would have set.[23]

Likewise, you do not wrong a terminally ill relative by refusing them your bone marrow. Their need for it, no matter how urgent, is just a mere wish. Your organs are not *their* means, so your refusal does not take anything 'away' from them that they already had. For the same reason, a 'Process and Production Method' regulation that excludes a foreign trader from selling a certain product in the jurisdiction is not coercive, because that trader does not have a right to market her goods there. The trader might very much *want* to sell her goods there, but this is a 'mere wish' which the regulating state is under no obligation to help achieve.

Thus conceived, there are just two ways another may commit a tort against you: (1) she may deprive you of your means; or (2) she may use your means for her purposes rather than yours.[24] For the first category, you must have been deprived of the means itself.[25] Merely reducing the *value* of your means – say, of your business – does not deprive you of it, but simply changes the world around you in such a way that makes your means unsuitable for the purposes you had intended. It is therefore unrecoverable as pure economic loss. In contrast, harm is irrelevant for the second category of wrongful use because it does not involve you actually 'losing' anything.[26] Your nocturnal visitor's trespass is not inconsistent with your possessing and using your house because, quite obviously, you still have the house. Rather, it is wrongful because he accomplished *his* purposes by using *your* means, and this is inconsistent with your status as a free person not at the disposal of another.

Next, recall Kant's 'rational billiard ball' model of corrective justice introduced in chapter one, according to which coercion is wrongful when it hinders freedom, but rightful when deployed as a hindrance to that hindrance.

[22] *DR* 6:230, 387.
[23] Ripstein (n 5) 16.
[24] See A Ripstein, *Private Wrongs* (Cambridge, Harvard University Press, 2016) 43–52.
[25] *Ibid* 48–50.
[26] *Ibid* 46–48.

This in turn implies that the structure of the remedy is determined by that of the wrong it responds to. Accordingly, if someone wrongfully deprives you of your means, the remedy is that she must give it (or its value in money) back to you – *compensation*. This rationale cannot apply to remedy wrongful uses, for reasons explained rhetorically in an old English case:

> Suppose a gentleman has a paved walk in his paddock, before his window, and that a man walks up and down before the window of his house, and looks in while the owner is at dinner, is the trespasser to be permitted to say, 'here is a halfpenny for you, which is the full extent of the mischief I have done?' Would that be a compensation? I cannot say that it would be.[27]

Instead, if purposes are accomplished through the wrongful use of others' means, those 'gains' are wrongful, and must therefore be surrendered in *restitution*. For instance, if you lead tour groups through onyx caves partly lying under your neighbour's land, you must surrender a proportionate amount of the profits to that neighbour.[28]

In either case, the remedy is simply the right looked at from the other end. Despite their differences in orientation, however, restitution and compensation may sometimes turn out to bear a superficial resemblance. If someone spits in your face and you contract a disease from it, your remedy will 'include' your medical bills. This, however, is not because your claim to a remedy is predicated on a loss that 'consists' of medical expenses, but because erasing the tortfeasor's wrongful purpose includes setting back those expenses. The opposite does not hold for the first category. If you negligently run over your neighbour's rosebushes while rushing to collect your lottery winnings, you need only replace the rosebushes. You need not undo your purpose by handing over your winnings.

Such a description of the law of torts and its remedies may be unusual to students of English law where gain-based remedies in tort remain highly controversial.[29] It may also seem deeply unorthodox to, say, German lawyers, whose notion of restitution is the Thomistic or 'scholastic' idea of in kind return of things taken away, which is therefore structurally no different from

[27] *Merest v Harvey* (1814) 5 Taunt 442 (QB) 442; 128 ER 761, 761.

[28] *Edwards v Lee's Administrator* 96 SW 2d 1028; 265 Ky 418 (KY 1936). See also *Ministry of Defence v Ashman* [1993] 25 HLR 514 (CA) 519, where Hoffmann LJ held that a 'person entitled to possession of land can make a claim against a person who has been in occupation without his consent on two alternative bases. The first is for the loss which he has suffered in consequence of the defendant's trespass … The second is the value of the benefit which the occupier has received. This is a claim for restitution …'

[29] For instance, Jason Varuhas decries the fact that 'despite damages for trespass to land being classified as compensatory for nearly their entire history, under the influence of restitution theorists some courts have, in recent times, classified user damages as restitutionary …'. JNE Varuhas, *Damages and Human Rights* (Oxford, Bloomsbury Publishing, 2016) 57. For a celebrated exposition of the inadequacy of the traditional purely 'compensatory' model of English tort, see P Birks, 'Harassment and Hubris the Right to an Equality of Respect Modern Jurisprudence' (1997) 32 *Irish Jurist* 1.

compensation.[30] I say no more about restitution because it is a topic that could occupy many lifetimes, and because it is not essential to my argument.[31] Instead, I note simply that my distinction between wrongful damage and wrongful use, the role of harm in each, and their respective remedies, are all represented in the Roman private law by the delicts of *damnum iniuria datum* (loss given by a wrong) and *iniuria* (wrongs).[32]

It is also axiomatic that *damnum* pertains only to 'property' rights,[33] while *iniuria* attends to 'personality' rights. This may sound curious, given that one can damage another's body or use another's property. English lawyers for instance tend to think of trespass primarily as a violation of property rights, actionable the moment the trespasser sets foot on any part of your land,[34] but in the Roman law the injury corresponding to trespass is conceptualised as a *personal* wrong – a violation of *dignitas* – akin to an invasion of privacy.[35] Recall that your nocturnal visitor's conduct is not inconsistent with your possession of your house. Rather, what it is inconsistent with is 'your ability to be the one who determines how [the house] will be used'.[36] Conversely, and crucially for our inquiry, Roman law never recognised a direct action for careless damage to the body of a free man,[37] and the precise reason the jurist Ulpian gives for this

[30] See, eg, German Civil Code s 249 (1). R Zimmermann, *The Law of Obligations: Roman Foundations of the Civilian Tradition* (Oxford, Oxford University Press, 1996) 824–30; F Giglio, *The Foundations of Restitution for Wrongs* (Oxford, Bloomsbury Publishing, 2007) 155–62.

[31] I simply note that the theory of restitution described above is necessarily implied by the way Kant sets up rights and remedies as correlative relations of action and reaction ordered, unlike the Thomists, without reference to some moral standard that is 'out there' independently of the parties but knowable to them.

[32] See WW Buckland and AD McNair, *Roman Law and Common Law: A Comparison in Outline*, 2d edn (Cambridge, Cambridge University Press, 1965) 340–44.

[33] See P Birks and E Descheemaeker (eds), *The Roman Law of Obligations: The Collected Papers of Peter Birks* (Oxford, Oxford University Press, 2014) 195–98.

[34] Howell's State Trials reports Lord Camden CJ as holding that 'By the laws of England every invasion of private property, be it ever so minute, is a trespass.' *Entick v Carrington* (1765) 19 Howell's St Tr 1029 (KB) 1066. See also A Burrows, *Principles of the English Law of Obligations* (Oxford, Oxford University Press, 2015) 136 (s 2.10): 'Defamation protects reputation. Conversion protects property rights in goods. Trespass to land and private nuisance protect property rights in land.'

[35] Buckland and McNair (n 32) 102 (observing that trespasses are actionable in Roman delict only if the owner 'had expressly forbidden entry or if it was an enclosure, such as a dwelling-house, into which everyone knew that free entry would be forbidden … But it is a wrong against personality, not against property'). See also DL Carey Miller, 'Public Access to Private Land in Scotland' (2012) 15 *Potchefstroom Electronic Law Journal* 119, 120 (commenting that 'There is no delict of trespass in the Romanist common law of Scotland; the landowner has an enforceable right to require a trespasser to leave but there is no civil claim for the act of trespass *per se* as there is, on the basis of the 'tort of trespass', in English law.').

[36] Ripstein (n 5) 67.

[37] See Birks and Descheemaeker (n 33) 198. Instead of a direct action under the *Lex Aquilia*, which controlled all claims for damage, a freeman complaining of negligent damage to his body had to sue 'indirectly' through the *actio legis utilis Aquiliae*, a Praetorian intervention involving roping in his paterfamilias and arguing that by negligently harming his person, the wrongdoer had violated his father's 'property-like' right to his son in power. Another fiction was to construe the freeman as

is because '*dominus membrorum suorum nemo videtur*' – no one is to be seen as the owner of his limbs.[38] What this principle stands for is that property and personality are fundamentally distinct: 'Whatever meaning is given to 'property,' it is independent of personhood … a living person can be the holder of a property right but he or she cannot be the object of it.'[39]

The same rejection of self-ownership is fundamental to Kant's philosophy of right as demonstrated by the following crucial passage:

> An external object that in terms of its substance belongs to someone is his *property* (*dominium*), in which all rights in this thing inhere (as accidents of a substance) and which the owner (*dominus*) can, accordingly, dispose of as he pleases (*ius disponendi de re sua*). But from this it follows that an object of this sort can be only a corporeal thing (to which one has no obligation). So a man can be his own master (*sui iuris*) but cannot be the owner of himself (*sui dominus*) (cannot dispose of himself as he pleases) …[40]

Having ownership of some property means being able to dispose of it at your pleasure. Property is thus capable of being 'mine or yours' – it is always and everywhere *transmissible*.[41] As James Penner explains, the 'very idea of transmissibility [of property] is related to this idea of contingency – what is yours might as well be, and might come to be, not only mine, but his, hers, theirs, and so on'.[42] Your *person* is not like this: in the paradigmatic example, you cannot sell yourself into slavery. Note that the reason Kant gives for why such a contract must be void is not because it is immoral – even though it is certainly that as well – but because it is *juridically* incoherent. To sell yourself into slavery by contract is to purport to assume an obligation to become a thing, which by definition cannot be bound by obligations.[43] Such an act is therefore a legal

unaware of his status and serving another in good faith as a slave. See Zimmermann (n 30) 1014–17. Both of these partial commodifications are reminiscent of that involved in Kant's concept of a right to a person akin to a right to a thing.

[38] D.9.2.13.8 (Ulpian, 18 *On the Edict*).

[39] J Edelman, 'Property Rights to Our Bodies and Their Products' (2015) 39 *University of Western Australia Law Review* 47, 53. James Edelman frames his argument around the colourful English case of *R v Bentham* [2005] UKHL 18 (HL). The case concerned a defendant who, upon being confronted by the homeowner during a burglary, threateningly held his fingers under his jacket in the shape of a gun, for which he was convicted of an offence of possessing an imitation weapon. The conviction was reversed on appeal, with Lord Rodger of Earlsferry invoking the *dominus membrorum* principle to hold that if 'no-one is to be regarded as the owner of his own limbs … Equally, we may be sure, no-one is to be regarded as being in possession of his own limbs'. *Ibid*, para 4.

[40] *DR* 6:270, 421.

[41] *DR* 6:246, 401. Mary Gregor's translation is an improvement upon the original, which reads as 'mein und dein'. Harris explains that the concept of private property in land in English law requires three kinds of legal provisions: trespassory rules; transmission principles; and general use rules. JW Harris, 'Ownership of Land in English Law' in N MacCormick and P Birks (eds), *The Legal Mind: Essays for Tony Honoré* (Oxford, Clarendon Press, 1986) 145–46. Similarly, Birks argues that there is a necessary connection between freedom of alienation and property. P Birks, 'The Roman Law Concept of Dominium and the Idea of Absolute Ownership' (1985) *Acta Juridica* 1, 20–23.

[42] J Penner, 'On the Very Idea of Transmissible Rights' in James Penner and Henry Smith (eds), *Philosophical Foundations of Property Law* (Oxford, Oxford University Press, 2013) 256.

[43] *DR* 6:330, 472. See also Ripstein (n 5) 135–40.

nonsense, and can be of no force or validity. Thus, you are free whether you like it or not: independence operates as an *internal* constraint upon the structure of private law. Unlike property, personality rights cannot be disposed of at pleasure. They are *inalienable*.

If inalienability is the core of personality, it follows that your personality rights extend to more than just your body, but to all other things which cannot 'become' another's. In this sense, Kant describes a person's reputation as 'an innate external belonging … that clings to the subject as a person …'.[44] It is separate from you but cannot exist in separat*ion* from you.[45] Others may filch your good name from you just like they might steal your purse. Unlike your purse, however, *your* good name cannot become *their* good name. It remains yours, except that it is now a *bad* name. Similarly, the feats of courage you accomplish in your life cannot be left to your descendants as patrimony,[46] which is why Kant ridicules the idea of hereditary titles of nobility as being as silly as hereditary professorships.[47] Finally, the structure of property and personality rights is also reflected in that of the remedies for their violation. The contingency of property means that a wrongdoer can replace it. Accordingly, the remedy for wrongful damage is compensation. In contrast, personality rights cannot be taken from you, and therefore can be violated only by wrongful use. Thus, damage is irrelevant and the remedy is restitution.

B. The Three Defects in the State of Nature

As a social contractarian (of sorts), it is central to Kant that none of the legal relations described above can be realised as a matter of right in a condition of pure private interaction – the 'state of nature'.[48] This obtains even if persons in that state are rational and therefore know what proper legal relations are, and even if they have nothing but the best intentions. Instead, a combination of political institutions is required to address three structural defects in the state

[44] *DR* 6:295, 441.

[45] *cf ibid DR* 6:295-96, 441–43. Kant does maintain that a good reputation can survive its bearer's physical death in a way that his heirs are entitled to sue for defamation, but explains this as a function of that person's continuing to bear rights as a *homo noumenon*. The point that a reputation is not transmissible as property remains valid.

[46] *DR* 6:329, 471 ('if an ancestor had merit he could still not bequeath it to his descendants: they must acquire it for themselves …').

[47] *Ibid*. For similar critical comments about hereditary nobility and bondage, see *PP* 8:351, 232, and *DR* 6:348–49, 485–86. There is, however, one heritable status – citizenship. *DR* 6:343, 482.

[48] *DR* 6:256, 409. At *DR* 6:242, at 397, Kant qualifies this with the remark that 'a *state of nature* is not opposed to social but to a civil condition, since there can be society in a state of nature, but no *civil* society (which secures what is mine or yours by public laws).' What he means by this is that people in such a condition may very well refrain from interfering with others in ways contrary to right, but they will do this only as a matter of habit or convention, behind which there is no binding *civil* guarantee.

of nature: indeterminacy, non-reciprocity and unilateralism. While the first two can be dealt with expeditiously, the third requires closer examination because it is central to the discussion in section III below.

First, rights are 'indeterminate' without a non-partisan judge.[49] Suppose you and another genuinely believe that a particular thing is yours. In the absence of a neutral arbitrator, the only way to settle the dispute finally would be by fighting, or a game of chess, or by rolling dice. Victory, however, that does not mean your claim was correct, but only that you were a superior fighter, chess player or luckier gambler. As such, you might as well have taken it without making any pretence of a right to do so, and another even better fighter, chess player or gambler might come along and do the same to you.[50] Your right therefore remains undetermined, even unnecessary, because what ultimately controls is not the merits, but brute strength or sheer luck. The solution is a judiciary that issues binding decisions *publicly* and *systematically* – that is, in open court and according to principles applicable to all.[51]

Second, there is the defect of 'nonreciprocity'.[52] Being endowed with reason, you can know that you must not use arbitrary violence against others because such a maxim cannot be universalised consistently with the choice of all others under a universal law. However, you are prevented from *assuring* them of this, because you cannot be sure they will do the same for you. This is not a 'prisoner's dilemma' resulting from a lack of information but a moral one; by unilaterally disarming you place yourself at the mercy of others. This is not just imprudent, but immoral.[53] The solution is an executive with a monopoly on enforcement of determined rights, to be exercised once again publicly and systematically.

The third defect relates to the acquisition of property, and Kant's discussion of it contrasts profoundly with the natural law theories we saw in the previous chapter. The first relevant comparison is to Locke, whose 'proviso' about leaving enough and as good in common for others plays a prominent role in Benvenisti's sovereign duty of other-regardingness. Consider the canonical passage:

> Though the earth and all inferior creatures be common to all men, yet every man has a property in his own person; this nobody has any right to but himself. The labour of

[49] Ripstein (n 5) 168–72.

[50] See J Waldron, 'Kant's Legal Positivism' (1996) 109 *Harvard Law Review* 1535, 1540:

> The point of using force in the name of justice is to *assure* people of that to which they are entitled. But if force is being used to further contradictory ends, then its connection with assurance is ruptured. In such a situation, force is being used simply to represent the vehemence with which competing opinions about justice are held, and this use of force may well be worse than force not being put to the service of justice at all.

[51] Ripstein (n 5) 169–74. See also EJ Weinrib, 'Private Law and Public Right' (2011) 61 *University of Toronto Law Journal* 191, 197. ('The adjudication of liability manifests both publicness and systematicity. First, a court exercises its authority in a public manner by exhibiting justifications for liability that are accessible to public reason … Second, the court's decision partakes of the systematicity of the entire legal order.')

[52] Ripstein (n 5) 159–68.

[53] Ripstein (n 5) 161–66. See also *DR* 6:307, 452.

> his body and the work of his hands we may say are properly his. Whatsoever, then, he removes out of the state that nature hath provided and left it in, he hath mixed his labour with, and joined to it something that is his own, and thereby makes it his property. It being by him removed from the common state Nature placed it in, it hath by this labour something annexed to it that excludes the common right of other men. For this 'labour' being the unquestionable property of the labourer, no man but he can have a right to what that is once joined to, at least where there is enough, and as good as left in common for others.[54]

Of interest is Locke's notion of mixing labour as a first step to enclosing property, which gives rise to well-known difficulties.[55] If your labour is your 'unquestionable' property, does that mean – contrary to the first thing we learn in law school – that contracts for service are in principle conveyances of property?[56] In a memorable critique, Jim Harris argued that Locke commits a 'spectacular *non sequitur*' in the first sentence of the passage where he argues that because no one else keeps us as property, this must mean we must have property in ourselves. Instead, invoking the *dominus membrorum* principle we saw earlier, Harris points out that '[f]rom the fact that nobody owns me if I am not a slave, it simply does not follow that I must own myself. Nobody at all owns me, not even me'.[57]

In contrast to Locke, Kant distinguishes between personality and property rights by characterising them along the lines of *innate* and *acquired* rights to objects. An 'innate right is that which belongs to everyone by nature, independently of any act that would establish a right', whereas 'an acquired right is that for which such an act is required'.[58] Your body, reputation, and honour are innately yours. You do not have to account for how you came to possess them because they cannot have been anyone else's. In contrast, your right to your purse is an acquired right; if events had taken a different course they could very easily have been someone else's.[59] With this in mind, the first step to acquiring an external object in the state of nature is to engulf it with an innate object – by

[54] J Locke, 'Second Treatise of Government' in P Laslett (ed), *Locke: Two Treatises of Government*, Student Edition (Cambridge, Cambridge University Press, 1988) 287–88 (s 27, Ch 5).

[55] See JW Harris, *Property and Justice* (Oxford, Oxford University Press, 1996) 184–88. For a famous critique from a scholar otherwise generally sympathetic to Locke, see J Waldron, 'Two Worries About Mixing One's Labour' (1983) 33 *Philosophical Quarterly* 37.

[56] Harris, *ibid* 191–94. For an example of a judicial conflation of contractual and property rights, see *Lochner v New York* (1905) 198 US 45, 53 where the US Supreme Court held that the 'general right to make a contract in relation to his business is part of the liberty of the individual protected by the Fourteenth Amendment of the Federal Constitution … Under that provision no State can deprive any person of life, liberty or property without due process of law. The right to purchase or to sell labor is part of the liberty protected by this amendment, unless there are circumstances which exclude the right'.

[57] Harris, *ibid* 196.

[58] *DR* 6:237, 393.

[59] See Ripstein (n 5) 59–60.

picking up an apple and wrapping your fingers around it.[60] If you have done so, the only way another can get to the apple and make it theirs is by prising off your fingers. You can resist this because your fingers are innately yours.[61]

So far, Kant's concept of physical apprehension appears very much like Grotius's notion of bodily occupying a theatre seat. However, this is where the trouble starts for Grotius: your claim to the seat lasts only so long as you actually sit there. Mere physical possession or occupation is not enough for your control of the object to amount to 'ownership', because the moment you leave or let go, anybody else can take it.[62] A property right entails more than just a right not to be assaulted while occupying or holding the thing; it means being able to exclude others from the thing even when not in physical possession of it.[63] This, however, cannot be justified by simply ensuring others have enough and as good left for their needs. If you claim a right to exclude others from a certain plot of land because you have grown enough apples on it to feed everyone, they may justifiably retort that they prefer oranges and, in any event, that it was not for you to decide that they must have apples.

This reveals another problem with Grotian and Lockean natural law theories of original acquisition. Merely wrapping your fingers around the apple does not change the legal rights and obligations of others – they are already under an obligation not to interfere with your person. Claiming *property* in it, however, does change the legal rights and obligations of others – they are now obligated not to interfere with it even after you let go. No private person outside of a fiduciary can change another's legal position like this, and the encloser is certainly no fiduciary of the excluded. Harris accordingly identifies this as the 'fatal flaw' in the Grotian-Lockean approach: it 'presupposes a unilateral power to create new trespassory obligations'.[64] Such 'peremptory' obligations can rightfully be created only 'omnilaterally' – that is, by the whole of society coming together as one to back up your claim to exclude others from the thing even when you no longer physically occupy it.[65] The solution, then, is to magic up – 'postulate' – an institution capable of defining the 'signs' we must give one another to demonstrate taking control of a thing along with the intention to continue controlling it.[66] There is no property without law. To bind everyone, the law

[60] Kant puts it like this: 'The only condition under which a *taking possession* (*apprehensio*), beginning to hold (*possessionis physicae*) a corporeal thing in space, conforms with ... [external freedom] is the *first* taking possession (*prior apprehensio*), which is an act of choice.' *DR* 6:263, 415. See also *DR* 6:268, 419.

[61] *DR* 6:247–48, 402; Ripstein (n 5) 94.

[62] Harris illustrates this with an anecdote about a Home Counties man attending a cricket match in Yorkshire, who leaves his hat on his seat to get a drink. He returns to find his place taken by a native. Upon protesting, he is told: 'Nay, lad, up here it's bums that keep seats, not hats!' Harris (n 55) 214.

[63] *DR* 6:247, 402.

[64] Harris (n 55) 202.

[65] See Ripstein (n 5) 157–58.

[66] *DR* 6:265, 417.

must be made by an institution acting publicly and systematically as the voice of the united will of the community – a *legislature*.[67]

The three institutions operate in an interlocking fashion: the 'legislature must authorize all acts that change, enforce, or demarcate rights; the executive must enforce rights in accordance with law, and the judiciary must decide disputes and authorize remedies, again in accordance with law'.[68] The absence of one or more of these institutions leads to various pathologies: a system without an executive to enforce laws is an *anarchy*; one without a legislature to control government action is *despotic*; and one without a judiciary to settle legal disputes on the merits rather than force is *barbaric*.[69] The 'ideal' in which all three institutions obtain and function harmoniously is the *republic*, in which free citizens make law for themselves through an elected legislature.[70] However, like all ideals, this remains an aspiration that is forever unattainable. In the 'real', non-ideal world, much, much less is needed to give rise to a 'rightful condition' with binding and enforceable law. All that is needed is an ability to apply and enforce some semblance of the forms of private legal relations described above.[71] The existing institutions may be undemocratic, incompetent and even oppressive, but as long as they meet this very low bar, a rightful condition is 'constituted', and you are required to enter it. Just how defective the institutions can be before they cease to count as rightful conditions is left for chapter six.

The obligation to enter the rightful condition obtains not because it is so advantageous that it would be utterly irrational to remain outside, but because it is an offer you *cannot* refuse. Law and authority seem incompatible with freedom only if freedom is thought of as 'licence'; the ability to do whatever you want without constraint. If, however, freedom is understood as a civil guarantee that no one will dominate and instrumentalise you as a thing at their mercy, it becomes obvious that authority is *necessary* for freedom; it requires political institutions with authority to use force. One way to put it is that by remaining outside, you are purporting to reserve for yourself the opportunity to use violence against others as and when you please. Others need not abide this. Indeed they *must* not, for this would be inconsistent with *their* independence. Thus, the innate right to freedom of all persons means that others must compel you to enter into a condition with them where they will be assured of their independence. Another way to think of it is as the obverse of a slavery contract: consent to the 'original contract' is mandatory for the same reasons of juridical coherence for why consent to a slave contract is void. You *become* free by

[67] Ripstein (n 5) 157 ('my appropriation can only change your legal situation if everyone, including you, has conferred a power on me to appropriate. My act of appropriation is thus a unilateral exercise of an omnilateral power, rather than a unilateral act … my act genuinely binds them only when the general will has authorized it.').

[68] Ripstein (n 5) 173. See also *DR* 6:316, 459.

[69] See I Kant, RB Louden (ed) *Kant: Anthropology from a Pragmatic Point of View* (Cambridge, Cambridge University Press, 2006) 235 (7:330–31).

[70] *Ibid* 236 (7:331).

[71] *DR* 6:307, 451–52. Kant calls this minimal standard the 'postulate of public right'.

submitting to authority.[72] You cannot 'choose' not to submit, because choosing is only for the free. You are unfree if you decline, which means you can be forced – forced to be free.

C. Legislating on Property and Personality

The rightful condition consolidates and preserves innate and acquired rights under a system of lawfully constituted authority as property and personality rights.[73] To recall the previous section, property is by default transmissible, and personality by default inalienable. This, however, is not to deny the existence of 'inalienable' property rights such as fee tails, praedial servitudes or usufructs. Rather, transmissibility simply means that 'the same constraints on the conduct of others pass over to the new owner intact'.[74] A usufruct may not be alienated in gross, but you can always sell your life interest in it.[75]

Conversely, the inalienability of personality rights does not mean that you cannot donate your kidney. It means that you cannot sell your kidney as if it were property; stringent legal protections have to be in place ensuring that your decision to alienate it is not the product of domination. While the law of organ transplantation was beyond Kant's contemplation, something of what he might have said about it may perhaps be found in the infamous passages in the *Doctrine of Right* dealing with sexual intercourse. Kant begins by observing that because a 'human being cannot have property in himself, much less in another person', making use of another's body without infringing upon their dignity requires a 'morally necessary' purpose such as procreation, rather than plain enjoyment of another 'as a thing'.[76] Otherwise, sex becomes a 'cannibalistic' form of

> use by each of the sexual organs of another, [such that] each is actually a *consumable* thing (*res fungibilis*) with respect to the other, so that if one were to make oneself such a thing by *contract*, the contract would be contrary to law.[77]

Most legal systems fortunately do not pursue this principle to such extremes. Nevertheless, something of it is reflected in contemporary legal regimes

[72] *DR* 6:316, 459 ('one cannot say: the human being in a state has sacrificed a *part* of his innate outer freedom for the sake of an end, but rather, he has relinquished entirely his wild, lawless freedom in order to find his freedom as such undiminished, in a dependence upon laws, that is, in a rightful condition, since this dependence arises from his own lawgiving will').

[73] While 'people might come to recognize each other's claims to property or under contracts without an omnilateral authorization … whether or not they accept them depends on the matter of their choices'. Instead, only under a rightful condition do any rules or dispute resolution procedures possess 'genuine authority'. Ripstein (n 5) 157.

[74] A Ripstein, 'Property and Sovereignty: How to Tell the Difference' (2017) 18 *Theoretical Inquiries in Law* 243, 253.

[75] Birks clarifies that 'it is not nonsense to speak of ownership of a usufruct, a right definitionally temporary *and* inalienable. If the law declared sheep inalienable, the conclusion would have to be that you could not own sheep but only "sheepright": "sheepright" would be definitionally inalienable, whereas sheep are not.' Birks (n 41) 20–21.

[76] *DR* 6:359, 495.

[77] *DR* 6:359–60, 494–95.

governing sex work, organ transplantation and euthanasia. Where we permit such bodily alienations, contemporary legal regimes tend to prohibit them from being carried out on commercial terms. Where they are permitted on commercial terms, pains are taken to ensure that they result from genuine and informed choice, rather than vulnerability and exploitation.

In short, transmissibility and inalienability mean that property and personality raise exactly opposite problems for lawmakers. As regards property rights, the law trains its attention upon *acquisition* and the imposition of obligations upon others. As regards personality rights, the law trains its attention upon *alienation* and the relieving of others from their obligations.[78]

II. PUBLIC RIGHT: THE FIDUCIARY STATE

Although we now turn to sovereignty and public law, the private law concepts of damage, injury and fiduciary relations remain central. In particular, I agree with Benvenisti's characterisation of the sovereign state as a fiduciary, but, as explained above, not with his conception of what it means to *be* a fiduciary. For present purposes, the most important difference is that for Kant, the state is truly a 'person' in its own right.

A. The Separate, Public Person of the State

Despite long traditions of speaking about 'state personality', international lawyers often deploy that term as a mere placeholder for a collectivity of real, flesh-and-blood individuals. On this view, the state and its subjects are one and the same. For instance, Benvenisti describes the state as 'not more than the aggregate of individuals who define their and others' property rights through the political process'.[79] Similarly, in his defence of private law analogies for expounding legal relations between states, Hersch Lauterpacht observes that the 'analogy – nay, the essential identity – of rules governing the conduct of states and of individuals is not asserted for the reason that states *are like* individuals; it is due to the fact states *are composed* of individual human beings …'.[80] He then continues to explain that

> behind the mystical, impersonal, and therefore necessarily irresponsible personality of the metaphysical state there are the actual subjects of rights and duties, namely,

[78] See J Pallikkathayil, 'Persons and Bodies' in S Kisilevsky and MJ Stone (eds), *Freedom and Force: Essays on Kant's Legal Philosophy* (Oxford, Bloomsbury Publishing, 2017) 50.

[79] E Benvenisti, 'Sovereignty and the Politics of Property' (2017) 18 *Theoretical Inquiries in Law* 447, 448. See also Locke (n 54) 348 (s 120, Ch 8).

[80] H Lauterpacht, 'The Grotian Tradition in International Law' (1946) 23 *British Yearbook of International Law* 1, 27.

> individual human beings … [t]he individual is the ultimate unit of all law, international and municipal, in the double sense that the obligations of international law are ultimately addressed to him and that the development, the well-being, and the dignity of the individual human being are a matter of direct concern to international law.[81]

If state personhood is simply an aggregation of the personhoods of the individual human beings who are the 'ultimate unit of all law', then the former may presumably be picked apart and rearranged if conducive to the benefit of the latter. In this spirit, Nico Krisch claims that

> if public autonomy is to redeem its promise, it has to extend to the definition of the scope of the polity itself; individuals' choices, loyalties, and allegiances to particular polities demand respect in the construction of an institutional and jurisdictional framework.[82]

As such, Lauterpacht argues that beneath the reference to 'state personality', the state ought actually to be pictured 'like property, as dominion held under law', in a manner that 'deprive(s) it of the character of absoluteness and indivisibility'.[83] The same thought is put more colourfully by Geoffrey Howe: 'Sovereignty is not virginity, which you either have or you don't … [but] a bundle of sticks, and the subject of a never-ending series of transactions between nation-states, handing over some things and taking back others.'[84]

If the state is simply a collectivity of individuals, it would follow that sovereign or *public* obligations are in essence simply rights and obligations operating 'horizontally' between private parties. In this spirit, Henry Shue describes states as 'mediating' institutions for 'perfecting' pre-political rights and duties between private individuals to guarantee 'a few basics … when helpless to secure them for [themselves]',[85] and that 'negative' rights create corresponding duties on all persons public and private, while 'positive duties need to be divided and assigned among bearers in some reasonable way'.[86] Shue's vision of public right as a clearinghouse for rights and duties existing independently of institutions seem at variance with much contemporary human rights and constitutional rights practice. For instance, there are vanishingly few judicial decisions or constitutional provisions asserting the horizontality of human rights between private persons. Instead, the overwhelming trend is instead to find them as possessing 'indirect' horizontal effect in private legal relations, on grounds that the state must be presumed to have posited the private law in a manner consistent with its human rights and constitutional obligations.[87]

[81] *Ibid*.

[82] N Krisch, *Beyond Constitutionalism: The Pluralist Structure of Postnational Law* (Oxford, Oxford University Press, 2010) 298–99.

[83] Lauterpacht (n 80) 29–30.

[84] G Howe, 'Sovereignty and Interdependence: Britain's Place in the World' (1990) 66 *International Affairs* 675, 679.

[85] H Shue, 'Mediating Duties' (1988) 98 *Ethics* 687, 687.

[86] *Ibid* 690.

[87] For readings critical of this trend, see A Nolan, 'Holding Non-State Actors to Account for Constitutional Economic and Social Rights Violations: Experiences and Lessons from South Africa

This commonplace reflects deeper normative intuitions. To wit, if your neighbour were to drag you into her dungeon and waterboard you, we would ordinarily say she has committed a series of torts against you, rather than a violation of your human rights. We would say that your human rights have been violated only if your neighbour's conduct is not addressed by civil and criminal legislation, adjudication and enforcement. In other words, human rights violations require more than just private inconsistencies with right; they imply a *public* failure by your entire community. Moreover, this quality of publicness cannot be accounted for as an aggregation of many different horizontal claims against each and every individual community member, like a mass tort. Rather, human rights violations have the characteristic of a failure by someone whose job it is to take care of you – a *fiduciary*.

In contrast to this view of the state as an aggregation of private persons, Kant envisions the state as a distinct moral person.[88] The thought is perhaps most familiar from the idea that an orchestra is much more than just an aggregation of musicians playing particular notes on particular instruments at particular times, but instead constitutes 'a personified unit of agency in which [the musicians] no longer figure as individuals but as components …'.[89] Kant expresses this same thought when he argues that attribution and responsibility – the defining characteristics of personhood – must be traced not to individual people, but to the separate person of their state. This is why extracting reparations from the population of a defeated enemy state is illegal: 'to force individual persons to give up their belongings … would be robbery, since it was not the conquered people who waged the war; rather, the state under whose rule they lived waged the war *through the people* …'.[90]

As a separate person, the state occupies a uniquely *public* standpoint distinct from its subjects and officials. Contrary to Benvenisti, the state is not a forum for the celebration of its subjects' common sympathies, because these are necessarily private affairs. Again, this can be illustrated by analogy to an orchestra: its constituent musicians will invariably possess private habits, desires and aspirations that may be vastly different from each another. Nevertheless, as Ronald Dworkin memorably put it, we

> do not suppose that the orchestra also has a sex life, in some way composed of the sexual activities of its members, or that it has headaches, or high blood pressure, or

and Ireland' (2014) 12 *International Journal of Constitutional Law* 61, 65, 88, *passim*; S Woolman, 'The Amazing, Vanishing Bill of Rights' (2007) 124 *South African Law Journal* 762, 763.

[88] On a broadly 'liberal' reading of the *Perpetual Peace*, Tesón understands Kant to mean that the state 'does not acquire moral value greater than its components' and that the 'state as a moral person is just an analogy …'. Tesón draws this conclusion from I Kant, 'Toward Perpetual Peace' [hereinafter '*PP*'] in MJ Gregor (ed & tr), *Practical Philosophy: The Cambridge Edition of the Works of Immanuel Kant*, 9th edn (Cambridge, Cambridge University Press, 2006) 8:344, 318, which he concedes 'seems to conceive of the state in a holistic way as a moral person …'. FR Tesón, 'The Kantian Theory of International Law' (1992) 92 *Columbia Law Review* 53, 70–71.

[89] R Dworkin, *Sovereign Virtue: The Theory and Practice of Equality* (Cambridge, Harvard University Press, 2000) 226.

[90] *DR* 6:348, 485.

> responsibilities of friendship, or crises over whether it should care less about music and take up photography instead.[91]

Instead, the orchestra has just *one* purpose – making music. Likewise, the sole 'regulative principle' of the state is the provision of a rightful condition in which no member of the political community is subject to the will of anybody else, including the state.[92] The reason why the public person of the state may not establish an official religion is not limited to a concern that minorities may be discriminated against. It may not establish an official religion even if it is followed by the entire population, for such an act would express not the omnilateral will of the people, but only the 'parallel' wills of a multitude of private individuals.[93] Such a state would be just a private person writ large, and therefore unfit to wield public authority.

B. Human Rights and the Fiduciary State

The state wields authority over subjects; it claims an entitlement to determine their legal rights and duties and to bind them by its pronouncements. Public right contains no further or other duties than those conceivable in private law. Thus, the state is simply an extension of the private law concept of a fiduciary. Since it possesses its subjects, it may not also use them. Whatever decisions it makes in respect of its subjects must be consistent with purposes they could have set for themselves. Just as a principal requires the intercession of her fiduciary for the exercise of her rights, an individual requires the state to constitute the freedom that is her innate right. Equally, just as the private law contains a set of principles to ensure that private fiduciary relationships do not degenerate into self-dealing, public law contains a set of principles to ensure that authority does not degenerate into domination. These are *human rights*. Human rights are neither entitlements to the satisfaction of a set of basic interests, nor are they pre-political moral rights serving as the fount of the entire global legal order. Instead, their sole purpose is to ensure that those who possess us neither use us nor permit others to make us mere means to their ends.[94]

Accordingly, while I agree with Benvenisti that sovereigns are essentially fiduciaries, I contend that this relationship necessarily requires the state and its subjects as having separate personalities. In Birks's excellent phrase, the fiduciary

[91] Dworkin (n 89) 227.

[92] Kant argues that 'the well-being of a state must not be understood as the *welfare* of its citizens and their *happiness*; for happiness can perhaps come to them more easily and as they would like it to in a state of nature (as Rousseau asserts) or even under a despotic government. By the well-being of a state is understood … that condition in which its constitution conforms most fully to principles of right …'. *DR* 6:318, 461.

[93] Ripstein (n 5) 282–83. See also Dworkin (n 89) 223 (criticising a strand of communitarian thinking for 'suppos(ing) that a communal life is the life of an outsize person, that it has the same shape, encounters the same moral and ethical watersheds and dilemmas, and is subject to the same standards of success and failure as the several lives of the citizens who make it up').

[94] As Evan Criddle and Evan Fox-Decent put it, 'Human rights protect individuals against state domination and instrumentalization by entitling all persons to be treated in certain ways by public

obligation is 'inseverably compound':[95] the fiduciary duty of competence is inextricably linked to the duty of disinterestedness because, at its core, that office envisages one person taking 'positive steps in the interest *of another*'.[96] A fiduciary relationship cannot exist if there is a perfect identity between the class of fiduciaries and the class of principals. If the class of fiduciaries was one and the same as that of the principals, we would lack any criteria for judging the former's treatment of the latter. For the same reason, it would be deeply destructive of the human rights practice if the state and its interests were understood simply as aggregations of its subjects and their interests.

To illustrate, consider *A v Home Secretary*, the seminal UK Decision which examined the legality of 'control orders', through which the UK Government sought to detain indefinitely foreign nationals suspected of terrorist links, but who could not be deported to their home countries because they risked being tortured there.[97] The key question before the House of Lords was whether there was a 'public emergency threatening the life of the nation'[98] justifying a 'derogation' from the rights to liberty and trial guaranteed by the UK Human

institutions as a matter of rights. Human rights are thus claim-rights against public authorities.' EJ Criddle and E Fox-Decent, *Fiduciaries of Humanity: How International Law Constitutes Authority* (Oxford, Oxford University Press, 2016) 106. Ariel Zylberman expresses the similar idea through the remark that the 'unifying thought of the relational approach is that the *point* of specific human rights is not to minimize suffering in the world or to protect some independent good. Rather, the point of human rights is making real a social world governed by reciprocal relations of respect among equally independent persons.' A Zylberman, 'Why Human Rights? Because of You' (2016) 24 *Journal of Political Philosophy* 321, 342. An anonymous reviewer helpfully observes that my characterisation of the relation between state and subject as 'fiduciary', together with my frequent analogies to parental rights in order to explain the rights of states, might lead readers to think that Kant imagines the state to stand in the objectionable role of a parent over an infantilised people. This impression would be unwarranted: Kant specifically criticises paternalistic government as 'the most despotic of all (since it treats citizens as children).' *DR* 6:317, 460. It is important to acknowledge that whatever else its faults (and there are many) Kant's account of parenthood is strikingly original in that it conceptualises it as a legal relationship entailing rights and obligations modelled upon *negotiorum gestio*, rather than as a despotic office of absolute power over children. See *DR* 6:281–82, 429–30. Moreover, I use parental analogies in the technical sense of analogy and not as a metaphor; that is, as a perfect identity between two sets of relations rather than a partial similarity between the relata. In other words, I am not saying that the state is like a parent or the subject is like a child, but that the *relationship* between the state and the subject is fundamentally just like the *relationship* between the parent and the child, which, incidentally, is also just like the relationship between the trustee and beneficiary, the CEO and the company, innkeeper and guest, *etc*. All of these are manifestations of the same basic form of a 'right to a person akin to a right to a thing'. It is in this sense that Kant begins his discussion of the right to a person akin to a right to a thing with the example of parental rights over their children, and later begins his discussion of the right of nations by describing the 'natives of a country' as being '*in an intellectual sense* … born of the same mother (the republic) they constitute as it were one family (*gens, natio*)…' *DR* 6:343, 482 (emphasis added). In this way, while Kant reviles paternalism in government, it might be said that he nonetheless, and despite his distressing views about women, approves of maternalistic rule!

[95] P Birks, 'The Content of Fiduciary Obligation' (2000) 34 *Israel Law Review* 3, 33.

[96] *Ibid* 37–38 (emphasis added).

[97] *A and others v Secretary of State for the Home Department*; *X and another v Secretary of State for the Home Department* [2004] UKHL 56 (HL).

[98] The classic definition of the phrase is as 'an exceptional situation of crisis or emergency which affects the whole population and constitutes a threat to the organised life of the community of which the State is composed'. *Lawless v Ireland (No 3)* (1961) 1 EHRR 15, para 28.

Rights Act 1998 and the European Convention on Human Rights. In his speech, Lord Hoffmann observed that

> The 'nation' is a social organism, living in its territory ... under its own form of government and subject to a system of laws which expresses its own political and moral values ... The life of the nation is not coterminous with the lives of its people. The nation, its institutions and values, endure through generations. In many important respects, England is the same nation as it was at the time of the first Elizabeth or the Glorious Revolution. The Armada threatened to destroy the life of the nation, not by loss of life in battle, but by subjecting English institutions to the rule of Spain and the Inquisition. The same was true of the threat posed to the United Kingdom by Nazi Germany in the Second World War.[99]

As such, while 'fanatical groups of terrorists [might] kill and destroy' individual subjects,[100] this in itself was insufficient to 'threaten the life of the nation'.[101] Instead, the 'real threat to the life of the nation, in the sense of a people living in accordance with its traditional laws and political values' comes not from terrorism but from arbitrary measures such as the control orders.[102]

In exactly this spirit, Kant remarks that people who have united themselves into a society and therefore share a general will must regard the state as existing in perpetuity.[103] The state lives and dies by its fiduciary purpose: its immortality is 'a pure normative requirement, grounded in its ability to speak and act for everyone' notwithstanding changes in membership.[104] Thus, contrary to a prominent trend in contemporary human rights literature,[105] a strong personification of the state is not only compatible with the human rights practice, but essential to it. Interpreting human rights and sovereignty along such lines allows one to picture human rights as integrated with and mutually supporting the rule of law and democracy, rather than as eternally opposed to one another. However, it contradicts a central tenet of the human rights

[99] *A and others v Secretary of State* (n 97) para 91.
[100] *A and others v Secretary of State* (n 97) para 96.
[101] *A and others v Secretary of State* (n 97) para 96.
[102] *A and others v Secretary of State* (n 97) para 96. The Inter-American Court has held that an armed conflict may justify a declaration of a state of emergency only if finite in duration, thus prohibiting open-ended emergency rule. *Judicial Guarantees in States of Emergency (Arts 27(2), 25 and 8 American Convention on Human Rights)* IACHR Series A No 9, IHRR 3443 (IACHR 1987). See also Criddle and Fox-Decent (n 94) 136–37, arguing that 'terrorist violence will rarely justify a state's recourse to emergency powers' because a 'threat to the organized life of the community' lies in the 'disrupt[ion of] the state's ability to guarantee its subjects' secure and equal freedom' rather than the danger to the lives of individual subjects.
[103] *DR* 6:326, 468.
[104] Ripstein (n 5) 272–73.
[105] For instance, Peters contends that post-Cold War developments in international law 'definitely ousted the principle of sovereignty from its position as the *Letztbegründung* (first principle) of international law' and that the doctrine of sovereign personality 'remains foundational only in a historical or ontological sense ...'. A Peters, 'Humanity as the A and Ω of Sovereignty' (2009) 20 *European Journal of International Law* 513, 514. See also L Henkin, 'That S Word: Sovereignty, and Globalization, and Human Rights, Et Cetera' (1999) 68 *Fordham Law Review* 1, 2: 'a state is not a person, but an abstraction – and its relation to other abstractions, such as the governments which represent states, has inevitably brought distortion and confusion'.

movement – that they are pre-political and held purely in virtue of being human.[106] Rather, human rights are fully political, and held in virtue of a very particular status; that of being a *subject*. As will be argued in chapter six, this theoretical claim is largely substantiated in the contemporary practice of human rights law, and particularly so in the European variant thereof.

III. INTERNATIONAL LAW: PROPERTY AND PERSONALITY

The next step is a theory of proper legal relations between one state and another. The starting point is that as persons, states also have an innate right to independence from the arbitrary choice of others. Sovereignty is simply 'the legal translation of the political notion of independence … the freedom of the state to exercise as it sees fit the powers at its disposal'.[107] Just like natural persons, this freedom is unrealisable in an international state of nature but requires a rightful condition.[108] Benvenisti's fourth normative ground is correct. Subjection to international law is not just compatible with sovereignty, but necessary for it.

Kant's international state of nature differs from its domestic counterpart in that there is only one defect rather than three.[109] The defect common to both conditions is the indeterminacy of rights. For the same reasons that apply to natural persons, states can never settle their disputes through war; 'right cannot be decided by war and its favorable outcome, *victory* …'.[110] In this respect, the gulf between Kant and Grotius could not be wider. Under the 'regular war' tradition inaugurated by Grotius, war was *the* means by which sovereigns obtained a final and binding judgment in disputes between them. As Oona Hathaway and Scott Shapiro have recently argued, Grotius's theory of 'regular war' as a procedure for settling disputes prevailed until 1928 when war was 'outlawed' by the Kellogg-Briand Pact. As a result, they observe that

> In the modern era, it is not uncommon for observers to wonder whether international law is really law when there are no police to enforce it … Few recognize that this problem is so vexing because it is so new. During the Old World Order, international law did not need police. International law was backed by the very real threat of war.[111]

[106] For instance, Simmons states that '*Human* rights are rights possessed by all human beings (at all times and in all places), simply in virtue of their humanity … [as] natural rights that are innate and that cannot be lost (that is, that cannot be given away, forfeited, or taken away).' AJ Simmons, *Justification and Legitimacy: Essays on Rights and Obligations* (Cambridge, Cambridge University Press, 2001) 185. Beitz calls this the 'orthodox' position. C Beitz, 'Human Rights and the Law of Peoples' in Deen K Chatterjee (ed), *The Ethics of Assistance: Morality and the Distant Needy* (Cambridge, Cambridge University Press, 2004) 196.

[107] H Ruiz Fabri, 'Human Rights and State Sovereignty: Have the Boundaries Been Significantly Redrawn?' in P Alston and E MacDonald (eds), *Human Rights, Intervention, and the Use of Force* (Oxford, Oxford University Press, 2008) 34.

[108] *DR* 6:344, 482.

[109] Ripstein (n 5) 227–28.

[110] *PP* 8:355, 326.

[111] OA Hathaway and SJ Shapiro, *The Internationalists: How a Radical Plan to Outlaw War Remade the World* (New York, Simon and Schuster, 2017) 44–45.

Grotius, along with Pufendorf and Vattel, was the main pillar upon which this 'Old World Order' was built. For this reason, Kant in the *Perpetual Peace* excoriates all three as 'only sorry comforters', whose counsel merely encouraged crowned heads to start endless wars over often incredibly petty squabbles.[112]

For Kant, neither an executive nor a legislature feature in the international rightful condition. The absence of an international analogue to a domestic executive empowered to enforce binding laws is a common feature of Enlightenment-era proposals for international peace,[113] and Kant's reason for not having one at the international level is because unlike private persons, republican democracies are supposed to be fully rational. Whereas private persons must surrender the enforcement of their rights to an executive because they are a seething mess of mutually incompatible passions, republican democracies need not do so because they are constituted for the single purpose of providing a rightful condition. Peace between such states is guaranteed as a matter of reason, because in such political communities the persons deciding upon whether or not to go to war are the same – the *public* – as those who will do the actual fighting and the repayment of war debts, rather than unaccountable monarchs or military-industrial lobbies.[114]

Once again, legislatures are our main concern, but this time the question is why the ideal international order lacks one. This claim might seem controversial given that Kant describes the international rightful condition as taking the form of a '*permanent congress of states*'[115] which is 'expected to make collectively binding decisions'.[116] The crucial point, however, is the nature of those binding decisions; that is to say, the problem they are supposed to solve. Earlier, we saw that the task of a legislature was to make property rights possible. In contrast, Kant's extremely cursory remarks on the international congress describe its role emphatically as of *dispute resolution*:

> Only by such a congress can the idea of a public right of nations be realized, one to be established for deciding their disputes in a civil way, as if by lawsuit, rather than in a barbaric way (the way of savages), namely by war.[117]

[112] *PP* 8:355, 326. See also Hathaway and Shapiro, *ibid* 38–44, on the types of reasons given in 'War Manifestos', which included unpaid debts, questions over dynastic succession and stolen queens.

[113] See, eg, P Niesen, 'The West Divided? Bentham and Kant on Law and Ethics in Foreign Policy' in D Chandler and V Heins (eds), *Rethinking Ethical Foreign Policy: Pitfalls, Paradoxes, and Possibilities* (Abingdon-New York, Routledge, 2007) 97.

[114] *PP* 8:350–51, 324. Various scholars have attempted to prove or debunk the so-called 'democratic peace' theory as an empirical matter. See MW Doyle, 'Kant, Liberal Legacies, and Foreign Affairs' (1983) 12 *Philosophy & Public Affairs* 205; T Schwartz and KK Skinner, 'The Myth of the Democratic Peace' (2002) 46 *Orbis* 159. These arguments misunderstand Kant's purpose. The theorem is offered not as a verifiable factual claim, but as a 'transcendental' idea of reason against which the democratic credentials of any political community may be judged. See G Cavallar, 'Kantian Perspectives on Democratic Peace: Alternatives to Doyle' (2001) 27 *Review of International Studies* 229.

[115] *DR* 6:350, 487.

[116] Niesen (n 113) 97.

[117] *DR* 6:351, 488.

As such, by way of exclusion one can deduce that there is no legislature at the international rightful condition because rightfully constituted states *do not have property*. Contrary to Benvenisti's third normative intuition, sovereigns are not 'proprietors' of sections of the earth's surface. In fact, they are not proprietors of anything.

A. Territory: Property or Body?

Recall that property rights are acquired rights to external objects of choice; that is, things that could very well have been another's if events had panned out differently. At the beginning of § 61 of the *Doctrine of Right*, Kant does say that in a state of nature among nations, just as in a state of nature among individuals, 'anything external that is mine or yours which states can acquire or retain by way, are merely *provisional*'.[118] Just as for individual human beings, entry into a rightful condition transforms these provisional rights into peremptory rights. What Kant leaves unsaid, however, is whether all such provisional rights are made peremptory, and whether they retain the same qualities.[119] I contend that they do not: upon entry into the international rightful condition the previously provisional 'property' rights of states in external things do become peremptory, but also lose quality of being mine or yours, and therefore transform into innate 'bodily' rights.

To illustrate, consider that if you and your friend were to exchange all your belongings, your lifestyles would be transformed, perhaps immeasurably, but the two of you could still carry on with the identities you normally present to the world. Not quite if you exchanged bodies. Similarly, Ruritania and Cagliostro as states would not simply be changed if they exchanged their lands, natural endowments and people. They would simply cease to exist as Ruritania or Cagliostro. This is Kant's point in the *Perpetual Peace* when he claims that 'a state is not (like the land on which it resides) a belonging (*patrimonium*) …'.[120] Instead,

> [l]ike a trunk, it has its own roots; and to annex it to another state as a graft is to do away with its existence as a moral person and to make a moral person into a thing, and so to contradict the idea of the original contract, apart from which no right over a people can be thought.[121]

The qualifier 'like the land on which it resides' should not be read to mean that while the *state* is not property, the land might be. While Kant does say that title to the state's land is held by the head of state acting as the 'supreme proprietor',[122]

[118] *DR* 6:350, 487.
[119] Niesen (n 113) 106.
[120] *PP* 8:344, 318.
[121] *PP* 8:344, 318.
[122] *DR* 6:323, 466.

he describes that role as consisting solely in organising the 'division' of the land, rather than as an 'aggregation' of private ownership claims therein.[123] Instead, '[a]ll land belongs only to the people (and the people taken distributively, not collectively …)'.[124] This point is also reflected in the controversial passage in the *Doctrine of Right* where Kant permits states to unite together to launch pre-emptive strikes against 'unjust enemy' states whose publicly expressed will would render any condition of peace among nations impossible. This exorbitant privilege stops short of the coalition members dividing the territory of the unjust enemy between themselves in a way that would 'make the state, as it were, disappear from the earth …'.[125] As such, the state does not *own* its territory – it simply *is* the territory.

Admittedly, the fact that there is no inhabited spot on earth over which sovereignty has not changed hands on multiple occasions may lead one to think that territory must be transmissible in the manner of property. Moreover, textbooks of international law almost uniformly describe the law of territory as being based upon the Roman law of immovable property.[126] As with most things in contemporary international law, the *locus classicus* on this subject is Lauterpacht, who was instrumental in burying the model of 'territory-as-body', or, as he termed it, the 'object' theory of territory.[127] Lauterpacht acknowledges a number of its attractive features: it avoids the problem of the patrimonial state discussed above,[128] and territory and state indeed appear to be an 'inseparable unity'.[129] Nevertheless, he dismisses these problems by resorting to the device of the state as an aggregation of individuals already discussed above:

> If we think of the State not in terms of an absolute and mystical entity but as the totality of the individuals organised as a State, then there is nothing artificial in regarding the State as the owner of territory. The individuals, in their collective capacity as a State, own the territory of the State. The State owns its territory.[130]

The bulk of Lauterpacht's argument for modelling territory on property was contemporaneous state practice, which recognised that forms of territorial title

[123] *DR* 6:323–24, 466.

[124] *DR* 6:324, 466.

[125] *DR* 6:350, 487. Instead, all they can do is change the unjust enemy state's constitution to one disinclined to aggression.

[126] See, eg, RY Jennings, *The Acquisition of Territory in International Law* (Manchester, Manchester University Press, 1963) 3; JL Brierly, Andrew Clapham (ed), *Brierly's Law of Nations: An Introduction to the Role of International Law in International Relations*, 7th edn (Oxford, Oxford University Press, 2012) 168–69; Malcolm N Shaw, *International Law*, 8th edn (Cambridge, Cambridge University Press, 2017) 361–63.

[127] H Lauterpacht, 'Property Relations Between States. State Territory' in E Lauterpacht (ed), *International Law: Volume 1, The General Works: Being the Collected Papers of Hersch Lauterpacht* (Cambridge, Cambridge University Press, 1970) 367.

[128] *Ibid.*

[129] *Ibid* 367–68. Lauterpacht explicitly recommends the *dominus membrorum* rule as intuitively preferable to Lockean 'body-extension' theories of property. *Ibid* 368.

[130] *Ibid* 368.

modelled on property such as international mandates, territorial leases, grants in perpetuity and condominia. In particular, Lauterpacht's prime example was the United States' purchase of the Danish West Indies for US$25 million in 1917.[131] Another leading authority for the property-model of territory was the *Island of Palmas* arbitration, which, as we saw in the previous chapter, is relied upon by Benvenisti for his contention that sovereigns have been 'allocated' different sections of the earth's surface. The ratio of that award was that territory could be acquired by 'acquisitive prescription' in a manner essentially identical to adverse possession of private property in land.[132]

Students of international law will know that the years since *Island of Palmas* have witnessed a sea change in the law: the current leading case of *Frontier Dispute (Burkina Faso v Mali)* emphatically rejects prescription by *effectivités* (effective administration) by one state of the territory of another and instead requires the positive acquiescence of the latter.[133] While inaction might controversially constitute affirmative evidence of acquiescence or recognition,[134] the rule is definitively no longer one of unilateral prescription. This departure from private property principles has led some to question the entire enterprise of using private law analogies for explicating international law.[135] There is, however, another possibility: that property is simply the wrong analogy, and that the correct one is to personality.

Kant's specific response to Lauterpacht would be that his very examples reveal precisely what is so wrongful about the property model of territory, even by the low standards of an international state of nature.[136] The exploitation inherent in the various systems of international mandates has been written about extensively,[137] while the few leased territories that exist today are

[131] *Ibid* 367–68.

[132] *Island of Palmas Case (or Miangas), US v Netherlands* (1928) 2 (1949) RIAA 829, 839 (holding that international law had to recognise acquisitive prescription of territory out of necessity, given that even municipal law felt unable to do so without adverse possession of land despite possessing a 'complete judicial system' enabling it to 'recognize abstract rights of property as existing apart from any material display of them …').

[133] *Frontier Dispute, Burkina Faso v Mali*, Merits [1986] ICJ Rep 554, para 63. ('Where the territory which is the subject of the dispute is effectively administered by a State other than the one possessing the legal title, preference should be given to the holder of the title.') See also R O'Keefe, 'Legal Title versus *Effectivités*: Prescription and the Promise and Problems of Private Law Analogies' (2011) 13 *International Community Law Review* 147, 176–77.

[134] *Sovereignty over Pedra Branca/Pulau Batu Puteh, Middle Rocks and South Ledge, Malaysia v Singapore*, Judgment (Merits) [2008] ICJ Rep 12, para 121 ('silence may also speak, but only if the conduct of the other State calls for a response'). At paras 11–13 of their joint dissenting Opinion, Judges Simma and Abraham criticise the majority's approach as effectively the former rule of acquisitive prescription in everything but name.

[135] O'Keefe (n 133) 187–88.

[136] P Niesen, 'Restorative Justice in International and Cosmopolitan Law' in K Flikschuh and L Ypi (eds), *Kant and Colonialism: Historical and Critical Perspectives* (Oxford, Oxford University Press, 2014) 187.

[137] The example most familiar to international lawyers is the Australian mandate over Nauru, during which excessive phosphate mining rendered the island an environmental wasteland.

known primarily as places of dispossession, torture and lawlessness.[138] New Hebrideans living under the British-French condominium over their islands used to joke that it was more accurately described as 'pandemonium'.[139] The core of the problem is that for a 'patrimonial' sovereign to buy, sell, devise or give away territory is to give away the land *with* the people on it, which is to treat them as chattels. Lauterpacht notes that 'it is easier for a State to part with some of its territory with *impunity* – and, in some cases, with beneficent results – than for an individual to part with his body'.[140] This is true only if the people who live there, or who have property there, are considered uniquely disposable. As such, Lauterpacht's object theory of territory appears to be simply another example of Harris's spectacular *non sequitur*. From the fact that a state is independent if no other colonial or imperial power owns its territory, it simply does not follow that the state or its people must own the territory collectively. In fact, *nobody* owns the territory, not even the independent state.

Moreover, unlike the mercenary terms in which colonial possessions were sold or exchanged, independent states treat the transfer of territory as a matter of utmost legal and political sensitivity.[141] In fact, this is arguably true even of Lauterpacht's prime example: the Danish West Indies were sold only after approval by the very first referendum in Denmark, in which the Faroese and Danes abroad, and even women and servants were called upon to vote.[142] A happier reprise occurred as this book was being written: another US administration offered to purchase Greenland from Denmark in what was touted as 'essentially a real estate deal'.[143] In an act of courage the Danish Prime Minister

This became the subject of a dispute before the International Court of Justice (ICJ) that was eventually settled out of court. See K Highet and G Kahale III, 'Certain Phosphate Lands in Nauru' (1993) 87 *American Journal of International Law* 282. The deeper objection to mandate systems is that they tend to entrench colonial structures and systems in administered territories while ostensibly claiming to prepare them for sovereignty. See A Anghie, *Imperialism, Sovereignty and the Making of International Law* (Cambridge, Cambridge University Press, 2005) 179–94.

[138] A particularly poignant report relates to how a Chagos Islander characterises the 'deal' by which Mauritius agreed to the hiving off of the Chagos Islands in exchange for independence as one where 'Mauritius got independence because it sold my mother's land'. L Jeffrey and D Vine, 'Sorry, Sadness, and Impoverishment: The Lives of Chagossians in Mauritius' in S Evers and M Kooy (eds), *Eviction from the Chagos Islands: Displacement and Struggle for Identity Against Two World Powers* (Leiden, Brill, 2011) 83.

[139] M Bennett and J Harewood, *Vanuatu* (Melbourne, Lonely Planet, 2003) 14.

[140] Lauterpacht (n 127) 368 (emphasis added).

[141] The Supreme Administrative Court of Egypt recently issues a Decision declaring as unconstitutional a treaty effectively 'selling' certain Red Sea islands to Saudi Arabia. *President of the Republic et al v Ali Ayyoub et al* [2017] Supreme Administrative Court of Egypt Judgment, on appeal No 74236/62 J S. Reported in G Le Moli, 'President of the Republic et al. v. Ali Ayyoub et al' (2019) 113 *American Journal of International Law* 791.

[142] The only people whose consent was not sought were the actual inhabitants of the islands. 'A Historic Referendum' (*The Danish West-Indies*), www.virgin-islands-history.org/en/history/sale-of-the-danish-west-indian-islands-to-the-usa/a-historic-referendum. I am grateful to Ivy Wanjiru Gikonyo for bringing this to my attention.

[143] M Pengelly, 'Trump Confirms He Is Considering Attempt to Buy Greenland' *The Guardian* (18 August 2019).

Mette Frederiksen declined the offer and, in what one hopes will be taken to reflect a new rule of customary law, added that 'Thankfully, the time where you buy and sell other countries and populations is over'.[144]

Kant's overriding reason why territory cannot be held as or analogised to property is the imperative of peace. If territories are treated as chattels to be bought and sold, this gives rise to the possibility of disputes arising from such transactions. If on top of this, one accepts the Grotian consolation that war is a suitable means for prosecuting rights or for settling disputes, this gives rise to the prospect of endless war.[145] For such reasons, the ICJ has held that existing borders must be respected even if former colonisers drew them without attention to ethnic boundaries, simply 'to prevent the independence and stability of new States [from] being endangered by fratricidal struggles provoked by the challenging of frontiers …'.[146] Kant expresses the same fear of fratricidal warfare in the *Perpetual Peace*. Writing in the wake of the Austrian Wars of Succession – a series of world wars set off by a disagreement over the inheritance laws of an ancient Frankish tribe – he observes that:

> Everyone knows into what danger the presumption that acquisition can take place in this way has brought Europe, they only part of the world in which it is known … that states can marry each other, partly as a new industry for making oneself predominant by family alliances even without expending one's forces, and partly as a way of extending one's possession of land.[147]

Accordingly, the Second Preliminary Article to the *Perpetual Peace* is captioned: 'No independently existing state (whether small or large) shall be acquired by another state through inheritance, exchange, purchase, or donation.'[148]

B. No Property, Only Personality

Kant goes further: the sovereign not only does not hold territory, resources and people as property, it does not hold property *at all*. The category of property relations does not exist at international law because

> the idea of the right of nations involves only the concept of an antagonism in accordance with principles of outer freedom by which each can preserve what belongs to it, but not a way of acquiring, by which one state's increase of power could threaten others.[149]

[144] E Helmore, 'Trump Cancels Denmark Trip after PM Says Greenland Is Not for Sale' *The Guardian* (21 August 2019).
[145] See A Ripstein, 'Just War, Regular War, and Perpetual Peace' (2016) 107 *Kant-Studien* 179, 188.
[146] *Frontier Dispute, Burkina Faso v Mali, Merits* (n 133) para 20.
[147] *PP* 8:344, 318.
[148] *PP* 8:344, 318.
[149] *DR* 6:347, 485.

As described earlier, the core of property ownership is the *ius disponendi de rea sua* – the despotic right to dispose of a thing at will.[150] If the state cannot properly have any purpose other than the equal freedom of its subjects, then it is constitutionally – that is to say, *internally* – restrained from even *thinking* about controlling external objects in this way.[151]

As Peter Niesen puts it, states 'cannot lay claim to external objects; all that can concern them is their internal set-up'.[152] Accordingly, the state's possessory rights in things cannot be the same as that which private persons have over their property.[153] Instead, they are akin to the powers fiduciaries possess over their principals, or the rights private persons have over their bodies: that is, not *dominium* or ownership, but administration – *imperium*. Something of this is suggested by the passage in the *Doctrine of Right* stipulating that the sovereign 'cannot have any land at all as his private property (for otherwise he would make himself a private person)'.[154] Kant is more explicit in the *Naturrecht Feyerabend* lectures, where he is recorded by a student as teaching that '*Summa jurium in proprium* is *dominium*, lordship, and he who possesses this right is *dominus*, proprietor. He is the owner of another human being. For this reason, Augustus never accepted being called "*dominus*".'[155] As such, Kant stakes a position completely the opposite of Grotius, Lauterpacht and Benvenisti, but more in accordance with the Stoic principle that *omnia rex imperio possidet singuli dominio*.[156] Whereas private persons have full-blooded rights of ownership over particular things, the sovereign has rights over everything, but only of administration. Property and sovereignty are not just distinct but antithetical. A sovereign may neither have property nor may a proprietor be sovereign.

[150] Harris (n 55) 31: 'Ownership interests, at any point on the spectrum, entail both open-endedness and permitted self-seeking … within the terms of the relevant property institution, [the owner] may defend any use or exercise of power by pointing out that, as owner, he was at liberty to suit himself.'

[151] Harris (n 55) 105. Harris remarks that 'the privileged domain [regarding dealings with state funds or chattels] afforded to officials falls nowhere along the ownership spectrum since it lacks the crucial feature of legitimate, self-seeking exploitation …'. That said, while Harris claims that states only have quasi-ownership rights in the domestic sphere, he notes in conclusory fashion that 'within the arena of public international law, self-seeking exploitation is allowed', and 'trespassory rules [of international law] protect 'State territory' and 'State territorial sea', concepts which, in this respect, are frankly modelled on private property ownership interests …'. Harris (n 55) 105. These statements assume without argument the conventional idea of sovereigns as domestically public but internationally private, which I show below to be incorrect.

[152] Niesen (n 136) 181.

[153] See, eg, *Van Brocklin v Tennessee* 117 US 151, 158–59 (1886):

> The United States do not and cannot hold property as a monarch may, for private or personal purposes. All the property and revenues of the United States must be held and applied, as all taxes, duties, imposts and excises must be laid and collected, to pay the debts and provide for the common defence and general welfare of the United States (internal citations omitted).

[154] *DR* 6:323–24, 466.

[155] I Kant, L Vinx (tr) 'Naturrecht Feyerabend' (1784) 34 (27:1345).

[156] Seneca, M Griffin and B Inwood (trs), *On Benefits* (Chicago, University of Chicago Press, 2011) 170 (s 4.2, bk 7).

All this might appear to be completely irreconcilable with contemporary international law, given not just the predominant theory of territory as property discussed above, but also the existence of treaties with names like the 'United Nations Convention on Jurisdictional Immunities of States and *Their Property*'.[157] To be clear, my claim is not that rightfully constituted states cannot hold titles of property created under *their* law. They can and do, but only *de jure gestionis* rather than in sovereign capacity. Rather, my claim is that *international law* does not create or recognise property titles in states. With this clarification in mind, a closer look at the doctrinal materials reveals some surprising results. A recent monograph on the 'international law of property' observes that the 'conventional wisdom is that international property law does not exist as a category',[158] and, despite its title, its discussion consists almost entirely of international rules on the protection or recognition of domestically created private property rights.[159] The only example I have been able to identify that unambiguously qualifies as a property right created at international law is the United Nations Convention on the Law of the Sea (UNCLOS) regime on title to minerals mined from the seabed.[160] Even then, these are held by private persons, not states.

More interestingly, the topic of international property rights was broached in recent International Court of Justice (ICJ) litigation between Australia and Timor-Leste arising out of Australia's seizure of 'documents, data, and other property' from Timor-Leste's legal advisers in Australia.[161] Acting for Timor-Leste, Sir Eli Lauterpacht asserted that Timor-Leste's 'property' rights in those documents were 'entitled to full respect on the international plane in whatever State they may be located ... no matter what special provisions may be asserted by Australian law against them',[162] and even that the seizure of such sovereign

[157] UN Convention on Jurisdictional Immunities of States and their Property 2004, UN Doc A/59/508, art 1. Tzeng observes that the purpose of that treaty is to 'codify the rules of foreign sovereign immunity applicable in national courts' rather than to set out an international law of property. P Tzeng, 'The State's Right to Property under International Law' (2016) 125 *Yale Law Journal* 1805, 1809. In fact, it does not even define that term.

[158] JG Sprankling, *The International Law of Property* (Oxford, Oxford University Press, 2014) 349.

[159] Tzeng (n 157) 1806, fn 8.

[160] Sprankling (n 158) 162–64, citing Agreement relating to the implementation of Part XI of the United Nations Convention on the Law of the Sea of 10 December 1982 (adopted and entered into force 28 July 1994) 1836 UNTS 3, Annex; and UN Convention on the Law of the Sea (adopted 10 December 1982, entered into force 16 November 1994) 1833 UNTS 3 1982, Annex III, art 1. Internationally designated satellite orbits might appear to be another example of the creation of property rights by international law. See Sprankling (n 158) 191–92. These rights do not appear to be freely transferrable, which makes them just non-proprietary licences to use particular trajectories in the atmosphere. And again, the rights belong to private satellite operators, not states. See UN Agreement Governing the Activities of States on the Moon and Other Celestial Bodies (adopted 5 December 1979, entered into force 11 July 1984) [1979] 1363 UNTS 3, arts 5(1)-(2).

[161] 'Application Instituting Proceedings, Timor-Leste v Australia (17 December 2013)' (2013) para 2, at www.icj-cij.org/files/case-related/156/17962.pdf.

[162] 'Timor-Leste v Australia, Verbatim Record (20 January 2014, 10:00 AM)' (2014) 27–28, at www.icj-cij.org/files/case-related/156/156-20140120-ORA-01-00-BI.pdf.

'property' was tantamount to invading its territory.[163] Australia readily conceded that it had taken the documents,[164] but denied liability on grounds that 'an absolute, unqualified right of property at international law', allowing each state 'an absolute right of property in all documents produced by it or its agents in the territory of another State … inviolable and immune from any judicial or executive action in that other State' would constitute recognition of 'a new form of extraterritoriality'.[165] The litigation was eventually settled out of court, so no authoritative precedent exists on this question. Nevertheless, a commentator admits that as 'absurd as it may sound, Australia is correct'.[166] To admit of such international property rights would 'allow a State adventitiously to expand its sovereignty into the territory of other States'.[167] For instance, Ruritania might ship military vehicles into Cagliostro's territory without the latter's permission, and then seek to prohibit the other from moving it as 'sovereign property' immune from the latter's laws.[168] This would be an intolerable method of generating permissions from wrongs.

But perhaps the most fruitful area for tracing the ancient idea that sovereigns have no property in contemporary positive international law might be the law of state responsibility. If the state has no property rights, but only personality rights, this means that wrongs against it must sound in injury, and remedies in restitution. This is the position reflected, albeit imperfectly, in the authoritative *Articles on State Responsibility for Internationally Wrongful Acts*. Actual loss is irrelevant in assessments of international wrongfulness: 'there is no general

[163] *Ibid* 31.

[164] 'Counter-Memorial of Australia, Timor-Leste v Australia (28 July 2014)' (2014) para 1.2, at www.icj-cij.org/files/case-related/156/18702.pdf.

[165] 'Timor-Leste v Australia, Verbatim Record (21 January 2014, 10:00 AM)' (2014) 11–12, at www.icj-cij.org/files/case-related/156/156-20140121-ORA-01-00-BI.pdf. See also 'Counter-Memorial of Australia, Timor-Leste v Australia (28 July 2014)' (n 164) para 5.64.

[166] Tzeng (n 157) 1805. Tzeng comes to this conclusion reluctantly because in his view, the lack of property rights at international law prolonged litigation on what 'should have been a simple issue'. *Ibid* 1811–19. I disagree with this last point. Instead of characterising Australia's seizure of the documents as a deprivation of property, it may be characterised as an outrage against Timor-Leste's personality, like a violation of privacy, or of the right to the confidentiality of attorney-client communications, both of which are implied by Timor-Leste's status as a free equal in the international order.

[167] 'Timor-Leste v Australia, Verbatim Record (21 January 2014, 10:00 AM)' (n 165) 12.

[168] *cf* statements in Parliament by the Singaporean Defence Minister, following the Chinese seizure of 'Terrex' military vehicles purchased by Singapore that were being shipped through the Hong Kong Special Administrative Region without the appropriate clearances having been sought. Parliament Deb 9 January 2017, vol 94, sess 1, sitting no 30:

> The legal position is that the SAF Terrexes and other equipment detained in Hong Kong are the property of the Singapore Government. They are protected by sovereign immunity, even though they were being shipped by commercial carriers. This means that they are immune from any measures of constraint abroad. They cannot legally be detained or confiscated by other countries.

requirement ... that a State should have suffered material harm or damage before it can seek reparation for a breach'.[169] As for remedies, the *Articles* state that

> because restitution most closely conforms to the general principle that the responsible State is bound to wipe out the legal and material consequences of its wrongful act by re-establishing the situation that would exist if the act had not been committed, it comes first among the forms of reparation.[170]

Clearly, the meanings of 'injury' and 'restitution' in the *Articles* do not correspond perfectly to the concepts as they are used in this chapter. In particular, the concept of 'restitution' in the law of state responsibility is not the Roman idea of surrendering wrongful gains but the Thomistic idea of in kind return.[171] Concerning injury, however, the similarities are greater, and its resilience is attested to by the fact it was retained in the *Articles* despite considerable opposition. For instance, the Drafting Committee of the International Law Commission (ILC) in 2000 proposed a definition of 'injury' as consisting 'of any damage, whether material or moral, arising in consequence of the internationally wrongful act of a State'.[172] Instead, the final version of the Commentary to the *Articles* now reads that injury '*includes*', rather than 'consists' of any damage.[173] This may be explained through the example given earlier in section I.A, where if someone wrongs you by spitting in your face and you contract a disease from it, your remedy for an injury 'includes' your medical costs rather than consists of it.

A clarification must be made which will become important for the next chapter. Regarding the attempts by certain ILC members to ground the concept of international wrongs in material damage, James Crawford rightly defends the traditional approach by invoking the difference between harms and wrongs using arguments broadly similar to those made in the previous chapter.[174] Nevertheless, in the course of arguing for the rejection of liability for purely 'legal injuries' – that is, for mere breach of an international obligation – Crawford comments that such liability conflicts with the 'natural meaning' of the word injury, which according to him lies in 'harm, material or moral, suffered by the victim as obligee or beneficiary of the obligation breached'.[175]

[169] International Law Commission, 'Draft Articles on Responsibility of States for Internationally Wrongful Acts, Adopted by the Commission at Its Fifty-Third Session in 2001' (2001) UN Doc A/56/10, art 31, comment 7 [hereinafter *ARS*].

[170] *Ibid*, art 35, comment 3.

[171] See, eg, Zimmermann (n 30) 824–30.

[172] (2000) 2(2) UNYBILC, UN Doc A/CN.4/Ser.A/2000/Add.1 (Part 2)/Rev1, 68.

[173] *ARS* (n 169) art 31(2) (emphasis added).

[174] J Crawford, *State Responsibility: The General Part* (Cambridge, Cambridge University Press, 2013) 485–87.

[175] *Ibid* 490. See also *Rainbow Warrior Affair, New Zealand v France* (1990) 20 RIAA 217, para 109 (recording the parties' agreement that material damage is not a precondition for liability for international wrongs, but that 'injury' may lie in 'legal' or 'moral' damage).

Crawford's invocation of the concept of 'moral damage' is premised upon the exact assumption he rejected only a few paragraphs earlier: that is, that wrongs are always grounded upon some form of harm. The incoherence of moral damage is perhaps best illustrated by going back to *Baget c Rosenweigh*, the French case that first established it as a legal concept.[176] The plaintiffs were licensed Paris pharmacists intervening as civil parties in criminal proceedings against unlicensed pharmacists. The plaintiffs were unable to establish any quantifiable material damage as required for delictual actions.[177] A number of the defendants operated in neighbourhoods where there was no licensed pharmacist who could even claim that his business had suffered losses.[178] Nevertheless, the Court held the defendants liable for a *civil* wrong, on the grounds that 'l'exercice illégal de la pharmacie porte nécessairement un dommage aux pharmaciens, puisqu'il constitue une usurpation des droits qui leur sont garantis par la loi …'.[179] The circularity is obvious: the reasoning (1) begins with an assumption that a *right* to recover exists only if the plaintiff has suffered 'harm'; (2) proceeds to find such harm has indeed been suffered in the form of 'moral damage'; and (3) defines the nature of that damage as consisting of the violation of a right.[180] In contrast, the Procurer-General's presentation of the case makes it clear that the concept of 'moral damage' is quite literally the result of an attempt to shoehorn the idea of *iniuria* – a violation of a personality right – into the language of damage.[181] As we shall see in chapter five, it is not the only such example.

The idea of a wrong is deeper and conceptually prior to that of harm. Likewise, the core of the concept of an international wrong is not a harm but a wrong. And that, Kant explains, is a coercive act inconsistent with a person's innate right as a free equal, subject to the will of no other.

IV. CONCLUSION

For a monograph ostensibly dealing with the EU's legal relations with the wider world, I have gone quite a while without mentioning the European Union. As stated earlier, however, this long detour was necessary to set out the core

[176] *Baget c Rosenweigh* (1833) Sirey 1833.I.458 (Cassation, Chambre Réunies).

[177] French Civil Code ss 1382–83.

[178] *Baget c Rosenweigh* (n 176) 460.

[179] *Baget c Rosenweigh* (n 176) 462–63.

[180] The same circularity infects Lord Holt CJ's dissent in *Ashby v White*, where he held that 'surely every injury imports a damage, though it does not cost the party one farthing, and it is impossible to prove the contrary; for a damage is not merely pecuniary, but an injury imports a damage, when a man is thereby hindered of his right'. *Ashby v White* (1703) 87 ER 808 (KB) 816. The dissent subsequently formed the basis of the reversal by the House of Lords. *Ashby v White* (1703) 91 ER 665 (HL).

[181] *Baget c Rosenweigh* (n 176) 461–62 ('L'action des pharmaciens, à part et avant l'intérêt pécuniare, poursuit la reparation d'un préjudice tout *moral*, la conservation de l'honneur de l'exercice consciencieux de la profession …').

principles of republican international legal order central to the coming chapters. To recapitulate, these are: (1) the fiduciary nature of the relationship between sovereigns and their subjects; (2) that factual 'harms' cannot be central in ascertaining the international rights of sovereigns, because these can only be rights in personality, violations of which are not predicated upon damage; and (3) the right of all sovereigns to use coercion to ensure that they are not subject to the will of another. With this, all the necessary machinery has been wheeled onto the stage to provide: (1) a partial justification of the EU's unilateral measures providing global public goods; (2) a theory of the EU's extraterritorial human rights obligations; and (3) a critique of jurisprudence and doctrines internal to EU law insulating it from fulfilling these obligations.

Before we can proceed, some obvious objections need to be addressed. It was stated in the introduction that this book was an attempt at an immanent critique taking conventional human rights, public international law and EU law practices seriously, with a view to identifying internal contradictions within them. Such an approach neither assumes nor aims at providing wholesale validation for those practices, so it is to be expected that the normative picture will depart from the positive practice in some respects. It may have been expected at the outset, for instance, that while a few peripheral doctrines of international law might not be reconciled with the normative account, most of the paradigmatic doctrines would 'fit'. It turns out, however, that the gaps between the theory and the practice are numerous, glaring and deep.

Kant's theory of republican international order envisions a *foedus pacificum* – a loose congress of democratic republics bound together only by a mandatory judicial dispute settlement. That congress is 'only a voluntary coalition ... which can be dissolved at any time, not a federation (like that of the American states) which is based on a constitution and cannot be dissolved'.[182] In the international legal order we actually have, the pre-eminent international institution is accorded legal personality, as do many other international organisations.[183] Moreover, the UN's central component – the Security Council – was designed as a permanent, unaccountable and unchallengeable world executive, but now also strays into legislating.[184] In contrast, its judicial department has no mandatory jurisdiction over disputants. Of the scholars critical of the structure of the international institutional order, few have been as assiduous as Benvenisti. In a recent piece, he characterises the 'functionalist' development of the law of international organisations as being premised upon:

(1) the recognition of international organisations as possessing legal personality distinct from those of Member States;

[182] *DR* 6:311, 488.

[183] *Reparation for Injuries Suffered in the Service of the United Nations*, Advisory Opinion [1949] ICJ Rep 174, 178.

[184] See, eg, S Talmon, 'The Security Council as World Legislature' (2005) 99 *American Journal of International Law* 175.

(2) a steady expansion of the powers conferred upon such organisations through broad interpretations of the treaty provisions conferring them, doctrines of implied powers, and even reference to subsequent practice in a manner 'exact(ly) opposite to domestic public law doctrines of *ultra vires* and abuse of rights';
(3) an understanding that external legal restraints upon such organisations come from a body of international law pertaining specifically to international organisations rather than to states generally;
(4) the immunity of international organisations from domestic review; and
(5) permitting Member States to avoid their domestic obligations by 'laundering' their acts through international organisations.[185]

In numerous other writings, Benvenisti argues that the current state of global governance is characterised by a deep despotism standing in stark contrast to the complacent faith of a past generation of international civil servants that international organisations had transcended the conflicts and contradictions of the nation-state.[186] In particular, he singles out for particular criticism the Hammarskjöldian argument against judicial scrutiny of international organisations, on the grounds that unlike domestic decisionmakers, international civil servants supposedly possess an independence and impartiality allowing them to rise above their 'personal sympathies and antipathies'.[187] As we shall see in chapters five and seven, a similar position is taken by EU institutions and particularly the ECJ based on the EU's 'supranational' nature.

More importantly, neither can the EU be likened to Kant's *foedus pacificum*, even in embryonic form. The EU is not a voluntary coalition, but – as is now officially enshrined in Article 47 of Treaty on European Union (TEU) as inserted by the Lisbon Treaty – a person capable of bearing obligations and of placing others under obligations in its own name.[188] At the same time, however, various actors and the ECJ in particular have also adamantly resisted its assimilation into the mode of a democratic republic. The critique here differs from that offered by Garrett Wallace Brown, who argues that the restriction of EU membership to

[185] E Benvenisti, 'Upholding Democracy Amid the Challenges of New Technology: What Role for the Law of Global Governance?' (2018) 29 *European Journal of International Law* 9, 18.

[186] See particularly the discussion of the UN Mission in Kosovo (UNMIK) in *ibid* 26–30. See also E Benvenisti, *The Law of Global Governance* (Leiden, Brill-Nijhoff, 2014) Ch 2; and E Benvenisti, *Sharing Transboundary Resources: International Law and Optimal Resource Use* (Cambridge, Cambridge University Press, 2002) Ch 4.

[187] Benvenisti (n 185) 10.

[188] Article 335 TEU provides that 'In each of the Member States, the Union shall enjoy the most extensive legal capacity accorded to legal persons under their laws; it may, in particular, acquire or dispose of movable and immovable property and may be a party to legal proceedings.' The principle had been developed in the jurisprudence as long ago as the early cases of Case 6/64 *Costa v ENEL* [1964] ECR 585, 593; Case 22/70 *Commission v Council (ERTA)* [1971] ECR 273, paras 13–14.

liberal democracies and the legal protection of freedoms to trade conform to the Kantian requirements of constitutional right and international right, but that the EU falls short of the requirements of cosmopolitan right with respect to its restrictions on the free movement of non-EU Member State citizens.[189] Rather, I argue that the EU fails at the very first step of constitutional right.

Recall that Kant criticises the disaggregation of states as inconsistent with the idea of the original contract apart from which no right over a people can be thought. In the *Doctrine of Right*, he defines a colony as a people with their own constitution, laws and land, but whose executive power has been taken by or alienated to another people.[190] At its core, the Kantian plan for eternal peace is premised upon independent, indivisible republican democracies settling their disputes on the merits rather than by violence. This is very different from the EU's method for achieving the same result through 'pooling sovereignty'; that is to say, by taking states at different levels of dysfunctionality, undermining their capacity for violence by disassembling their internal institutional arrangements, and reassembling them at the 'supranational' or 'intergovernmental' level into a 'new legal order'.[191] Unsurprisingly, the entity that has arisen from this process has been described variously as a 'constitutional monstrosity'[192] and a 'leviathan of shreds and patches'[193] whose sheer complexity gives rise to both a 'democratic deficit' and executive paralysis.

Of the voluminous literature critiquing EU integration, perhaps the most famous is Joseph Weiler's account of the EU as beginning as a cartel between post-war French and German heavy industry – for which, like for all cartels, democratic scrutiny was anathema – that then developed by picking apart Member States' domestic institutions and reassembling them at the EU level, in the process greatly increasing the powers of national executives and courts at the expense of national parliaments.[194] The same charge of a fundamentally anti-democratic ethos was made more recently by Quinn Slobodian, who traces

[189] GW Brown, 'The European Union and Kant's Idea of Cosmopolitan Right: Why the EU Is Not Cosmopolitan' (2014) 20 *European Journal of International Relations* 671.

[190] *DR* 6:348, 486.

[191] The classic dicta in *Van Gend en Loos* describes the EU as 'a new legal order of international law for the benefit of which the States have limited their sovereign rights, albeit within limited fields …'. Case 26/62 *NV Algemene Transport- en Expeditie Onderneming van Gend & Loos v Nederlandse administratie der belastingen* [1963] ECR 1, 2. Similarly, the ECJ in *Costa v ENEL* ascribes to the EU very 'real powers stemming from a limitation of sovereignty or a transfer of powers from the States to the Community …'. Case 6/64 *Costa v ENEL* (n 188) 593.

[192] N Krisch, 'Europe's Constitutional Monstrosity' (2005) 25 *OJLS* 321.

[193] P Allott, 'Epilogue: Europe and the Dream of Reason' in JHH Weiler and M Wind, *European Constitutionalism Beyond the State* (Cambridge, Cambridge University Press, 2003) 202.

[194] See JHH Weiler, 'The Political and Legal Culture of European Integration: An Exploratory Essay' (2011) 9 *International Journal of Constitutional Law* 678, 679–81; JHH Weiler, 'The Transformation of Europe' (1991) 100 *Yale Law Journal* 2403.

the origins of the EU and the World Trade Organization to a Geneva-based coterie of post-war reactionary economic and political theorists who identified national democratic politics as obstacles to the ultimate end of free trade, thus necessitating an international or supranational constitutional order to encase the regulatory impulses of new democracies, both within Europe but more importantly outside of it. In Slobodian's telling, the main model for this legal order was none other than the Austro-Hungarian Empire many of them had been born and raised in.[195]

Alongside the democratic deficit, there is the perennial complaint that the EU's internal constitution fails to provide clarity over who bears final decision-making power – the problem of *Kompetenz-Kompetenz* – in numerous areas, such that those individuals ultimately cannot know who to hold accountable. As Weiler observed in a piece written just as the Lisbon reforms were coming into force,

> it is difficult to point to a single instance of accountability for political failure … in the annals of European integration. This is not, decidedly not, a story of corruption or malfeasance …. [Instead, the] failure is rooted in the very structure of European governance. It is not designed for political accountability.[196]

Instead, Weiler describes European governance as 'governance without government … there is no 'government' to throw out'.[197] In relation to the EU's external relations, the slipperiness of the EU was captured in the question traditionally attributed to Henry Kissinger: 'Who do I call if I want to call Europe?' Certainly, successive treaty re-negotiations have attempted to make up for losses in Member State democratic accountability by multiplying and expanding the powers and roles of the EU Parliament, creating mechanisms for national parliaments to scrutinise proposed EU legislation. In addition, the (partial) eradication of the pillar structure in Lisbon was intended to provide clarity over decision-making powers, while the solution to the 'Kissinger-question' was supposed to be provided by the appointment of an effective EU Foreign Minister in the form of the High Representative of the Union for Foreign Affairs and Security Policy. Finally, and crucially, clarity and accountability relating to the EU's relations with the wider world was supposed to have been provided by consolidating the previously fissiparous constitutional materials under Article 3(5) TEU.[198] Most of these legal and political questions regarding relating

[195] Q Slobodian, *Globalists: The End of Empire and the Birth of Neoliberalism* (Cambridge, Harvard University Press, 2018).

[196] Weiler, 'The Political and Legal Culture of European Integration' (n 194) 680.

[197] Weiler, 'The Political and Legal Culture of European Integration' (n 194) 680.

[198] See, eg, M Cremona, 'Coherence through Law: What Difference Will the Treaty of Lisbon Make?' (2008) 3 *Hamburg Review of Social Sciences* 11, 30; P van Elsuwege, 'EU External Action after the Collapse of the Pillar Structure: In Search of a New Balance between Delimitation and Consistency' (2010) 47 *CML Rev* 987, 1014–15.

purely to the EU's internal constitution remain outside the scope of this book. In chapter eight, however, we shall see that as far as the EU's rightful relations with distant strangers is concerned, seeking to place the EU under an obligation remains very much an exercise in chasing a phantom. Moreover, far from leading to greater legal accountability, Article 3(5) TEU is the precise tool that renders *legal* accountability impossible.

Thus, far from being an imperfect realisation of Kant's federation of peace, the EU might have rather more in common with Kant's dystopia of a 'soulless despotism' or 'universal monarchy' which, 'after it has destroyed the seed of the good, finally deteriorates into anarchy'.[199] Recall that despotism and anarchy are technical terms for pathological forms of government that obtain respectively when a legislature and when an executive is lacking.[200] Given this state of affairs, it may be asked whether it makes sense at all to analyse the EU against the framework of Kant's philosophy of right. The answer has to be 'no'. Kant's idealist and 'metaphysical' legal theory was nevertheless written with a view to its practical implementation, and in this regard the crucial role utopias play in our moral and political imagination is by pointing out the direction for reform.[201] As such, Kant in the *Perpetual Peace* remarks that a

> moral politician will make it his principle that, once defects that could not have been prevented are found within the constitution of a state or in the relations of states, it is a duty … to be concerned about how they can be improved as soon as possible and brought into conformity with natural right …[202]

The thought behind this is the idea that imperfect and defective things are to be governed according to the same rules that apply to their ideal versions. Accordingly, it is irrelevant that the EU cannot account for its political legitimacy in the same way as a sovereign state. The fact that the EU meets the low bar of making law for individuals with more than a minimal degree of success places it in the same position of a republican democracy *vis á vis* all others, state and non-state. As such, the same 'regulative principles' that pertain to democratic republics must also govern irregular federations as disordered as the EU. The fact that the EU is not internally constituted as a democratic republic does not allow it to evade the obligations of sovereigns. This basic principle applies regardless of whether that authority is exercised within the territory of the Member States or upon persons located abroad. Where and to the extent its defective internal constitution

[199] *PP* 8:367, 336.

[200] The terms 'despotism' and 'anarchy' have distinct technical meanings in Kant's vocabulary: *despotism* is the condition where there is 'Law and power without freedom', while *anarchy* is a condition of 'Law and freedom without power …'. Kant and Louden (n 69) 235 (7:331).

[201] See A Pinheiro Walla, 'Global Government or Global Governance? Realism and Idealism in Kant's Legal Theory' (2017) 13 *Journal of Global Ethics* 312, 315–16.

[202] *PP* 8:372, 340.

prevents the fulfilment of these obligations, this is inconsistent with right. Conversely, the EU's lack of an internal constitution even remotely resembling the republican ideal does not disqualify it from exercising the *external* rights of sovereigns. Accordingly, the next chapter returns to the topic of the unilateral assertion of extraterritorial jurisdiction to provide global public goods. There, it is argued that the EU's measures in this regard are, in fact, largely defensible.

5

Extraterritorial Jurisdiction to Provide Global Public Goods

As mentioned in previous chapters, contemporary international legal scholarship tends to discuss 'global public goods' in terms borrowed from the economic sciences; that is, as things that generally advance utility or other substantive goods, but which require public intervention due to certain structural features of non-excludability and/or non-rivalrousness resulting in private undersupply. We also saw prominent scholars theorise the assertion of extraterritorial jurisdiction by the EU on this understanding of public goods. This chapter begins from a different, distinctly *juridical* conception of public goods, and on this basis provides a theory of extraterritorial jurisdiction that accounts for and critiques in part such assertions by the EU. Specifically, it defends the longstanding refusal of the European Court of Justice (ECJ), over repeated exhortations by numerous Advocates General, to rely upon the 'effects doctrine'. The 'critique' on the other hand is of the ECJ's equally longstanding rejection of attempts to subject the EU to external, international judicial scrutiny. Building up towards these conclusions, however, will once again require considerable discussion of subjects not immediately related to EU law. This is necessary because the EU's rights of jurisdiction over the rest of the world are necessarily determined not internally by the EU legal order, but externally by public international law. The EU may not unilaterally set the terms by which it interacts with the wider world.

I begin by setting out the alternative conception of public goods. Using roads as an archetype, Arthur Ripstein develops the Kantian insights discussed in the previous chapter to provide a normative conception of public goods as those things a political community – ideally a state – must provide to constitute the freedom of all its members.[1] Such things must be provided *publicly*; they may not be supplied or held privately even if this would lead to increased utility or efficiency, simply because to do so would result in the members of the public being placed at the mercy of a private person. Conduct that frustrates the equal freedom of subjects, or which interferes with the state's ability

[1] A Ripstein, *Force and Freedom: Kant's Legal and Political Philosophy* (Cambridge, Harvard University Press, 2009) Ch 8.

to ensure their equal freedom are wrongs against the state in 'public' nuisance. Unlike private nuisances against private persons, public nuisances have the character not of property damage but of injury, and are therefore actionable in the absence of material damage. Note that the terms 'public nuisance' and 'private nuisance' are employed in a non-technical sense; they are not intended to import wholesale the private or criminal law of any particular jurisdiction or legal tradition.

This theory of domestic public goods is then extrapolated to the international sphere. If, as argued in chapter three, the state is a moral person whose sole purpose is to ensure the freedom of its subjects, and all other persons are under a duty of mandatory cooperation with the regulating state to this end, it follows that every state has the right to prescribe laws necessary to provide public goods for its subjects, including those asserting authority over distant strangers. The rationale behind the regulation of domestic public nuisances applies equally to a state's right to regulate 'global' public nuisances caused by non-subjects outside the territory. Measures taken for this purpose do not wrong other persons – state or non-state – because they are all under a duty of mandatory cooperation with respect to the regulating state in the fulfilment of its single purpose. Finally, like domestic public nuisances, global public nuisances also have the nature of injuries – they are actionable in the absence of demonstrable material damage.

These contentions may seem to contradict several well-known legal doctrines, in particular, the 'no-harm' principle of international environmental law. This chapter demonstrates that these doctrines are problematic: they can be sustained only with great strain, and are being challenged by new doctrines better accounted for under the theory of global public goods set out here. More fundamentally, this chapter runs against the widely held notion that cross-boundary problems arising as a result of globalisation require the ouster of sovereignty from its place as the organising principle of international law. Instead, it is argued that a robust vision of sovereigns as free and equal persons in the international legal order is vital to solving problems of global magnitude. The irony, then, is that the main international actor putting this theory into practice should be one whose internal constitution, as we saw in the previous chapter, is anything but democratic or republican.

I. RIPSTEIN'S ROADS

Ripstein's theory of public goods begins with a thought experiment. Imagine you live in a libertarian paradise where every square inch of land is privately owned, such that there is no way to travel from one part of the territory to another without obtaining the permission of each intermediate landowner. Under these conditions, your ability to leave your house, communicate with others, or get back to your house if you have left, are all completely at the mercy of your neighbours.

This is intolerable, but not necessarily for welfare reasons: your house may be so vast, your curiosity so limited, or your fear of sickening from the plague outside so overpowering, that you are perfectly happy never to leave your compound.[2] Rather, it is the mere fact that you need your neighbour's permission to leave your land that constitutes a standing affront to your dignity.[3] The objection is not that productive transactions between community members will be difficult to make or that valuable relationships will be hard to form, but that '*somebody else* gets to decide' when or whether you may engage in either of these – as if you were a serf under their lordship.[4] Moreover, this capacity to dominate you is transferrable; your neighbours can alienate it by selling their plots. In this way, your condition resembles that of the class of mediaeval serfs known as *glebae adscripti*, title to whom ran with that of the land, which they were naturally prohibited from leaving.[5] Unlike a feudal lord, however, your neighbours are just as subject to your arbitrary choice as you are to theirs. As such, everybody in this community systematically dominates and is dominated by everybody else. Rather than you and your fellow community members being the masters of your land, your land is, in reality, the master of you.

Note that there is no solution to this problem in private law. A landowner who refuses another passage over their land neither wrongfully deprives the refusee of her land nor wrongfully uses the refusee's land. Instead, he merely uses his land in a manner which makes the refusee's land unsuitable for her desired projects.[6] As such, refusing to allow another to cross one's land is non-coercive in the same way as one state declining to trade with another, and therefore constitutes neither damage nor injury. Additionally, neither can the systemic problem be solved by automatically encumbering property titles with easements of necessity in favour of all other persons. Such a stratagem would render all landowners subject to the arbitrary choice of anyone who might want to cross it. They would, for instance, have to obtain the individual permission of each member of the community before they could build an extension.[7]

[2] *Ibid* 248.
[3] *Ibid* 247–48.
[4] *Ibid* 246, 248.
[5] Kant mentions them in two places in the *Doctrine of Right*, in the first of which he describes them as '*grunduntertänig*'. Kant, 'The Doctrine of Right' [hereinafter '*DR*'] in MJ Gregor (ed & tr), *Practical Philosophy: The Cambridge Edition of the Works of Immanuel Kant*, 9th edn (Cambridge, Cambridge University Press, 2006) 6:324, 466 and 6:330, 471. See also *Horwood v Millar's Timber and Trading Co Ltd* (1917) 1 KB 305, 311. The case involved a money-lending contract whose terms placed almost total control of the debtor's property and productive capacity in the hands of the creditor. Holding them invalid for restraint of trade, Lord Cozens-Hardy MR commented:

> Is it open for a man in consideration of a sum of cash to bind himself not to leave the house where he is[?] … It seems to me that if as a matter of construction I come to the conclusion that the contract is one which puts the covenantor in the position – I cannot think of a better word at the moment to express my view – of *adscriptus glebae*, as the villein used to be called in mediaeval times, on the ground of public policy the law will not recognize such a thing.

[6] Ripstein (n 1) 245–46.
[7] Ripstein (n 1) 252.

Instead, the solution to this conundrum lies in a system of *publicly* administered spaces for all persons to travel upon – *roads*. The state's *obligation* to provide public goods also implies that it has the *rights* to provide those roads, and to compel subjects into doing what is necessary to maintain them. It may impose taxes, expropriate land under eminent domain, and allow others to use or even destroy others' property in emergencies.[8] This is part of the offer that cannot be refused. You are unfree – a prisoner in your own home – unless you agree to the scheme of public provision. As such, force may be used against you to secure your cooperation, which is the same thing as your freedom. Similarly, because property rights are possible only within a rightful condition, claims of property rights cannot be maintained if doing so is incompatible with the preservation of the rightful condition.[9] Something of this is captured in the ancient rule that an action does not lie against someone who pulls down your house to prevent a fire from spreading.[10] Echoes of that principle may be found in *Pesce and Others*, where the ECJ upheld a phytosanitary measure that sought to prevent the spread of the *Xylella fastidiosa* bacterium by requiring the destruction, potentially without compensation, of privately owned olive trees.[11] A more apposite example, because it emphasises the *public* nature of the limitation upon private rights, is provided by the English rule that persons travelling on a public highway may traverse onto private property adjoining it in the event of a flood. This exception does not apply if it is a *private* easement that has become impassable.[12]

Finally, the state's obligation to provide public goods endows it with rights in '*public* nuisance' against persons who subject the entire community to their

[8] Ripstein (n 1) 253.

[9] The best illustration of this is in Kant's explication of the law of market overt. Ordinarily, a person who buys something from a thief must surrender to the person it was stolen from, even if the purchase was in good faith and for value. One cannot ordinarily pass better title than one has, and the thief has no title at all. An exception obtains if the sale took place in an open market. Kant explains this problem not by recourse to the usual but implausible argument that original owners can be expected to observe all sales taking place in open markets, but by reference to the systematic nature of secure ownership. If the onus was on purchasers to ensure that their vendors could demonstrate good title, they would also have to satisfy themselves that their vendors' suppliers also had good title, and those suppliers' suppliers, such as 'would go on to infinity in an ascending series'. *DR* 6:301, 447. This would undermine security of title in anything bought at a market, and thus defeat the entire point of markets itself. As such, the original owner's property right is defeated by innocent purchase for value at an open market. For useful discussion, see EJ Weinrib, 'Private Law and Public Right' (2011) 61 *University of Toronto Law Journal* 191, 199–203.

[10] D.9.2.49.1 (Ulpian, 9 *Disputations*).

[11] Joined Cases C-78/16 and C-79/16 *Pesce and Others* ECLI:EU:C:2016:428 (9 June 2016), concerning Commission Implementing Decision (EU) 2015/789 of 18 May 2015, as regards measures to prevent the introduction into and the spread within the Union of Xylella fastidiosa [2015] OJ L125/36. The measure did not contain any express provision for compensating the owners for the destruction of their trees. Notwithstanding Article 17(1) of the EU Charter of Fundamental Rights, which allows for expropriation in the public interest but only 'subject to fair compensation being paid in good time', the ECJ held that a general principle of EU law 'requiring compensation to be paid in all circumstances cannot be inferred from that fact'. See para 85, citing the Charter of Fundamental Rights of the European Union [2000] OJ C364/1, art 17(1).

[12] *Taylor v Whitehead* (1781) 99 ER 475, 477 (KB).

arbitrary choices. Public nuisances may take two forms: (1) they either interfere with public goods directly, or (2) they undermine the state's ability to provide its subjects with public goods. Such rights in public nuisance are structurally distinct from the complaint of an individual subject in *private* nuisance. This may be illustrated by reference to the Anglo-American common law of public nuisance, which is not simply an aggregation of harms suffered by multiple private persons.[13] Instead, a claim for public nuisance lies only for interference with a 'public right' – that is, 'an indivisible resource shared by the public at large, like air, water, or public rights of way'.[14] Moreover, whereas private nuisance is always premised upon damage, public nuisances, in contrast, have the character of outrages against personality and are actionable even without damage. To demonstrate, if you and your friends cause a massive traffic jam by playing football in the middle of a highway, the people you hold up in traffic may suffer significant inconvenience, but they do not ordinarily have any civil claim against you. Your conduct may harm them, but it does not necessarily wrong them. However, with respect to public nuisance, the state could hold you to be liable even if, miraculously, your football match did not disrupt any traffic at all. At this point, a caveat is required. English law acknowledges a private right to pass and repass on public roads and navigable waters, which if blocked, gives rise to a *civil* claim known as a private action for public nuisance.[15] Such claimants may recover only if they can demonstrate that they have incurred 'special damage' as a result of their being prevented from passing and repassing, and what exactly this special damage consists of is notoriously vexed.[16] However, concerning the *crime* of public nuisance – say, for playing football in the middle

[13] See, eg, Restatement (Second) of Torts (1979) s 821B, cmt g: 'Conduct does not become a public nuisance merely because it interferes with the use and enjoyment of land by a large number of persons.'

[14] *State v Lead Industries Association* 951 A2d 428, 448 (RI 2008), citing *City of Chicago v American Cyanamid Co* 823 NE 2d 126, 131 (IL 2005). See also TW Merrill, 'Is Public Nuisance a Tort?' (2011) 4 *Journal of Tort Law* 1, 10 ('blockage is … an injury common to the general public. It does not matter whether the road or the waterway is actually used by everyone or indeed by anyone at all').

[15] In an early case, the deterioration of the plaintiff's coals caused by the defendant obstructing a highway was held to constitute 'special' damage. *Iveson v Moore* (1699) 91 ER 486 (KB). In a later case, a barge owner was allowed to recover special damages from a defendant whose obstruction of a canal required him to transport goods overland at great cost. *Rose v Miles* (1815) 105 ER 773 (KB). Finally, in *Tate & Lyle Industries Ltd v Greater London Council* (1983) 2 AC 509 (HL), the defendant's construction of ferry terminals on the Thames river caused water surrounding the plaintiff's landing stage to silt up. The plaintiff was allowed to recover in public nuisance for interference with the plaintiff's public right of navigation, leading to the plaintiff having to pay for dredging, thus incurring special damage.

[16] Merrill argues that the special damage rule is the result of a misreading of a 16th century case, and consequently, that public nuisance should not be a distinct private tort at all. Merrill (n 14) 13–15, citing *Anonymous decision* (1535) YB Mich 27 Hen VIII, fo 27 pl 10. In contrast, Jason Neyers argues that the private action for public nuisance has a firm basis in well-established *public* rights to pass and repass highways and waterways. JW Neyers and A Botterell, 'Tate & Lyle: Pure Economic Loss and the Modern Tort of Public Nuisance' (2015) 53 *Alberta Law Review* 1031; JW Neyers, 'Reconceptualizing the Tort of Public Nuisance' (2017) 76 *CLJ* 87.

of the highway – questions of harm and damage do not even arise.[17] This follows for two reasons. First, to recall the previous chapter, the state acting in sovereign capacity does not have any property that can be damaged. Second, the wrongfulness of a public nuisance lies in its frustration of the state's *status* as the public fiduciary ensuring the equal freedom of its subjects. As such, it is at its core an outrage against personality.

Ripstein's theory of public goods thus stands in stark contrast to 'conventional' approaches to public goods. Ultimately, highways are designated as 'public' goods not because they facilitate substantive goods such as navigability or commerce or because they repair market failures, but because they fulfil the core task of ensuring that members of the public are not systematically dependent upon each other's arbitrary choices. In fact, the question of private 'undersupply' is wholly irrelevant – even if private parties were generally happy to step forward and supply private highways on a non-profit basis, the fact remains that any such roads provided would remain arbitrary gifts. While certain modalities of this task may allow for considerable private 'outsourcing', ultimate responsibility for ensuring their provision rests with the 'public' person of the state.[18] In this regard, the argument of this chapter resembles the account given by Avihay Dorfman and Alon Harel of 'inherently public goods' – such as the punishment of crimes and prosecution of wars – which can be provided only by public officials. There is, however, a slight difference in emphasis: it is not so much that the 'value' of such things lies entirely in their being undertaken by persons acting on behalf of the community, but because delegating them to even well-meaning and competent private persons necessarily implies transforming the political community into a system of pure private domination. Even under the best circumstances, a private bearer of the power cannot adopt the perspective of the political community as a whole, but can only do what is good and right in his own eyes.[19]

Other plausible precursors of Ripstein's theory of public goods include the Roman concept of a *res publica*, as well as the 'public trust doctrine' most prominently associated with US environmental law. In Roman law, the question of whether a body of water qualified as a public river, say, for the purpose of interdicting private works upon it, did not turn upon whether it was navigable.[20]

[17] See, eg, Merrill (n 14) 12–16.

[18] Dorfman and Harel argue that a state may legitimately delegate significant aspects of the job of repairing roads and highways to private parties, because road maintenance 'can be realized by virtually any skilled repairperson, regardless of the question of in whose name this person is acting'. A Dorfman and A Harel, 'The Case Against Privatization' (2013) 41 *Philosophy & Public Affairs* 67, 90.

[19] *Ibid* 94.

[20] D.43.13.1.2–3 (Ulpian, 68 *On the Edict*). See also *Van Niekerk & Union Government (Minister of Lands) v Carter* 1917 AD 359, 373 (Supreme Court of Appeal, South Africa). ('So far as their public character was concerned, the Roman law drew no distinction in principle between navigable and non-navigable rivers, though they were in some respects separately dealt with by the Praetor's Edicts.')

As for the public trust doctrine, Joseph Sax observes in the seminal article that synthesised that doctrine that of the three strands of precedent it draws from, the one 'with the greatest historical support' focuses upon the idea 'that certain interests are so intrinsically important to every citizen that their free availability tends to mark the society as one of citizens rather than of serfs'.[21] That said, a crucial point about the public doctrine concerns its suggestion that the state is a bearer of *property* rights, even if only in 'paper' title.[22] Listing a number of pernicious effects of this approach, Sax rejects the 'rather dubious notion that the general public should be viewed as a property holder',[23] but instead contends that the fundamental problem with, for instance, privatising riverbeds is not that it is incompatible with the people's beneficial ownership rights in property, but because through such actions, the state may effectively 'divest itself of authority to govern the whole of an area in which it has a responsibility to exercise its police power … in effect, to abdicate legislative authority over navigation'.[24] In other words, the concern is with the state's *status* as a public authority.

Interestingly, this question does not arise in jurisdictions based on the Roman law, where the concept of fiduciary obligation is not seen as a matter of property ownership, but of personal status.[25] This may sometimes have curious results, for instance in the South African case of *Mostert Snr v S*,[26] which concerned two farmers who were, in addition to other statutory offences, convicted of theft for illegally abstracting water from the Lomati river. On appeal, the Supreme Court of Appeal held that '[p]ublic water, running in a river or a stream, was recognised [in the Roman law] as being *res communes* and therefore incapable

[21] JL Sax, 'The Public Trust Doctrine in Natural Resource Law: Effective Judicial Intervention' (1970) 68 *Michigan Law Review* 471, 484.

[22] As the Supreme Court of Wisconsin put it, the 'equitable title to those submerged lands vests in the public at large, while the legal title vests in the state, restricted only by the trust, and the trust, being both active and administrative, requires the law-making body to act in all cases where action is necessary, not only to preserve the trust, but to promote it'. *City of Milwaukee v State* 193 Wis 423, 449 (WI 1927).

[23] Sax (n 21) 484. Given that governments are constitutionally obligated to compensate owners for takings of property, and that the beneficial owners of the things subject to the public trust are the people, Sax surmised that then governments, as representatives of the people, may presumably just pay themselves after selling them off. Sax (n 21) 479–80. Besides, the designation of a river or field as 'trust property' entails a kind of irrevocability, which Sax considers contrary to law and policy. Sax (n 21) 482.

[24] Sax (n 21) 489.

[25] Commenting upon the possible emergence of a principle of international public trusteeship in international environmental law, Peter Sand observes that civilian systems had difficulties in adopting the doctrine due to the lack of proper analogues to the English concept of a trust. Nevertheless, 'there are some striking similarities to the concept of *domaine public* in French public/administrative law, which has been identified as a parallel to the Anglo-American public trust, investing the state with custodianship (*droit de garde*, rather than ownership) …'. PH Sand, 'Principle 27: Cooperation in a Spirit of Global Partnership' in JE Viñuales (ed), *The Rio Declaration on Environment and Development: A Commentary* (Oxford, Oxford University Press, 2015) 626–27.

[26] *Mostert Snr and another v State* [2010] 2 All SA 482 (Supreme Court of Appeal, SA).

of being owned …'.[27] This meant that 'it was also incapable of being stolen', leading to the defendants' theft convictions being quashed.[28] Notwithstanding its counterintuitive result, *Mostert* is correct. If rivers and other public goods are considered property, this means they may be alienated, and if so, potentially to just one person, thus 'putting it in the power of one man to lay waste a whole country'.[29]

A. Expanding the Concept: Other Public Goods

The structure of Ripstein's argument for the state obligation to provide roads and waterways can be applied to other fields, such that many other things considered public goods under the commonplace economic definition also qualify as such on Ripstein's definition. Antitrust and competition regulation qualifies a public good not because it leads to greater efficiencies or maximises consumer welfare, but because it ensures a market whose participants are not at the mercy of dominant actors. For this reason, agribusiness concentration in food supply chains is a problem even if food is in plentiful supply. Likewise, cartelisation or collusion are objectionable in themselves, regardless of whether they actually reduce the welfare of consumers.

Second, social welfare systems for education and housing are public goods. Illiteracy enslaves: a person who cannot read street signs or house numbers will be systematically dependent upon the kindness of literate passers-by to figure out how to get anywhere. Because she is thus effectively confined to familiar neighbourhoods, her illiteracy makes her just as much an *adscriptus glebae* as a member of Ripstein's roadless community. More broadly, people without education are very likely rendered unable to participate in the political life of their community and therefore condemned to live their lives passively at the mercy of technocratic elites or demagogues.[30] Thus, the state is obligated to ensure meaningful access to basic education, and the school system accordingly constitutes a public good. The converse problem is presented by homelessness. If a homeless person commits the wrong of trespass by sleeping upon the private property of another, his doing so on the streets is equally wrongful as a public nuisance.

[27] *Ibid*, para 22.

[28] *Ibid*, para 23. The defendants' convictions for other criminal offences were not disturbed. *Ibid*, para 36.

[29] *Magistrates of Linlithgow v Elphinstone* (1768) 3 Kames' Decisions 331 (SC) 332. The High Court of Australia has similarly observed that a 'right to use the water of a stream (and all the water thereof if that can lawfully be done) is illusory if the flow of the stream can be diminished at will by another person. A positive right in a landowner to the use of the water of a stream prima facie invites a right to present such interference with the stream as would prevent him from using the water.' *H Jones & Co Pty Ltd v Kingborough Corporation* (1950) 82 CLR 282 (High Court of Australia), para 18.

[30] Ripstein (n 1) 293–95.

Thus, if other persons decide to insist upon their rights against him, he becomes the obverse of an *adscriptus glebae* – a human being who does wrong simply by standing in one place. Accordingly, for the original contract to be capable of being consented to, it must imply a corresponding obligation upon the state to supply the means of sustenance to those who are unable to provide for even their 'most necessary natural needs'.[31]

Third, as will become briefly relevant at a crucial point in the next chapter, money is a public good. Under the conventional definition, money counts at best as 'impure public goods' like park benches because they are eminently both rivalrous and excludable.[32] On the Kantian conception, however, money qualifies as a fully-fledged public good because like roads, it is necessary for intercourse between the members of a political community, and must be provided and organised publicly. As Kant states in the *Doctrine of Right*, the 'real definition' of money is as 'the universal *means by which men exchange their industriousness with one another*'.[33] For this reason, 'counterfeiting money or bills of exchange, theft and robbery, and the like are public crimes, because they endanger the commonwealth and not just an individual person'.[34]

Finally, and most pertinently for our present purposes, the above rationale can be leveraged into explaining why environmental regulation counts as a public good. The structures of systematic domination that arise in the absence of public environmental regulation are the same as those we encountered in our consideration of the roadless community. A polluter affects the ability of the individuals in his vicinity to make use of their means – their bodily health and property. However, trespass requires tangible physical invasion,[35] while private nuisance requires non-negligible loss of use of property and the tracing of

[31] *DR* 6:326, 468. This and the surrounding passages are unusual in that Kant seems to be directly invoking questions of interests and needs. Addressing this, however, is beyond the scope of this chapter. See generally EJ Weinrib, 'Poverty and Property in Kant's System of Rights' (2002) 78 *Notre Dame Law Review* 795; Ripstein (n 1) Ch 9; and E Fox-Decent and EJ Criddle, 'The Fiduciary Constitution of Human Rights' (2009) 15 *Legal Theory* 301, 330–32.

[32] C Felber, *Money: The New Rules of the Game* (Cham, Springer International Publishing, 2017) 29–30.

[33] *DR* 6:287, 435. Christian Felber adopts more or less this rationale in arguing that money constitutes a 'pure' public good in the sense of 'a 'public service', a modern 'commons' and a '*Res publica*'. Felber, *ibid* 29. Fundamentally, the point of money is to 'create trust between people who do not know each other …'. Felber, *ibid* 30.

[34] *DR* 6:331, 473.

[35] Clifford Rechtshaffen and Denise Antolini argue that '(i)n the environmental context, a key issue in a trespass action is whether an appropriate "object" has indeed entered plaintiff's property. Traditionally, the thing has to be "tangible," that is visible – such as shrapnel from a bullet, a utility line, or an arm – and it must have caused "direct" interference …'. While they note that some courts have 'loosened up' on the directness requirement in the wake of scientific advances regarding 'dust, vibration, and smoke', they also acknowledge that '(m)any courts have been reluctant to extend trespass in this direction because it would produce 'too much liability' (internal citations omitted). C Rechtschaffen and DE Antolini, 'Common Law Remedies: A Refresher' in C Rechtschaffen and DE Antolini (eds), *Creative Common Law Strategies for Protecting the Environment* (Washington, Environmental Law Institute, 2007) 14–15.

causation to individual polluters,[36] both of which are all but impossible to prove if many different polluters contribute to environmental degradation slowly over time.[37] Thus, just like the inhabitants of Ripstein's roadless community, victims of pollution living under a system of pure private right have no solution at private law, and so will be frustrated not just in the achievement of particular projects, but made systematically subject to the will of polluters.

This calls for a public and systematic solution which the state as the public fiduciary has an obligation to provide: environmental regulation. A state's failure to provide a clean environment therefore constitutes a breach of its duties as the public fiduciary, thus entitling its subjects to bring claims against it in human rights.[38] Within the contemporary European legal order, the Strasbourg Court has on several occasions interpreted the right to family life in Article 8 of the European Convention on Human Rights (ECHR) as also implying a right to a clean environment.[39] Moreover, the claim of a violation of the right to a clean environment does not require proof of loss or damage: in *Tătar v Romania*, the Strasbourg Court found a violation of Article 8 ECHR even though there was no proven causal link between emissions of sodium cyanide into a nearby river by a private gold mine operator and the applicant's asthma.[40] Instead, the Court relied upon the precautionary principle to hold that the state had a positive

[36] The connection between private nuisance and property is particularly pronounced in English common law, where a plaintiff cannot bring a nuisance claim unless she holds a property title in the land. See FH Newark, 'The Boundaries of Nuisance' (1949) 65 *LQR* 480, 488–89. For a while, this basic principle was challenged by the Court of Appeal Decision in *Khorasandjian v Bush* [1993] QB 727 (CA), where a plaintiff who was living with parents without any property title was allowed to recover in private nuisance against a harasser sending her unwanted phone calls. However, the House of Lords overruled *Khorasandjian* in *Hunter v Canary Wharf Ltd* [1997] UKHL 14, [1997] 1 AC 655 (HL). Similarly, the German 'Law of Neighbours' is situated in the part of the Civil Code dealing with property, at BGB (German Civil Code) s 906. French law seems to be an exception to this general rule, in that the *trouble de voisinage* is available merely on the basis of being in the vicinity. See C van Dam, *European Tort Law* (Oxford, Oxford University Press, 2013) 448–49.

[37] See, eg, JR Allum, '"An Outcrop of Hell": History, Environment, and the Politics of the Trail Smelter Dispute' in RM Bratspies and RA Miller (eds), *Transboundary Harm in International Law: Lessons from the Trail Smelter Arbitration* (Cambridge, Cambridge University Press, 2006) 19–20. Allum describes the development of Canadian jurisprudence on environmental torts as one where the onset of the industrial revolution in the early 20th century led to polluter's liability being assessed against the productive value of the polluting activity, such that courts 'demanded absolute proof of "tangible economic injury" before granting compensation and only reluctantly imposed conditions on the future operations of even the most egregious offenders'.

[38] This was not Kant's own view: he envisions socio-economic and other forms of public provision only as an imperfect duty on the part of the state, with no corresponding legal right on the part of the subject. The reasons for this cannot be explored here.

[39] In *López Ostra v Spain*, Merits and just satisfaction [1994] ECHR 46, the Strasbourg Court found an Article 8 ECHR violation in a case where the applicant suffered from fumes from a leather factory that had been allowed to operate without a licence. In *Fadeyeva v Russian Federation*, Merits and just satisfaction [2005] ECHR 376, the Court found an Article 8 ECHR violation where the state had not offered assistance in finding alternative housing for the applicant living in the vicinity of the largest steel smelting plant in Russia.

[40] *Tătar and Tătar v Romania*, Merits and just satisfaction, App no 67021/01 (ECtHR, 27 January 2009).

obligation to take effective steps even in the absence of scientific certainty about the effects of such emissions. Interpreted in this light, the imperative in Article 191(2) on the Treaty on the Functioning of the European Union (TFEU) that 'Union policy on the environment shall aim at a high level of protection' is exactly right. A clean environment is indeed a priority which every political community must set for itself and pursue, because it is necessary for the equal freedom of its subjects.

B. Limitations upon the Right to Provide Public Goods

Because the state's right to provide public goods derives from its public, fiduciary office, the measures it takes may be challenged for lack of (1) public purpose, or (2) necessity. The first limitation arises from the nature of the state as a public person. In this respect, Ripstein's theory of the law of public goods possesses resources unavailable to the conventional 'economic' approaches to the same. Under the latter, public promotion of arts and culture through the provision of museums and theatres would qualify as public goods because they advance general utility while being privately undersupplied. However, this same rationale could also justify the public enforcement of religious rituals and dress codes as public goods on the grounds that they advance the utility of ethnic or religious majorities, while being at the same time difficult to achieve without official compulsion.[41] Under Ripstein's conception, however, neither of these things would qualify as public goods, for the reason that they do not pursue the public purpose of ensuring the equal freedom of the people. Regarding museums and theatres, states have the discretion to provide them in accordance with the democratic approval of the people, because museums and theatres are things a free people can choose to fund and enjoy. In contrast, public enforcement of religious observances and dress codes is not only unnecessary but, for the reasons adumbrated in the previous chapter, wholly incompatible with the rightful condition.

The second limitation follows from the first. Recall that coercion is compatible with right only 'as a *hindering of a hindrance to freedom*'.[42] As such, the state cannot invade or exact any more than is necessary for the provision of equal freedom. Anything in excess must be deemed as being for a private purpose.[43] One may rationalise the general principle of proportionality in EU law in this light. As the ECJ observed in *Pesce and Others*, the principle of proportionality

> requires that measures adopted by EU institutions should not exceed the limits of what is appropriate and necessary to attain the legitimate objectives pursued by the

[41] Ripstein (n 1) 259–60.
[42] *DR* 6:231, 388.
[43] Ripstein (n 1) 254.

> legislation in question, and where there is a choice between several appropriate measures, recourse must be had to the least onerous, and the disadvantages caused must not be disproportionate to the aims pursued.[44]

II. GLOBAL PUBLIC GOODS

The previous paragraphs accounted for a state's right to redress 'public bads' occurring within its territory. What if the threat to the state's ability to provide a rightful condition comes from outside? The following section argues that states can neither be prohibited from enacting regulation nor reduced to hoping for the cooperation of other persons, because either of these would leave it at the mercy of all other persons – state and non-state – in the fulfilment of its single purpose, thus violating *its* dignity. In short, nothing that a state does which is necessary to provide a rightful condition can ever be wrongful as against any other person. All other persons are under a duty of mandatory cooperation with the regulating state.

The state's right of jurisdiction regarding 'global' public goods thus bears essentially the same structure as its purely domestic counterpart: it is not premised upon harm or loss, and it is circumscribed by criteria of public purpose and necessity. Moreover, like domestic public goods, global public goods are those things that are necessary for (1) a sovereign to ensure its subjects' freedom, or (2) to preserve its ability to do so. While most of the global public goods mentioned in the introduction fall under the second category, their rationale may be explicated by considering those coming under the first. In this regard, the most convenient example to proceed from would be the global analogues of roads: the high seas, rights of passage and other things necessary for international travel.

A. The Right to Regulate Global Public Goods

Just as persons have constitutional rights as citizens to visit other members of their community, they also have *cosmopolitan* rights as 'citizens of the world' to visit distant strangers.[45] Once again, these rights are justified not by reference to the advantages of free trade or the mind-broadening effects of travel.

[44] Joined Cases C-78/16 and C-79/16 *Pesce and Others* (n 11) para 48. See also Case C-101/12 *Schaible v Land Baden-Württemberg* EU:C:2013:661 (17 October 2013), para 29.

[45] *DR* 6:352, 489. Importantly, this is simply a right to visit, not a right to be welcomed. I Kant, 'Toward Perpetual Peace' [hereinafter '*PP*'] in MJ Gregor (ed & tr), *Practical Philosophy: The Cambridge Edition of the Works of Immanuel Kant*, 9th edn (Cambridge, Cambridge University Press, 2006) 8:357–58, 328–29.

Kant was in fact more than just a little dubious of such rationalisations.[46] Instead, the justification of cosmopolitan right is again entirely formal. A person cannot be prevented from attempting to interact with distant others at the mere whim of another without good reason, and the only reasons that are good are those that are non-dominating. Visiting with hostile purposes is incompatible with the equal freedom of the hosts and so may be prohibited – Kant accordingly approves of the closure by China and Japan of their borders to predatory European trading companies.[47] In contrast, a refugee cannot be turned away because that would 'destroy them'; that is, leave them outside a rightful condition.[48] Within these limits, persons have rights '*to try to* establish community with all and, to this end, to *visit* all regions of the earth', which cannot be annulled despite the possibility of abuse.[49] A state may not deny a visitor the chance simply to 'present oneself for society',[50] for this would amount to treating her as an untouchable.

Thus described, cosmopolitan right implies the provision and maintenance of international 'roads' for all to travel upon – the seas and deserts.[51] Contrary to Grotius, the reason why the high seas cannot rightfully be reduced to property or sovereignty is not that they are by nature non-excludable and non-rivalrous.[52] Rather, it is because the seas have to be kept open to give effect to the right to travel.[53] Pirates and brigands threaten these global thoroughfares, rendering the exercise of cosmopolitan right by individual travellers subject to their arbitrary will. They are, in a sense, global public nuisances. As the fiduciaries of their subjects, states may rightfully employ coercion to hinder their hindrance to their subjects' freedom. Accordingly, they have jurisdiction to punish pirates and brigands anywhere as enemies of mankind.[54]

[46] The section in the *Perpetual Peace* discussing cosmopolitan right contains a famously blistering passage noting the curious fact that European trading companies somehow always seemed to be teetering on the edge of bankruptcy despite practising the 'cruelest and most calculated slavery' in the Sugar Islands. *PP* 8:359, 330. Instead, Kant speculates that their real function was to train sailors for wars back home in Europe on behalf of princes who 'make much ado of their piety … while they drink wrongfulness like water …' *ibid*.

[47] *PP* 8:359, 329–30.

[48] *PP* 8:358, 329.

[49] *DR* 6:353, 489.

[50] *PP* 8:358, 329.

[51] *PP* 8:358, 329.

[52] Indeed, the whole point of the *Free Sea* was to challenge the legality of Portuguese closure of sea lanes. W Werner, 'Mankind's Territory and the Limits of International Law-Making' in R Liivoja and J Petman (eds), *International Law-Making: Essays in Honour of Jan Klabbers* (Abingdon, Routledge, 2014) 108. Moreover, we have definitely possessed the technology to mark off exclusive economic zones and to build artificial islands since the 1950s. See SJ Shackelford, 'The Tragedy of the Common Heritage of Mankind' (2009) 28 *Stanford Environmental Law Journal* 109, 122–24.

[53] 'Although the seas might seem to remove nations from any community with one another, they are the arrangements of nature most favoring their commerce by means of navigation …' *DR* 6:352–53, 489.

[54] *PP* 8:358, 329.

The same rationale can be leveraged to justify the use of state regulatory powers to address climate change. As Evan Fox-Decent puts it, climate change leaves 'peoples living in coastal regions threatened by rising water levels, others threatened by ever-more-frequent and violent storms, and yet others whose agricultural or hunter-gatherer ways of life are threatened by diminishing rains and other climactic changes'.[55] At best, these may ground a claim for damage on the part of the affected private persons, assuming they can hale the distant polluters into their courts, and overcome the insurmountable evidential obstacles, let alone execute on any judgments. As against states, however, climate change-inducing pollution constitutes injury akin to public nuisance, because it leaves their subjects systematically dependent upon the choices of distant polluters.[56] That climate change violates the personality rights of states is demonstrated perhaps most starkly by the fact that certain low-lying or island states will disappear completely as a result of rising sea levels. As against these states, climate change is a mortal threat to their very existence.

Neither the state's entitlement to redress threats against it nor the structure of that entitlement is altered by the fact that the polluter is located outside the jurisdiction. In the *Perpetual Peace*, Kant states that if a measure is necessary 'for its security' – that is, to safeguard its capacity to provide a rightful condition – the state 'can and ought to require the others to enter with it into a constitution similar to a civil constitution, in which it can be assured of its right'.[57] The burdens placed upon others by such unilateral measures are not wrongful as against other private persons, because the invitation to join a rightful condition is an offer that cannot be refused. Nor is it wrongful as against other states whose nationals are burdened by extraterritorial jurisdiction, because nothing one state does to preserve its rightful condition can constitute a wrong against another.

Note that this feature is unique to the international rightful condition. An analogue does not exist for it in its domestic counterpart. No private person in a domestic order can take it upon herself to make legislative determinations about the modalities of public provision for another private person. Even if they were to act out of the best of intentions after the most exhaustive deliberations, any such determination would still be *unilateral*, and hence incapable of binding another. Within a domestic rightful condition, public goods must be

[55] E Fox-Decent, 'From Fiduciary States to Joint Trusteeship of the Atmosphere: The Right to a Healthy Environment through a Fiduciary Prism' in K Coghill, C Sampford and T Smith (eds), *Fiduciary Duty and the Atmospheric Trust* (Abingdon, Routledge, 2013) 259.

[56] As Fox-Decent puts it, 'vulnerable peoples … are left to negotiate as best they can with those who are indifferent to the effects of environmental degradation … The vulnerable are left to beg more powerful parties for compensation that is given as charity, if it is given at all …' *ibid* 264. Fox-Decent also claims that Pacific 'islanders' rights to their lands are "illusory" if the unilateral actions of other states are permitted to cause global warming and rising sea levels' *ibid* 259–60.

[57] *PP* 8:354, 326.

provided publicly; that is to say, omnilaterally. Why does this same argument not also apply to the international sphere? That is to say, why is one state's determinations of the types and amounts of global public goods necessary to ensure the freedom of its subjects not be seen as acts of unilateral domination of non-subject individuals and other states? Leaving aside Kant's opposition to global government, the answer once again lies in property. To recall the previous chapter, the impetus for the setting up of the rightful condition lies in the fact that for human beings, innate right requires the acquisition of external things; in order to establish purposes and pursue them, one first has to have the means to do so, which in turn requires one to have rights to those means, and those rights have to be consistent with like rights on the part of everyone else. The acquisition of external things implies excluding others from those same things, which implies placing others under obligations not to interfere with those things. This, as argued in the previous chapter, cannot be accomplished rightfully by the excluder alone, because the purposes of the excluder are diametrically opposed to those of the excluded, such that subordinating the latter to the former constitutes an act of domination. Instead, we require a legislature capable of speaking omnilaterally; that is, representing the united will of both the excluder *and* the excluded at the same time.

A similar institution has no place in the international rightful condition because states as moral persons do not have property. The problems of originally acquiring external things do not arise for states because, as explained in the previous chapter, territory is not an external thing acquired to advance some desired end. Rather, it is 'innate' in that the territory just *is* the state; it is the physical space in which the state manifests itself. As such, in the same way as human beings in the state of nature need not set up a legislature before defending their persons, states in the international rightful condition need not set up a world legislature to provide global public goods. This can be expressed differently. Human beings, as described in the previous chapter, are a seething mess of divergent passions and projects. As such, we need a common powerful will to express a public standpoint systematically unavailable to us as private individuals. In contrast, states are public persons *ideally* with no purpose other than ensuring the independence of their subjects. Recall that independence is not a 'value' that can be maximised or bought at the cost of another people's servitude. Rather, it is the organising principle of all interpersonal relations, such that nobody is truly independent unless everybody is. As such, states must be taken as engaged in the same collective project of creating and maintaining a global order in which no person anywhere on this earth is at the mercy of any other person elsewhere on it.[58] It is in this sense that sovereigns are trustees of

[58] *DR* 6:354, 491 ('… morally practical reason pronounces in us its irresistible *veto*: *there is to be no war*, neither war between you and me in the state of nature nor war between us as states …'). See also Alice Pinheiro Walla, 'Global Government or Global Governance? Realism and Idealism in Kant's Legal Theory' (2017) 13 *Journal of Global Ethics* 312, 314 ('… the civil condition must not be

humanity. Accordingly, states are entitled to a presumption – rebuttable at a later stage – that they act in furtherance of this purpose.

This basic rationale is apparent in An Hertogen's revisionist interpretation of the *Lotus* Decision as stating a 'residual rule … that sovereignty should be exercised so as to ensure co-existence and cooperation between independent states'.[59] As regards the *dictum* that limits upon prescriptive jurisdiction cannot be presumed, Hertogen argues that a contrary

> requirement of permission [would be] problematic not because the acting state will have a de facto veto right over a rule that prohibits its actions but, rather, because the state will have a de facto veto right over the creation of any rule that permits an affected state to respond.[60]

Similarly, Mattias Kumm argues that because certain types of 'cross-border effects' give rise to 'areas in which states lack legitimate authority to effectively control what may or may not be done', this means that

> no injustice is done to states when they are subject to legal obligations without having consented to them. On the contrary, deep legitimacy questions arise when individual states have the capacity to effectively veto the emergence of universally binding obligations in contexts where the behavior of an individual state raises justice-sensitive externality concerns.[61]

The rationale of independence generates one limitation upon the right of jurisdiction central to the *Lotus* doctrine. Recall that a state's territory is analogous to body; it is simply the space in which the state manifests itself. As such, it follows that the regulating state must wait for the individual private polluter or their assets to enter its territory. The same point can be put differently. Because the individual polluter and its national state are separate persons, such that the conduct of the former is not attributable to the latter, to exercise enforcement jurisdiction upon the territory of the polluter's national state would be tantamount to coercion against an innocent third party. Accordingly, no state can exercise its jurisdiction in the territory of another without the latter's affirmative consent. Such consent must not amount to capitulation: it must be informed and circumscribed to preserve the independence of the consenting state, as well as its continuing responsibility for activity occurring in its territory.[62]

restricted to a particular polity; since there is a state of nature outside its borders, this state of nature must also be overcome. In the end, the civil condition must encompass *all areas and inhabitants of the earth*').

[59] A Hertogen, 'Letting Lotus Bloom' (2015) 26 *European Journal of International Law* 901, 917.

[60] *Ibid* 915.

[61] M Kumm, 'Sovereignty and the Right to Be Left Alone: Subsidiarity, Justice-Sensitive Externalities, and the Proper Domain of the Consent Requirement in International Law' (2016) 79 *Law and Contemporary Problems* 239, 251.

[62] Umut Özsu argues in a series of writings that a core principle of Turkey's submissions before the Permanent Court of International Justice in the *Lotus* proceedings was to abolish the extraterritorial consular regime or 'capitulations' originally granted *ex gratia* by the Ottoman sultan, but which had assumed the aspect of treaty obligations as the empire weakened in the 19th century.

In this light, we may revisit the cases Benvenisti relied upon in chapter three in support of his proposed obligation of costless accommodation. To recall, these were the *Iron Rhine Arbitration*, *Right of Passage over Indian Territory*, the *Lake Lanoux Arbitration* and the *Dispute Regarding Navigational and Related Rights* between Costa Rica and Nicaragua. The precedent most congenial to Benvenisti's and Ryngaert's equitable approach is the *Iron Rhine Arbitration*, which concerned a dispute between the Netherlands and Belgium regarding the reactivation of a disused railway line linking the two countries.[63] In the complex treaty arrangements under which the railway line was built, a right of transit had been granted to Belgium over Dutch territory, subject to the Netherlands retaining certain regulatory powers.[64] One question before the tribunal was whether a diversion proposed by the Netherlands for environmental reasons was compatible with the Belgian right of transit.[65] In its award, the tribunal held that Belgium could not 'reasonably withhold its consent', especially if the Netherlands offered to bear the extra costs incurred as a result of the diversion.[66] This contradicts Benvenisti's restricted *Pareto* criterion, according to which states are prohibited from accepting side payments in exchange for accommodating others' interests. In *Right of Passage*, the International Court of Justice (ICJ) found that Portugal had acquired rights of passage over Indian territory between its then Indian enclaves, largely due to historical use rather than any deeper principle.[67] This is incompatible with the current rule against acquisitive prescription of territory as discussed in chapter four.

In contrast to these two precedents, consider *Lake Lanoux*, a dispute between France and Spain concerning French plans to divert a shared river to construct a hydroelectric dam. The relevant treaty provided that any party seeking to carry out works on the river had to obtain the approval of the other. France proposed a hydroelectric project involving works wholly within its territory that would not have imposed any costs upon Spain. Spain nevertheless withheld its approval, ostensibly in order to extract from France a larger share of water and electricity.[68] The crucial passages in the award state that

> To admit that jurisdiction in a certain field can no longer be exercised except on the condition of, or by way of, an agreement between two States, *is to place an essential*

U Özsu, 'De-Territorializing and Re-Territorializing Lotus: Sovereignty and Systematicity as Dialectical Nation-Building in Early Republican Turkey' (2009) 22 *Leiden Journal of International Law* 29; and U Özsu, 'The Ottoman Empire, the Origins of Extraterritoriality, and International Legal Theory' in A Orford and F Hoffmann (eds), *The Oxford Handbook of the Theory of International Law* (Oxford, Oxford University Press, 2016).

[63] *Iron Rhine Arbitration (Belgium v Netherlands)* (Award) (2005) 27 RIAA 35, para 2.

[64] *Ibid*, paras 28–43.

[65] *Ibid*, para 3.

[66] *Ibid*, para 232.

[67] *Right of Passage over Indian Territory (Portugal v India)* (Judgment, merits) [1960] ICJ Rep 6, 37–38.

[68] E Benvenisti, 'Sovereigns as Trustees of Humanity: On the Accountability of States to Foreign Stakeholders' (2013) 107 *American Journal of International Law* 295, 323.

> *restriction on the sovereignty of a State*, and such restriction could only be admitted if there were clear and convincing evidence. Without doubt, international practice does reveal some special cases in which this hypothesis has become reality … But these cases are exceptional, and *international judicial decisions are slow to recognize their existence, especially when they impair the territorial sovereignty of a State*, as would be the case in the present matter.
>
> In effect, in order to appreciate in its essence the necessity for prior agreement, one must envisage the hypothesis in which the interested States cannot reach agreement. In such a case, it must be admitted that *the State which is normally competent has lost its right to act alone as a result of the unconditional and arbitrary opposition of another State. This amounts to admitting a 'right of assent'; a 'right of veto', which at the discretion of one State paralyses the exercise of the territorial jurisdiction of another*[69] (emphasis added).

At their core, these passages indicate that the panel was not concerned with the balancing of interests or the maximisation of utility. Rather, its sole interest was in preventing France from being rendered subject to Spain's arbitrary choice.

Finally, consider *Dispute Regarding Navigational and Related Rights*, where the ICJ was called upon to construe a treaty between Nicaragua and Costa Rica, under which Costa Rica had been given navigational rights 'for the purposes of commerce' along a river designated as entirely within Nicaraguan territory. The issue was whether certain villagers on the Costa Rican bank could rely upon that exception to make use of the river 'to meet the basic requirements of everyday life, such as taking children to school or … giv[ing] or receiv[ing] medical treatment …'.[70] The topography of the region was such that inland travel would have been prohibitively expensive for those communities. The ICJ refused to strain the word 'commerce' to include non-commercial activity. Instead, it held that

> it cannot have been the intention of the authors of the [treaty] to deprive the inhabitants of the Costa Rican Bank of the river, of the right to use the river to the extent necessary to meet their essential requirements, even for activities of a non-commercial nature, given the geography of the area … [T]he parties must be presumed … to have intended to preserve for the Costa Ricans living on that bank a minimal right of navigation for the purposes of continuing to live a normal life in the villages along the river.[71]

Once again, the analysis does not turn on interests that can be accommodated at no cost or of requests which cannot be refused in good conscience. Although Nicaragua appears never to have argued it, its interests may very well have been set back by increased river traffic. Instead, the ICJ's discussion of 'presumed'

[69] *Lake Lanoux Arbitration (France v Spain)* (1957) 12 (1963) RIAA 281, 128.

[70] *Dispute Regarding Navigational and Related Rights (Costa Rica v Nicaragua)* (Judgment on the merits)[2009] ICJ Rep 213, para 74.

[71] *Ibid*, para 79.

consent is distinctly reminiscent of the Kantian idea of mandatory cooperation. The navigational rights simply had to be accorded by Nicaragua, because otherwise, a community of Costa Ricans would have been turned into *glebae adscripti* – prisoners in their own homes.

These precedents reveal considerable support in positive legal practice for the normative conception of global public goods advocated in this chapter. They also suggest the outline of a strategy for defending extraterritorial assertions of jurisdiction to provide global public goods from within positive international legal materials. This outline will be fleshed out in the next two sub-sections. After this, we will be in a position to compare the EU's particular mode of asserting extraterritorial jurisdiction against this outline to ascertain whether and to what extent it is justifiable.

B. The Irrelevance of Harm

The closure of a necessary passage may be likened to false imprisonment. Acts of transboundary environmental pollution may be likened to batteries upon the body of the state. Both false imprisonment and battery are actionable regardless of damage. By the same analogy, a state's right to enact extraterritorial measures to provide global public goods also cannot be contingent upon a requirement of harm or loss. This might sound controversial given that international environmental law is often described as premised upon a 'no-harm' or 'harm-prevention' principle.[72] According to conventional accounts, the principle made its first appearance in international legal practice in *Trail Smelter*, a mid-twentieth century arbitration between the US and Canada, where it was expressed as a prohibition against the causation of harm to the territory of other states, such harm having to be 'of serious consequence and the injury … established by clear and convincing evidence'.[73] Over time, the 'no-harm' principle was adopted in seminal international judicial decisions and international instruments, and two main lines of development are evident.[74] The first is that

[72] A leading textbook describes the principle as expressed in Principle 21 of the Stockholm Declaration as 'the cornerstone of international environmental law'. P Sands and J Peel, *Principles of International Environmental Law*, 4th edn (Cambridge, Cambridge University Press, 2018) 201.

[73] *Trail Smelter Arbitration, United States v Canada* (1941) 3 RIAA 1905, 1965.

[74] *Corfu Channel, United Kingdom v Albania*, Judgment [1949] ICJ Rep 4, 22 (describing 'every State's obligation not to allow knowingly its territory to be used for acts contrary to the rights of other States'); *Legality of the Threat or Use of Nuclear Weapons*, Advisory Opinion [1996] ICJ Rep 226, para 29. ('The existence of the general obligation of States to ensure that activities within their jurisdiction and control respect the environment of other States or of areas beyond national control is now part of the corpus of international law relating to the environment.') For international instruments, see Stockholm Declaration of the United Nations Conference on the Human Environment 1972 (UN Doc A/CONF48/14/Rev1, 3; UN Doc A/CONF48/PC/6) [hereinafter '*Stockholm Declaration*'], principle 21; Rio Declaration on Environment and Development 1992 (UN Doc A/CONF151/5/Rev1; UN Doc A/CONF151/26/Rev1 Vol1, Annex I) [hereinafter '*Rio Declaration*'], principle 2; and Articles on Prevention of Transboundary Harm from Hazardous

the principle no longer contemplates only harm to the territory of states but also the 'global commons'.[75] The second and more interesting development has been an attenuation of the concept of harm.

The obvious reason for this is the fact that the concerns of international environmental law have shifted from inter-state disputes over polluted water or air, but to the uniquely global problem of climate change. If the original *Trail Smelter* requirements of serious harm and demonstrability were to be insisted upon, we would, quite simply, all be dead. As such, Jutta Brunnée has written that the practical impossibility of tracing particular harmful emissions of particular emitters suggests that climate change is simply 'not the kind of transboundary pollution contemplated by the no harm rule',[76] while Benoît Mayer observes that 'the no-harm principle has rarely been explicitly invoked in international responses to climate change'.[77] Notwithstanding this difficulty, international environmental lawyers have attempted to retain the original focus on harm by rebranding the no-harm principle as the 'harm prevention' principle, entailing two distinct 'substantive' and 'procedural' sub-obligations.[78] According to this innovation, the 'substantive' no-harm obligation requires states to refrain from causing actual transboundary damage, while the 'procedural' no-harm obligation requires states 'to notify, warn, inform, or consult states potentially affected by transboundary impacts, to undertake (transboundary) environmental impact assessments … and monitor or report performance …'.[79]

The distinction between substantive and procedural harm prevention obligations was first posited in the *Pulp Mills* case, where the ICJ was tasked with construing a treaty between Argentina and Uruguay concerning the river Uruguay.[80] In interpreting what it termed the 'procedural' aspects of the treaty,

Activities: Text adopted by the Commission at its fifty-third session, in 2001 (Final Outcome) 2001 (UN Doc A/56/10, 370), article 3.

[75] KA Brent, 'The Certain Activities Case: What Implications for the No-Harm Rule?' (2017) 20 *Asia-Pacific Journal of Environmental Law* 28, 35–39. Brent traces the start of this expansion to Principle 21 of the *Stockholm Declaration*.

[76] J Brunnée, 'The Global Climate Regime: Wither Common Concern?' in A Seibert-Fohr et al (eds), *Coexistence, Cooperation and Solidarity: Liber Amicorum Rüdiger Wolfrum*, vol 1 (Leiden-Boston, Brill, 2011) 722.

[77] B Mayer, 'The Relevance of the No-Harm Principle to Climate Change Law and Politics' (2016) 19 *Asia-Pacific Journal of Environmental Law* 79, 79. Instead, Mayer argues that the no-harm principle has been supplanted in the climate change discourse by the concept of 'common but differentiated responsibility' which seeks to apportion the climate change-related obligations of states according to their historical contributions to it. *Ibid* 82–83.

[78] See, eg, U Beyerlin and T Marauhn, *International Environmental Law* (Oxford, Bloomsbury Publishing, 2011) 39–46; P-M Dupuy and JE Viñuales, *International Environmental Law* (Cambridge, Cambridge University Press, 2015) 54; J Brunnée, 'Procedure and Substance in International Environmental Law' (2020) 405 *Receuil des cours* 81.

[79] J Brunnée, 'International Environmental Law and Community Interests: Procedural Aspects' in E Benvenisti and G Nolte (eds), *Community Obligations across International Law* (Oxford, Oxford University Press, 2018) 154.

[80] *Pulp Mills on the River Uruguay, Argentina v Uruguay* [2010] ICJ Rep 14.

the Court took cognisance of the customary obligation of due diligence, which it understood as implying a requirement 'to undertake an environmental impact assessment where there is a risk that the proposed industrial activity may have a significant adverse impact in a transboundary context, in particular, on a shared resource'.[81] The Court observed further that a violation of a procedural obligation under the treaty did not necessarily also imply a violation of a substantive obligation,[82] and contrariwise that 'the fact that the parties [may] have complied with their substantive obligations does not mean that they are deemed to have complied *ipso facto* with their procedural obligations, or are excused from doing so'.[83]

The procedural/substantive divide was pursued further in the *Certain Activities carried out by Nicaragua in the Border Area* litigation between Costa Rica and Nicaragua, which, among other things, was concerned with whether Nicaragua had violated a procedural obligation to conduct an environmental impact assessment and to notify Costa Rica of its results before commencing dredging on a boundary river.[84] The Court ultimately held that it did not, on grounds that the dredging did not pose a sufficiently significant environmental risk.[85] It then went on to hold that Nicaragua had also not violated its substantive obligations under the no-harm principle. In her separate Opinion in *Certain Activities*, Judge Donoghue criticised this entire procedural/substantive distinction as unhelpful and unnecessarily complicated, and instead advocated that the 'requirement to exercise due diligence' be taken to constitute the single 'governing primary norm … that applies to all phases of a project (e.g., planning, assessment of impact, decision to proceed, implementation, post-implementation monitoring)'.[86] A failure to exercise due diligence in the planning phase could 'engage the responsibility of the State of origin even in the absence of material damage to potentially affected States'. Moreover, if

> at a subsequent phase, the failure of the State of origin to exercise due diligence in the implementation of a project causes significant transboundary harm, the primary norm that is breached remains one of due diligence, but the reparations due to the affected State must also address the material damage caused to the affected State.[87]

[81] *Ibid*, paras 204. The ICJ also observed that 'the principle of prevention, as a customary rule, has its origins in the due diligence that is required of a State in its territory. It is "every State's obligation not to allow knowingly its territory to be used for acts contrary to the rights of other States."'… A State is thus obliged to use all the means at its disposal in order to avoid activities which take place in its territory, or in any area under its jurisdiction, causing significant damage to the environment of another State.' *Ibid* para 101 (internal citations omitted).

[82] *Ibid*, paras 71–74.

[83] *Ibid*, paras 78.

[84] *Certain Activities carried out by Nicaragua in the Border Area; Construction of a Road in Costa Rica along the San Juan River, Costa Rica v Nicaragua*, Judgment [2015] ICJ Rep 665, paras 101–12.

[85] *Ibid*, paras 112.

[86] *Ibid*, para 9 (separate Opinion of Judge Donoghue).

[87] *Ibid*.

I agree with the growing number of international environmental lawyers who think Judge Donoghue is right.[88] My objection to the idea of 'procedural' and 'substantive' harm prevention principles is not that there is no intelligible distinction to be made between procedure and substance.[89] Rather, the reason why that distinction is unintelligible in *this* case is because it is being invoked to preserve a questionable premise. Recall the example given earlier of playing football in the middle of a highway miraculously without causing any traffic disruption. It would be strange to account for your criminal liability in public nuisance as a function of you making 'procedural' nuisances of yourselves notwithstanding the lack of a substantive traffic jam. Instead, it would be better to say that the wrong is complete the moment you and your associates usurp – that is, make wrongful use of – a *public* space. As such, potential damage is entirely secondary – something that exacerbates the wrong rather than constitutes it.[90] The same rationale applies to the regulation of global public goods. A failure to exercise due diligence is an international wrong complete in itself; it *includes* rather than consists of any actual environmental damage. The idea of a 'procedural' obligation not to cause harm, like the notion of 'moral' damage we saw in the previous chapter, is simply an attempt to shoehorn what is really an injury into the language of damage. There is only one obligation – a substantive obligation to exercise due diligence to ensure that activities taking place within the territory do not threaten the status of other states as of free equals in the international rightful condition. This quality of sovereignty itself derives solely from a political community's provision of a domestic rightful condition for their subjects, of which an important aspect is the provision of a clean environment, which includes both state territory and the global commons.

Now, this is not to say that questions of harm are entirely relevant. Rather, the claim is that placing harms front and centre leads to incoherence. These are particularly evident in harm-based accounts of the precautionary principle, precisely because it is impossible to weigh the cost of regulation against the unknown harms and benefits of proposed hazardous conduct. As Cass Sunstein has argued in a series of articles and books critical of the precautionary principle, any 'balancing' or 'weighing' of presently unquantifiable interests is

[88] For instance, Mayer concludes that the 'most coherent interpretation of the no-harm principle is as a due diligence obligation …' and that this 'conclusion is suggested by the wording of the no-harm principle in the Stockholm and Rio declarations as an obligation 'to ensure …' Mayer (n 77) 93. See also *Responsibilities and Obligations of States Sponsoring Persons and Entities with Respect to Activities in the Area, Advisory opinion, ITLOS Case No 17* [2011] ITLOS Rep 10, paras 112–16; Brent (n 75) 33–34; L-A Duvic-Paoli, *The Prevention Principle in International Environmental Law* (Cambridge, Cambridge University Press, 2018) 336–39; S Maljean-Dubois and V Richard, 'The International Court of Justice's Judgement of 20 April 2010 in the *Pulp Mills on the River Uruguay (Argentina v. Uruguay)* Case' in P Almeida and J-M Sorel (eds), *Latin America and the International Court of Justice: Contributions to International Law* (Abingdon-New York, Routledge, 2016) 311–13.

[89] *cf* Maljean-Dubois and Richard, *ibid* 312.

[90] Ripstein (n 1) 262.

logically impossible because potential harms and benefits fall on both sides of the scale. Instead, he submits that invocations of the principle usually reflect little more than irrational impulses and cultural prejudices.[91] Worse, Sunstein points to differences between the EU and the US in the policy areas where the precautionary principle is deployed – hormones in beef and genetically modified beef for the EU, compared to mad cow disease (BSE) and carcinogens in food for the US – to argue that it simply serves as a cover for biases in favour of particular industrial lobbies.[92] Benvenisti remarks that the precautionary principle is inherently conservative and 'conveys the potentially erroneous message that present uses are *a priori* safe'.[93] Sunstein goes one step further, and claims that the ultimate result of the precautionary principle is policy paralysis – 'it stands as an obstacle to regulation and nonregulation, and to everything in between'.[94]

These problems are avoided if one conceives of the purpose of law as guaranteeing freedom from domination, rather than the maximisation of utility or the avoidance of harm. The transfer of the burden of proof under the precautionary principle may be rationalised in the same way as the transfer of the burden of proof in actions for defamation.[95] At common law, a plaintiff in a libel action never has to demonstrate that she has suffered or will suffer damage as a result of an insulting statement.[96] Instead, it is for the defendant to establish its truth, or to withdraw it.[97] If the burdens were otherwise, you would potentially have to spend your life putting out small fires started by others, rendering you effectively at the mercy of everyone else's arbitrary choices. Questions of harm play a role only when considering whether the statements complained of are of a

[91] CR Sunstein, 'Beyond the Precautionary Principle' (2003) 151 *University of Pennsylvania Law Review* 1003, 1035–54.

[92] *Ibid* 1015–16.

[93] E Benvenisti, *Sharing Transboundary Resources: International Law and Optimal Resource Use* (Cambridge, Cambridge University Press, 2002) 110–11.

[94] Sunstein (n 91) 1028.

[95] At first glance, this aspect of the precautionary principle may appear to contradict an aspect of the innate right to independence, which Kant calls the right to be 'beyond reproach', that is, to be presumed to have 'done no wrong to anyone'. *DR* 6:238, 394. Ordinarily, if anyone accuses you of doing wrong, they bear the burden of proving it, not you. This basic principle structures private causes of action and the criminal law. For the reasons described in the text, however, defamation constitutes the one exception to this basic case, such that all you need is to show before a court that someone has imputed a wrong to you, which they must then prove or retract.

[96] Windeyer J explained in the High Court of Australia that a plaintiff 'gets damages because he was injured in his reputation, that is simply because he was publically defamed'. *Uren v John Fairfax & Sons Pty Ltd* 117 CLR 118 (High Court of Australia) 150. Lord Hoffmann has similarly held that because a man's 'reputation is a part of his personality, the "immortal part" of himself', it is right that he should be entitled to vindicate his reputation and receive compensation for a slur upon it without proof of financial loss'. *Jameel v The Wall Street Journal Europe Sprl* [2006] UKHL 44, [2007] 1 AC 359 (HL), para 91.

[97] This remains the rule in almost the entire English-speaking world outside of the United States. *Belt v Lawes* (1882) LJQB 359, 361; *Hill v Church of Scientology of Toronto* [1995] 2 SCR 1130 (Supreme Court of Canada); *Khumalo v Holomisa* 2002 (5) SA 401 (Constitutional Court, SA); *The Age Co Ltd v Elliott* [2006] 14 VR 375 (Court of Appeal, Victoria).

type that may cause reasonable persons to think worse of her. Similarly, in the case of public goods, the only role harmfulness plays is in whether the conduct proposed is of a type that tends to threaten the rightful condition by privatising a public thing. Whether it *actually* leads to damage is secondary. This rationale justifies the prohibition of conduct that is strongly suspected but not proven to be harmful under the precautionary principle. The state can legitimately expect a party proposing *prima facie* harmful activity to prove its harmlessness if such activity presents a risk of leaving its subjects at the mercy of distant polluters.[98] This is not just a collective interest or common 'concern' but an individual *right* inhering in the state.

In conclusion, while harm-based theories of jurisdiction face tremendous difficulties in accounting for central doctrines of contemporary environmental law, 'reliance on Kant's legal theory allows [one] to trade fruitfully on the Kantian distinction between harms and wrongs' in explicating legal solutions to problems like climate change that are 'gradual and non-linear in progression, severely affecting at present a relatively small portion of the earth's population'.[99] The crucial factor justifying these conceptual moves is the recognition of a unified public standpoint that is more than just an aggregation of private interests or choices. One cannot ordinarily hold another liable just because they might, at some point, drop a brick on your foot. To make the leap from the redress of actual harm to the regulation of risks of harm, we require the idea of a threat to a public good. Without damage or imminence thereof having to be proved, however, there is the concern that rights of extraterritorial jurisdiction may become untethered to any limiting principle. I now turn to this question.

C. Public Purpose and Necessity

Recall the anti-colonialism of the *Perpetual Peace*. In the *Doctrine of Right*, whose brief discussion of cosmopolitan right consists almost entirely of a condemnation of colonialism, Kant excoriates certain commentators justifying coercion against foreign peoples so that 'these crude peoples will become civilized' thereby.[100] The fundamental problem with relying upon selfless intervention by hegemonic states to advance global interests or values is not that such interventions are unlikely to be selfless or competently undertaken. Rather, it is

[98] See Transboundary Haze Pollution Act 2014 (Singapore) s 8(2):

> [W]here – (a) it is proved, or presumed by the operation [the act], that an entity owns or occupies any land situated outside Singapore; and (b) it is further proved, or presumed by operation of [the act], that any haze pollution in Singapore involves smoke resulting from any fire on that land outside Singapore, it shall be presumed, until the contrary is proved, that the entity which is the owner or occupier of the land engaged in conduct, or engaged in conduct that condones any conduct by another, which caused or contributed to that haze pollution in Singapore.

[99] Fox-Decent (n 55) 260.

[100] *DR* 6:353, 490.

because ends do not justify means: 'all these supposed good intentions cannot wash away the stain of injustice in the means used for them'.[101] Therefore, even if it is wrongful in the highest degree to remain outside an international rightful condition, neither international nor cosmopolitan right allows for the coercion of another people simply to drag them into civilisation.[102] Coercion is never justified merely because it produces 'good' results, but only as a hindrance to a hindrance to freedom. As such, it cannot be deployed if 'neither nature nor chance' has brought that state into contact with 'a people that holds out no prospect of civil union with it ...'.[103]

Instead, it must be demonstrated that the extraterritorial conduct complained of is of a type that tends to threaten the regulator's *domestic* rightful condition. This means that the same criteria governing the domestic provision of public goods also apply at the international level. Assertions of extraterritorial jurisdiction are legitimate only if *necessary* for accomplishing the state's sole public purpose of securing the equal freedom of its subjects. They can neither pursue the common sympathies or private conceptions of the good peculiar to a particular community, nor even a 'global value' shared by every single state and political community in the world (if such a thing even exists.) The requirement of a public purpose means that unlike in the domestic rightful condition, a state may not enact extraterritorial measures to pursue aims that are compatible with, but unnecessary for a domestic rightful condition. Cagliostro may not levy taxes upon the citizens of Ruritania to set up a national opera house there, even if Ruritanians really could do with a bit of cultivation. Such a decision requires Ruritanian democratic approval, which Cagliostro does not possess.

Moreover, a state may not enact extraterritorial measures that pursue proper public purposes, but impose greater burdens on distant strangers than strictly needed. Anything in excess can only be for a private purpose. For this reason, unilateral assertions of extraterritorial jurisdiction may have to be 'flexible', or sensitive to changes in other states' regulatory regimes in the manner conceived by the preamble to the EU Emissions Trading Directive as discussed in chapter three.[104] To facilitate this flexibility and sensitivity, it may be prudent to invite the participation of foreign stakeholders in domestic policymaking processes. Benvenisti and Ryngaert are therefore correct to advocate these things.

[101] *DR* 6:353, 490.

[102] At *DR* 6:344, 482, Kant remarks that even though remaining in the international state of nature is 'wrong in the highest degree, and states neighboring upon one another are under an obligation to leave it', it is still the fact that 'no state is wronged by another in this condition (insofar as neither wants anything better) ...'.

[103] *DR* 6:266, 417.

[104] Parliament and Council Directive 2003/87/EC of 13 October 2003 establishing a scheme for greenhouse gas emission allowance trading within the Community and amending Council Directive 96/61/EC [2003] OJ L275/32; E Benvenisti, 'Legislating for Humanity: May States Compel Foreigners to Promote Global Welfare?' in R Liivoja and J Petman (eds), *International Law-making: Essays in Honour of Jan Klabbers* (Abingdon, Routledge, 2014) 13.

Aside from the above substantive criteria, there is one institutional requirement: the judicial settlement of disputes. As argued in chapter four, the sole defect in an international state of nature is the indeterminacy of rights, meaning that the one institution required in the international rightful condition is an international court where states may settle their disputes through lawsuits rather than by war. Therefore, a state enacting extraterritorial measures to provide a global public good must submit itself to the jurisdiction of an international court where it may answer legal challenges regarding necessity or public purpose. No state can expect others simply to accept its protestations of good faith.[105] Of course, compulsory general jurisdiction does not exist in international law as it currently stands. However, nothing *prevents* a state from accepting the jurisdiction of the ICJ, or of other courts or arbitral tribunals. If states avail themselves of this facility, there will be no further grounds to question the legitimacy of their extraterritorial measures in pursuit of global public goods. If these criteria are fulfilled, all other states will be under an obligation of mandatory cooperation with the regulating state. 'Blocking statutes' will be illegal.

III. APPRAISING THE EU

The previous paragraphs set out a normative theory of public goods, of unilateral jurisdiction to provide global public goods and outlined how these normative claims might translate into positive legal argument. Against this background, we may now appraise the EU's unique methods of asserting extraterritorial jurisdiction. I cannot examine each and every example of EU regulation in these areas to see whether they indeed pursue ends that qualify as republican public purposes and whether their impositions are necessary and proportionate. Rather, my purpose has been to set out in the general principles by which such measures may be enacted or defended. Whether individual measures are proper and legitimate is something that has to be examined on a case by case basis, which is beyond the scope of this book.

That said, my first conclusion is that despite its deeply imperial overtones, the technique of territorial extension in EU extraterritorial competition and environmental regulation turns out to be – to a significant extent – a valid form of asserting jurisdiction defensible under a republican theory of international legal order. The same is true of the ECJ's steadfast refusal to invoke either the effects doctrine or the no-harm principle, as well as its commitment to the precautionary principle. On the republican model of international legal order,

[105] *cf* Benvenisti (n 68) 317–18 (rejecting the claim that sovereigns may be allowed to abide by their own judgment without giving others any reasons, but not requiring compulsory judicial settlement of disputes).

extraterritorial jurisdiction is better justified on what international lawyers call the 'protective principle', rather than on some extrapolation of the territorial principle. In this regard, it is important that much of the EU's extraterritorial jurisprudence and legislation centres around climate change, environmental and marine pollution, maritime transport, air transport, financial services and competition, all of which can be conceived of as public goods in Ripstein's understanding.

That said, certain instances of EU extraterritorial regulation are almost certainly incompatible with the republican model, for instance, the extraterritorial animal welfare measures discussed in chapter two. Animal welfare measures, like measures catering for museums and theatres, fall under the category of goods that are compatible with but not necessary for the rightful condition. A states' competence to legislate them depends upon democratic approval. The EU therefore has every right to legislate them 'domestically', but not extraterritorially. There is one final delicious irony. As argued above, the reason why the EU need not demonstrate harm or loss before imposing its environmental regulation upon distant strangers is because environmental pollution is structurally akin to bodily injury rather than to property damage. Like territory, the environment is like body, not property. However, we find that the centrepiece of the EU's strategy for tackling aviation pollution relies upon a commodification of the environment – the trading of rights to emit carbon into the atmosphere.

Notwithstanding these complaints around the edges, there are grounds to assert that the EU is probably the single political organisation of jurisdiction providing effective regulation for the preservation of various forms of global commons, be it the environment, competitive markets, or cyberspace. Concerning the last, the current system of private control over the most popular social media platforms arguably provides the perfect illustration of the perils of leaving 'public things' wholly in private hands. Quite small groups of people possess the ability to compromise political processes by 'pollut(ing) … the marketplace of ideas'[106] with misinformation, which the massive corporations controlling these platforms appear to have not just no interest, but no ability to address. In a recent book, Siva Vaidhyanathan describes how the harvesting of user data by Facebook to facilitate targeted advertising has given rise to unprecedented levels of social fragmentation and alienation as a result of the fact that, like *adscripti glebae*, users of Facebook and other social media platforms become ensnared in their own peculiar bubbles and echo chambers.[107] Short of nationalising these

[106] E Benvenisti, 'Upholding Democracy Amid the Challenges of New Technology: What Role for the Law of Global Governance?' (2018) 29 *European Journal of International Law* 9, 67.

[107] S Vaidhyanathan, *Antisocial Media: How Facebook Disconnects Us and Undermines Democracy* (Oxford, Oxford University Press, 2018). See also Angela Nagle, *Kill All Normies: Online Culture Wars From 4Chan And Tumblr To Trump And The Alt-Right* (Alresford, Zero Books, 2017).

social media platforms as public goods, one solution would be to give users control over what is done with their data. In this connection, Vaidhyanathan remarks that

> The least we should is embrace European-style data protection laws worldwide. Individuals should have a right to be informed how data about them … will be used by private companies. People should have the power to remove data from the dossiers that companies like Facebook and Google keep on every user. The foundations for these rights exist in the latest versions of European privacy and data protection law. Other major states such as Brazil, India, Australia, Canada, Mexico, Japan, and the United States should follow and model data protection laws after the European Union's.[108]

Similarly, Benvenisti believes that 'the EU has been the vanguard in setting limits' to this ungoverned space as a result of enacting data protection measures of exterritorial application.[109]

A far more serious problem concerns the institutional requirement of international adjudication. The hybrid status of the EU as neither state nor international organisation raises profound difficulties: the EU is not a member of the UN, and therefore not a party to the ICJ Statute. Neither may it submit to the jurisdiction of the court on an *ad hoc* basis, because Article 34 of the ICJ Statute provides that only states can appear in proceedings before it.[110] As Advocate General Wathelet observed in his Opinion in *Western Sahara Campaign*, these considerations mean that

> review of the external action of the European Union does not fall within the jurisdiction of an international court or even of the International Court of Justice. Consequently, even if its action infringed a peremptory norm of international law within the meaning of Article 53 of the Vienna Convention on the Law of Treaties or the obligations '*erga omnes*' of customary international law, no international court would have jurisdiction to adjudicate on such an agreement.[111]

To be sure, the EU is a member of several international organisations and before whose judicial mechanisms it can be brought. For instance, as a longstanding party to United Nations Convention on the Law of the Sea (UNCLOS), the EU regularly takes part in international arbitrations before the International Tribunal for the Law of the Sea (ITLOS).[112] Moreover, there is also the possibility

[108] Vaidhyanathan, *ibid* 216.

[109] Benvenisti (n 106) 65, citing the General Data Protection Regulation (GDPR). Regulation 2016/679/EU of the European Parliament and of the Council of 27 April 2016 on the protection of natural persons with regard to the processing of personal data and on the free movement of such data, and repealing Directive 95/46/EC [2016] OJ L119/1.

[110] Case C-266/16 *Western Sahara Campaign UK, The Queen v Commissioners for Her Majesty's Revenue and Customs, Secretary of State for Environment, Food and Rural Affairs* ECLI:EU:C:2018:1 (10 January 2018), Opinion of AG Wathelet, para 81.

[111] *Ibid*, para 82.

[112] Esa Paasivirta, 'The European Union and the United Nations Convention on the Law of the Sea' (2015) 38 *Fordham International Law Journal* 1045, 1055–58.

of an EU measure being challenged indirectly by bringing a lawsuit against the Member State implementing that measure.[113] That said, a particular problem arises from the fact that many measures central to the provision of global public goods, such as the combating of piracy on the high seas, are taken under the Common Foreign and Security Policy (CFSP) pillar, which sets out the specialised regime for enacting measures on questions of international peace and security. According to the second paragraph of Article 24 (1) of Treaty on European Union (TEU) and the first paragraph of Article 275 TFEU, the ECJ cannot, in principle, adjudicate upon acts adopted in the context of the CFSP pillar. The only role played by EU courts concerning such measures is to police 'competence-creep' – that is, to prevent the use of the CFSP regime for measures that could have been enacted under other competences – and to police restrictive measures against individuals – that is, *Kadi*-style targeted sanctions.[114]

Most interesting for our purposes, however, is the longstanding tendency in ECJ jurisprudence of interpreting internal constitutional doctrines to prevent the EU from joining international organisations, precisely to insulate the EU legal order and its institutions from external judicial review or accountability. The prime examples of this are the two 'opinions' delivered by the ECJ on the legality of the EU's accession to the ECHR, a topic which will be relevant for the next chapter. In the first of these, *Opinion 2/94*, the Court held that the then European Communities were prohibited from acceding to the ECHR on grounds that the treaties did not confer any such competence upon it,[115] and that accession to the ECHR was too profound a constitutional development to be carried out without explicit treaty amendment.[116] The Lisbon Treaty set out to fix this in Article 6(2) TEU by explicitly providing that the Union shall accede to the ECHR and that such accession shall be carried out in a way that does not affect its internal competences. Notwithstanding this treaty change, the ECJ invalidated a second attempt to accede to the ECHR in *Opinion 2/13*, on the grounds that the form of accession as envisaged in the Draft Accession Agreement was 'liable adversely to affect the autonomy and effectiveness' of the preliminary reference procedure, and consequently, also 'liable adversely to affect the specific characteristics of EU law and its autonomy'.[117]

Instead of simply requiring greater assurances that the ECHR bodies would not muscle into the territory of the ECJ by issuing binding interpretations on questions of EU law,[118] the Court opined that accession to the ECHR would 'upset the underlying balance of the EU and undermine the autonomy of EU law',[119] effectively rendering Article 6(2) TEU an impossible constitutional

[113] See *ibid* 1055.
[114] Article 275 TFEU, Article 40 TEU.
[115] *Opinion 2/94* [1996] ECR I-1759, paras 23–30.
[116] *Ibid*, paras 33–35.
[117] *Opinion 2/13* ECLI:EU:C:2014:2454 (18 Dec 2014), paras 199–200.
[118] *Ibid*, paras 183–87.
[119] *Ibid*, paras 194.

command.[120] It began this line of its reasoning by observing that the ECHR had traditionally been open only to states, which the EU emphatically was not.[121] Despite the amendment of the ECHR to include non-state entities, the Court rehearsed the *Van Gend en Loos* dogma of the EU being a 'new kind of legal order' to claim that it could not accede to the ECHR in the same way as a state.[122] Once again, the Court's exact words merit close reading:

> The approach adopted in the agreement envisaged, *which is to treat the EU as a State and to give it a role identical in every respect to that of any other Contracting Party*, specifically disregards the intrinsic nature of the EU and, in particular, fails to take into consideration the fact that the Member States have, by reason of their membership of the EU, accepted that relations between them as regards the matters covered by the transfer of powers from the Member States to the EU *are governed by EU law to the exclusion, if EU law so requires, of any other law*.[123]

In the Court's view, the main structural feature of the EU 'new legal order' preventing it from acceding to the ECHR in the ordinary manner of states was the 'principle of mutual trust between the Member States', according to which the Member States are 'required to presume that fundamental rights have been observed by the other Member States', such that 'save in exceptional cases, they may not check whether that other Member State has actually, in a specific case, observed the fundamental rights guaranteed by the EU'.[124] What then prevents the EU legal order from degenerating into a vast conspiracy of silence? The ECJ's guardianship of fundamental rights within the new legal order. According to the ECJ, however, membership of the ECHR alongside its Member States would disturb this 'underlying balance' by allowing – or, in the Court's alarmist depiction – 'requir[ing]' every Member State 'to check that another Member State has observed fundamental rights' in areas governed by EU law.[125]

This reasoning has been criticised as dubious because inter-state disputes before the ECHR are in any case exceedingly rare,[126] and because in addition to the ECHR requirements of domestic exhaustion of remedies, there are already tools available at EU law for keeping disputes between the Member States 'inside the house' even if the EU is not itself a member of the corresponding

[120] T Isiksel, 'European Exceptionalism and the EU's Accession to the ECHR' (2016) 27 *European Journal of International Law* 565, 565.

[121] *Opinion 2/13* (n 117) paras 155–56.

[122] *Opinion 2/13* (n 117) paras 158.

[123] *Opinion 2/13* (n 117) para 193 (emphasis added).

[124] *Opinion 2/13* (n 117) para 192 (emphasis added).

[125] *Opinion 2/13* (n 117) para 194.

[126] Judge Spielmann, then at the Strasbourg Court, commented extrajudicially that 'Inter-State cases have been few, although they have not really been far between. Rather, they have tended to come in waves, and the Court is experiencing one such wave at present', and further speculated that that particular wave arrived for political and strategic reasons. Dean Spielmann, 'Speech to Gray's Inn: The European Court of Human Rights as Guarantor of a Peaceful Public Order in Europe' (7 November 2014) 1, www.echr.coe.int/Documents/Speech_20141107_Spielmann_GraysInn.pdf.

international organisation.[127] Moreover, the draft accession agreement contained a 'prior involvement procedure' prohibiting national constitutional courts from pronouncing on the ECHR compliance of measures implementing EU law before the ECJ had had an opportunity to do so.[128] On top of this, there is the '*Bosphorus* presumption' – a longstanding policy of the Strasbourg Court not to review measures implementing EU law on the charitable assumption that the EU provides a comparable level of rights protection as Strasbourg.[129] For these and similar reasons, commentators have largely condemned *Opinion 2/13* as little more than a brazen political manoeuvre by the ECJ to protect its bailiwick.[130]

This, however, raises the question of how the EU's internal constitution lends itself so easily to such misuse. In an incisive article, Turkuler Isiksel argues that the ECJ's attitude

> is nourished … from deep sources within the founding philosophy of European integration, according to which supranational institutions are possessed of political judgment that, while not inerrant, is capable of rising above the distortions of moral particularism and *raison d'état* that ensnare nation states.[131]

The supranationalism of the EU is, on this view, reason enough for it to be utterly convinced of its rectitude: 'a commitment to reason, universalism, and respect for law are held to be immanent within the structure of supranational governance and to constitute a sufficient safeguard against'[132] wrongful conduct. On the other hand, the 'nebulous concept' of the 'new legal order' also allows the ECJ to depict the EU as a system of abstract norms whose purity

[127] See, eg, the *Mox Plant* Decision, Case C-459/03 *Commission v Ireland* [2006] ECR I-4635. In that case, the Commission brought infringement proceedings against Ireland for submitting a dispute between itself and the UK regarding the interpretation of UNCLOS provisions on marine pollution to arbitration before ITLOS. The CJEU held that because the then European Community had ratified and incorporated UNCLOS into the EU legal order, Ireland's submission of the dispute with the UK to an external tribunal was in violation of Article 292 TEC (now 344 TFEU), which recognises the exclusive jurisdiction of EU courts 'to resolve disputes concerning the interpretation and application of provisions of Community law …' which in turn gave rise to 'a manifest risk that the jurisdictional order laid down in the Treaties and, consequently, the autonomy of the Community legal system may be adversely affected'. *Ibid*, paras 152–54.

[128] C Eckes, 'EU Accession to the ECHR: Between Autonomy and Adaptation' (2013) 76 *MLR* 254, 268–69.

[129] *Bosphorus Hava Yolları Turizm ve Ticaret Anonim Şirketi v Ireland*, App no 45036/98 (30 June 2005), paras 155–56.

[130] See, eg, E Spaventa, 'A Very Fearful Court? The Protection of Fundamental Rights in the European Union after Opinion 2/13' (2015) 22 *Maastricht Journal of European and Comparative Law* 35, 37 ('… the priorities of the Court post-Charter have not changed: EU integration and the defence of the Court's own hermeneutic monopoly seem to be the guiding principles before and above fundamental rights protection'); J Odermatt, 'A Giant Step Backwards – Opinion 2/13 on the EU's Accession to the European Convention on Human Rights' (2014) 47 *New York University Journal of International Law and Politics* 783.

[131] Isiksel (n 120) 578.

[132] Isiksel (n 120) 567.

can be maintained only by sealing it off from external scrutiny. The result is an 'overconfident belief that the EU, under the Court's own stewardship, has transcended the political and institutional flaws that typically generate' wrongs.[133] In this way, the ECJ 'keeps other institutional actors involved in European integration – including member states – guessing as to what may or may not be compatible with its basic structure, while reserving for itself the authority to pronounce on' the same.[134] In chapter seven, I develop upon Isiksel's insight to argue that the EU's ephemeral, changeling nature comes equally to its aid in its relations with distant strangers.

IV. CONCLUSION

A sovereign's sole purpose of ensuring its subjects' dignity implies obligations and consequently rights to provide public goods for its subjects, which are simply those things that must be provided publicly to ensure that no subject is left at the mercy of anybody else. This fundamental purpose cannot be frustrated by the arbitrary non-cooperation of other persons, state or non-state, domestic or foreign. All others must mandatorily cooperate with it to fulfil that purpose. In enforcing such cooperation seemingly 'unilaterally', the state need not demonstrate damage, because it has no property that can be damaged. The state must, however, subject itself to the jurisdiction of an international court where it must answer legal challenges concerning necessity and proper purpose, thereby curing such measures of their unilateralism. And so, despite its very different Kantian premises, this chapter ends by agreeing with Benvenisti's conclusions as discussed in chapter three. Just like for Benvenisti, the germ of the argument lies in a belief in the vital necessity of states as political institutions and of their fiduciary office, and also culminates in the possibility of sovereigns bearing fiduciary obligations toward distant strangers. However, while Benvenisti's model conceives of sovereigns as owing fiduciary obligations to humanity directly, my republican model holds instead that sovereigns owe fiduciary obligations first and foremost only to their subjects, but that in the course of fulfilling these obligations, they make themselves fiduciaries of the rest of humanity constructively. There is no need for other-regardingness, selflessness or philanthropy. Extraterritorial jurisdiction on republican principles is possible even for a nation of devils, if only they have understanding.

[133] Isiksel (n 120) 573.
[134] Isiksel (n 120) 577.

The extraterritorial assertion of 'jurisdiction' – understood in the proper sense as 'law speaking' – implies one more thing. As argued in the previous chapter, political authority is a fiduciary office, such that the assertion of political authority over subjects entails obligations in human rights towards them. Extraterritorial assertions of authority over distant strangers, such as in measures to provide global public goods, give rise to human rights obligations towards them. I turn to this in the next chapter.

6

Extraterritorial Human Rights Obligations

THE EU OWES perfect human rights obligations towards the distant strangers over whom it asserts authority. In contrast, where the EU merely asserts 'power' over distant strangers, it has no such obligations towards them whatsoever, no matter how devastating the factual effects may be. These two claims build upon arguments already presented, namely: (1) that the technique of 'territorial extension' employed the EU in extraterritorial legislation is essentially a claim of *authority* over distant strangers; (2) that authority is a fiduciary office entailing obligations of accountability towards subjects; and (3) that in so far as they are *legal* rights – that is, juridical entitlements to place others under obligations – human rights are simply accountability demands made by persons of their political authorities. This description is of course not intended as a transcendental account valid across time and space – that would be almost certainly impossible given that there appears to be little historical continuity in the use of the term 'human rights'[1] – but as an immanent description of the structure and rationale of the juridical claims going under that name in the contemporary 'European' legal practice. Put simply, I take human rights as they feature in the legal practice and make an interpretive claim as to where they 'fit' best within the scheme of Kant's philosophy of right.

My normative theory includes a claim that many readers might find distressing: the orthodoxy that human rights are possessed by all human beings at all times and in all places simply by virtue of being human is simply not true. If human rights and corresponding obligations arise from relations of authority, then 'jurisdiction' – a relation of authority and obedience – is the threshold that has to be crossed before any claim in human rights can obtain. Human rights are, like all rights, political. Moreover, I contend that this is not simply a practical threshold, but a conceptual one: without jurisdiction, human rights and the corresponding obligations are not just unachievable, but inconceivable. Outside of a minimal institutional context, human rights cannot even be *thought*. As such, if you are not a subject of authority, you have no rights at all.

[1] A famous recent work argues that the contemporary human rights movement traces its beginnings to no earlier than the 1970s. S Moyn, *The Last Utopia* (Cambridge, Harvard University Press, 2012).

Subsequent sections turn to positive law to demonstrate my normative claims in contemporary human rights legal doctrine, and particularly in the case law on the concept of 'human rights jurisdiction' as developed by the Strasbourg Court. Contrary to widespread literature and rhetoric, that practice does not actually treat the claims it calls human rights either as timeless, pre-institutional entitlements inhering in all human beings simply by virtue of their humanity but as presupposing a condition of political authority. Moreover, this cannot be explained as a practical consideration for making human rights 'feasible'; obligations under the European Convention on Human Rights (ECHR) have been imposed upon states with hardly any ability to do anything in the circumstances.

The choice of Strasbourg for illustrative purposes might strike the reader as odd given not just the repeated blocking of EU accession to the ECHR by the European Court of Justice (ECJ) as discussed in the previous chapter, but also the consecration of the EU Charter of Fundamental Rights ('EU Charter') as the EU's 'official' bill of rights by the Lisbon Treaty.[2] The first thing to note is that despite its rejection of the Strasbourg Court's jurisdiction in *Opinion 2/13*, the ECJ reiterated that according to 'Article 6(3) TEU, fundamental rights, as guaranteed by the ECHR, constitute general principles of the EU's law' even if the ECHR 'does not constitute a legal instrument which has been formally incorporated into the legal order of the EU'.[3] Moreover, Article 6(3) of the Treaty on European Union (TEU) speaks of the ECHR's normativity as a source of general principles of EU law on par with the 'constitutional traditions common to the Member States'. As such, it may be said that the ECJ views the ECHR jurisprudence as the most authentic articulation of the practice of human rights law. Second, the Strasbourg jurisprudence is far more developed than any other comparable body on questions of extraterritoriality, while that same subject has almost never been broached even in the scholarly literature on the EU Charter.[4] In fact, the lack of scholarly interest in the extraterritorial application of the EU Charter might simply be a reflection of the strength of ECHR extraterritoriality jurisprudence. For these reasons, the Strasbourg jurisprudence will continue to be an unavoidable point of reference, particularly on the issue of extraterritorial human rights obligations.[5]

[2] Article 6(1) TEU.

[3] See Case C-2/13 *Opinion 2/13* ECLI:EU:C:2014:2454 (18 December 2014), para 179, citing C-571/10 *Kamberaj v Istituto per l'Edilizia sociale della Provincia autonoma di Bolzano* ECLI:EU:C:2012:233 (26 April 2012), para 60; C-617/10 *Åklagaren v Åkerberg Fransson* ECLI:EU:C:2013:105 (26 February 2013), para 44.

[4] The only other major scholarly work in a language accessible to the author specifically examining the extraterritoriality of the EU Charter is a book chapter by Moreno-Lax and Costello. V Moreno-Lax and C Costello, 'The Extraterritorial Application of the EU Charter of Fundamental Rights: From Territoriality to Facticity, the Effectiveness Model' in S Peers et al (eds), *The EU Charter of Fundamental Rights* (Oxford, Bloomsbury, 2014).

[5] L Bartels, 'The EU's Human Rights Obligations in Relation to Policies with Extraterritorial Effects' (2014) 25 *European Journal of International Law* 1071, 1077.

I. HUMAN RIGHTS AS PUBLIC FIDUCIARY RIGHTS

A useful way to explicate my Kantian, 'political' conception of human rights would be by contrasting it against 'moral' theories of the same. What follows is explicitly not a refutation of such accounts – nothing remotely approaching that can be accomplished here – but merely an outline of the main points of difference. The contrast is perhaps best captured in the old saw about the temperamental difference between foxes and hedgehogs. Whereas what I describe as 'moral' theories display a sophisticated vulpine taste for richness and complexity, my Kantian account has a naïve and decidedly porcupine preference for unity.

A. 'Moral' Theories of Human Rights Law

Generally speaking, moral theories of human rights tend to begin by designating certain ends – normative agency,[6] satisfaction of basic needs[7] and facilitation of capabilities and functionings[8] – as ultimately valuable, such that human beings are variously ascribed 'moral' rights or obligations in respect of them, from which legal rights and obligations are derived taking into account the social context. As such, human rights *law* serves as 'efficient means' for the achievement of 'background' moral rights, which may themselves represent even more fundamental ends.[9] John Tasioulas, one of the most pre-eminent contemporary theorists of human rights, proposes that 'human rights are first and foremost moral standards and that IHRL's formative aim is to give those standards appropriate legal expression and effect'.[10] Tasioulas plumbs very deeply for philosophical justification: he starts from 'the idea of each and every individual human being as an ultimate focus of moral concern' to contend that human beings are, 'in virtue of our standing as human beings, *equipped with the capacity to realize certain values in our lives*, [such that] we possesses certain rights, independently of whether or not they are actually enforced or even recognized socially'.[11] As such, the 'idea' of human rights cannot 'ultimately consist in a system of [legal] principles, but in a distinctive *ethical* sensibility'.[12] Law is, in a

[6] See J Griffin, *On Human Rights* (Oxford, Oxford University Press, 2008).

[7] See H Shue, *Basic Rights: Subsistence, Affluence, and U.S. Foreign Policy*, 2nd edn (Princeton, Princeton University Press, 1996).

[8] See A Sen, *Development as Freedom* (New York, Knopf Doubleday, 2011).

[9] A Zylberman, 'Why Human Rights? Because of You' (2016) 24 *Journal of Political Philosophy* 321, 321.

[10] J Tasioulas, 'Saving Human Rights from Human Rights Law' (2019) 52 *Vanderbilt Journal of Transnational Law* 1167, 1207.

[11] J Tasioulas, 'Towards a Philosophy of Human Rights' (2012) 65 *Current Legal Problems* 1, 4.

[12] *Ibid* (emphasis added).

sense, secondary: the 'formative aim' of human rights *law* is to express or give effect to this sensibility. As such, Tasioulas remarks that

> Given that what is at issue are moral obligations corresponding to universal moral rights, there is no reason in principle to restrict the bearers of these obligations exclusively to states. Individuals, corporations, international organisations and other agents may also be directly subject to human rights obligations.[13]

Tasioulas's description of how these ethical sensibilities translate into legal rights and obligations is exquisitely intricate. Notwithstanding our supposedly innate human capacities to realise ultimate moral values, there are nevertheless on the first level 'pervasive frailties that afflict the human condition – ignorance, lack of empathy and imagination, laziness and inertia, the impulse to dominate, illegitimate self-preference, scarce resources, and so on' that prevent us from 'grasping those standards or adhering to their demands in practice'.[14] Leaving this aside, there is also the problem of explaining how general ethical norms are to be specified into 'directed' rights and obligations owed by one human being to another. Tasioulas describes this process of individuation essentially in terms of *allocation*: 'an obligation, which is the content of a right, will only exist if it is feasible, which is in turn a matter of it being *possible* to comply with and not *unduly burdensome*'.[15] He eventually develops a complex multi-part test requiring examination of: (1) the 'scope' of a right in terms of 'identification' with human interests; (2) the 'possibility' of advancing these rights through coercive obligations; (3) whether the obligations may be 'unduly burdensome'; and (4) whether the obligations may be complied with 'holistically' as a group, rather than on a 'one-on-one' basis.[16]

Each of these levels presents further mysteries.[17] The human interests involved at level (1) refer to a potentially 'irreducible plurality of values' whose *objective* importance 'is not conditional on their being objects of desire or preference on the part of those for whom they are good'.[18] The notion of a 'burden' at level (3) is similarly 'not simply to be explicated in terms of such factors as market

[13] J Tasioulas, 'Minimum Core Obligations: Human Rights in the Here and Now' (World Bank, 2017) 5, http://elibrary.worldbank.org/doi/book/10.1596/29144.

[14] Tasioulas (n 10) 1168.

[15] Tasioulas (n 13) 22. Tasioulas claims a slight Kantian inspiration in that he likens the process of 'progressive realization' of minimum core rights to Kant's description of how certain preliminary articles of the treaty for Perpetual Peace are merely *leges latae* to be implemented over time. See Tasioulas (n 13) 12–13, citing I Kant, 'Toward Perpetual Peace' [hereinafter '*PP*'] in MJ Gregor (ed & tr), *Practical Philosophy: The Cambridge Edition of the Works of Immanuel Kant*, 9th edn (Cambridge, Cambridge University Press, 2006) 8:347, 320–21.

[16] See, eg, J Tasioulas, 'Working on the Core: A Response to Commentators' (15 June 2018), http://jamesgstewart.com/working-on-the-core-a-response-to-commentators/. The number of parts to the test is somewhat unclear. In the 'Executive Summary' to the report, Tasioulas describes the test as having three parts. Tasioulas (n 13) vi. In a subsequent blog responding to critics, however, there seem to be four. Tasioulas, 'Working on the Core', *ibid*.

[17] Tasioulas (n 10) 1182 ('All three of these elements require complicated explication …').

[18] Tasioulas (n 10) 1181–82.

price or psychological commitments …'[19] Given these qualifications at every step, Tasioulas had written earlier that the process of specifying individual human rights takes more than what 'unaided moral reasoning can generate from within its own resources',[20] but requires resort to 'some form of social fiat, such as convention or positive law, to supplement the deliverances of natural reason'.[21] That said, social fiat and legalisation appear to bring difficulties of their own. In his earlier work, Tasioulas was concerned that the process of 'incarcerating human rights within a legal framework' might obscure 'the tremendous diversity of ways of life in which they are given shape and force'.[22] More recent work, however, complains that far from incarcerating it, human rights law has burst the bounds of human rights morality by inflating the number of recognised rights[23] and by conferring too much power upon unelected judges capable neither of deep moral introspection nor of empirical research.[24]

Samantha Besson, another prominent contemporary theorist of human rights law, similarly conceives the relationship between human rights obligees and obligors in terms of allocation.[25] She begins from a two-part premise about human rights as moral rights representing qualifying 'interests' to claim, first, that certain interests are vulnerable to 'standard threats', which then implies an 'abstract right' to the protection of that interest, which exists without the corresponding duty-bearers first having to be identified.[26] Second, she then turns to a parallel argument grounding human rights upon interests not according to their vulnerability to standard threats, but on the basis that they 'constitute part of a person's well-being in an objective sense',[27] such 'objectivity' being a function of their 'normative status' as an 'equal member of the moral-political community'.[28] Thus defined, human rights subsequently give rise to directed duties through a three-part process,[29] and only then – finally – are duties 'allocated'. This allocation is modelled on Shue's three-part typology of duties to respect, protect and fulfil, and 'takes place in context and at a specific time and place'.[30] While Besson argues, taking inspiration from Hannah Arendt, that

[19] Tasioulas (n 10) 1182.

[20] J Tasioulas, 'Human Dignity and the Foundations of Human Rights' in JC McCrudden (ed), *Understanding Human Dignity* (Oxford, Oxford University Press, 2013) 298.

[21] *Ibid.*

[22] Tasioulas (n 11) 2.

[23] Tasioulas (n 10) 1186–89.

[24] Tasioulas (n 10) 1202–206.

[25] See S Besson, 'The Allocation of Anti-Poverty Rights Duties: Our Rights, but Whose Duties?' in K Nadakavukaren-Schefer (ed), *Poverty and the International Economic Legal System* (Cambridge, Cambridge University Press, 2013).

[26] *Ibid* 413–14.

[27] *Ibid* 414.

[28] *Ibid.*

[29] *Ibid* 414–15.

[30] *Ibid* 416.

political institutions must be the 'primary duty-bearers' for claims of human rights,[31] she nevertheless claims that private individuals nevertheless come under 'residual or subsidiary' duties 'when their institutions have failed or before they have set up their institutions'.[32]

This same notion of human rights as background ethical objectives concretised in or allocated through law may be discerned in the text of the EU treaty provisions at the heart of this study. To recall, Article 21(2)(b) TEU speaks of human rights as objectives for which the EU is required to '*define* and pursue common policies … [and] work for a high degree of cooperation in all fields of international relations' to '*consolidate* and support …' (emphasis added). In a recent book on the incorporation of human rights considerations in investment treaties between the EU and third countries, Vivian Kube interprets these and like provisions as setting out a broad framework where the promotion or advancement of human rights constitute abstract foreign policy 'objectives'.[33] In contrast to other commentators who have generally been sceptical of the utility of the listed foreign policy objectives because of the vagueness with which they are formulated, Kube suggests that numerous mechanisms – from the reports by the EU Ombudsman to 'impact assessments' – may help sharpen or define the specific implications of each abstract foreign policy objective in the formulation of external policy.[34] As such, she urges that 'concrete obligations can be derived from the EU human rights framework when viewed against the factual context and in conjunction with other applicable EU law as well as the applicable international human rights law.'[35]

Finally, and perhaps of greatest relevance for this chapter, the notion that human rights and obligations are concretised and allocated moral principles also animates Marko Milanovic's widely-cited text on the extraterritorial application of human rights treaties. Milanovic notes that

> Universality and human dignity are undoubtedly the foundational principles of international human rights law, affirmed in binding treaties and non-binding declarations alike. But universality and human dignity are concepts that are too amorphous, in and of themselves, to overcome the threshold of state jurisdiction that is found in most human rights treaties.[36]

Like Tasioulas, Milanovic conceives of 'human dignity' in terms of well-being, but whereas Tasioulas conceives of well-being as lying in an open-ended

[31] Ibid 418–21. See also S Besson, 'The Right to Have Rights: From Human Rights to Citizens' Rights and Back' in M Goldoni and C McCorkindale (eds), *Hannah Arendt and the Law* (Oxford, Bloomsbury, 2012) 341–44.

[32] Besson (n 25) 421.

[33] V Kube, *EU Human Rights, International Investment Law and Participation: Operationalizing the EU Foreign Policy Objective to Global Human Rights Protection* (Cham, Springer, 2019).

[34] *Ibid* 55–75.

[35] *Ibid* 67.

[36] M Milanovic, *Extraterritorial Application of Human Rights Treaties: Law, Principles, and Policy* (Oxford, Oxford University Press, 2011) 56.

plurality of values,[37] Milanovic instead restricts this to simple utilitarian concepts of pleasure and pain.[38] The treaty provisions on 'state jurisdiction' are legally significant not simply because the instruments say so, but because, according to Milanovic, they serve to 'limit the obligations of contracting states to those situations where these [abstract] obligations could realistically be met and human rights effectively protected'.[39] On these lines, Milanovic proposes a three-part set of rules: 'negative' obligations to respect are territorially unlimited because it does not take much effort or resources to refrain from actively harming others outside the territory, while 'positive' obligations to do certain proactive things are 'limited to those areas that are under the state's effective control'.[40] In addition, Milanovic also proposes a third class of positive human rights obligations that do apply extraterritorially: 'prophylactic and procedural obligations' to investigate killings potentially perpetrated by state officials and agents on foreign territory.[41] Milanovic explains this last category as arising first because such obligations are closely connected to universally applicable negative obligations, and second, because all that is required of the duty-bearer is control and knowledge of the actions of its own agents.[42]

B. Human Rights as Legal and Directed all the Way Down

An authentically Kantian theory of human rights law differs radically from those described above. The first obvious point of departure is that for Kant, interests, needs, or other aspects of material well-being are not analytically basic. To recall once again the paradigmatic example from previous chapters, there is something objectionable in the condition of a well-kept slave whose needs, interests or functionings are extravagantly catered for by a kindly master, and even if the slave is entirely happy with this arrangement. Instead, the single organising principle of Kant's legal philosophy is the simple idea that a person's only natural right lies in not being a thing at the mercy of another. Previous chapters have established the idea that freedom thus conceived requires political institutions entitled to use force. Another less-explored feature of Kant's philosophy of right is the conceptual priority of law before ethics. As briefly introduced in chapter one, the thought is that we must first work out how to be free before even thinking about how to be good. This means, *pace* Tasioulas, that legal rights and

[37] Tasioulas (n 11) 26.

[38] See, eg, M Milanovic, 'The Drowning Child' (*EJIL: Talk!*, 3 September 2015).

[39] Milanovic (n 36) 56.

[40] Milanovic (n 36) 263.

[41] Milanovic (n 36) 215–19.

[42] Milanovic (n 36) 215–16, citing *R (on the application of Middleton) v West Somerset Coroner* [2004] UKHL 10 (HL), para 3.

obligations cannot be specified or individuated expressions of ultimate moral standards discerned through 'ordinary moral reasoning' because such moral reasoning is itself the artificial product of legally ordered institutions. Moreover, the reason why moral reasoning requires law and institutions is not because human beings are marked by pervasive frailties, but because *morality* would be incomplete. Without institutions, the demands of morality would be so self-contradictory that even a host of angels could not meet them. The fault is not just in ourselves, but also in the stars.

To illustrate, imagine you have absent-mindedly taken someone else's thing – say, a toothbrush. The intuitive, 'proper' thing to do would be to return the toothbrush, both because taking things habitually used and possessed by another is incompatible with your habitually using and possessing things, as well as incompatible with that other's fundamental right not to have themselves and their things subjected to the determining choice of anybody else. In a system of pure private interaction without institutions, however, such ordinary moral reasoning breaks down. Suppose you return the toothbrush 'unilaterally' – out of the kindness of your heart, concern for her welfare, or even just fidelity to the moral law. Because the sole motivation is the kindness of *your* heart, *your* concern for her welfare, *your* fidelity to the moral law, your attempt to 'do the right thing' still leaves the other's use and possession of the toothbrush at *your* mercy, and as such, goes nowhere in reversing the violation of their independence. At the same time, you are also prevented from allowing her to reclaim the toothbrush from you forcefully, for this would be to recognise a unilateral power on her part to designate you as a wrongdoer. Even if she is 'correct' in this determination, this remains an act of subjection to her sole determination. You would be entitled – even required – to resist her by force of your own.

In this way, 'ordinary moral reasoning' outside of institutions issues mutually incompatible demands, and so, ultimately none at all. The solution lies in postulating into existence a set of institutions to transform each person's unilaterally acquired external objects into peremptory property rights, to adjudicate disputes over rights according to a public procedure built around the presumption that no one has done wrong, and to guarantee these rights publicly by force.[43] Only if some semblance of this institutional context exists does returning the toothbrush cease to be just an act of unilateral charity and become a matter of rights. This is arguably reflected in the Universal Declaration of Human Rights' (UDHR) exhortation that 'Everyone has duties to the community *in which alone* the free and full development of his personality is possible.'[44] Rightful relations

[43] I Kant, 'The Doctrine of Right' [hereinafter '*DR*'] in MJ Gregor (ed & tr), *Practical Philosophy: The Cambridge Edition of the Works of Immanuel Kant*, 9th edn (Cambridge, Cambridge University Press, 2006) 6:307, 452.

[44] Article 29 UDHR.

are not just inconvenient in a system of pure private interaction; they are, in a sense, not fully *conceivable*.

The same applies to human rights as well. Recall Besson's claim that private persons come under residual or subsidiary 'human rights duties' relating to poverty before political institutions come into being or if they have failed. If the concept of duty implies at the very least a reason to criticise persons for non-fulfilment, then it becomes difficult to imagine how this could be correct. To tell persons caught in the middle of a civil war that they had duties, say, to build a bit of a hospital, seems deeply thoughtless no matter how residual, subsidiary or otherwise defeasible the duty is imagined, because one cannot judge them for fleeing altogether. To the contrary, their successful flight would be something to be welcomed, even to congratulate them for. Not for nothing does Kant declare that the

> greatest difficulty in the right of nations has to do precisely with right during a war; it is difficult even to form a concept of this or to think of law in this lawless state without contradicting oneself (*inter arma silent leges*).[45]

As such, contrary to the prevalent trend in the law and scholarship on the relationship between human rights and humanitarian law, a Kantian would contend that human rights law presumptively has no application in a pure context of armed conflict, where there is no suggestion of institutions.[46]

Accordingly, a Kantian account of human rights does not, and cannot start with an inquiry into what interests or values constitute universal or ultimate ends to be advanced through law. Rather, the starting point must be about how persons can interact with one another in a manner where no one is subject to the determining choice of another, such that each person can freely choose those ends for themselves. Such interaction, as explained in chapter four, is possible only in three *legal* forms, maintained by force by institutions whose relation to their subjects itself falls under the fiduciary form. As such, again contrary to Tasioulas, human rights, like all rights, are first and foremost *juridical*. A Kantian account of human rights thus has the salutary advantage of obviating the need for a curious feature of the alternative accounts of human rights law explored above: the multiple foundations, intricate multi-part balancing tests (which aren't really balancing tests), the host of abstract newly-invented abstract concepts which have themselves to be explained or limited by further newly-invented abstract concepts, all of which deliverances still require supplementation by analysis of facts peculiar to the circumstances.

[45] *DR* 6:347, 485.

[46] See, eg, *Legality of the Threat or Use of Nuclear Weapons, Advisory Opinion* [1996] ICJ Rep 226, para 25. See also Janina Dill's recent book chapter arguing that human rights law in principle applies all the time, but that it is displaced by humanitarian law due to epistemic and volitional gaps that arise in the onerous conditions of warfare. J Dill, 'Towards a Moral Division of Labour between IHL and IHRL during the Conduct of Hostilities' in Z Bohrer, J Dill and H Duffy (eds), *The Law Applicable to Armed Conflict* (Cambridge, Cambridge University Press, 2020).

Indeed, these immense difficulties faced by the conventional approaches may be a function of the fact that 'interests', 'needs' or 'values' are *monadic* concepts, while 'rights' and 'obligations' are *relational*. Because the former concepts pertain to one person alone, any theory of rights as expressions or manifestations of a particular person's welfare or of a subset of her interests ultimately renders them as non-correlative as the concepts of welfare and interests themselves.[47] In contrast, a Kantian account of human rights law does not have to fit the square peg of an interest or need into the round shape of a right, simply because its organising principle of independence is itself an irreducibly relational concept. From this irreducibly relational nature of human rights (indeed of all rights), it follows that rights and obligations are not contingently allocated according to the needs of the obligee or the convenience of the obligor, but that there is a necessary juridical reason why it is *this* obligor, rather than another, that can be compelled to make some performance to *that* obligee, rather than another.

In this regard, recall the general agreement between the various alternative accounts explored above on the idea that states and other organisations of jurisdiction are the 'primary' obligors; that is to say, the *public* aspect of human rights claims. This too is not contingent: there is a reason why it is this category of person that first comes to mind when we think about human rights obligors rather than say, powerful private multinational corporations. To recall a point from chapter four, human rights do not respond primarily to *private* moral or legal failures, regardless of how devastating their effects might be for your interests, needs or other aspects of material well-being. If 'human rights' have any purchase separate and distinct from other departments of law, it is that they attend to matters of *public* and systematic importance. To call yourself a victim of a human rights violation is to claim that your entire community has failed you. The human right to torture is thus not a right against all others to refrain from torturing you, but a right to a reasonable social guarantee that no one – including the provider of the guarantee – shall torture you. It is in this sense that human rights are 'basic' rights: they 'capture some of our basic ideals about life in society' and 'articulate the conditions required for realizing a social world under which we can relate to one another as equally independent'.[48] In another sense, however, human rights are not at all basic, but in fact the most awesome and extravagant demands one could ever make as of right. They presume the existence of public institutions, not only for their practical fulfilment but for their *conceptual* possibility. The corollary, however, is that there can be no rights whatsoever in the state of nature.

[47] See EJ Weinrib, *Corrective Justice* (Oxford, Oxford University Press, 2012) 21–22. For an illustration of the multiple logical hurdles facing the derivation of relational normative concepts from non-relational ones, see Zylberman (n 9) 323–26.

[48] A Zylberman, 'Human Rights and the Rights of States: A Relational Account' (2016) 46 *Canadian Journal of Philosophy* 291, 312.

Needless to say, the above account has several features readers might find objectionable. One might be that a cold indifference to interests and needs results in an empty theory that effectively takes 'the human out of human rights',[49] particularly given that the connection between urgent interests and human rights seems so very intuitive. It might appear self-evident that the wrongfulness of torture lies in the fact that 'Victims of torture not only suffer excruciating pain, their physical and mental health is threatened',[50] that the 'human right to a fair trial serves one's interest in liberty, the human right to health serves one's interest in health, and so on …'.[51] That 'status-based' theories of human rights would deny these apparently obvious intuitions are, for Tasioulas, their most 'egregious' flaw.[52] Second, the central role of the state in my political account of human rights might sound ludicrous, even offensive, to activists and practitioners whose experience may have taught them that it is precisely the state that is the root of all evil.[53]

Leaving aside the difficulty of deriving relational rights out of monadic interests, to accord foundational importance to interests also seems to produce a deflationary effect. On a suffering-based conception of torture, it would intuitively follow that the distinction between the right against torture and the right against inhuman and degrading treatment lies primarily in 'a difference in the intensity of the suffering inflicted'.[54] This, however, not only seems to miss something important but also appears to sanction – or at least not object to – interrogation techniques designed around thresholds of physical pain.[55] Similarly, the right to food does not appear primarily explicable in terms of avoiding the pain of hunger. Rather, a crucial element is that food be accessible and available so that people may feed themselves.[56] To construe it as

[49] A Buchanan, *Human Rights, Legitimacy, and the Use of Force* (Oxford, Oxford University Press, 2010) Ch 2.

[50] Tasioulas (n 11) 13.

[51] Tasioulas (n 11) 13.

[52] Tasioulas (n 11) 7.

[53] Tasioulas (n 11) 24 (observing approvingly that 'the language of human rights is often deployed by those implacably opposed to the state, or to its assertions of legitimacy …').

[54] *Ireland v UK* [1978] ECHR 1, para 167, citing Declaration on the Protection of All Persons from being Subjected to Torture and Other Cruel, Inhuman or Degrading Treatment or Punishment, UNGA Res 3452 (XXX) (9 December 1975) art 1 ('Torture constitutes an aggravated and deliberate form of cruel, inhuman or degrading treatment or punishment'). See also *Krajina, Prosecutor v Brđanin* (Judgment) ICTY-99-36-T (1 September 2004) ICL 121, para 483. ('The seriousness of the pain or suffering sets torture apart from other forms of mistreatment.')

[55] EJ Criddle and E Fox-Decent, *Fiduciaries of Humanity: How International Law Constitutes Authority* (Oxford, Oxford University Press, 2016) 107–10. See also US Department of Justice, Office of Legal Counsel, *Memorandum for Alberto R Gonzales Regarding Standards of Conduct for Interrogation under 18 USC §§ 2340-2340A* (1 August 2002) 1, www.justice.gov/sites/default/files/olc/legacy/2010/08/05/memo-gonzales-aug2002.pdf ('Physical pain amounting to torture must be equivalent in intensity to the pain accompanying serious physical injury, such as organ failure, impairment of bodily function, or even death.').

[56] General Comment No 12 – 'The Right to Adequate Food (Art 11)' (Committee on Economic, Social and Cultural Rights) UN Doc E/C 12/1999/5 paras 7–8, 12–13.

'a right to be fed' would imply a profound 'humiliation of those who are being fed'.[57]

As for the centrality of the state, recall Tasioulas's claim that the 'process of delineating and assigning counterpart duties' to *moral* human rights is unlikely to be 'entirely a matter resolved by pure moral reasoning', and that we need 'some form of social fiat, such as convention or positive law, to supplement the deliverances of natural reason'.[58] On what basis is this social fiat supposed to be issued? Could different societies issue different fiats? For such reasons, Evan Criddle and Evan Fox-Decent worry that this move 'does not resolve the problem so much as surrender to it …'.[59] Rather than roping in social fiat or any other conceptual phlogiston, Criddle and Fox-Decent prefer, as do I, to proceed from a 'conception of legality that has moral deliverances of its own'.[60] On the Kantian approach, all human rights – in fact, all rights – are explained by reference to the single idea that no one is to be subject to the will of another. To reiterate, this is not an interest or a value, but a status. Inhuman and degrading treatment consists in being treated as a thing incapable of choice, or as a thing whose choices are beneath consideration.[61] Torture, in contrast, lies in being instrumentalised: in being turned into a thing physically incapable of choosing. Once again, the sole guiding principle is freedom from domination, which gives rise to rights that cannot even be imagined in a system of pure private interaction. As Ariel Zylberman puts it, the reason why public authorities are legitimate not because of their instrumental effectiveness in securing needs, interests or goods, but because they are 'partly constitutive of our independence'.[62] Human rights supply the juridical means to ensure this independence, but they presuppose and depend upon a relationship of political authority and obedience.

[57] K Tomaševski, 'Human Rights Indicators: The Right to Food as a Test Case' in K Tomaševski and P Alston (eds), *The Right to Food* (Dorderecht, Martinus Nijhoff, 1984) 148. See also RE Robertson, 'The Right to Food – Canada's Broken Covenant' [1989] *Canadian Human Rights Yearbook* 185, 188 ('… the right to food is not synonymous with the right to be fed, for that implies an unhealthy dependence upon others').

[58] Tasioulas (n 20) 298. See also Besson (n 31) 342. Besson remarks that

> What makes it the case that a given individual interest is sufficiently fundamental or important to generate a duty … may be found in the normative status of each individual *qua* equal member of moral-political community. A person's interests merit equal respect in virtue of her status as a member of the community; those interests are recognised as socio-comparatively important by members of the community, and only then can they be recognised as human rights.

[59] Criddle and Fox-Decent (n 55) 93.

[60] Criddle and Fox-Decent (n 55) 93.

[61] See *Woodson v North Carolina* 428 US 280, 304 (1976) (declaring mandatory death penalty unconstitutional as cruel and unusual punishment on grounds that it treats convicted persons 'not as uniquely individual human beings, but as members of a faceless, undifferentiated mass to be subjected to the blind infliction of the penalty of death').

[62] Zylberman (n 48) 296.

C. Human Rights as Rights and as Philanthropy

Kant's strict separation of law from ethics, identification of law solely with the morality of interpersonal coercion, denial of rights outside of a lawful condition, and general boosting of sovereign states may at first glance appear to make his legal philosophy totally antithetical to the spirit of Articles 3(5) and 21 TEU, and the other provisions examined in chapter two. This, however, would be the wrong conclusion to draw, because while a state's legal obligations are one thing, its *ethical* duties are another matter altogether. The limitation of the EU's legal human rights obligations to instances where it creates legal effects in no way precludes a discussion of what it owes distant strangers as a question of foreign policy. This is a *political* matter requiring reflection upon the values that purportedly inspired the EU's creation and development. Moreover, my claim that human rights norms are not legal expressions or instantiations of ethical norms does not entail that foreign policy norms pertaining to human rights cannot be 'translated' into legal norms. Where EU internal constitutional rules dictate that its policymakers take account of, conduct impact assessments on, or consult stakeholders regarding any particular objective, then those rules arguably comprise administrative norms *internally* binding upon the EU.

As such, the account offered here does not totally contradict Kube's arguments regarding foreign policy objectives in the formulation of investment treaties between the EU and third countries. Instead, it is concerned with fundamentally different questions altogether. As stated in the introduction, this book deals with rightful relations between the EU and distant strangers; in other words, rights and obligations. The question of whether the EU possesses the *competence* to take any particular measure concerning distant strangers, is different from the question of whether that measure is rightful or wrongful as against those distant strangers. Put differently, to attack an EU measure for failure to advance human rights or any other enumerated foreign policy objective is not to claim that the EU has *wronged* the distant stranger, but to claim that it has acted beyond its competences or failed to comply with all procedural requirements.[63] As such, the complaint is not that the measure does wrong, but that it is *ultra vires*, and so, not properly an act of the EU at all. As will be explained in the next chapter, it is precisely this confusion of internal *vires* with external wrongfulness – of the 'right to act' with the 'rightfulness of the act' – that undermines the General Court's otherwise defensible Decision in *Polisario*.[64]

For similar reasons, the rich and fascinating literature on human rights conditionality in the EU's treaty relations with third states is also not relevant. The 'human rights clauses' routinely included as 'essential elements' in such

[63] *cf* C Ryngaert, 'EU Trade Agreements and Human Rights: From Extraterritorial to Territorial Obligations' (2018) 20 International Community Law Review 374, 388–89.

[64] Case T-512/12 *Front Polisario v Council* ECLI:EU:T:2015:953 (10 December 2015).

treaties since the 1990s purport to give one party the right to take 'appropriate measures' – often including the suspension of the agreement – in the event the other party fails to comply with specified human rights norms or violates democratic principles.[65] In the leading case on the subject, the ECJ defied the advice of the Advocate General and interpreted such a clause as creating a right on the part of the EU to take measures upon a triggering event; not an *obligation* to do so, let alone one personal to victimised persons in the third state.[66] Just as in *Commune de Champagne*,[67] a treaty between the EU and a third state does not, without more, create any legal relation between the EU and the distant strangers, much less a fiduciary relation. For this reason also, it would not be inconsistent with right for the EU to invoke clauses on labour rights conditionality, say, as a means of eliminating trade barriers.[68] This is not to say that blatantly self-interested invocations are unproblematic, but only that they are not problematic as human rights violations.

II. AUTHORITY AND HUMAN RIGHTS JURISDICTION

This section demonstrates the extent to which my above theoretical claims are reflected in the positive jurisprudence of the Strasbourg Court. To recall chapter two, the concept of human rights jurisdiction – or 'state jurisdiction' in the parlance of Article 1 ECHR – serves as a threshold in the contemporary human rights practice, such that states (and other comparable political organisations of jurisdiction such as the EU) have obligations corresponding to human rights only for claims arising within what is described as their 'jurisdiction'. Recall also that the concept of human rights jurisdiction has often been conflated with the general rules of jurisdiction in international law,[69] resulting in the criteria for human rights jurisdiction being identified with territorial control – in Besson's phrase, 'boots on the ground'.[70] In contrast, this chapter argues that the fundamental criterion for meeting the threshold of human rights jurisdiction is a claim of authority over a person, rather than some function of 'power' such as an ability to advance welfare or to control territory. This approach provides a clear answer for when the EU is under direct human rights obligations

[65] L Bartels, *Human Rights Conditionality in the EU's International Agreements* (Oxford, Oxford University Press, 2005) 23–26.

[66] Case C-268/94 *Portugal v Council* [1996] ECR I-6177, paras 27–28; *cf* Case C-268/94 *Portugal v Council*, Opinion of AG La Pergola [1996] ECR I-6180, para 28.

[67] Case T-212/02 *Commune de Champagne v Council* [2007] ECR II-2023.

[68] As suggested by the Advocate General in *Opinion 2/15 (EU-Singapore FTA)*, Opinion of AG Sharpston ECLI:EU:C:2016:992 (21 December 2016), paras 489–90.

[69] See Milanovic (n 36) 21–34.

[70] S Besson, 'The Extraterritoriality of the European Convention on Human Rights: Why Human Rights Depend on Jurisdiction and What Jurisdiction Amounts To' (2012) 25 *Leiden Journal of International Law* 857, 868.

towards distant strangers, and when it is not. Where the EU creates legal effects over distant strangers extraterritorially – pre-eminently via the method of territorial extension – it acquires obligations toward them in human rights, even if no boots ever touch the ground. Where the EU merely creates factual effects upon distant strangers, however, it is under no human rights obligations towards them whatsoever, regardless of how devastating those 'factual' effects may be.

Conceiving human rights jurisdiction in this way explains both how it differs from general jurisdiction in international law, as well as how the two concepts are related: Ordinarily, governments make law for their subjects – citizens, denizens, residents, visitors – for which the concept of 'territory' serves as shorthand. Therefore, their human rights jurisdiction ordinarily extends only over their territory. However, states exceed these bounds from time to time – sometimes legally, such as when they assert authority extraterritorially pursuant to a justified ground of jurisdiction such as the provision of a global public good, and sometimes illegally, for instance when they aggress upon and occupy other states' territories. In these exceptional situations, the state's human rights jurisdiction expands accordingly, regardless of whether the assertion of authority was itself legal. Thus, the correct measure of human rights jurisdiction is not the scope of the state's authority under the rules of jurisdiction in international law, but that claimed by the particular actor's municipal legal order, legally or not.[71]

These claims will be defended by a process of comparing and contrasting with other prominent theories of human rights jurisdiction that generally assume that a state's obligations depend upon its ability to exercise 'power'. While the same is also fundamentally true of Besson's account of human rights jurisdiction, her Arendtian commitments to the centrality of politics lead her to argue, as I do, that human rights jurisdiction is associated with authority, or as she terms it, 'normative power'.[72] Moreover, Besson's conception of authority is Razian, which, despite starting from very different premises, is capable of agreeing with the Kantian conception of authority as a fiduciary office.[73] Thus, despite fundamental theoretical disagreements, there are many superficial similarities between my Kantian account of human rights jurisdiction and Besson's. There are, needless to say, also some differences.

[71] *Ibid* 870 ('the state jurisdiction at stake in Article 1 ECHR is clearly a matter of law, but it is a matter of domestic law and not of international law …'). Similarly, Michał Gondek observes that 'a person may in certain circumstances be within the jurisdiction of a state party to a human rights treaty when he or she is outside state territory and an act of state affecting such person would not pass a test of what is legal under the international law of jurisdiction'. M Gondek, *The Reach of Human Rights in a Globalising World: Extraterritorial Application of Human Rights Treaties* (Cambridge, Intersentia, 2009) 56–57.

[72] Besson (n 70) 865.

[73] See, eg, J Raz, *The Morality of Freedom* (Oxford, Clarendon Press, 1986) 5 ('[Governments] do not have a legitimate interest of their own. The only interest a government is entitled to pursue is that of its subjects.'). On Besson's Razian inspirations, see S Besson, 'The Authority of International Law: Lifting the State Veil' (2009) 31 *Sydney Law Review* 343, 351–57.

The starting point for the doctrinal discussion of human rights jurisdiction is the 2011 Decision of the Strasbourg Court in *Al-Skeini*.[74] To recall chapter two, the Strasbourg jurisprudence on human rights jurisdiction took many turns after *Banković*, culminating eventually in *Al-Skeini*, where the Court discarded two of the central holdings of the *Banković* Decision. These were, first, that a state party had to be able to protect all the rights specified in the Convention for Article 1 of the ECHR jurisdiction to arise, rather than a 'divided and tailored'[75] version of it. Second, *Banković* had also held that the ECHR applied only within something called the '*espace juridique*' of the Council of Europe.[76] The *Al-Skeini* Court did away with this confabulation and held instead that state jurisdiction under Article 1 ECHR obtained anywhere in the world the Convention parties exercised (1) state agent authority and control over persons,[77] or (2) effective control over territory.[78] It then went on to find that the facts of the case fell within the first of these categories, on grounds that

> following the removal from power of the Ba'ath regime and until the accession of the interim Iraqi government, the United Kingdom (together with the United States of America) assumed in Iraq the exercise of some of the public powers normally to be exercised by a sovereign government. In particular, the United Kingdom assumed authority and responsibility for the maintenance of security in south-east Iraq. In these exceptional circumstances, the Court considers that the United Kingdom, through its soldiers engaged in security operations in Basra during the period in question, exercised authority and control over individuals killed in the course of such security operations, so as to establish a jurisdictional link between the deceased and the United Kingdom for the purposes of Article 1 of the Convention.[79]

A. Capability

The first theory of human rights jurisdiction of interest is offered by Yuval Shany, who links human rights obligations more or less with the 'capability' of parties to international human rights treaties to advance the material welfare of persons, regardless of where they are.[80] A long-time member and current vice-chair of the UN Human Rights Committee (HRC), Shany interprets the

[74] *Al-Skeini and ors v UK, Merits and just satisfaction* (2011) 53 EHRR 18.
[75] *Banković and ors v Belgium* (2001) ECHR 890, para 75, overruled by *Al-Skeini*, *ibid*, para 137.
[76] *Banković*, *ibid*, para 80, overruled by *Al-Skeini* (n 74) para 142.
[77] *Al-Skeini* (n 74) 133–37.
[78] *Al-Skeini* (n 74) paras 138–40.
[79] *Al-Skeini* (n 74) para 149.
[80] Y Shany, 'Taking Universality Seriously: A Functional Approach to Extraterritoriality in International Rights Law' (2013) 7 *Law & Ethics of Human Rights* 49, 54–60. See also O Ben-Naftali and Y Shany, 'Living in Denial: The Application of Human Rights in the Occupied Territories' (2003) 37 *Israel Law Review* 17, 71–76 (arguing from HRC jurisprudence that individuals fall within a state's human rights jurisdiction if the projection of that state's power has potential impacts that are direct, significant and foreseeable).

above passage from *Al-Skeini* as incorporating the HRC's jurisprudence on matters of extraterritorial application, in particular, he has in mind *López Burgos v Uruguay*, which involved the kidnapping of an Uruguayan national from Argentina, and his subsequent detention, and torture in Uruguay by Uruguayan paramilitaries.[81] In that communication, the HRC found Uruguay responsible for the International Covenant on Civil and Political Rights (ICCPR) violation taking place on Argentinian soil on the grounds that 'it would be unconscionable to ... interpret responsibility under [the ICCPR] as to permit a State Party to perpetrate violations of the Covenant on the territory of another State, which violations it could not perpetrate on its own territory'.[82] The *López Burgos* formula was adopted by the Strasbourg Court in the *Issa*, *Pad* and *Isaak* line of cases, where it held that 'Article I of the Convention cannot be interpreted so as to allow a State party to perpetrate violations of the Convention on the territory of another State, which it could not perpetrate on its own territory.'[83]

Additionally, Shany recalls *General Comment No 31*, the 'most authoritative summary to date of the HRC's position on the extraterritorial application',[84] where the HRC observed that

> a State party must respect and ensure the rights laid down in the Covenant to anyone within the power or effective control of that State Party, even if not situated within the territory of the State Party ... This principle also applies to those within the power or effective control of the forces of a State Party acting outside its territory, regardless of the circumstances in which such power or effective control was obtained, such as forces constituting a national contingent of a State Party assigned to an international peace-keeping or peace-enforcement operation.[85]

According to Shany, the *Al-Skeini* Decision adopts this HRC principle: he interprets the dispositive paragraph in *Al-Skeini* to indicate that 'the Court did not explicitly base its decision ... on the belligerent occupation of Basra by the Coalition forces ... or on the legal obligations that ensued from this particular state of affairs',[86] but on the fact that

> the UK substituted in a functional sense the authority of the local Iraqi government. Put differently, the Court found that the UK was both capable and particularly well

[81] UNHRC, *López Burgos v Uruguay* UN Doc CCPR/C/13/D/52/1979, UN Doc A/36/40 Annex XIX (29 July 1981).

[82] *Ibid*, para 12(3). See also UNHRC, *Lichtensztejn v Uruguay* (Merits) UN Doc CCPR/C/18/D/77/1980 (31 March 1983), para 6(1); UNHRC, *Celiberti de Casariego v Uruguay* UN Doc CCPR/C/13/D/56/1979, UN Doc CCPR/C/OP/1, 92 (29 July 1981), para 10(3)–11.

[83] *Issa and ors v Turkey, Merits* (2004) 41 EHRR 567, para 71. See also *Pad and ors v Turkey, Admissibility*, App no 60167/00 (28 June 2007), para 54; *Isaak v Turkey, Admissibility*, App no 4458798 (28 September 2006), para 19.

[84] Shany (n 80) 53.

[85] UNHRC, 'General Comment No 31: The Nature of the General Legal Obligation Imposed on States Parties to the Covenant' (2004) UN Doc CCPR/C/21/Rev.1/Add.13, para 10.

[86] Shany (n 80) 60.

situated to assume government responsibilities *vis-à-vis* the population of Basra, including its obligations to protect their human rights.[87]

If Shany is right that the British were capable or well-situated in Southern Iraq, one may wonder if it is ever possible to be incapable or poorly-situated. That precise contention had been characterised earlier by the English Court of Appeal as 'utterly unreal'.[88] The correct reading of that passage is precisely the interpretation that Shany rejects: the UK's obligations stemmed from its participation in the belligerent occupation of Basra. Reading the dispositive paragraph, it is apparent that uppermost in the Court's mind was not the fact the Coalition forces were 'capable' or 'well-situated' to exercise governmental powers, but that they had actually *done* so: they 'assum*ed*' public powers, and 'exercis*ed*' authority and control over the victims. It was irrelevant whether they had the wherewithal to do it well. More importantly, the language of *Al-Skeini* differs from the HRC's in a subtle but important respect: not 'power and effective control', but '*authority* and control'.

The most obvious objection to Shany's approach is that human rights obligations – for that matter all legal obligations – are not imposed just because they *can* be imposed.[89] Shany tries to address this critique by countering that feasibility is merely the first criterion.[90] Instead, he insists that in addition to being in a position where they are able to do so, it must either be shown that: (1) the impact of the obligation not being imposed must be 'direct, significant and foreseeable'; or (2) there must be a 'legitimate expectation' that the state in question will intervene, arising from 'special legal relations' between the state and the individual involved.[91] Additional criterion (1) is a requirement of urgency, which does indeed address the concern that human rights obligations are imposed too lightly. Unfortunately, it accomplishes this rather too well; the requirements of directness and significance reduce human rights obligations to humanitarian obligations, precluding less spectacular violations from redress. Moreover, the 'special legal relationship' in additional criterion

[87] Shany (n 80) 60.

[88] *Al-Skeini and ors, R (on the application of) v Secretary of State for Defence* [2005] EWCA (Civ) 1609 (CA), para 124.

[89] For a similar approach, see the 'Maastricht Guidelines on Violations of Economic, Social and Cultural Rights' (1998) 20 *Human Rights Quarterly* 691, s 18:

> The obligation to protect includes the State's responsibility to ensure that private entities or individuals, including transnational corporations over which they exercise jurisdiction, do not deprive individuals of their economic, social and cultural rights. States are responsible for violations of economic, social and cultural rights that result from their failure to exercise due diligence in controlling the behaviour of such non-state actors.

See also M Scheinin, 'Just Another Word? Jurisdiction in the Roadmaps of State Responsibility and Human Rights' in M Langford, *Global Justice, State Duties: The Extraterritorial Scope of Economic, Social, and Cultural Rights in International Law* (Cambridge, Cambridge University Press, 2013); and Moreno-Lax and Costello (n 4).

[90] Shany (n 80) 70.

[91] Shany (n 80) 69–70.

(2) appears not to be a normative relationship, but one where the state is 'particularly well-situated to protect that said individual'.[92] It is, in effect, a second capability threshold; a state must not only be capable of bearing extraterritorial human rights obligations but also be 'particularly well-situated', the quality of well-situatedness being 'captured by the tests of directness, significance and foreseeability (eg effective control over the territory in which the individual in question resides or physical control over his or her person) …'.[93]

Nonetheless, Shany's discussion of the conditions in which it is legitimate to expect a state party to intervene does at times indicate that there might be more to it than just the effective delivery of outputs. For instance, he speaks of a second category of 'special legal relationships, which … generate strong expectations that it would do so by virtue of the special legal position of the state *vis-à-vis* the individual',[94] but provides no further explanation as to how or on what basis such special relations arise. This, however, effectively ignores arguably the most interesting paradox presented by the idea of extraterritorial human rights jurisdiction in situations of illegal occupation, thereby giving rise to an objection that Naz Modirzadeh expresses particularly powerfully:

> while I understand the short-term gains of demanding that the British respect human rights law in their actions in Iraq, … I do not *want* an occupying power that has invaded my State to be recognized by the international community as having a 'rights-based' relationship with my population. I do not want that State to be in a position to argue that it has to engage in certain institutional changes in order to be able to comply with its human rights obligations back home. I do not want a State that has no relationship to civil society in my country, has no long-term understanding of my population, its history, its religious values, etc, to have a hand in shaping its human rights framework simply by virtue of its choice to invade.[95]

In short, to justify obligations merely on capability is to ride roughshod over the self-determination of distant strangers. Even if one were to assume that human rights and corresponding obligations are merely contingently related, the 'demand-side' of the equation would still require an analysis of the 'supply-side' considerations; that is, of 'egalitarian and … democratic decision-making on those complex moral issues of allocation of human rights obligations and responsibilities for human rights'.[96] Ignoring such considerations may very well undermine any sense of legitimacy. As a practical matter, measures imposed from on high are unlikely to be internalised and are liable to be abandoned at the first opportunity. Thus, the notions of 'legitimate expectation' and 'special legal

[92] Shany (n 80) 69.
[93] Shany (n 80) 69.
[94] Shany (n 80) 69.
[95] N Modirzadeh, 'The Dark Side of Convergence: A Pro-Civilian Critique of the Extraterritorial Application of Human Rights Law in Armed Conflict' (2010) 86 *International Law Studies (US Naval War College)* 349, 375.
[96] Besson (n 25) 430.

relationships' simply require a normative account of authority and obedience, especially in situations where the claim to authority is fundamentally defective.

In this regard, while otherwise fundamentally irreconcilable with my Kantian framework, Raz nevertheless suggests a viable way of understanding how an illegal invader might acquire obligations of accountability in human rights in the same way as a properly constituted authority, while at the same time denying recognition of their title to govern as rightful. Raz distinguishes between two different senses of the word 'authority': (1) 'authority to perform actions' – *authorisation*; and (2) 'authority over persons' – that is, the claim of an entitlement to tell people what to do and force them to do as told. This distinction, in turn, gives rise to a further distinction between *de jure* and *de facto* authority. '*De jure* authority' combines 'authority to perform actions' and 'authority over persons',[97] in that it illustrates the sense in which assertions of authority by officials belonging to institutions governed by a legal framework are themselves carried out 'under authority'. In contrast, *de facto* authority consists solely of authority over persons. It is not itself 'authorised'; that is, valid in terms of pedigree. A judge who improperly issues an injunction against you does so without authorisation, but you are nonetheless bound by it until and unless it is discharged. Despite having no legal authorisation, the judge has acted as if she does: though *ultra vires*, her acts are nevertheless carried out 'under colour of law'. In this way, *de facto* authorities do not simply 'exert naked power (e.g. through terrorizing a population or manipulating it)' but 'act … under the guise of legitimacy'.[98] The necessary and sufficient condition for human rights obligations, on this view, is 'authority over persons', not 'authority to perform actions'. On the Razian approach, the 'supply-side' of authority is irrelevant.

In a forthcoming book, Arthur Ripstein expresses a similar but explicitly relational idea by imagining the example of a relationship between a kidnapper and a child abducted at a very early age. Kidnapping a child is, without doubt, a highly wrongful and defective means of establishing a relationship with it. Equally, without doubt, the rightful thing for the kidnapper to do is to return the child to its parents, but this is entirely beside the point. Instead, the relevant inquiry is to ascertain what is morally required within the relationship between the kidnapper and the child, notwithstanding its fundamental wrongfulness. A moment's thought reveals that the kidnapper owes that child exactly the same obligations of a loving parent: she must not just refrain from abusing the child,

[97] J Raz, 'Legitimate Authority' in *The Authority of Law: Essays on Law and Morality*, 2nd edn (Oxford, Oxford University Press, 2009) 19–20. See also E Fox-Decent, *Sovereignty's Promise: The State as Fiduciary* (Oxford, Oxford University Press, 2011) 90–91 (defining '*de facto* sovereignty' as the 'brute ability to govern through effective institutions' and '*de jure* sovereignty' as 'the state's authority to do so', the latter further separating into *legal* and *political* bases of sovereignty).

[98] J Raz, 'The Problem of Authority: Revisiting the Service Conception' (2006) 90 *Minnesota Law Review* 1003, 1005 (citations omitted).

but must actively care for its safety, nutrition and education. She must do all this for no reason other than that she has held herself out as a parent toward that child. It is conceivable that the kidnapper might care for the child even better than the child's rightful parents would have done. While this is relevant to the question of whether the kidnapper fulfils her obligations *in her role* as a parent, it in no way justifies or redeems the wrong by which she *became* a parent. The original act of kidnapping is and remains utterly unforgivable.[99]

These notions translate to the analysis of human rights obligations in instances of occupation, legal or not. To wit, an occupier who does not harm or even advances the material interests of the inhabitants nonetheless wrongs them formally:

> Alien control renders a people vulnerable to the will of another state or agency and undermines the ability of the dominated people's institutions to govern and represent their members … Ultimately, alien control of a nation dominates the nation's members as well as the nation's collective legal personality.[100]

Nevertheless, even within that deeply wrongful condition, claims of right can be made. For the Kantian, it is not so much that the 'supply side' falls away, but the fact of the occupier's assumption of a role – whether licit or not – that matters. Where an occupation is illegal, the occupying power 'is subject to the same general set of obligations that attach to any exercise of political power over human beings'.[101] Where the occupation is legal, the occupant's 'moral obligations in governing are the same as they would have been if it were legitimately in the role of an occupying power. Those obligations, in turn, are just the obligations that it would have as a legitimate ruler'.[102] Human rights obligations, therefore, arise upon the *actual* 'exercise of some of the public powers normally to be exercised by a sovereign government', not the capacity or well-situatedness to advance welfare. In this way, human rights obligations prevent political institutions from treating the human beings they assert *de facto* political authority over as *de jure* outsiders.[103] They may not be heard to disclaim

[99] A Ripstein, 'Kant and the Law of War' (Manuscript on File with Author) (28 June 2018) 99–100.

[100] E Fox-Decent and EJ Criddle, 'The Fiduciary Constitution of Human Rights' (2009) 15 *Legal Theory* 301, 333.

[101] Ripstein (n 99) 100.

[102] Ripstein (n 99) 100.

[103] Shany voices a version of this concern in an earlier piece co-authored with Orna Ben-Naftali, contending that human rights law properly applies in the occupied territories concurrently with protections under humanitarian law. Ben-Naftali and Shany (n 80). Citing the fact that some of the most outrageous Nazi atrocities were directed precisely against individuals in occupied territories, Ben-Naftali and Shany correctly reject the Israeli Government's then legal argument that 'jurisdiction' for the purpose of human rights are obtained 'only between a State and its *citizens*'. Ben-Naftali and Shany (n 80) 62. In order to get around this problem, they expand the concept of jurisdiction to include factual power; that is, the 'actual or potential exercise of governmental power vis-à-vis all affected individuals'. Ben-Naftali and Shany (n 80) 61–63. My response has been instead to elaborate the relations states may have with human beings that are analogous to the authority-relation they have with their citizens.

their responsibility on municipal legal grounds, by alleging their own turpitude (say, in cases of illegal occupation), or raising logistical or other difficulties. Human rights jurisdiction is therefore properly limited to situations involving actual exercises of authority, and not mere factual capability to improve material well-being.

B. Control

The second account of human rights jurisdiction of interest is that offered by Marko Milanovic, whose 2011 monograph is, as already noted, by far the most well-known and widely cited work on the topic. After an exhaustive study of numerous human rights treaties but with an emphasis on the ECHR, Milanovic concludes that the term 'jurisdiction' in human rights treaties is best understood as denoting 'state control over territory, and perhaps individuals'.[104] From this premise, as already introduced above, Milanovic constructs a three-part model where: (1) negative obligations to respect are territorially unlimited; (2) positive obligations to protect and fulfil are 'limited to those areas that are under the state's effective control';[105] (3) a special class of positive obligations termed 'prophylactic and procedural obligations' also apply on foreign territory requiring state parties to investigate killings potentially perpetrated by state officials and agents.[106] Thus, despite claiming to supply a principled account of extraterritorial human rights obligations, what Milanovic actually provides is a deeply pragmatic compromise between competing policy considerations, where what ultimately counts is the factual ability to achieve particular states of material well being.[107]

At one point, Milanovic anticipates something that sounds a bit like the authority-based theory of human rights jurisdiction offered here, but rejects it on the basis that limiting human rights jurisdiction only to those instances where states act pursuant to some legal authorisation 'would open the door to abuse' by allowing them to get away with clandestine violations committed solely through brute power.[108] While

> an exercise of a legal power or authority by a state over an individual outside its territory would suffice to satisfy the jurisdictional threshold … *[l]imiting* the personal model to such purported exercises of legal power … would be entirely arbitrary, and would only serve to undermine the rule of law by creating a perverse incentive for states to act outside their own legal system if they wish to violate human rights.[109]

[104] Milanovic (n 36) 262.
[105] Milanovic (n 36) 263.
[106] Milanovic (n 36) 215–19.
[107] Milanovic (n 36) 263 (describing his rule as providing 'the benefit of clarity and predictability, [and] the best balance among its competitors between the conflicting demands of universality and effectiveness'). See generally Milanovic (n 36) Ch 3, on 'Policy Behind the Rule'.
[108] Milanovic (n 36) 206–207.
[109] Milanovic (n 36) 207.

This claim does not actually undermine the theory provided here because, to put it in Razian terms, the relevant sense of authority for human rights obligations is 'authority over persons', *not* 'authority to perform actions'. Any act creative of legal effects over a person suffices to give rise to human rights jurisdiction, even if that act was itself *ultra vires* per the internal constitution of the actor. In other words, there is no incentive for states to subvert their internal legal rules because they are obligated regardless of the legality of their acts under municipal law.

The more pressing issue for our purposes concerns Milanovic's classification of human rights obligations into negative and positive obligations. As mentioned above, he invents an exceptional set of positive obligations – 'prophylactic and procedural obligations' to investigate killings – that do apply extraterritorially. Milanovic explains these as obtaining first because such obligations are closely connected to universally applicable negative obligations, and second, because all that is required of the duty-bearer is control and knowledge of the actions of its own agents.[110] On his view, a state is not required to investigate an extraterritorial human rights violation in which its agents did not participate at all, unless the act was committed in a territory under its effective control.[111] In other words, the obligation to investigate a killing arises from the possibility that it may have been committed by a state agent. Attribution is therefore central to explaining them. While Milanovic distinguishes between the concepts of attribution and human rights jurisdiction and rightly criticises early Strasbourg cases for conflating them, 'prophylactic and procedural obligations' are, on his scheme, an instance where attribution is a prerequisite for jurisdiction.[112]

Milanovic's text was written in the doctrinally unstable period after *Banković* was handed down, and can be described as a richly deserved polemic against it.[113] Nevertheless, despite his prediction that his would be 'the only model of state jurisdiction and extraterritorial application that is stable in the long run',[114] the doctrinal settlement that emerged after *Al-Skeini* does not resemble Milanovic's model very much nor does this appear likely to change. *Banković* would still

[110] Milanovic (n 36) 212–16.

[111] See Milanovic (n 36) 217 (arguing that the 'positive procedural' obligation to investigate killings would not obtain 'were they done by third parties, be they insurgents or indeed the soldiers of an allied country ... since they took place in an area outside its jurisdiction, and it would in fact be exceedingly difficult, if not impossible, for the [state party] to conduct an effective investigation without having control over the territory').

[112] Milanovic (n 36) 51–52. On the difference between human rights jurisdiction and state responsibility, see generally Milanovic (n 36) 41–52.

[113] See, eg, Milanovic (n 36) 264. ('Let me conclude by saying that I certainly do not suffer from the naïve belief that my proposed model of extraterritorial application will be adopted any time soon. At least when it comes to Strasbourg, it requires a major departure from existing jurisprudence, above all from *Bankovic*.')

[114] Milanovic (n 36) 263.

be decided the same way if it came before the Court today, albeit on different reasoning.[115] While there was some reason to think otherwise following the *Issa*, *Pad* and *Isaak* line of cases mentioned earlier, these precedents are isolated in the jurisprudence, and can no longer be treated as persuasive following *Al-Skeini*.

Specifically, Milanovic's theory of prophylactic and procedural obligations was rejected in *Jaloud v Netherlands*, which involved a fatal shooting of an Iraqi by a Dutch soldier at a checkpoint manned by a Dutch battalion participating in the United States and United Kingdom-led military coalition, assisted by Iraqi troops under their command.[116] As in *Al-Skeini*, it was not the shooting itself that was at issue, but the subsequent failure by the relevant Dutch military officials to investigate it. In fact, the Court acknowledged there were severe obstacles to carrying out such an investigation, with one concurring opinion criticising the majority for not making it clearer that the complaint was not about the conduct of the Dutch soldiers, but that of the Dutch military courts.[117] The Court emphatically (if somewhat incorrectly) maintained 'that the test for establishing the existence of "jurisdiction" under Article 1 of the Convention has never been equated with the test for establishing a State's responsibility for an internationally wrongful act under general international law'.[118] This point was driven home in Judge Spielmann's concurring opinion, which rebuked the majority for even mentioning the topic.[119] Instead, the Court held that the Netherlands' human rights jurisdiction arose simply because the applicant 'met his death when a vehicle in which he was a passenger was fired upon while passing through a checkpoint manned by personnel under the command and direct supervision of a Netherlands Royal Army officer'.[120]

Despite the Court's perspicuity on the matter, Milanovic nevertheless insists that 'attribution is an issue in *every single case*, *Jaloud* included … [because for] a state to be responsible for any violation of the Convention, the conduct

[115] M Milanovic, 'Al-Skeini and Al-Jedda in Strasbourg' (2012) 23 *European Journal of International Law* 121, 132 ('… drone operations in Yemen or wherever would be just as excluded from the purview of human rights as under *Bankovic*'). See also J Dyson, 'Essex Lecture 2014: The Extraterritorial Application of the European Convention on Human Rights' (2014), www.judiciary.gov.uk/wp-content/uploads/JCO/Documents/Speeches/lord-dyson-speech-extraterritorial-reach-echr-300114.pdf ('It is likely that, if it were faced with the facts of *Bankovic* today, the Court would reach the same conclusion as it did in 2001, but its analysis would now depend on the degree of authority and control the respondent State exercised over the applicants, not where they were located or whether their cases could be squeezed into one of the exceptional categories to territorial jurisdiction.').

[116] *Jaloud v Netherlands* (2014) ECHR 1292.

[117] *Ibid*, para 226. See also *ibid*, para 4.

[118] *Ibid*, para 154, citing *Catan v Moldova and Russian Federation* (2012) ECHR 1827, para 115.

[119] *Jaloud* (n 116) (Concurring Opinion, Judge Spielmann) paras 5, 7 (criticising the majority's discussion of attribution as being 'ambiguous, subsidiary, and incomprehensible', as well as unnecessary and likely to confuse).

[120] *Jaloud* (n 116) para 152.

of some human being has to be *attributed* to that state'.[121] Milanovic rightly distinguishes between the concepts of attribution and human rights jurisdiction: '*Attribution of conduct* is a question of whether the acts or omissions of a living, breathing human being (or group of human beings) should *in law* be regarded as the conduct of a state ….' According to him, however, human rights jurisdiction, on the other hand,

> poses two different questions – does a state exercise effective control of an area or territory in which the victim of the alleged human rights violation is located (spatial model of jurisdiction), or does the state, through its agents, exercise authority and control over the individual victim of the alleged human rights violation (personal model of jurisdiction).

He also once again correctly distinguishes between 'jurisdiction-establishing conduct' and 'violation-establishing conduct'. The Court could not have decided as it did without attributing both forms of conduct to the Netherlands, but for Milanovic, this means *Jaloud* must have involved 'not one, *but two*, attribution inquiries'.[122]

Because physical 'control' or the factual ability to achieve levels of well-being is the touchstone of his theory, Milanovic places great importance upon *causal* links between the putative rights-claimants and corresponding duty-bearers. Attribution is key: he sees 'jurisdiction-establishing conduct' in terms of 'acts or omissions by which a state, through its organs or agents, establishes control over an area or control over an individual'.[123] As such, 'When a state exercises jurisdiction, i.e. control over a foreign territory or individuals, it by definition needs to do so through its agents, i.e. persons whose acts are attributable to it.'[124] From this, it must follow that there can be no Dutch human rights jurisdiction if: (1) there can be no imaginable involvement by Dutch soldiers in the shooting: or (2) any such acts of involvement were attributable to the United Kingdom, under whose orders its soldiers operated. If there was no imaginable Dutch involvement in the shooting, nothing the Netherlands did could have had any bearing upon the claimants' well-being. Even if there was some bearing on the claimants' well-being, the Netherlands would not have been accountable, since its soldiers were under the direction of the United Kingdom.

The flaw in this reasoning can be revealed by expressing two different senses of the word 'responsible', where 'attribution' pertains to one sense and 'jurisdiction' to the other. The question of 'Who is responsible?' can be taken to mean 'Who did this?' – an inquiry into *attribution*. However, that same question

[121] M Milanovic, 'Jurisdiction and Responsibility: Trends in the Jurisprudence of the Strasbourg Court' in A van Aaken and I Motoc (eds), *European Convention on Human Rights and General International Law* (Oxford, Oxford University Press, 2018) 105.

[122] *Ibid* 107.

[123] *Ibid* 106. One wonders how physical control over areas or individuals may be established by omission.

[124] Milanovic (n 36) 51.

can also be taken as asking 'Who is in charge?' – the question of *jurisdiction*. Milanovic identifies being 'in charge' with having physical control over territory or persons, but a moment's thought reveals that this cannot be right. As demonstrated by the discussion of territorial extension in chapter two, it is possible to effect profound changes in a place purely through *legal* effects; that is, by exercising what international lawyers call 'prescriptive jurisdiction' over persons there. If the notion of responsibility relevant for human rights jurisdiction is understood in terms of claiming to be 'in charge', rather than of doing things or controlling those who do things, then the link between attribution and jurisdiction is broken. It becomes possible to explain *Jaloud* without claiming that the Strasbourg judges were twice engaging in attribution analysis despite vehemently denying it. There is no need to trace or manufacture causation to potential acts relating to territory or persons. A parent has a positive obligation to rescue her child from drowning in a puddle, not because it was she who most likely pushed it into that puddle, but simply because she is that child's fiduciary. The responsibility involved here is not causal, but *managerial*. Likewise, it could legitimately have been expected of the Netherlands, having held itself out as a public authority over people passing through the checkpoint, that a shooting occurring under its nose would not go un-investigated, regardless of who did it. Authority implies liability for omissions, just like the fiduciary obligation of loyalty.

Even if the Dutch soldiers had been placed 'at the disposal' of the United Kingdom or of any other power,[125] the Netherlands could not have disclaimed responsibility on the grounds that its soldiers were only following orders.[126] Once again, the criterion for human rights obligations is not authority to perform acts but authority over persons. The 'supply side' pedigree or chain of authorisation is irrelevant. If the Dutch troops concerned had indeed been at the disposal of the United Kingdom, the proper solution would have been to find that both the Netherlands' and the United Kingdom's human rights jurisdiction had arisen. The finding of human rights jurisdiction has nothing to do with traceability of consequences to a particular actor's agency or with its being the last link in a chain of command, but everything to do with its having held itself out as an authority over an individual.

There is even a sense in which one can be considered 'in charge' even if one is completely unable to exert *any* factual control over a situation.[127] Such a notion arguably underlies the pre-*Al-Skeini* Decision of *Ilaşcu*, where the Court held

[125] The Court found otherwise. *Jaloud* (n 116), para 151.

[126] This was indeed the approach taken in *Behrami*, where France successfully denied jurisdiction because its actions in Kosovo were ultimately attributable to NATO. *Behrami and Behrami v France, Saramati v France, Germany and Norway, Admissibility* (2007) 45 EHRR 10, paras 132–43, 151. See M Milanović and T Papić, 'As Bad as It Gets: The European Court of Human Rights's *Behrami and Saramati* Decision and General International Law' (2009) 58 *ICLQ* 267.

[127] See DL Attanasio, 'The State Obligation to Protect' (PhD thesis, University of California, Los Angeles, 2015) 105–109.

that despite having lost control over a portion of its territory to the Russian-sponsored Transdniestrian puppet government, Moldova nevertheless had a positive obligation to use all of the diplomatic, economic, judicial and other measures within its ability to secure the ECHR rights of individuals held in the breakaway region.[128] The Court reaffirmed this reasoning eight years later in *Catan*, which involved violations of the right to education in Transdniestria.[129] A similar position was taken by the Inter-American Court in *Pueblo Bello Massacre v Colombia*, which held Colombia responsible for human rights violations committed by rebel paramilitaries in a region where the central government exercised only very tenuous control.[130]

Notwithstanding its firm establishment in the Strasbourg jurisprudence and beyond, the *Ilaşcu-Catan* line of cases is almost universally criticised by scholars taking the conventional approach. This is understandable given their premises: if legal rights and obligations are merely instruments for pursuing deeper moral goals more effectively, then it makes no sense to allocate obligations where it is vanishingly unlikely that they will attain those ends. Milanovic thus concludes that *Ilaşcu* should 'be rejected, as it undermines the broader principle that it is only the state's capacity to act, and not its territorial title, that should matter'.[131] While they agree on very little else, Besson would also appear to espouse this opinion, for example when she argues that in order to give rise to human rights jurisdiction, the claim of authority by the putative duty-bearer must be accompanied by 'effective power' and 'overall control [which] should be effective and exercised, and not merely claimed'.[132] At times, she even expresses this thought in superficially Kantian terms, for instance when she remarks that 'the feasibility of duties is [both] part of their concrete requirements (following the principle 'ought implies can') *and a condition for their existence*'.[133] The most well-developed critique of *Ilaşcu*, however, is by Lea Raible, and begins with the thought that the term 'jurisdiction' has not one, but many meanings.[134] As used by human rights lawyers, 'jurisdiction', in Raible's view, refers to a threshold or 'trigger' activating states' obligations.[135] As used by general international lawyers, however, that same word refers instead to the bundle of entitlements states ordinarily have in their territory, which Raible describes as 'not entirely unlike property'.[136] Importantly, Raible then argues that 'title

[128] *Ilaşcu and ors and Romania (intervening) v Moldova and Russian Federation, Admissibility* (2004) ECHR 318, paras 332–52.

[129] *Catan* (n 118) para 110.

[130] *Case of the Pueblo Bello Massacre v Colombia, del Carmen Álvarez Blanco and ors v Colombia, Merits, reparations and costs* [2006] IHRL 1524, paras 119–27.

[131] Milanovic (n 36) 107.

[132] Besson (n 70) 873.

[133] Besson (n 70) 868 (emphasis added).

[134] L Raible, 'Title to Territory and Jurisdiction in International Human Rights Law: Three Models for a Fraught Relationship' (2018) *Leiden Journal of International Law* 315.

[135] *Ibid* 320.

[136] *Ibid* 322.

to territory and jurisdiction in international human rights law serve different purposes'.[137] The law of territory is primarily concerned with maintaining international stability,[138] while human rights law is concerned with 'allocation' of entitlements and duties between individuals and states, a task for which some effective control over territory is crucial.[139] As such, Raible contends that occupation of a state's territory by another cannot in and of itself extinguish title, so the state retains 'jurisdiction' within the meaning of general international law of territory, but where a state's territory has been occupied by another, it no longer has any ability to advance the welfare of, or provide normative guidance to the people there, so the question of 'jurisdiction' within the meaning of human rights law does not even arise. The problem with *Ilaşçu* and *Catan* then, is that they treat human rights obligations as 'allocated' automatically along with title to territory as determined in international law, such that territorial 'title always results in [human rights] jurisdiction, regardless of whether the latter's criteria are met or not …'.[140]

An authentically Kantian theory of human rights law objects to these arguments at every step. The most fundamental objection is that rights and obligations are linked to one another as a function of the external forms of interpersonal relations, rather than as a function of the matter or substance of the choices persons make in their relations with one another.[141] For this reason, it rejects at the outset the construction of legal obligations as contingently 'allocated' according to the obligor's ease and convenience. To the contrary, the very concept of a 'duty' lies in its being morally required regardless of one's inclinations. It is in this sense that Lord Dyson notes extrajudicially that if a 'Contracting State has taken over control of the civil administration of the foreign territory then its inability to control the situation is not a ticket out of the Convention.'[142]

At a level closer to the surface, a state's territory is, contrary to Raible, *entirely* unlike property. Sovereign states are not real estate conglomerates; they violate their regulative principles to the extent they behave as such. Rather, as *public* fiduciaries, all three fundamental characteristics of sovereignty – personhood under international law, jurisdiction over territory, and rulership over their subjects – are inalienable aspects of their 'status'; that is to say, of their very persons. None of them is property disposable at will.[143] 'Jurisdiction' means exactly the same thing at general international law and

[137] *Ibid* 323.
[138] *Ibid* 322–23.
[139] *Ibid* 325, 327–28.
[140] *Ibid* 329.
[141] *DR* 6:230, 386–87.
[142] See Dyson (n 115) 20.
[143] The early 20th century international lawyer Alfred von Verdross specifies treaties prohibiting a state from protecting its citizens abroad as one category of treaty forbidden by international law. A von Verdross, 'Forbidden Treaties in International Law' (1937) 31 *American Journal of International Law* 571, 576.

human rights law – 'law-speaking'. A claim of sovereignty over territory is just the same thing as claiming authority over residents there, which in turn is just the same thing as having obligations of accountability towards them. The rights and obligations are inseverably compound – two sides of the same fiduciary coin. As such, *Ilasçu* and *Catan* are correctly decided because it is not consistent with right for a state to lay claim to a territory and at the same time deny obligations of accountability towards the people on it. As a matter of pure external relations, all that needs to be said is that a state holding itself out as the political authority over certain persons ought to act like it. Its pretensions, even if risible, create obligations.

It makes no difference if the territory was not abandoned but wrongfully seized by another state or rebel group because its subjects' rights to authority survive their violation. As long as the state and its population exist, the subjects have rights to the state's 'status' as their public fiduciary, which are neither in the power of the state to give away unilaterally nor defeasible by the wrongs of third parties. Properly applied, the 'ought implies can' principle governs the specification of the content of obligations in the light of the circumstances – which is possible only after determining the form of the relation between the putative obligee and obligor.[144] At the 'jurisdictional' stage, an obligor is saddled with human rights obligations towards subjects simply because it has pretended to have authority over them. The onerousness of these obligations in no way negates their existence. What the *content* of these obligations are, and whether or not the obligor has fulfilled or breached them are separate questions to be examined in light of the concrete circumstances of each case; that is, at the *merits*. Some excuse might lie if a state really cannot fulfil its obligations, but it bears the burden of proving it tried.[145] Given its total lack of physical control over Transdniestria, Moldova might not have been able to do very much for its subjects there, but it still owed them something. Hence the obligation – incumbent upon no other state – to take all 'diplomatic, economic, judicial or other measures' still feasible within its limited power.[146]

C. Arendt's Loophole

Equally, 'negative' obligations to respect are not owed universally to everyone, but only to subjects. Both types of obligation are subject to the same

[144] See A Pinheiro Walla, 'Global Government or Global Governance? Realism and Idealism in Kant's Legal Theory' (2017) 13 *Journal of Global Ethics* 312, 318. ('The saying "ought implies can" attributed to Kant is usually taken to mean that it cannot be my duty to do something impossible. However, Kant understood it the other way around: because something is commanded by reason, it *is* possible.')

[145] *Al-Skeini* (n 74) para 166 (holding that compliance with positive duties is an obligation of means rather than result, meaning the duty-bearer must demonstrate due diligence).

[146] *Ilaşcu* (n 128) para 331.

jurisdictional rules. Besson observes that international human rights treaties ultimately serve a constitutional purpose of 'securing a minimal right to political membership and hence a right to have (human) rights in that political community …'.[147] She then proceeds from this Arendtian insight to observe that

> military occupation with effective control over a territory need not imply jurisdiction, because it may lack the normative element of reason-giving and appeal for compliance. Another example may be effective personal control by troops without, however, any normative appeal besides the use of coercion.[148]

In other words, because authority is the wellspring of human rights obligations, a state has no human rights obligations if it controls a foreign territory without any pretence of legitimacy, but through brute force alone.

Some comfort may be drawn from the likely fact that controlling an area through brute power alone must be incredibly exhausting, and that a conqueror has an incentive to lighten its load by claiming a moral obligation of compliance on the part of the occupied.[149] It is not effective control of territory that is needed for authority, but authority that is needed for effective control. As such, 'effective control of territory' should be understood as setting up a presumption that the putative duty-bearer exercises not just power but also authority over the individuals there, which the state cannot be heard to deny.[150] Further grounds for optimism may lie in the general acceptance that pockets of political order may arise even during active conflicts, thus addressing or at least ameliorating the problems of 'black sites' and that of the treatment of civilians during armed conflicts. For instance in *Hassan*, the Strasbourg Court held that the taking of an Iraqi civilian into British custody gave rise to human rights obligations on the part of the UK, notwithstanding that this took place during the active hostilities phase of an international conflict.[151] Even though the events in *Hassan* and *Jaloud* occurred during active conflicts, the requirement of 'authority over persons' was fulfilled because the state party essentially claimed an entitlement to tell the victims what to do and to force them to do as told, thus giving rise to a 'metaphysical' rather than 'empirical' interval of peace.

[147] Besson (n 70) 863–64.

[148] Besson (n 70) 876.

[149] See J Raz, 'Authority and Justification' in J Raz (ed), *Authority* (New York, New York University Press, 1990) 117. ('Acquiescence seems relevant to the explanation of *de facto* authority rather than to legitimate authority. To have effective political control requires, in the circumstances of our world, a high degree of acquiescence.')

[150] *Al-Skeini* (n 74) paras 138–39. ('Where the fact of such domination over the territory is established, it is not necessary to determine whether the Contracting State exercises detailed control over the policies and actions of the subordinate local administration.'). See also V Tzevelekos, 'Reconstructing the Effective Control Criterion in Extraterritorial Human Rights Breaches: Direct Attribution of Wrongfulness, Due Diligence, and Concurrent Responsibility' (2014) 36 *Michigan Journal of International Law* 129, 150 ('Although the factual element of effectiveness recedes, the question of control remains intact. The sole difference is that it now depends on a presumption that does not need to be tested …').

[151] *Hassan v UK* (2014) ECHR 1162, para 77.

Nevertheless, the problem persists: both Besson's and my theory of human rights jurisdiction would not cover exercises of pure brute force involving no claims of *de facto* authority over the victims; such as a campaign of aerial drone strikes upon villagers in a faraway land. As the law stands, it is almost certain that the victims of the strikes would have no recourse before the Strasbourg Court, but would be thrown out immediately for lack of jurisdiction. In this regard, consider the *obiter* discussion towards the end of *Al-Skeini*, where the Court considered a gloss on the facts of the earlier *Issa* Decision, which involved an incursion by Turkish soldiers into Iraq where they allegedly shot a number of shepherds. The claim was ultimately dismissed because the allegations were not proven. In *Al-Skeini*, the Court recalled the *Issa* fact pattern and opined that Article 1 ECHR state jurisdiction would not have arisen on it, but that it might have if the Iraqi shepherds had been taken by Turkish forces to a nearby cave before they were shot.[152] This distinction would be absurd under either the models advocated by Shany and Milanovic because it is eminently within a state's ability not to shoot someone no matter where they may be located. However, an explanation can be provided on Besson's and the Kantian theory where human rights obligations obtain only in relations of authority. In the second situation where the shepherds were ordered into a van and driven to a cave for a brief period, it can be said, however implausibly, that they were, however briefly, *governed*. In contrast, if the shepherds had simply been shot where they stood, they would merely have been 'affected' in exactly the same way as the victims in *Banković*.[153]

To be sure, this is not to deny that drone strikes may be wrongful for other reasons; say, as war crimes or as crimes against humanity. What it is *not*, though, is a violation of any rights belonging to the individual victims. As unsettling as it may sound, this was more or less predicted by Arendt, who, in a celebrated critique of the UDHR, observed that

> The paradox involved in the loss of human rights is that such loss coincides with the instant when a person becomes a human being in general – without a profession, without a citizenship, without an opinion, without a deed by which to identify and specify himself – … representing nothing but his own absolutely unique individuality which, deprived of expression within and action upon a common world, loses all significance.[154]

On this point, Arendt's republicanism is almost at one with Kant's.[155] Political institutions are constitutive of our independence. Outside of them, rights cannot

[152] *Al-Skeini* (n 74) para 136.

[153] See Milanovic (n 115) 130. ('While the ability to kill is 'authority and control' over the individual if the state has public powers, killing is not authority and control if the state is merely firing missiles from an aircraft.')

[154] H Arendt, *The Origins of Totalitarianism* (Cleveland-New York, Meridian Books, 1958) 302.

[155] The salient difference is that while Arendt's 'right to have rights' is a right to a *political* identity, Kantian innate right is merely a right to juridical personhood.

be fully imagined. Thus, the moment you are nothing more than a human being – a bare life – is also the very instant you have no rights whatsoever.

III. TERRITORIAL EXTENSION AND HUMAN RIGHTS JURISDICTION

We are finally in a position to answer the question of whether the EU has any extraterritorial human rights obligations. If human rights obligations arise out of claims of authority over persons, then the technique of 'territorial extension' described in chapter two, whereby the EU asserts prescriptive jurisdiction in a geographically unbounded fashion, must necessarily give rise to the entire spectrum of human rights obligations, negative and positive. This is in fact already established in Strasbourg jurisprudence. The idea that human rights obligations depend upon factual effects is a mistake resulting from the fact that the most prominent extraterritoriality cases before the Strasbourg Court have tended to involve military occupation of foreign countries.[156] That this is a misconception may be demonstrated by comparing the two little-known cases that have so far come before the Court where a human rights violation was alleged purely on the basis of intangible extraterritorial effects: *Ben El Mahi*[157] and *Kovačič*.[158]

Ben El Mahi was brought by Moroccan applicants challenging the publication in Denmark of a newspaper caricaturing the prophet Muhammad. *Kovačič* was brought by Croatian foreign currency depositors at a Zagreb branch of a Slovenian bank – the Ljubljana Bank – who had been prevented by Slovenian legislation from withdrawing funds from certain foreign currency accounts. Those accounts had been opened with the Ljubljana Bank before the breakup of Yugoslavia and had begun to be frozen from 1998 onwards due to increasing hyperinflation. Following the breakup, the Government of newly-independent Slovenia legislated to require the Ljubljana Bank to retain its liability for all foreign currency accounts regardless of whether they were held in branches on Slovenian territory or in branches in the other former Yugoslav republics.

[156] Indeed, the Strasbourg Court itself arguably assumed this misconception in *Al-Skeini* when, in discussing *Öcalan v Turkey*, *Issa*, *Al-Saadoon and Mufdhi v UK* and *Medvedyev*, it observed that it did 'not consider that jurisdiction in the above cases arose solely from the control exercised by the Contracting State over the buildings, aircraft or ship in which the individuals were held. What is decisive is the exercise of physical power and control over the person in question'. See *Al-Skeini* (n 74) para 136, citing *Öcalan v Turkey* (2005) 41 EHRR 45, para 91, *Al-Saadoon and Mufdhi v UK, Admissibility*, App no 61498/08 (ECtHR, 30 June 2009), paras 86–89; *Medvedyev and ors v France* (2010) 51 EHRR 39, para 67.

[157] *Ben El Mahi v Denmark, Admissibility* (2006) ECHR XV-2006.

[158] *Kovačič and ors v Slovenia, Admissibility*, App no 44574/98, App no 45133/98, App no 48316/99 (ECtHR, 9 October 2003). This chapter does not consider *White v Sweden* (2006) ECHR 793 or *von Hannover v Germany* (2004) ECHR 294. These cases concerned defamations that arguably 'took place' in the territory of the ECHR contracting party, even if the claimant was located in Mozambique or Monaco and Paris respectively. Moreover, the Court did not consider the issue of jurisdiction in either of these cases.

In *Ben El Mahi*, the Court declared the application inadmissible by repeating the *Banković* formula; that is, that jurisdiction arising under Article 1 of the ECHR is the same as jurisdiction at international law, and that it obtained outside of state territory only in exceptional circumstances. In *Kovačić*, however, the Third Chamber of the Strasbourg Court held unanimously that the matter fell within Slovenia's human rights jurisdiction, notwithstanding the then-recent *Banković* Decision. Slovenia had introduced measures 'addressing the issue of foreign-currency savings deposited with branches of Slovenian banks outside Slovenian territory …',[159] leading the Court to find that the 'applicants' position as regards their foreign-currency savings deposited with the Zagreb Main Branch are and continue to be affected by that legislative measure'.[160] Ultimately, the Court held that the matter fell within Slovenia's human rights jurisdiction because 'the acts of the Slovenian authorities continue[d] to produce effects, albeit outside Slovenian territory, such that Slovenia's responsibility under the Convention could be engaged'.[161]

To date, several authors have remarked upon the apparent incompatibility between these two cases.[162] The incompatibility disappears if one bears in mind the distinctions between 'affecting' and 'governing'; that is, the distinction between factual effects and legal effects.[163] Note that despite some confusion in the language between 'responsibility' and 'jurisdiction' in *Kovačić*, neither the Court nor the applicants invoked the principles of state responsibility and attribution. It was never claimed either by the applicants or by the Court that the Ljubljana Bank was controlled by or acting upon the instruction of Slovenia, such that the freezing of the funds was somehow an act of the Slovenian state. Instead, the applicants' complaint was that by enacting such legislation, 'Slovenia had chosen to interfere in [the Ljubljana Bank's] private-law relationship to the detriment of non-Slovenian savers'.[164] Accordingly, the crucial factor was that Slovenian legislation had 'addressed' the operation of bank accounts in Croatia, thus creating *legal* effects there, even if such legislation merely recognised a pre-existing set of circumstances.

This crucial factor distinguishes *Kovačić* from *Ben El Mahi*. In the latter, the Moroccan applicants did not, indeed could not, claim that Denmark had altered

[159] *Kovačič, Admissibility, ibid* para 4(c).
[160] *Kovačič, Admissibility, ibid* para 5 (c).
[161] *Kovačič, Admissibility, ibid*.
[162] See Bartels (n 5) 1077–78; M Den Heijer, 'Procedural Aspects of Shared Responsibility in the European Court of Human Rights' (2013) 4 *Journal of International Dispute Settlement* 361, 361, 366, fn 26.
[163] See M Den Heijer and R Lawson, 'Extraterritorial Human Rights and the Concept of "Jurisdiction"' in M Langford et al (eds), *Global Justice, State Duties: The Extraterritorial Scope of Economic, Social, and Cultural Rights in International Law* (Cambridge, Cambridge University Press, 2013) 179 (examining a group of post-*Banković* cases including *Kovačić*, and concluding that 'the factual exercise of authority appeared decisive in enlivening the State's human rights obligations').
[164] *Ibid*, para 5(b).

their legal position. In contrast, the Slovenian legislation did not merely affect the Croatian depositors; it also governed them. Indeed, given that the freezing of the accounts had begun *before* the breakup of Yugoslavia, one might say that the Slovenian legislation created only *legal* effects upon the claimants and no factual effects at all.[165] It is immaterial that the measures were addressed solely to Slovenian banks. In so far as it is a debt, a bank account has the character of a contract, and one cannot alter the legal position of one party to a contractual relationship without also doing the same for the other. Slovenia therefore owed human rights obligations towards the Croatian applicants, including positive obligations to prevent their rights from violation by the Ljubljana Bank.[166] As a result of the Slovenian measures, the Croatian depositors were legally barred from reclaiming their deposits exactly as if those measures had been enacted by Croatia. For this reason, they qualify, in the language of *Al-Skeini*, as exercises of public powers normally to be exercised by a sovereign government. More relevantly, the measures also count as examples of territorial extension *par excellence*, in that they determined the legal rights and duties of persons in Croatia in a way that could only have been accomplished by a geographically unbounded claim of prescriptive jurisdiction. Finally, given that the measure was taken to preserve the monetary system, the Slovenian measures also qualify as exercises of extraterritorial jurisdiction to provide a public good.[167]

Thus, as a matter both of normative theory and positive ECHR practice, where the EU presumes authority over the rest of the world – even if only by non-physical methods, and even if enforcement is postponed until entry on EU territory or perhaps indefinitely – it acquires human rights obligations to distant strangers who become 'constructive' subjects of its authority. The rule in *Commune de Champagne*, which, to recall chapter two, claims that acts of the EU cannot and do not create legal effects outside the territory of EU

[165] *cf* D Augenstein and D Kinley, 'When Human Rights "Responsibilities" Become "Duties": The Extra-Territorial Obligations of States That Bind Corporations' in S Deva and D Bilchitz (eds), *Human Rights Obligations of Business: Beyond the Corporate Responsibility to Respect?* (Cambridge, Cambridge University Press, 2013) 287–88. Augenstein and Kinley understand *Kovačić* to mean that 'what is decisive for the determination of extra-territorial human rights obligations to protect against corporate violations is not the state's exercise of de jure authority, but its assertion of de facto power over the individual rights-holder. More specifically, it is an act or omission of the state in relation to a corporate actor that brings the individual under the power of the state and triggers corresponding obligations to protect his or her human rights against corporate violations'. Such an interpretation is irreconcilable with *Al-Skeini*, *Ben El Mahi* or the *Banković* rejection of a human rights 'effects doctrine', as well as with the facts of the *Kovačić* itself – the Slovenian legislation had no factual effect upon the applicants. Those accounts had become inaccessible during the Yugoslav regime itself.

[166] *Kovačić, Admissibility* (n 158) para 5(c). The applicants were eventually unsuccessful due to new information coming before the Court. *Kovačić and ors v Slovenia, Struck out of the List*, App no 44574/98, App no 45133/98, App no 48316/99 (6 November 2006) paras 257–69.

[167] Whether or not they met the necessity requirements as set out in chapter five cannot be examined here.

Member States, commits the same fallacy as the *espace juridique* doctrine in *Banković*. They both confuse the statement 'State X *shouldn't* assert jurisdiction extraterritorially' with the statement 'State X *doesn't* assert jurisdiction extraterritorially'. Accordingly, the rule in *Commune de Champagne* must go the same way as *Banković*. Instead, as demonstrated by *Kovačić*, a state may exercise authority by causing legal effects overseas without its agents ever setting foot there.[168] Distinctions between the instrumentalities of authority are irrelevant. All that matters is that authority is claimed, and that there is some meaningful attempt to enforce it. The EU's human rights obligations cover the entire complement of positive and negative obligations, with questions regarding their specific scope and whether or not breach has occurred being determined at the merits by reference to the particular facts of each case.

IV. CONCLUSION

Here, at long last, are the answers to the two hypothetical situations introduced at the very beginning of chapter one. In the scenario concerning the wiping out of the livelihoods of farmers in developing countries as a result of agricultural subsidies awarded to European farmers, the EU has no human rights obligations towards affected distant farmers whatsoever. Substantive or procedural objections may be interposed on grounds of failures by policymakers to take account of negative impacts, conduct impact assessments, and such like, but these are administrative questions about whether the EU has compiled with its internal procedures and acted within its defined competences. They are irrelevant to 'external' questions of rightful relations between the EU and the Ruritanian farmers. In contrast, the hypothetical concerning the supermarket merger does indeed give rise to human rights obligations towards distant farmers. In so far as territorial extension is relied upon to assert jurisdiction over the foreign supply chains in which they are enmeshed, EU competition law creates *legal* effects upon them. The EU thus stands as an authority in relation to the Ruritanian farmers and therefore owes those distant strangers the obligations of a public fiduciary. Accordingly, the Commission must therefore place appropriate conditions upon the merger, or even block it if necessary. Put differently, the EU in its merger regulatory process regularly holds itself out as the competition authority for the entire world. It cannot act solely for the benefit of EU citizens, but for the benefit of every individual subject to its writ. To rule the world for the benefit of a metropolis is the very definition of imperialism.

[168] See FA Mann, *The Doctrine of Jurisdiction in International Law* (The Hague, AW Sijthoff, 1964) 14 (observing that while 'the mere exercise of prescriptive jurisdiction, without any attempt at enforcement, will not normally have to pass the test of international law … it is not difficult to visualize circumstances in which the exercise of legislative jurisdiction plainly implies the likelihood of enforcement that foreign States are entitled to challenge its presence on the statute book').

There is, of course, the fact that the EU blocking the merger as a result of alleged human rights obligations owed to Ruritanian farmers might appear to infringe Ruritania's 'sovereignty', understood loosely as its faculty of action. As argued in the previous chapter, a state or similar political organisation of jurisdiction has the right to do anything necessary to provide public goods for its subjects; nothing it does that is limited and proportionate to this goal can ever constitute a wrong against anyone else. Competition regulation is just one of these public goods. If the assertion of a right is not a wrong against another, neither is the fulfilment of obligations that arise from the assertion of that right. As such, the objection from Ruritanian 'sovereignty' must fail, because sovereignty has no meaning outside of an international rightful condition where each of its member states provide domestic rightful conditions for their subjects.

7

Closing the Courthouse Door: The Standing of Distant Strangers

RULES OF PROCEDURE, paradigmatically those governing standing to bring suit, lie at the very heart of what it means to be a rights-bearing subject. The previous chapters demonstrated that the EU routinely relies upon the provisions introduced in chapter two to claim authority over distant strangers. It was then argued, both normatively and as a matter of positive law, that such claims give rise to human rights obligations towards those distant strangers. This final chapter argues that the EU's internal constitution effectively insulates EU institutions and policymakers from these obligations of accountability. As such, it turns out that Bartels' instincts regarding the significance of the provisions are largely correct, but not for creditable reasons. Indeed, they might be worse than empty platitudes: as we shall see, the courts of the EU deploy the provisions – which, to recall, commit the EU to the advancement and promotion of human rights, the rule of law and democracy in all its relations with the wider world – for the very purpose of avoiding the obligations of accountability the EU owes to the distant strangers it purports to govern.

These no doubt strong claims will be defended by reference to the recent *Polisario* and *Western Sahara Campaign* litigations before the various EU courts. The various decisions and opinions arising from this litigation constitute the latest instalments of the decades-long legal and political struggle over the Western Sahara between Morocco and the local national liberation movement known as the Frente Popular de Liberación de Saguía-el-Hamra y Río de Oro ('Front Polisario'), which began with the Advisory Opinion of the International Court of Justice (ICJ) in 1975.[1] All of these cases before the EU courts concerned various treaties between the EU and Morocco, which currently occupies all but a small part of the Western Sahara. The first set of materials – the *Polisario* litigation – was brought under the 'judicial review' procedure, and comprises a judgment of the General Court, an Opinion by Advocate General (AG) Wathelet, and a judgment by the European Court of Justice (ECJ). In December 2015, the General Court partially annulled a Council Decision adopting a modification of the EU-Morocco Association Agreement that applied to fisheries and other agricultural exports coming from the territory of the

[1] *Western Sahara* (Advisory Opinion) [1975] ICJ Rep 12.

Western Sahara.[2] The General Court held that the Front Polisario had the requisite standing to bring a judicial review of the Council Decision directly, as well as that the concerned measure needed to be annulled in part due to a failure by the EU institutions to assess the implications of the Association Agreement for the exploitation of natural resources and the human rights of the inhabitants of the Western Sahara. Second, there is the Advisory Opinion by AG Wathelet, in which he offered three different theories, the first two of which would have reversed the General Court's Decision, and the last which would have preserved it.[3] In its judgment issued in December 2016, the ECJ adopted the first of AG Wathelet's theories, which – bizarrely – denied the Front Polisario standing to seek judicial review of the contested measure, but proceeded to interpret it in a fashion effectively annulling its application over the Western Sahara anyway.[4]

The second set of materials is the *Western Sahara Campaign* litigation, which consists of an Opinion by AG Wathelet issued in January 2018[5] and a judgment of the ECJ little more than a month later in February 2018, which constitutes the first preliminary ruling effectively examining the validity of an international agreement concluded by the EU or of its acts of implementation.[6] The application was made by a private voluntary organisation by way of preliminary reference from the English courts and sought to examine the validity of measures taken by the United Kingdom to implement the EU-Morocco Fisheries Partnership Agreement ('FPA'),[7] as amended by a 2013 Protocol.[8]

[2] Case T-512/12 *Front Polisario v Council* ECLI:EU:T:2015:953 (10 December 2015), partially annulling the Council Decision 2012/497/EU of 8 March 2012 on the conclusion of an Agreement in the form of an Exchange of Letters between the European Union and the Kingdom of Morocco concerning reciprocal liberalisation measures on agricultural products, processed agricultural products, fish and fishery products, the replacement of Protocols 1, 2 and 3 and their Annexes and amendments to the Euro-Mediterranean Agreement establishing an association between the European Communities and their Member States, of the one part, and the Kingdom of Morocco, of the other part [2012] OJ L241/2. See also Euro-Mediterranean Agreement establishing an association agreement between the European Communities and their Member States, of the one part, and the Kingdom of Morocco, of the other part [1996] OJ L70/2. Simon and Rigaux observe that the General Court inaccurately describes the contested measure as adopting a 'conclusion' of the EU-Morocco Association Agreement. D Simon and A Rigaux, 'Le Tribunal et Le Droit International Des Traités : Un Arrêt Déconcertant (Trib. UE, 10 Déc. 2015, Aff. T 512/12, Front Polisario c Conseil)' (2016) n° 2 *Europe: actualité du doit de l'union européenne* 5, para 2.

[3] Case C-104/16 P *Council v Front Polisario* ECLI:EU:C:2016:677 (13 September 2016), Opinion of AG Wathelet.

[4] Case C-104/16 P *Council v Front Polisario* ECLI:EU:C:2016:973 (21 December 2016).

[5] Case C-266/16 *Western Sahara Campaign UK, The Queen v Commissioners for Her Majesty's Revenue and Customs, Secretary of State for Environment, Food and Rural Affairs* ECLI:EU:C:2018:1 (10 January 2018), Opinion of AG Wathelet.

[6] Case C-266/16 *Western Sahara Campaign UK, The Queen v Commissioners for Her Majesty's Revenue and Customs, Secretary of State for Environment, Food and Rural Affairs* ECLI:EU:C:2018:118 (27 February 2018), paras 48–51.

[7] Fisheries Partnership Agreement between the European Communities and the Kingdom of Morocco [2006] OJ L141/4 (hereinafter 'EU-Morocco FPA').

[8] Protocol between the European Union and the Kingdom of Morocco setting out the fishing opportunities and financial contribution provided for in the Fisheries Partnership Agreement between the European Union and the Kingdom of Morocco [2013] OJ L328/2.

The FPA purported to accord various types of advantageous treatment to Moroccan fisheries products, and the crux was whether the phrases 'waters falling within the sovereignty or jurisdiction of the Kingdom of Morocco',[9] 'Moroccan fishing zones'[10] and 'waters under Moroccan jurisdiction'[11] included the waters adjacent to the Western Sahara. As will be explained below, AG Wathelet interpreted these phrases as having been intended to include Western Saharan waters, and on this basis opined that the EU-Morocco FPA and the other contested measures were invalid due to incompatibility with peremptory norms of international law. In contrast, the ECJ upheld the measures through 'conform interpretation' with those same norms. Following the handing down of *Western Sahara Campaign*, the General Court dismissed a second application for annulment made by the Front Polisario by an order issued on 19 July 2018.[12]

Before we proceed, it must be made clear that I do not take any position on the merits of the Sahrawi national liberation movement or the Moroccan position that the Western Sahara constitutes an integral part of its sovereign territory. Instead, all that this chapter attempts is to show the gap between the EU's professed rhetoric and its acts of legal significance in the wider world, and to critique the methods by which the EU courts have rationalised either of these things.

I. STANDING IN EU LAW

Before the substantive critiques of this chapter can be set out, it may be useful to explain briefly the law governing how individuals may challenge EU measures before the courts of the EU. The most well-known of these methods is the reference for a preliminary ruling under Article 267 of the Treaty on the Functioning of the European Union (TFEU). In Morten Broberg's and Niels Fenger's useful summary, a 'reference for a preliminary ruling is a request from a national court of a Member State to the [ECJ] to give an authoritative interpretation on an EU act or decision or a decision on the validity of such an act'.[13] Under this procedure, the ECJ does not actually settle disputes; 'it makes judgment neither on the facts in the main proceedings nor on the interpretation and application of national law … [nor does] it pronounce … on the concrete application of EU law in the main proceedings before the referring court'.[14] Instead, it operates as

[9] EU-Morocco FPA (n 7) art 2(a).

[10] EU-Morocco FPA (n 7) art 2(a).

[11] EU-Morocco FPA (n 7) art 11.

[12] Case T-180/14 *Front Polisario v Council (Polisario II)* ECLI:EU:T:2018:496 (19 July 2018).

[13] M Broberg and N Fenger, *Preliminary References to the European Court of Justice*, 2nd edn (Oxford, Oxford University Press, 2014) 1.

[14] *Ibid*.

a 'Kelsenian' constitutional court pronouncing purely in abstract terms upon the meaning of EU law norms, which the referring Member State court must then follow in settling the dispute before it.[15] As is well known, the preliminary reference procedure is how most EU litigation arises and has historically been the engine of the vast majority of seminal EU jurisprudence, as well as a major driving force behind EU integration by ensuring the uniform interpretation and application of EU law by Member State courts.[16]

The second and, for our purposes, most relevant method is the Article 263 TFEU procedure, which – in contrast to the 'indirect' preliminary ruling method described above – allows individual applicants to seek direct 'judicial review' of EU measures in the courts of the EU. The kinds of measures subject to judicial review are specified in the first subparagraph of Article 263 TFEU:

> The Court of Justice of the European Union shall review the legality of legislative acts, of acts of the Council, of the Commission and of the European Central Bank, other than recommendations and opinions, and of acts of the European Parliament and of the European Council intended to produce legal effects vis-à-vis third parties. It shall also review the legality of acts of bodies, offices or agencies of the Union intended to produce legal effects vis-à-vis third parties.

A. The Requirement of Legal Effects

The first step to seeking judicial review under Article 263 TFEU is to demonstrate that the contested EU measure produces 'legal' rather than just 'factual' effects.[17] In other words, the measure must not simply purport to 'affect' someone but to *govern* her. That the point of Article 263 TFEU judicial review is to remedy improper exercises of political authority can be seen in the grounds of review, which are listed in Article 263(2) TFEU as 'lack of competence, infringement of an essential procedural requirement, infringement of the Treaties or of any rule of law relating to their application, or misuse of powers'. Notwithstanding the centrality of political authority to Article 263 TFEU judicial review, EU courts have sometimes been quite flexible in their understanding of the concept of a

[15] For a useful description of the differences between Kelsenian constitutional review and appellate review, see A Stone Sweet, 'Why Europe Rejected American Judicial Review – And Why It May Not Matter' (2002) 101 *Michigan Law Review* 2744.

[16] As a leading textbook states, 'Article 267 TFEU is one of the most important Treaty provisions. There would have been few, at the inception of the Treaty, who would have guessed its significance in shaping EU law … [It] is the "jewel in the Crown" of the Court's jurisdiction.' P Craig and G de Búrca, *EU Law: Text, Cases, and Materials*, 5th edn (Oxford, Oxford University Press, 2015) 464. See also M Rhimes, 'The EU Courts Stand Their Ground: Why Are the Standing Rules for Direct Actions Still So Restrictive' (2016) 9 *European Journal of Legal Studies* 103, 160.

[17] See, eg, Case C-583/11 *Inuit Tapiriit Kanatami v Parliament and Council* ECLI:EU:C:2013:625 (3 October 2013), para 56; Case 60/81 *IBM v Commission* [1981] ECR 2639, para 9; Case 22/70 *Commission v Council (ERTA)* [1971] ECR 273 para 41.

legal effect, in a manner that betrays perhaps a little conceptual confusion.[18] For instance, in her Opinion in *Inuit II*, AG Kokott suggested doing away with the legal effects requirement because applicants had 'perfectly correctly' been recognised as possessing standing to challenge state aid authorisations and merger approvals, which she characterised as producing only factual effects.[19] Although technically correct, her advice misses an important point. The effects of such official decisions to authorise new concentrations or issue subsidies to particular firms are unlike other factual effects in a distinctive respect: they do not simply affect the factual position of other market participants, say, like a competitor coming up with a better product, or a supplier demanding a higher price for an input. Rather, they modify the very terms on which the market participants interact with one another and can, therefore, be taken only by a public authority. The decision-maker is not on an equal footing to the complainants but occupies a hierarchically superior position to them. In this sense, the market participants are not just 'affected' by the decisions of the Commission but *governed* by them. As such, the Commission in its role as a merger or state aid regulator is akin to the class of persons such as physicians, investment advisers and bailees. As we saw in chapter four, such persons are properly fixed with fiduciary obligations even if they do not technically alter their principals' legal rights and obligations, because they 'possess' their patients, clients and guests all the same.

Now, there are other means by which individuals may conceivably challenge EU measures. Article 277 TFEU allows parties to plead the illegality or inapplicability of EU acts in proceedings brought against them by EU institutions. They may also seek redress for wrongful losses caused by EU institutions through actions for damage under Article 340 TFEU.[20] Nevertheless, the tradition is that Article 267 TFEU and Article 263 TFEU alone supply everything an applicant could ever want – the 'complete system of remedies'. As the ECJ put it in *Rosneft*:

> The review of the legality of acts of the Union that the Court is to ensure under the Treaties relies, in accordance with settled case-law, on two complementary judicial procedures. The FEU Treaty has established, by Articles 263 and 277, on the one hand, and Article 267, on the other, a complete system of legal remedies and procedures designed to ensure judicial review of the legality of European Union acts, and has entrusted such review to the Courts of the European Union.[21]

[18] See, eg, Case 34/86 *Council v Parliament* [1986] ECR 2155. The ECJ held that a declaration by the President of the European Parliament relating to the final adoption of the general budget of the then European Community was productive of legal effects upon third parties, and therefore reviewable.

[19] Case C-583/11 *Inuit Tapiriit Kanatami v Parliament and Council* ECLI:EU:C:2013:21 (17 January 2013), Opinion of AG Kokott, para 71.

[20] Craig and de Búrca (n 16) 583 ('In any developed legal system there must be a mechanism whereby losses caused by governmental action may be recovered by an action brought by an individual … Compensation against the EU is governed by Article 340 TFEU (ex Article 288 EC).').

[21] Case C-72/15 *PJSC Rosneft Oil Company v Her Majesty's Treasury* ECLI:EU:C:2017:236 (28 March 2017), para 66.

The crucial point to bear in mind is that Article 263 TFEU judicial review serves a fundamentally different purpose than abstract, constitutional review carried out under Article 267 TFEU. As Broberg and Fenger note, the Article 267 TFEU preliminary reference is – in principle at least – not 'a dispute resolution procedure … [but] a non-contentious stage in the procedure before the national court'.[22] In contrast, Article 263 TFEU judicial review *is* contentious and adversarial – it

> entitles certain (natural or legal) persons to institute legal proceedings before the Court of Justice in order that in this way they may safeguard their rights under EU law. In contrast, Article 267 gives national courts a right to ask the Court of Justice about the interpretation or validity with respect to EU law thereby ensuring the correct and uniform application of EU law.[23]

Put differently, Article 263 TFEU is about individuals seeking *their* rights, while Article 267 TFEU is about courts ensuring compliance with a system of abstract norms.

B. Direct and Individual Concern under Article 263 TFEU

After listing several 'privileged applicants' – Member States and EU institutions – allowed standing on easier terms, the fourth subparagraph of Article 263 TFEU provides that

> Any natural or legal person may, under the conditions referred to in the first and second subparagraphs, institute proceedings against an act addressed to that person or which is of direct and individual concern to them, and against a regulatory act which is of direct concern to them and does not entail implementing measures.

This provision, and in particular the concept of a 'regulatory act', was introduced by the Lisbon treaty using language lifted *verbatim* from Article III-365(4) of the failed Treaty on a Constitution for Europe ('Constitutional Treaty'). Before Lisbon, the regime under Article 230 of the Treaty on the European Communities (TEC) allowed ordinary applicants to seek judicial review of EU measures only if they were either explicitly addressed to them or if they were of 'direct and individual concern' to them. As is well known, the ECJ had interpreted these requirements extremely narrowly, and in a manner that systematically excluded

[22] Broberg and Fenger (n 13) 279–80. In practice, however, the preliminary reference procedure often takes on the character of adversarial dispute settlement. For instance, in references 'concerning the validity of an EU act, it would be wrong to view the preliminary procedure as purely non-contentious proceedings where it is solely for the referring court to establish the facts. In reality, such preliminary cases have significant adversarial elements in which the EU institution that has issued the contested act behaves more like a defendant than a neutral observer' (at 370).

[23] Broberg and Fenger (n 13) 219.

most applicants.[24] According to that jurisprudence, which still constitutes binding precedent, a measure was of 'direct concern' if, in addition to producing legal effects, its operation involved no 'autonomous will' interposing itself between the EU and the applicant. This could either be because the measure was directly effective, or because it '[left] no room for any discretion' on the part of any intermediaries.[25] The direct concern requirement was left unchanged by Lisbon.[26]

The more onerous, and for our purposes interesting requirement is that of 'individual concern.' In the infamous *Plaumann* Decision, the ECJ held that this required the challenged measure to 'affect [the applicant] by reason of certain attributes which are peculiar to them or by reason of circumstances in which they are differentiated from all other persons'.[27] In that case, an importer of clementines had challenged a decision not to lower import taxes on that particular fruit in circumstances where it was evident that the measure would have had effects uniquely upon the importer and nobody else. Nonetheless, the plaintiff was found to lack standing because, in principle, any other undertaking could have chosen to enter that market. The stringency of the individual concern requirement was demonstrated subsequently in *Codorníu*, which involved a direct challenge by a Spanish producer of sparkling wine against an EU measure prohibiting producers outside France and Luxembourg from calling their product 'crémant'.[28] Unlike the applicant in *Plaumann*, the applicant in *Codorníu* satisfied the individual concern requirement because it had obtained a trademark over that appellation in Spain, thereby effectively creating a new market which no other Spanish producer could enter. In short, under the old Article 230 TEC regime, standing to bring judicial review was available only against measures effectively amounting to bills of attainder: the challenged measure had either to address the applicant personally by name, or it had to single her out with such surgical precision that it might as well have identified her by name.

[24] For representative readings, see A Arnull, 'Private Applicants and the Action for Annulment under Article 173 of the EC Treaty' (1995) 32 *CML Rev* 7; C Koch, 'Locus Standi of Private Applicants under the EU Constitution: Preserving Gaps in the Protection of Individuals Right to an Effective Remedy' (2005) 30 *EL Rev* 511; P Craig, 'Standing, Rights, and the Structure of Legal Argument' (2003) 9 *European Public Law* 493.

[25] Case 294/83 *Parti écologiste 'Les Verts' v Parliament* [1986] ECR 1339, para 31.

[26] See, eg, Case T-694/14 *European Renewable Energies Federation (EREF) v Commission* ECLI:EU:T:2015:915 (23 November 2015), para 17; *Inuit*, Opinion of AG Kokott (n 19) paras 68–69; Case T-262/10 *Microban v Commission* [2011] ECR II-7697, para 32; K Lenaerts, I Maselis and K Gutman, *EU Procedural Law* (Oxford, Oxford University Press, 2014) 335–36 (s 7.109); Rhimes (n 16) 106–35.

[27] Case 25/62 *Plaumann v Commission* [1963] ECR 95, 107. See Lenaerts, Maselis and Gutman, *ibid* 326 (s 7.100) ('An applicant can show in only limited ways that it is individually concerned by a measure of general application.'); Rhimes (n 16) 145 ('As is known, it is nearly impossible to show individual concern in relation to [a legislative] act.').

[28] Case C-309/89 *Codorníu SA v Council* [1994] ECR I-01853.

Unsurprisingly, this state of affairs elicited such overwhelming criticism from academia,[29] the General Court[30] and numerous Advocates General,[31] that change was felt to be necessary by the time of the Constitutional Treaty.[32] This was the context in which the current Article 263 TFEU came into being. The solution envisaged by Article 263 TFEU was to add a third category to the pre-Lisbon regime: applicants may now challenge a 'regulatory act which is of direct concern to them and does not entail implementing measures' without having to satisfy the individual concern requirement. However, the Lisbon drafters omitted one rather important thing: the critical term 'regulatory act' was left undefined, thus giving rise to a need for judicial clarification.[33] This was duly provided in *Inuit II*, where the General Court, Advocate General and ECJ all agreed in defining regulatory acts as 'acts of general application other than legislative acts'.[34] In short, the rationale was that 'regulatory act' had to be understood in contradistinction to 'legislative act', a term mentioned in the first paragraph of Article 263 TFEU and defined in Article 289 TFEU as acts jointly passed by the Parliament and the Council, as well as by some other procedures.

For legislative acts not addressed to the applicant, the old, exacting standards of direct and individual concern continue to apply. In her Opinion in *Inuit II*, AG Kokott justified this on the basis that such acts deserved a measure of special deference because they were taken by the EU Parliament and the Council – bodies, in her view, endowed with 'particularly high democratic legitimation'.[35] Needless to say, some might dispute the characterisation of the Parliament and Council as particularly democratic bodies,[36] as well as contest the theory of legislative deference on which it is grounded.[37] Moreover, she

[29] See sources listed in n 24.

[30] See Case T-177/01 *Jégo-Quéré v Commission* [2002] ECR II-2365.

[31] See, eg, Case C-50/00 *Unión de Pequeños Agricultores v Council* [2002] ECR I-6681, Opinion of AG Jacobs; Case C-358/89 *Extramet v Council (Admissibility)* [1991] ECR I-2507, Opinion of AG Jacobs; Case C-491/01 *British American Tobacco (Investments) Ltd and Imperial Tobacco* [2002] ECR I-11461, Opinion of AG Geelhoed.

[32] *Inuit*, Opinion of AG Kokott (n 19) paras 1–2.

[33] *Inuit*, Opinion of AG Kokott (n 19) para 30; D Chalmers, G Davies and G Monti, *European Union Law: Text and Materials*, 3rd edn (Cambridge, Cambridge University Press, 2014) 414–15.

[34] Case T-18/10 *Inuit Tapiriit Kanatami v Parliament and Council* [2011] ECR II-05599, para 56; *Inuit*, Opinion of AG Kokott (n 19) para 47; *Inuit* (n 17) para 60.

[35] *Inuit*, Opinion of Advocate General Kokott (n 19) para 38. See B Libgober, 'Can the EU Be a Constitutional System without Universal Access to Judicial Review' (2014) 36 *Michigan Journal of International Law* 353 (defending the EU's claim to be a constitutional order adhering to the rule of law, because the rules of standing for judicial review of legislation are equally, if not more strict in many EU Member States).

[36] See, eg, *Unión de Pequeños*, Opinion of AG Jacobs (n 31) para 86.

[37] Rhimes makes the interesting point that AG Kokott's deference argument proves 'too little', because the Council – whose members are not directly elected – carries as much weight as the Parliament in the ordinary legislative procedure under Article 289(1) TFEU, as well as 'too much' because legislative acts can be challenged indirectly anyway. Rhimes (n 16) 142–43.

added that sufficient judicial protection was afforded anyway by the preliminary reference procedure and by Article 277 TFEU,[38] even though she acknowledged with respect to the former that 'merely indirect examination of the lawfulness of a legislative act' might not constitute 'an adequate substitute for the lack of a direct legal remedy',[39] and with respect to the latter that an individual ought not to be required to run the risk of legal sanctions in proceedings brought against them to contest the legality of EU acts.[40] The ECJ concurred with her in the Decision that followed, holding that the relevant *travaux préparatoires* for the Constitutional Treaty envisaged a general liberalisation of standing rules, but not for challenges against legislative measures.[41]

The measure challenged in *Polisario* was a 'legislative act' within the terms of Article 263(4) TFEU not directly addressing the Front Polisario. As such, the *Plaumann* standard applied in full.[42] Obviously, neither the Front Polisario nor individual Sahrawis have ever conferred any democratic imprimatur upon the EU Parliament and Council. It is also not possible for preliminary references to be requested from non-EU Member State courts, nor is it compatible with the dignity of individual Sahrawis to have to depend upon the charity of well-meaning non-governmental organisations to seek preliminary references from EU Member State courts on their behalf. As such, the crucial question is whether the measures such as the EU-Morocco Association Agreement and the FPA can be said to create legal effects upon – that is, to govern – individual Sahrawis. If so, then the criteria of direct and individual concern must be seen as unjustifiable restrictions upon the ability of individual Sahrawis in vindicating their rights.

II. THE EU-MOROCCO AGREEMENTS: TRUSTEES *DE SON TORT* OF HUMANITY

This section argues that the international agreements at the heart of *Polisario* and *Western Sahara Campaign*, and by extension the measures adopting them, constitute extraterritorial assertions of authority. They create legal effects not just over the Front Polisario, but over individual Sahrawis as well. Recall the *Commune de Champagne* Decision from chapter two, which was understood by Bartels to stand for the notion that the EU either cannot or does not unilaterally create legal effects outside its borders, thus leading him to speculate that individual distant strangers may likely never meet the standing requirements required by Article 263 TFEU. We return to this case here, because it serves

[38] *Inuit*, Opinion of AG Kokott (n 19) para 117.

[39] *Inuit*, Opinion of AG Kokott (n 19) para 118.

[40] *Inuit*, Opinion of AG Kokott (n 19) para 118.

[41] *Inuit* (n 17) para 59, citing Secretariat of the European Convention, 'Final Report of the Discussion Circle on the Court of Justice of 25 March 2003' CONV 636/03, para 22 and 'Cover Note from the Praesidium to the Convention of 12 May 2003' CONV 734/03, 20.

[42] *Polisario* (n 2) para 71–73.

as a useful foil against which the fact pattern of *Polisario* and *Western Sahara Campaign* may be compared.

In *Commune de Champagne*, the General Court denied certain Swiss applicants standing to challenge an act of the EU approving a series of international agreements between the EU and Switzerland, which prohibited wines from the Commune of Champagne in the Swiss Canton of Vaud from being marketed within the EU under the name of 'Champagne'. It is important to note that it was not the international agreement itself that was challenged. As a bilateral act, it was not judicially reviewable under the then Article 230 TEC.[43] Instead, the proper subject of judicial review was the EU act adopting those agreements into EU law.[44] It was in this context that the General Court interpreted the principle of sovereign equality in Article 2(1) of the UN Charter (UNC), read in the light of the then Article 299 TEC (now Article 355 TFEU), to find that 'an act of an institution adopted pursuant to the [EC] Treaty, as a unilateral act of the Community, cannot create rights and obligations outside the territory thus defined'.[45] As chapters two to five have hopefully demonstrated, this broad statement is mistaken both at positive law and at normative theory.

Another Decision relevant for our discussion is *Brita*, a preliminary reference which concerned whether goods produced in Israeli settlements in the West Bank were entitled to types of preferential treatment provided for under the terms of a treaty between the then European Communities and Israel.[46] The central issue in that case was the relative effect of treaties or *pacta tertiis nec nocent nec prosunt*, a principle enshrined in Article 34 of the Vienna Convention on the Law of Treaties (VCLT) and which is broadly understood to prohibit parties to a treaty creating rights or obligations for a third party without its assent.[47] The ECJ held that goods from West Bank settlements were not entitled to the advantages under the EC-Israel Association Agreement, because interpreting that treaty to allow for that would infringe upon rights that had been accorded to Palestinian authorities under a separate agreement between the EC and the Palestinian Liberation Organization (PLO). The reasoning was twofold. On the one hand, the EC-Israel Agreement did not positively require Member State authorities to accord preferential treatment to goods produced in West Bank settlements. On the other hand, the EC-PLO agreement obligated the same Member State authorities to provide preferential treatment to goods produced

[43] Case T-212/02 *Commune de Champagne v Council* [2007] ECR II-2023, para 86–87. The treaty concerned was the Agreement on Scientific and Technological Cooperation, of 4 April 2002 on the conclusion of Seven Agreements with the Swiss Confederation [2002] OJ L114/132.

[44] *Ibid* para 88. The measure reviewed was the Council and Commission Decision 2002/309/EC, Euratom as regards the Agreement on Scientific and Technological Cooperation, of 4 April 2002 on the conclusion of seven Agreements with the Swiss Confederation [2002] OJ L114/1.

[45] *Commune de Champagne* (n 43) paras 89–90.

[46] Case C-386/08 *Firma Brita GmbH v Hauptzollamt Hamburg-Hafen* [2010] ECR I-1289.

[47] *Ibid* paras 101–12. Vienna Convention on the Law of Treaties 1969, 1155 UNTS 331, Article 38 contains an exception for *erga omnes* obligations and customary rules of international law.

in the territory of the West Bank only on the basis of certificates issued by PLO authorities.[48]

Curiously, no mention was made of *Commune de Champagne* in the General Court's *Polisario* Decision or the *Western Sahara Campaign* Opinion and judgment, despite its obvious relevance. However, in the appeal from the General Court's *Polisario* Decision before the ECJ, the Council cited *Commune de Champagne* in Bartelsian terms, as meaning that a 'Council decision relating to the conclusion of an international agreement between the European Union and a third State has no legal effect in the territory of the other party to that agreement' such that 'the situation of such a territory is governed solely by the provisions adopted by that other party in the exercise of its sovereign powers'.[49] In the Advisory Opinion, however, AG Wathelet interpreted *Commune de Champagne* more narrowly as being relevant only to international agreements whose proper territorial scope of application was not contested.[50] AG Wathelet's reading is preferable. Strictly speaking, the General Court's statement in *Commune de Champagne* is both *obiter* and overbroad. The General Court was indeed correct to find that the Swiss applicants lacked standing to seek judicial review, because whatever factual effects the EU measure adopting the international agreement may have had upon them, the change in their legal position was traceable solely to Switzerland.[51] In other words, if the applicants had a problem with that international agreement, they should have taken it up with their sovereign representative, not the EU. The EU did not by its internal, unilateral act produce legal effects upon the applicants in *that* particular instance. However, as established in chapter two, there are many other occasions when it does, most evidently in EU extraterritorial legislation in the areas of competition, data privacy, environmental and financial regulation utilising the method of territorial extension.

The problem, however, is that neither the EU-Morocco Association Agreement nor the FPA fits this mould. The question then is whether there is any other way these international agreements can be described as assertions of political authority over distant strangers. That this is indeed the case may be illustrated by contrasting the fact pattern of *Commune de Champagne* with those of *Polisario* and *Western Sahara Campaign*.

On the conception of dignity as independence, persons normally may not unilaterally change the legal rights and obligations of others; that is to say, exercise authority over each other. If that were generally possible, all persons would

[48] *Brita* (n 46) paras 44–45, 52, 56–58.

[49] *Council v Front Polisario* (n 4) para 78. See also *Council v Front Polisario*, Opinion of AG Wathelet (n 3) para 55.

[50] *Council v Front Polisario*, Opinion of AG Wathelet (n 3) paras 55–56. The ECJ avoided settling this debate by maintaining that the reference to the territory of Morocco was not to be interpreted as including the Western Sahara. *Council v Front Polisario* (n 4) para 92–99.

[51] *Commune de Champagne* (n 43) para 91.

become subject to the arbitrary choices of everyone else – they would dominate and be dominated by all others. The relative effect of treaties can be explained in such terms: two international persons cannot by agreement between themselves alter the legal rights and obligations of a third person. To hold otherwise would be to treat that third international person as a thing at the disposal of the treaty parties, which is contrary to their dignity as a free equal in the international legal order. As has also been established by now, authority is a fiduciary office – the 'possession' of a person is compatible with right only if that person is not also 'used'. To possess and use a person simultaneously is to treat them wholly as means and not as an end also. By conceptualising (1) juridical dignity in terms of independence; (2) the unilateral creation of legal effects as implying a claim of political authority; and (3) political authority in terms of fiduciary accountability, we can simultaneously explain why *Commune de Champagne* was correct to hold that the EU did not produce any legal effects upon the Swiss applicants in that case, as well as why the opposite should apply for both the Front Polisario and an individual Sahrawi applicant.

In the *Commune de Champagne* fact pattern, a treaty between international parties can be analogised to a contract between two private trustees. Ordinarily, legitimate political authorities/trustees are presumed to be entitled to modify the legal positions of their subjects/beneficiaries, so each counterparty to the contract/treaty has no reason or standing to question the other's decision or motivations behind entering into the agreement. Therefore, all changes in any individual subject's legal position are traceable to their particular sovereign.

This default model ceases to apply if one party has affirmative knowledge that the counterparty is violating their obligations to their subjects. The situation may be analogised to dishonest or knowing assistance in procuring a breach of trust in English law, under which a trustee's

> legal power and control over the trust property … may no doubt be extended in equity to others who are not properly trustees, if they are found either making themselves trustees *de son tort*, or actually participating in any fraudulent conduct of the trustee to the injury of the *cestui que trust*.[52]

Similarly, the law on international responsibility of states and international organisations recognises secondary liability for aiding or assisting international wrongs when states and international organisations have: (1) knowledge of the circumstances of the internationally wrongful act; and (2) that act would be wrongful if committed by the state or international organisation itself.[53] While there is a lively debate between common lawyers as to whether the

[52] *Barnes v Addy* (1874) 9 LR Ch App 244 (CA) 251–52.

[53] International Law Commission, 'Articles on Responsibility of States for Internationally Wrongful Acts, Adopted by the Commission at Its Fifty-Third Session in 2001' (2001) UN Doc A/56/10, 43, art 16 [hereinafter *ARS*]; International Law Commission, 'Articles on the Responsibility of International Organizations, Adopted by the Drafting Committee in 2011 (Final Outcome)' (2011) UN Doc A/CN.4/L.778, art 14.

standard for knowing assistance in a breach of trust is dishonesty or mere negligence,[54] the consensus at international law is that 'the aid or assistance must be given with a view to facilitating the commission of the wrongful act, and must actually do so'.[55] This is an incredibly high standard which can be satisfied only in the most unusual of cases. Thus, despite proceeding from very different premises, I ultimately agree with Bartels' conclusion that 'it is doubtful that a party negotiating a trade agreement will ever know with the requisite degree of certainty that a given obligation will result in a violation of human rights obligations'.[56] I agree also with the exception suggested by Bartels to this general position: an agreement to export instruments of torture gives rise to human rights obligations (and liability) because it knowingly assists and procures the importing state's breach of its human rights obligations.[57]

At this point, it must be emphasised that the procedural question of admissibility before the EU courts does not depend upon the substantive question of what constitutes assisting an international wrong in international law. The procedural question is, in some sense 'primary': does the EU owe the claimant an obligation of accountability because it has established itself as an authority over them? This is not the secondary, substantive question of whether it has *breached* those obligations. That comes later – at the merits. The question is not whether international wrongs committed by Morocco in the exploitation of the Western Sahara are attributable to the EU as a matter of international law,[58] but whether the EU, by entering into the Association Agreement with Morocco, has placed itself in a kind of relationship with individual Sahrawis where it might legitimately be expected to hear their grievances and owe them the courtesy of a reply.

Thus expressed, the legal analysis is as follows: in a *Commune de Champagne* scenario, the primary obligation of accountability is contingent upon

[54] See *Royal Brunei Airlines v Tan* [1995] UKPC 4 (holding the correct standard as dishonesty rather than negligence or unconscionability); *Farah Constructions Pty Ltd v Say-Dee Pty Ltd* [2007] HCA 22 (requiring a more fine-grained assessment of the third party's and the trustee's dishonesty) (High Court, Australia). See also *Dubai Aluminium Company Ltd v Salaam* [2002] UKHL 48 (HL) and *Air Canada v M & L Travel Ltd* (1993) 3 SCR 787 (Supreme Court, Canada).

[55] J Crawford, *The International Law Commission's Articles on State Responsibility: Introduction, Text and Commentaries* (Cambridge, Cambridge University Press, 2002) 149, para 5. See also H Aust, *Complicity and the Law of State Responsibility* (Cambridge, Cambridge University Press, 2011) 235 ('It thus appears that the ILC wants Article 16 [*ARS*] to be interpreted narrowly so that the 'knowledge' element turns into something more akin to a requirement of wrongful intent.'); *Application of the Convention on the Prevention and Punishment of the Crime of Genocide, Bosnia and Herzegovina v Serbia and Montenegro* (Judgment) [2007] ICJ Rep 43, para 421 ('There is no doubt that the conduct of an organ or a person furnishing aid or assistance to a perpetrator of the crime of genocide cannot be treated as complicity in genocide unless *at the least* that organ or person acted knowingly, that is to say, in particular, was aware of the specific intent (*dolus specialis*) of the principal perpetrator.') (Emphasis added.).

[56] L Bartels, 'The EU's Human Rights Obligations in Relation to Policies with Extraterritorial Effects' (2014) 25 *European Journal of International Law* 1071, 1081.

[57] *Ibid.*

[58] The Council attempted to argue this before the General Court. See *Polisario* (n 2), para 230.

affirmative knowledge of a substantive breach by the treaty counterparty. The EU is accountable to a distant stranger only if it is affirmatively aware that that person's sovereign would rely upon the treaty to violate her rights. However, in a scenario like *Polisario* or *Western Sahara Campaign* – that is, when the EU enters into a treaty that purports to dispose of things and persons upon the territory of a *third state not a party to the agreement* – this configuration is disrupted in two different ways. First, by concluding the agreement, both the EU and the counterparty hold themselves out as fiduciaries of the third state. Second, the EU also holds itself out as a fiduciary of the individual subjects of the third state, because the presumption that the counterparty speaks for the people of that territory ceases to hold.

That the EU-Morocco Association Agreement and the FPA both produce legal effects can be demonstrated normatively as a matter of interpersonal interaction. Consider a scenario of two persons agreeing between themselves that a third person, X, is to be placed under an obligation to make some performance. The maxim upon which the contractors appear to be acting is that they somehow consider themselves 'in charge' of X; they must imagine themselves entitled to determine her legal position. Otherwise, the agreement cannot even begin to be understood. Now, the contractors may be entirely incorrect in presuming themselves to be 'authorised' to dispose of X in this way, thus giving X a cause of action against them in injury. X is entirely free to characterise the contractors' conduct as a civil wrong against her.

As the master of her claim, however, X also has the option of 'overlooking' the contractors' lack of authorisation, and instead seek to hold them accountable as her fiduciaries under a theory of constructive trust or *negotiorum gestio*. If she takes this route, it is obviously impermissible for the *contractors* to raise *their* lack of authorisation and transform their agreement into a nullity, because no one can be heard to plead their own wrong. The contractors remain bound by the ostensible maxim of their action. Moreover, if X is herself a fiduciary of others, such that the contractors have intermeddled in the relationship between X and her beneficiaries, then the beneficiaries themselves become entitled to hold the contractors accountable to them as fiduciaries. To recall chapter three, the fiduciary's status is an acquired right in the hands of the beneficiary just as much as an item of their property or a performance owed them under contract. In so far as the contractors have 'taken' this status by usurping the fiduciary's office, they must now fulfil that office. This is the rationale behind *Mara v Browne*, in which Smith LJ held that

> if one, not being a trustee and not having authority from a trustee, takes upon himself to intermeddle with the trust matters or to do acts characteristic of the office of trustee, he may therefore make himself what is called in law a trustee of his own wrong – ie a trustee *de son tort*…[59]

[59] *Mara v Browne* [1896] 1 Ch 199 (CA) 209.

This rationale is also illustrated in the basic principles of the international law of occupation. Article 42 of the Hague Regulations 1907 provides that 'Territory is considered occupied when it is actually placed under the authority of the hostile army',[60] while Article 43 of the same imposes upon such an occupant an obligation to maintain order and public life in the territory.[61] This has traditionally been understood as meaning that the occupant is in a fiduciary relationship with the ousted sovereign. As a leading textbook puts it,

> occupation does not transfer sovereignty. Instead, it transfers to the occupant the authority to exercise some of the rights of sovereignty. The occupant, therefore, exercises a temporary right of administration, on a trusteeship basis until the occupation ceases in one way or another.[62]

This, however, is not the end of the occupant's fiduciary obligations. As Benvenisti explains, the current Fourth set of Geneva Conventions build on the Hague Regulations to envisage a much more expansive role for the occupant with regards to governing the territory, whereby it is 'a proactive regulator, [and] no longer the disinterested watch guard envisioned in the Hague Regulations'.[63] In this spirit, Benvenisti argues that 'the emerging principles of self-determination, of human and minority rights' mean that 'the occupant's status is conceived to be that of a trustee' not just of the ousted sovereign, but also of the population under occupation.[64]

These basic principles were specifically brought to bear in the context of the Western Sahara in the 'Corell Memorandum', a legal opinion issued by Hans Corell, the UN Under-Secretary-General for Legal Affairs and Legal Counsel.[65]

[60] This provision has been preserved in subsequent treaties and has become customary international law. See E Benvenisti, *The International Law of Occupation*, 2nd edn (Oxford, Oxford University Press, 2012) 44, citing *Tuta and Štela, Prosecutor v Naletilić (Mladen) and Martinović (Vinko)* (Trial judgment) ICTY-98-34-T (31 March 2003), para 217.

[61] The authentic text of Hague (IV) Regulations respecting the Laws and Customs of War on Land of 1907, 205 CTS 277, Article 43 provides that 'L'autorité du pouvoir légal ayant passé de fait entre les mains de l'occupant, celui-ci prendra toutes les mesures qui dépendent de lui en vue de rétablir et d'assurer, autant qu'il est possible, l'ordre et la vie publics …'. The first English version mistranslated the phrase 'la vie publics' as 'safety'. See Benvenisti (n 60) 68, fn 1.

[62] G von Glahn and JL Taulbee, *Law Among Nations: An Introduction to Public International Law* (Abingdon, Routledge, 2015) 635. See also A Roberts, 'What Is a Military Occupation?' (1985) 55 *British Yearbook of International Law* 249, 294–95.

[63] Benvenisti (n 60) 74.

[64] Benvenisti (n 60) 6–7. See also Benvenisti (n 60) 72–76 (detailing the evolution of the occupant's duties from being mainly about preserving the rights of the ousted sovereign to becoming focused upon the welfare of the occupied people and protecting their human rights); EJ Criddle and E Fox-Decent, *Fiduciaries of Humanity: How International Law Constitutes Authority* (Oxford, Oxford University Press, 2016) 192–96 (describing the general recognition that occupants have human rights obligations towards the occupied people). In this regard, see the prohibition against pillage enshrined in Article 47, Hague Regulations. Finally, see the case law imposing a duty of vigilance upon the occupant. *Armed Activities on the Territory of the Congo, Democratic Republic of the Congo v Uganda* (Merits) [2005] ICJ Rep 168, paras 247–48.

[65] H Corell, 'Letter Dated 29 January 2002 from the Under-Secretary-General for Legal Affairs, the Legal Counsel, Addressed to the President of the Security Council' UN Doc S/2002/161.

On the question of the legality of Moroccan authorities entering into commercial contracts with foreign companies for the exploration of mineral resources in the Western Sahara, Corell opined that in virtue of the 'principle that the interests of the peoples of Non-Self-Governing Territories are paramount, and their well-being and development is the "sacred trust" of their respective administering Powers …'[66] leads to the conclusion that if 'exploration and exploitation activities were to proceed in disregard of the interests and wishes of the people of Western Sahara, they would be in violation of the principles of international law applicable to mineral resource activities in Non-Self-Governing Territories'.[67]

Unlike a sovereign, which can be presumed to have the same interests as its subjects, an occupying power 'must attend to at least three sets of interests: its own security interests, the interests of the ousted government, and those of the local population, which may be different from the interest of their legitimate government'.[68] This 'potential – if not inherent – conflict of interest between the occupant and occupied' obtains in all occupations, regardless of whether they are legal, illegal, 'belligerent', 'pacific', 'wartime' or 'military'.[69] While there is little positive law establishing the following claim (with the possible exception of the General Court's *Polisario* Decision as discussed below), the normative implications are clear. The conflict *inherent* to the occupier's rule means that any party entering into an agreement with it in respect of the occupied territory must be presumed to be aware of it. They are therefore put on immediate notice of the occupier's propensity for self-dealing both in the fiduciary relationship between the occupant and the ousted sovereign, and the fiduciary relationship between the occupant and the occupied population. There is, therefore, an affirmative duty on the part of the party to an agreement with an occupant to take reasonable steps to ensure the absence of exploitation. Failing this, it becomes a trustee *de son tort* of the ousted sovereign and the occupied population.

At this point, I reiterate that my focus in this chapter is simply whether or not certain types of international agreements produce extraterritorial legal effects such as are relevant to the procedural matter of admissibility before EU courts. It is *not* about the legality under international law of economic dealings with occupied territories. The question of the legality of any particular economic dealing by the EU is as irrelevant to my inquiry as questions about the legality of kidnapping are to whether a kidnapper must feed the kidnappee (to coin a phrase). Even if such economic dealings were completely illegal – as the ICJ

[66] *Ibid*, para 22.
[67] *Ibid*, para 25.
[68] Benvenisti (n 60) 69.
[69] Benvenisti (n 60) 3–4.

indicated in the *Namibia* Opinion[70] – this would not preclude the existence of obligations towards distant strangers in the occupied territory. Conversely, obligations towards distant strangers would obtain even if such economic dealings were fully permissible,[71] simply because the EU participates in a relationship with distant strangers that places them in a position of systematic vulnerability.

Thus, the EU-Morocco Association Agreement and the FPA produced legal effects over both the Front Polisario as well as over individual Sahrawi distant strangers. The Article 263 TFEU requirements of direct and individual concern for bringing judicial review are therefore illegitimate as applied against them. This, however, is by no means the full extent to which the courthouse doors are slammed shut. The next section sets out the reasoning by which the ECJ ultimately concluded that the concerned agreements created no extraterritorial legal effects, as well as of the use it made of Article 3(5) TEU in procuring this conclusion.

III. *POLISARIO* AND *WESTERN SAHARA CAMPAIGN*

The facts behind Morocco's presence in the Western Sahara following the departure of the Spanish colonial administration are reasonably well known. Formerly a colony of Spain, the then Spanish Sahara was added to the list of non-self-governing territories by the UN in 1963, following which the UN General Assembly called for a referendum to determine the future of the territory, with an option for full independence.[72] Morocco, which had long claimed the Western Sahara as an integral part of its territory, opposed the referendum and sought an Advisory Opinion on its legality from the ICJ in 1974. A year later, the ICJ opined that there existed no tie of territorial sovereignty between the Kingdom of Morocco and the Western Sahara such as might defeat the Sahrawi people's claim to self-determination and the formation of their own sovereign state.[73] Days later, Moroccan forces invaded the Western Sahara, following which an armed conflict broke out between those forces and the Front Polisario which

[70] See *Legal Consequences for States of the Continued Presence of South Africa in Namibia (South West Africa)* (Advisory Opinion) [1971] ICJ Rep 16, para 124 (finding an 'obligation to abstain from entering into economic or other forms of relation or dealings with South Africa on behalf of or concerning Namibia which may entrench its authority over the country').

[71] Kontorovich makes the sweeping claim that 'state practice has overwhelmingly found the ICJ's advice [in *Namibia*] to be inapplicable to other contexts, and suggests the *Namibia* Decision did not state a general or correct rule'. E Kontorovich, 'Economic Dealings with Occupied Territories' (2015) 53 *Columbia Journal of Transnational Law* 584, 591. This claim is made not through normative argument, but from the realist claim that the only thing that 'counts for international law [is] what countries do'. *Ibid* 593.

[72] UNGA Res 2229 (XXI) 'On the Question of Ifni and Spanish Sahara' UN Doc A/RES/2229(XXI) (20 December 1966).

[73] *Western Sahara* (n 1) para 162.

had been formed in the meantime. In February 1976, Spain withdrew from the Spanish Sahara and unilaterally relinquished all claims and obligations concerning the territory.[74] In 1979, the Front Polisario and Mauritania entered into an agreement whereby the latter relinquished its claims to the Western Sahara and withdrew its armed forces from the territory. Morocco entered into the vacuum left by the departing Mauritanian forces. Its subsequent annexation of the remainder of the Western Sahara was condemned by the UN General Assembly, which characterised the move as an 'occupation'.[75]

Morocco currently controls most of the Western Sahara; the sliver held by the Front Polisario is ruled from across the border in the Algerian town of Tindouf. Although the Front Polisario has been officially recognised by the UN as 'the representative of the people of Western Sahara',[76] Spain continues to be considered the *de jure* administering power in the territory notwithstanding its unilateral renunciation of its obligations.[77] It was in this context that the first EU-Morocco Association Agreement was concluded in 1996 and entered into force in 2000.

A. Case T-512/12 *Front Polisario v Council* – The General Court Decision

As mentioned above, the General Court held that the EU-Morocco Association Agreement had to be annulled on grounds of 'manifest errors of assessment' by the Council, as well as recognised the standing of the Front Polisario in seeking that annulment. One factor complicating the General Court's analysis was its diplomatic description of the Western Sahara as a 'disputed territory'. That characterisation of the Western Sahara territory is difficult to reconcile with the 'individual concern' requirement the Front Polisario had to fulfil to have standing, because it implies that there are at least two parties concerned with the status of that territory, such that any decision creating, or modifying legal rights or obligations in the territory would by definition have to be of concern to more than just the Front Polisario.[78] Instead, Fleury Graff offers the ingenious solution that 'Ce n'est, d'ailleurs, pas tant le "territoire" qui est disputé, que

[74] 'Letter Dated 26 February 1976 from the Permanent Representative of Spain to the UN Secretary-General' UN Doc A/31/56 – S/11997.

[75] UNGA Res 34/37 'On the Question of Western Sahara' UN Doc A/RES/34/37 (21 November 1979) art 5. See also UNGA Res 35/19 'On the Question of Western Sahara' UN Doc A/RES/35/19 (11 September 1980) art 3.

[76] UNGA Res 34/37, *ibid* art 7.

[77] UNSG, 'Report of 1 February 2016, Information from Non-Self-Governing Territories Transmitted under Art 73 (e) of the Charter of the United Nations' UN Doc A/71/68, annex.

[78] T Fleury Graff, 'Accords de Libre-Échange et Territoires Occupés: À Propos de l'arrêt TPIUE, 10 Décembre 2015, Front Polisario c. Conseil' (2016) 120 *Revue générale de droit international public* 263, 270. See also E Kassoti, 'The Front Polisario v. Council Case: The General Court, *Völkerrechtsfreundlichkeit* and the External Aspect of European Integration (First Part)' (2017) 2 *European Papers* 339, 352 ('another problematic aspect of the judgment is the examination of the substance of the action on the basis of the assumption that Western Sahara constitutes a

la "dispute" qui est "territoriale" du fait de son objet …',[79] and urges that the Western Sahara is more accurately described as an 'occupied territory.[80] Such a conclusion would follow from the General Court's explanation of the term 'disputed territory' as meaning 'a territory in fact controlled by a non-member State, without the sovereignty of that State over that territory being recognised by the European Union and its Member States or, more generally, by all other States'.[81] This is self-evidently not a territory that is disputed, but one that is occupied.[82]

The first substantive question the General Court had to deal with was whether the Front Polisario constituted a 'natural or legal person' for the purposes of Article 263(4) TFEU. The Council denied this basic question of capacity, on the grounds that the Front Polisario had not attached any constitutive documents of the sort enumerated under the Rules of Procedure of the General Court for applications made by legal persons governed by *private* law.[83] In response, the Front Polisario insisted that it was 'not a legally constituted body according to the law of any State, whether internationally recognised or not', and that as 'the incarnation of the sovereignty of the Sahrawi people' it could not be required 'to produce evidence of its constitution according to the national law of an internationally recognised State'.[84] In the end, the General Court accorded it personality recognised *under EU law*, on the basis of a jurisprudence emphasising twin criteria of independence and responsibility; that

"disputed territory" whose "international status is currently undetermined". In fact, the status of the territory is far from being undetermined …').

[79] Fleury Graff, *ibid* 270.

[80] Fleury Graff, *ibid* 269–72.

[81] *Polisario* (n 2) para 117. See also para 232, where the General Court describes the Western Sahara in particular as 'a territory … which is in fact administered by a non-member State, in this case the Kingdom of Morocco, although it is not included in the recognised international frontiers of that non-member State'.

[82] See Hague Regulations of 1907 (n 61), art 42 ('Territory is considered occupied when it is actually placed under the authority of the hostile army.'). See also Corell (n 65) para 6:

> On 14 November 1975, a Declaration of Principles on Western Sahara was concluded in Madrid between Spain, Morocco and Mauritania (the Madrid Agreement), whereby the powers and responsibilities of Spain, as the administering Power of the territory, were transferred to a temporary tripartite administration. The Madrid Agreement did not transfer sovereignty over the territory, nor did it confer upon any of the signatories the status of an administering Power – a status which Spain alone could not have unilaterally transferred.

[83] Rules of Procedure of the Court of First Instance of the European Communities [1991] OJ L136/1, Rule 44(5) provides that 'An application made by a legal person governed by private law shall be accompanied by: (a) the instrument or instruments constituting and regulating that legal person or a recent extract from the register of companies, firms or associations or any other proof of its existence in law …'.

[84] *Polisario* (n 2) paras 40–41. The Italian Court of Cassation has held that national liberation movements enjoy a form of 'objective legal personality' under international law independent of recognition by other sovereign states. *Arafat and Salah, Re*, (1988) 7 *Italian Yearbook of International Law* 295 (Italy, Supreme Court of Cassation, 1st Criminal Section).

is, in terms of being able to have one's actions attributed to oneself.[85] In particular, the General Court likened the Front Polisario to the applicant in *Groupement des Agences de voyages*, where an *ad hoc* association of travel agencies formed to respond to a tender was held to possess personality on grounds that

> the Commission could not challenge the capacity to institute proceedings of a body that it had allowed to participate in an invitation to tender and to which it had addressed a negative decision after a comparative examination of all the tenderers.[86]

Finally, the General Court cited *PKK and KNK v Council* – an action for annulment where two organisations challenged certain restrictive measures placed upon them for combating terrorism – for the contention that where an entity is regarded 'as having an existence sufficient to be the subject of … restrictive measures … consistency and justice required that that entity be recognised as having the capacity to challenge that decision'.[87]

The mislabelling of the Western Sahara as 'disputed territory', and its recognition of the Front Polisario as a person only under EU law, resulted in an extremely peculiar analysis of the issues regarding standing. Recall that the decision being challenged was a legislative act not explicitly addressed to the Front Polisario, such that the *Plaumann* doctrine was to apply in full.[88] In order to satisfy the 'individual concern' requirement, it had to be the case that no other person could lay claim to similar rights relating to the Western Sahara. The Court reasoned that the aforementioned 'effects on the legal position of the whole territory' were of direct concern to the Front Polisario because 'the definitive international status of that territory [had] not yet been determined and [had to] be determined in UN-led negotiations between the Kingdom of Morocco and, specifically, the Front Polisario'.[89] However, this only means that the Front Polisario had an *interest* in the conclusive determination of the legal rights concerning that territory, and 'interests' are not the same thing as rights.

Even if this objection is ignored, the fact that the Front Polisario plays an integral role in the UN-led negotiations would not be enough to satisfy the

[85] See *Polisario* (n 2) para 49 (finding that entities have personality when 'their constitutional structures were such as to endow them with the necessary independence to act as responsible bodies in legal matters …'), citing Case 175/73 *Union syndicale-Amalgamated European Public Service Union and others v Council* (1974) ECR 917, paras 9–17; Case 18/74 *Syndicat Général du Personnel des Organismes européens v Commission* [1974] ECR 933, paras 5–13. See also *Polisario* (n 2), para 51 citing Case 15/63 *Lassalle v Parliament* [1963] ECR 50, 51 (personality implies the possession of a measure of 'independence and responsibility, even if limited').

[86] Case 135/81 *Groupement des Agences de voyages v Commission* [1982] ECR 3800, paras 9–12. Cited at *Polisario* (n 2), para 48.

[87] Case T-229/02 *PKK v Council* (2008) II ECR 45, para 109–12. Cited at *Polisario* (n 2), para 50.

[88] *Polisario* (n 2) paras 71–73.

[89] *Polisario* (n 2) para 110.

individual concern requirement in and of itself. Recall that the applicant in *Plaumann* was denied standing because in principle any other person could have entered the clementine business, but that the applicant in *Codorníu* was recognised to have standing because, having taken out a trademark in Spain, it alone had the right to call its product 'crémant'. Therefore, for the Front Polisario to have standing, it had to be the case that *no one else* could rightfully have taken part in those negotiations. None of this would obtain if the Front Polisario was endowed with personality only under EU law in the manner of an ordinary private person. Instead, for the Front Polisario to have standing, one would have to take seriously its claim to be the incarnation of the Sahrawi people, and a person at international law.[90] The Council made precisely this argument before the ECJ, which AG Wathelet in principle agreed with in his second theory.[91] As we shall see, however, he would have denied the Front Polisario standing nonetheless.[92]

After disposing of these procedural questions thus, the General Court heard 11 different substantive pleas from the Front Polisario, of which it rejected all but one. Of particular interest for our purposes are the two instances where the General Court broached possible claims by individual Sahrawis. In the first, it considered whether the EU Charter of Fundamental Rights, read together with Article 6 TEU and Article 67 TFEU, could be invoked to invalidate the Association Agreement on grounds of human rights violations by Moroccan authorities.[93] It concluded that they could not, with the terse and conclusory remark that

> no absolute prohibition derives, either from those provisions or from those of the Charter of Fundamental Rights, which precludes the EU from concluding an agreement with a third State on trade in agricultural products, processed agricultural products, fish and fishery products which may also be applied to a territory controlled by that third State even though its sovereignty over that territory has not been internationally recognised.[94]

Second, it considered whether the EU was prohibited from entering into the Association Agreement by Articles 3(5) and 21 TEU, and Article 205 TFEU, which require the EU to protect and advance human rights in all its relations with the wider world. Again, it concluded that they did not, on the only marginally less opaque reasoning that because

> the EU institutions enjoy a wide discretion in the field of external economic relations which covers the agreement referred to by the contested decision … it cannot be accepted that it follows from the 'values on which the European Union is based', or

[90] Fleury Graff (n 78) 283.
[91] *Polisario*, Opinion of AG Wathelet (n 3) paras 184–85.
[92] *Polisario*, Opinion of AG Wathelet (n 3) paras 201, 212.
[93] *Polisario* (n 2) paras 143–48.
[94] *Polisario* (n 2) para 146.

> the provisions relied on by the Front Polisario …, that the conclusion by the Council of an agreement with a third State which may be applied in a disputed territory is, in all cases, prohibited.[95]

These pronouncements echo the General Court's major theme of the lack of an 'absolute' prohibition against economic dealings with 'disputed' (read 'occupied') territories.

Ultimately, the sole reason the Court gave for the annulment was an administrative omission:

> Given the fact, *inter alia*, that the sovereignty of the Kingdom of Morocco over Western Sahara is not recognised by the European Union or its Member States, or more generally by the UN, and the absence of any international mandate capable of justifying Moroccan presence on that territory, the Council, in the examination of all the relevant facts of the present case, with a view to exercising its wide discretion as to whether or not to conclude an agreement with the Kingdom of Morocco which may also apply to Western Sahara, should have satisfied itself that there was no evidence of an exploitation of the natural resources of the territory of Western Sahara under Moroccan control likely to be to the detriment of its inhabitants and to infringe their fundamental rights.[96]

The General Court dismissed the Council's argument that it was 'solely for the Kingdom of Morocco to ensure that the exploitation of the natural resources is beneficial to the inhabitants of the part of Western Sahara it controls',[97] and held instead that the duty of due diligence had special salience in the particular case of occupied territories like the Western Sahara.[98] Interestingly, the scope of the assessment required by the General Court appears to cover the entire catalogue of rights in the EU Charter of Fundamental Rights.[99] Because the Council had failed to carry out such an assessment, the EU institutions had committed not just an ordinary error, but a 'manifest' error of assessment, such that the Council Decision to adopt the EU-Morocco Association Agreement had to be annulled to the extent it applied to the Western Sahara.[100]

D. Case C-104/16 *Council v Front Polisario* – Before the ECJ

As is customary, the appeal before the ECJ produced two documents: an Advisory Opinion by AG Wathelet, followed by a judgment by the ECJ. As already mentioned, AG Wathelet gave the ECJ a choice of three options, two

[95] *Polisario* (n 2) para 165.
[96] *Polisario* (n 2) para 241.
[97] *Polisario* (n 2) para 240.
[98] *Polisario* (n 2) para 232.
[99] *Polisario* (n 2) para 228.
[100] *Polisario* (n 2) para 247.

of which would have reversed the General Court, and one which would have preserved it. The first of the three theories AG Wathelet presented – which eventually became the basis for the ECJ Decision – was pitted squarely against the General Court's premise that international agreements purporting to bind third parties are not 'absolutely' prohibited, and therefore implicitly permitted. Pointing to the Western Sahara's status as a non-self-governing territory under Article 73 UNC, as well as settled practice by the EU Member States and other states recognising the Western Sahara as such,[101] AG Wathelet rejected the General Court's 'disputed territory' terminology, and concluded instead that the Western Sahara 'cannot be part of the territory of the Kingdom of Morocco within the meaning of' the EU-Morocco Association Agreement.[102] From this point onwards, two sleights of hand take place.

In the second of his arguments, AG Wathelet invoked the relative effect of treaties, which, as mentioned above, prohibits parties to a treaty creating rights or obligations for a third party without its assent.[103] In its Decision below, the General Court had held that that principle was inapplicable because unlike in *Brita*, there was no parallel agreement between the EU and the Front Polisario from which the latter could derive rights that might be raised in opposition to the provisions of the EU-Morocco Association Agreement.[104] In contrast, AG Wathelet opined, and the ECJ agreed,[105] that as the Western Sahara was a non-self-governing territory rather than a 'disputed' one, it was by definition a third party to the EU-Morocco Association Agreement, and could therefore not be bound by that agreement without its consent. Such consent had not been given, so the treaty could not be interpreted as purporting to apply in the territory of the Western Sahara. Finally, since it did not apply to the Western Sahara, the Front Polisario had no legal interest in challenging the EU measure adopting it, and therefore lacked standing to do so.[106]

Next came a discussion of what was termed the '*de facto* application' of the agreement to the Western Sahara. By that, AG Wathelet and the ECJ meant: (1) the inclusion of, and extension of tariff preferences to 140 companies based in the Western Sahara in the list of approved foreign exporters contained in the schedules to the Association Agreement; and (2) the multiple visits by officials from the Commission's Food and Veterinary Office to the Western Sahara to

[101] *Polisario*, Opinion of AG Wathelet (n 3) paras 73–81.
[102] *Polisario*, Opinion of AG Wathelet (n 3) para 82.
[103] *Polisario*, Opinion of AG Wathelet (n 3) paras 101–12.
[104] *Polisario* (n 2) paras 95–97.
[105] *Council v Front Polisario* (n 4) para 106; *Polisario*, Opinion of AG Wathelet (n 3) paras 105, 108. The precise identity of 'it' is unclear. For the ECJ, the third party is the 'people' of the Western Sahara, while AG Wathelet's third party defines it as the 'territory', but then proceeds to refer interchangeably to that, the people, and their representatives.
[106] *Polisario*, Opinion of AG Wathelet (n 3) paras 105–12; *Council v Front Polisario* (n 4) paras 100–108.

ensure compliance by Moroccan authorities with EU health standards.[107] At no point did the Council or the Commission deny that these visits by EU officials to the Western Sahara actually took place. Before the General Court, the Commission 'confirm(ed) the presence on the list of approved exporters … of undertakings established in Western Sahara' but argued that they were merely there 'as a matter of convenience'.[108] Before the ECJ, the Council conceded that it knew that the preferential terms accorded by the Association Agreement were to be extended to exports coming from the Western Sahara, but argued that this did not amount to 'recognition, acquiescence or acceptance' of Morocco's claim to sovereignty over that territory.[109]

In the Opinion, AG Wathelet described this pejoratively as a strategy of 'application without recognition',[110] but ultimately concluded that the presence of 140 Western Sahara-based companies on the list of approved exporters was irrelevant, because 'those exporters are also established in Morocco, […] and for that reason are entitled to benefit from the [Association Agreement]'.[111] Neither did the visits by Commission officials constitute implementation of the Association Agreement in the Western Sahara, 'since they are not provided for' in the Association Agreement.[112] Instead, AG Wathelet reframed the discussion as a matter of subsequent practice possibly effecting a variation of a treaty,[113] and argued on this basis that the instances of '*de facto* application' did not qualify as such because the parties were not of one mind: Morocco viewed the Western Sahara as an integral part of its territory while the EU did not.[114] Once again, this meant that the EU-Morocco Association Agreement did not apply to the Western Sahara, such that the Front Polisario once again had no 'legal interest' in challenging the Council Decision adopting it.[115]

In the judgment, the ECJ adopted AG Wathelet's argument both on the relative effect and on '*de facto* application'. The first line of its findings observes that

> the conclusion of the General Court … that the Liberalisation Agreement 'also applies to the territory of Western Sahara' was based not on a finding of fact, but on a legal interpretation of that agreement made by the General Court on the basis of Article 31 of the Vienna Convention.[116]

[107] See *Polisario* (n 2) paras 79–80; *Polisario*, Opinion of AG Wathelet (n 3) paras 98–99. The ECJ is much more guarded, speaking only of 'the facts set out in paragraphs 77 to 87 of [the General Court] judgment'. *Council v Front Polisario* (n 4) para 117.

[108] *Polisario* (n 2) para 80.

[109] *Polisario*, Opinion of AG Wathelet (n 3) para 67.

[110] *Polisario*, Opinion of AG Wathelet (n 3) paras 67, 80.

[111] *Polisario*, Opinion of AG Wathelet (n 3) para 99.

[112] *Polisario*, Opinion of AG Wathelet (n 3) para 98.

[113] *Polisario*, Opinion of AG Wathelet (n 3) para 91, citing Joined Cases C 464/13 and C 465/13, *Europäische Schule München v Oberto and O'Leary* ECLI:EU:C:2015:163 (11 March 2015).

[114] *Polisario*, Opinion of AG Wathelet (n 3) paras 87–100.

[115] *Polisario*, Opinion of AG Wathelet (n 3) para 114.

[116] *Council v Front Polisario* (n 4) para 81, referring to *Polisario* (n 2) paras 73, 88, 98–102.

Following from this, the ECJ pointed out that

> in order to be able to draw correct legal conclusions from the absence of a stipulation excluding Western Sahara from the territorial scope of the Association Agreement, in interpreting that agreement, the General Court was bound not only to observe the rules of good faith interpretation ... pursuant to which the interpretation of a treaty must be carried out by taking account of any relevant rules of international law applicable in the relations between the parties ...[117]

These rules included the principle of self-determination, Article 29 VCLT on the territorial scope of treaties and the relative effect of treaties.[118] The first two of these meant that the phrase 'territory of the Kingdom of Morocco' contained in Article 94 of the Association Agreement was not to be interpreted as including the territory of Western Sahara,[119] while the relative effect of treaties meant that the Agreement could not apply to the Western Sahara in the absence of consultation of the Sahrawis.[120]

Second, because instances of '*de facto*' implementation of the Agreement 'would necessarily be incompatible with the principle that Treaty obligations must be performed in good faith, which nevertheless constitutes a binding principle of general international law applicable to subjects of that law who are contracting parties to a treaty',[121] it followed that recognising them as subsequent practice

> would necessarily have entailed conceding that the European Union intended to implement those agreements in a manner incompatible with the principles of self-determination and of the relative effect of treaties, even though the European Union repeatedly reiterated the need to comply with those principles ...[122]

This would 'necessarily be incompatible with the principle that Treaty obligations must be performed in good faith, which nevertheless constitutes a binding principle of general international law ...'.[123] Accordingly, the General Court erred 'in holding that the subsequent practice referred to in [its] judgment ... justified an interpretation of those agreements as meaning that they were legally applicable to the territory of Western Sahara'.[124]

As such, the ECJ's *Polisario* Decision does not simply narrow or block access to judicial review by throwing up the direct and individual concern requirements. By concluding and adopting the EU-Morocco Association Agreement,

[117] *Council v Front Polisario* (n 4) para 86, citing *Brita* (n 46), para 43 and Joined Cases C-402/05 and C-415/05 *Kadi v Council of the European Union and Commission of the European Communities* [2008] ECR I-6351, para 291.

[118] *Council v Front Polisario* (n 4) para 87.

[119] *Council v Front Polisario* (n 4) para 108.

[120] *Council v Front Polisario* (n 4) paras 106–107.

[121] *Council v Front Polisario* (n 4) para 124.

[122] *Council v Front Polisario* (n 4) para 123.

[123] *Council v Front Polisario* (n 4) para 124.

[124] *Council v Front Polisario* (n 4) para 125.

the EU placed itself in a fiduciary relationship with both the Front Polisario and individual Sahrawis; that is, a relationship of authority. Thus, in principle, both the Front Polisario and individual Sahrawis ought to have had standing to challenge the Council Decision adopting the Association Agreement. As such, the requirements of direct and individual concern would have posed unjustifiable barriers to both of them. In this regard, consider that AG Wathelet's second rationale acknowledged the Front Polisario as the legitimate representative of the Sahrawi people in the 'political process', and accordingly recognised that the Council Decision produced legal effects upon it.[125] Nevertheless, he advised that it still would not have standing due to the criteria of direct and individual concern, because the Council Decision might also have been of interest to the Kingdom of Spain as the entity officially tasked with administering the Western Sahara under Article 73 of the UNC.[126] Thus, the acknowledged legitimate representative of the Sahrawi people would nonetheless be denied standing on account of a speculative interest on the part of a colonial power that had abandoned any obligations relating to the Western Sahara more than three decades earlier.

According to the ECJ's rationale, however, the application would not be allowed to get even that far, but would instead be dismissed outright for lack of legal effects. The rule of the relative effect of treaties, meant to prevent two international persons from joining forces to exploit another, becomes a means by which the third person exploited by the arrangement is denied the right to complain of it.[127] As regards the instances of '*de facto* application', while AG Wathelet merely mischaracterised them, the ECJ Decision denied their reality outright. In both of these instances, the sleight of hand consists in sublimating the fact that the EU-Morocco Association Agreement was *actually* applied to the Western Sahara, with the question of whether it *should* have been applied there. The fact that there is a legal prohibition against others punching you does not mean they are factually incapable of doing so, or that the black eye you are left with is merely '*de facto*' and therefore somehow irrelevant. '*De facto* application' is just a euphemism for *illegal* application. The whole reason why the legal prohibition exists is because people are capable of punching each other and actually do so from time to time. Likewise, the fact that EU institutions may be *legally* prohibited from entering into an agreement with another state that it knows will be wrongfully applied upon the territory of yet another, does not mean that it *did not actually do so*, as the Council effectively conceded in its 'application without recognition' argument. The ECJ's invocation of the good

[125] *Polisario*, Opinion of AG Wathelet (n 3) paras 175, 185–86.

[126] *Polisario*, Opinion of AG Wathelet (n 3) paras 186–91, 201, 212.

[127] See G Van der Loo, 'Law and Practice of the EU's Trade Agreements with "Disputed" Territories: A Consistent Approach?' in I Govaere and S Garben (eds), *The Interface Between EU and International Law: Contemporary Reflections* (Oxford, Hart Publishing, 2019) 258.

faith principle to deny the reality of what transpired in the Western Sahara, is exactly the technique castigated earlier as absurd: the nullification of one's acts by alleging their wrongfulness.

C. Case C-266/16 *Western Sahara Campaign* – The Preliminary Reference

The final act in the piece is the *Western Sahara Campaign* Opinion and Decision, which, as mentioned above, came before the ECJ by way of a preliminary reference from the English courts. Specifically, the subject of the application was not just the FPA, but also a 2013 Protocol setting out the fishing zones subject to the FPA and the final contribution obligations, and Council Regulation 1270/2013 implementing the above.[128] Together, these instruments created an arrangement where Moroccan authorities permitted EU vessels to fish in Moroccan waters in exchange for monetary payments, as well as financial assistance to Morocco in setting up a national fisheries policy amounting to a total of €40 million.[129]

The key point of contention was the phrase 'waters falling within the sovereignty or jurisdiction of the Kingdom of Morocco'[130] repeated throughout the contested measures. In this regard, the essential complaint of the applicant was that the inclusion of Western Saharan waters in the scheme was contrary to the general principles of EU law and the Article 3(5) TEU obligation to contribute to the strict observance of international law and respect for the principles of the UNC – in particular, the right of self-determination, Article 73 UNC, the permanent sovereignty over natural resources and international humanitarian law.[131] Thus stated, the examination necessarily turned on the question of the legality in the light of public international law, and by extension of EU law, of the EU entering into economic dealings with occupied territories taking no account of the will of the people of the occupied territory or their recognised representatives.[132] Both the Opinion and the Decision came down strongly on the side that such agreements were illegal. Once again, I reiterate that this question is of no relevance to my argument in this chapter. What is relevant,

[128] Council Regulation 1270/2013/EU of 15 November 2013 on the allocation of fishing opportunities under the Protocol between the European Union and the Kingdom of Morocco setting out the fishing opportunities and financial contribution provided for in the Fisheries Partnership Agreement between the European Union and the Kingdom of Morocco [2013] OJ L328/40.

[129] EU-Morocco FPA (n 7) arts 2, 3 and 6. See Case *Western Sahara Campaign*, Opinion of AG Wathelet (n 5) paras 14–16.

[130] EU-Morocco FPA (n 7) art 2(a). See also Council Regulation 764/2006/EC of 22 May 2006 on the conclusion of the Fisheries Partnership Agreement between the European Community and the Kingdom of Morocco Fisheries Partnership Agreement between the European Communities and the Kingdom of Morocco [2006] OJ L141/1 recital 1; Council Regulation 1270/2013/EU (n 128) recital 2.

[131] *Western Sahara Campaign*, Opinion of AG Wathelet (n 5) para 26.

[132] *Western Sahara Campaign*, Opinion of AG Wathelet (n 5) paras 29–30.

though, is the subtle difference in the use made of Article 3(5) TEU between the Opinion and in the Decision.

The Opinion contained a lengthy and wide-ranging discussion on the relationship between EU law and international law, in which AG Wathelet adopted an attitude far removed from the indifferent list of possible options he provided in *Polisario*, but argued instead that the contested measures were clearly illegal. Starting from the premise that international treaties are to be read in their ordinary language in light of their object and purpose, AG Wathelet provided three reasons why this meant that the parties fully intended the FPA to apply in Western Saharan waters. The most arresting of these was a series of charts of the fishing zones contemplated under the 2013 Protocol, which clearly showed the waters adjacent to the Western Sahara as set aside for exploitative activities such as small-scale fishing, demersal fishing with longliners and trawlers, tuna fishing, as well as industrial pelagic fishing.[133] The other reasons were the fact that the 'genesis' of the FPA lay in a series of fisheries agreements concluded between Morocco and Spain before the latter joined the Union that were applied in Western Saharan waters, as well as affirmative knowledge by various EU institutions and Member States that Morocco intended the FPA to apply in Western Saharan waters.[134]

AG Wathelet then opined that an exception had to be made to the rule in *Air Transport Association* that individuals may seek review of EU measures for violation of customary international law only in cases of manifest error, and even then only of sufficiently precise rules. As discussed in chapter four, the EU is not a sovereign state and therefore unable to appear before the ICJ. Therefore, restricting the ability of applicants to rely on customary international law in the case of potentially illegal international treaties might be to exclude review altogether, even of those treaties violating *erga omnes* norms.[135] The Advocate General then proceeded to conduct a detailed examination of each of the rules of international law raised by the applicants and argued for the reviewability of the contested measures as against them.[136] He then advised that the concept of a 'de facto administering power' was unknown to international law,[137] and instead simply characterised Morocco as an occupying power in the Western Sahara.[138] Throughout all this, he constantly recalled the *Namibia* principle of neither recognising an illegal situation resulting from a breach of the right to self-determination nor rendering aid or assistance in maintaining the same, and argued that it had been incorporated into EU law through Article 3(5) TEU.[139]

[133] *Western Sahara Campaign*, Opinion of AG Wathelet (n 5) paras 66–69.
[134] *Western Sahara Campaign*, Opinion of AG Wathelet (n 5) paras 72–75.
[135] *Western Sahara Campaign*, Opinion of AG Wathelet (n 5) paras 76–87.
[136] *Western Sahara Campaign*, Opinion of AG Wathelet (n 5) paras 98–142.
[137] *Western Sahara Campaign*, Opinion of AG Wathelet (n 5) para 223. See also paras 221–33.
[138] *Western Sahara Campaign*, Opinion of AG Wathelet (n 5) paras 245–51.
[139] *Western Sahara Campaign*, Opinion of AG Wathelet (n 5) para 241.

Concerning the rule that an occupant is a mere usufructuary, allowed to exploit resources in the territory only for the benefit of the population,[140] the Advocate General noted that the FPA provided no means of ensuring that an appropriate portion of either the proceeds of fishing or of the financial contributions made by the EU would be allocated to the Saharawi population.[141] In the end, he advised the ECJ to find the arrangement under the FPA and the other contested measures 'incompatible with Article 3(5) TEU, the first subparagraph of Article 21(1) TEU, Article 21(2)(b) and (c) TEU and Articles 23 TEU and 205 TFEU in that they apply to the territory of Western Sahara and to the waters adjacent thereto'.[142]

In contrast to the prolixity of the Opinion, the ECJ issued a terse Decision that rejected several of AG Wathelet's premises. First, whereas AG Wathelet's distinguished the FPA from the Association Agreement in *Polisario* on the basis that the parties' intentions regarding the scope of territorial application were clear in the former, the ECJ instead held that the FPA was pursued as part of a project of fostering closer trade and economic links between the EU and Morocco, and therefore part of the same 'body of agreements' as the Association Agreement, such that the territorial scope of the FPA had to be determined by reference to that envisaged in the Association Agreement.[143] The Court then rehearsed its reasoning in *Polisario*: that is to say, because interpreting the territorial scope of the Association Agreement as including the Western Sahara would violate international norms such as the right of self-determination and the relative effect of treaties, neither could the territorial scope of the FPA be interpreted as including the Western Sahara.[144]

In essence, the question the applicants had sought an answer to was whether the FPA was 'rightful' under international law, and by extension EU law. AG Wathelet attempted to answer that specific question. In contrast, the ECJ 'redirected the question to the validity of the implementing legislation based on an interpretation of the agreements that would respect international law in the widest sense'.[145] Perhaps the most characteristic passage in the ECJ's Decision is the following:

> ... with respect to the expression 'waters falling within the sovereignty ... of the Kingdom of Morocco', used in Article 2(a) of the Fisheries Partnership Agreement,

[140] Hague Regulations of 1907 (n 61) art 55.

[141] *Western Sahara Campaign*, Opinion of AG Wathelet (n 5) paras 272–82.

[142] *Western Sahara Campaign*, Opinion of AG Wathelet (n 5) para 296.

[143] *Western Sahara Campaign* (n 6) paras 59–60.

[144] *Western Sahara Campaign* (n 6) paras 63–64. Strictly speaking, these paragraphs pertain to the phrase 'territory of Morocco' as stated in EU-Morocco FPA (n 7) art 11. The Court's reasoning was little different concerning the phrase 'waters falling within the sovereignty or jurisdiction' of Morocco. See Case *Western Sahara Campaign* (n 6) paras 65–68.

[145] J Larik, 'A Line in the Sand: The "Strict Observance" of International Law in the Western Sahara Case' (*Verfassungsblog*, 2 March 2018), https://verfassungsblog.de/a-line-in-the-sand-the-strict-observance-of-international-law-in-the-western-sahara-case/.

> it must be said that *it would be contrary to the rules of international law referred to in … the present judgment, which the European Union must observe* and which are applicable *mutatis mutandis* in this case, if it were agreed that the waters directly adjacent to the coast of the territory of Western Sahara were to be included within the scope of that agreement. *Consequently, the European Union could not properly support any intention* of the Kingdom of Morocco to include, by such means, the waters in question within the scope of that agreement.[146]

Or, to put it simply, *It would be wrong to do it, so we can't have done it.* Once again, the nullification of one's own acts by pleading their wrongfulness.

Recall that in the Opinion, AG Wathelet included certain maps showing that the waters off the Western Sahara had been demarcated for various categories of fisheries exploitation under the broad arrangement set out under the FPA. In the Decision, the ECJ dismissed their importance first by pointing to the fact that the geographical coordinates had been submitted *one day after* the deadline stipulated in the 2013 Protocol, and therefore formed no part of the agreement between the parties.[147] As preposterous as it may be to imagine that the EU and Moroccan negotiators had taken absolutely no view on the geographical scope of the Protocol until a day after the deadline, the ECJ ultimately went on to find that it would not have mattered even if they had been submitted on time, because

> in the light of the interpretation [of the expression 'Moroccan fishing zone' in] the present judgment and the reasoning supporting that interpretation, it must be held that, even if those geographical coordinates had been notified prior to the entry into force of the 2013 Protocol, they could in no way have called into question the interpretation of the expression 'Moroccan fishing zone' adopted in that paragraph nor have extended the scope of that protocol so as to include the waters adjacent to the territory of Western Sahara.[148]

It would not matter even if the parties had manifested their intention to fish in the Western Sahara by literally drawing it out on a chart. It presumably would not have mattered either if the Agreement had *actually* been implemented and EU-Member State ships had actually fished in Western Sahara waters for decades, any more so than it mattered in *Polisario* that the Commission actually sent officials to the Western Sahara pursuant to the EU-Morocco Association Agreement, or that 140 of the exporters listed in the schedules thereto were actually established in the Western Sahara.

Incredibly, this was the exact reasoning offered by the General Court in its recent *Polisario II* order, dismissing with costs an application by the Front Polisario seeking an annulment of the measure implementing the 2013

[146] *Western Sahara Campaign* (n 6) para 71 (emphasis added).
[147] *Western Sahara Campaign* (n 6) para 81.
[148] *Western Sahara Campaign* (n 6) para 82.

Protocol.[149] The General Court rejected the claim that the parties intended to fish in Western Saharan waters because

> il serait contraire aux règles de droit international visées au [cette] ordonnance, que l'Union doit respecter et qui s'appliquent *mutatis mutandis* en l'occurrence, d'inclure dans le champ d'application de l'accord de partenariat les eaux directement adjacentes à la côte du territoire du Sahara occidental au titre d'eaux relevant de la souveraineté du Royaume du Maroc.[150]

Accordingly, 'l'Union ne saurait valablement partager une intention du Royaume du Maroc d'inclure, à un tel titre, les eaux en question dans le champ d'application dudit accord.'[151] The General Court then proceeded to hold that the same argument also rendered irrelevant the Front Polisario's claim that the 2013 Protocol was *actually* being applied in Western Saharan territory at the time, through financial contributions made by the EU being used to fund Moroccan infrastructure there.[152] To admit the existence of

> une prétendue volonté de l'Union traduite par une pratique ultérieure et consistant à considérer désormais les accords d'association et de libéralisation comme étant juridiquement applicables au territoire du Sahara occidental aurait nécessairement impliqué d'admettre que l'Union entendait exécuter ces accords d'une manière incompatible avec les principes d'autodétermination et de l'effet relatif des traités.[153]

This would be intolerable because 'Une telle exécution serait nécessairement inconciliable avec le principe d'exécution des traités de bonne foi, qui constitue pourtant un principe obligatoire du droit international général applicable aux sujets de ce droit qui sont parties contractantes à un traité.'[154] In other words, *Western Sahara Campaign* raises an irrebuttable presumption of rectitude on the part of the EU, whereby the Union can do no wrong, even if proof of wrong is literally available in the form of a chart. It followed from this that the Front Polisario had no legal interest in seeking the annulment and was therefore denied standing under Article 263(4) TFEU.[155]

Consider a hypothetical case of a Sahrawi fisherman who complains that his livelihood has been adversely affected by overfishing as a result of the scheme created under the FPA. Of course, the FPA contains numerous expressions of

[149] See *Polisario II* (n 12) para 44. The contested measure was Council Decision 2013/785/EU of 16 December 2013 on the conclusion, on behalf of the European Union, of the Protocol between the European Union and the Kingdom of Morocco setting out the fishing opportunities and financial contribution provided for in the Fisheries Partnership Agreement between the European Union and the Kingdom of Morocco [2013] OJ L349/1.

[150] *Polisario II* (n 12) para 48.

[151] *Polisario II* (n 12) para 48 and 55–57.

[152] *Polisario II* (n 12) para 62.

[153] *Polisario II* (n 12) para 64.

[154] *Polisario II* (n 12) para 64.

[155] *Polisario II* (n 12) para 70.

a commitment to 'sustainable exploitation of fisheries resources',[156] but absent meaningful judicial review, there is no reason to credit these professions other than the bare word of the parties. The direct and individual concern requirements mean that he has no standing to bring judicial review of the relevant EU measures under Article 263 TFEU. This will not be a surprise for most EU lawyers. What is new though, is that on the now controlling reading of Article 3(5) TEU, EU courts would deny not just standing, but that anything untoward could have happened at all. He would be told that whatever the Commission's maps might show, the EU may not be understood to have agreed with Morocco to exploit the fisheries off the Western Sahara. As such, any overfishing occurring there is purely the responsibility of Morocco. Thus, we end up with a variant of the mistake in *Commune de Champagne* all over again.

Of course, this rationale cannot be applied to extraterritorial assertions of authority whose illegality cannot coherently be alleged by EU institutions, for instance, the Emissions Trading Directive[157] that was upheld in the *Air Transport Association of America* case.[158] It remains to be seen whether any individual applicants will be denied standing simply for failure to fulfil the requirements of direct and individual concern, or whether EU courts will find other 'creative' rationales for producing the same result.

IV. CONCLUSION

In the early days following the handing down of *Polisario*, there was a broad consensus that it was for the most part a blow for the international rule of law, human rights and democracy, not to mention for the self-determination of peoples and of their right to use their natural resources.[159] The Decision was justifiably described as a sensational 'victory through defeat' in that despite technically 'losing' on procedural questions of admissibility, the Front Polisario still secured its political objective of preventing the application of the Association Agreement over the Western Sahara, thus forcing a fundamental realignment

[156] See, eg, EU-Morocco FPA (n 7) Preamble ('DETERMINED to cooperate, in their mutual interest, in promoting the introduction of responsible fisheries to ensure the long-term conservation and sustainable exploitation of marine living resources …').

[157] Parliament and Council Directive 2003/87/EC of 13 October 2003 establishing a scheme for greenhouse gas emission allowance trading within the Community and amending Council Directive 96/61/EC [2003] OJ L275/32.

[158] Case C-366/10 *Air Transport Association of America and ors v Secretary of State for Energy and Climate Change* [2011] ECR I-13755.

[159] See, eg, A Rasi, 'Front Polisario: A Step Forward in Judicial Review of International Agreements by the Court of Justice?' (2017) 2 *European Papers* 967; P Hilpold, 'Self-Determination at the European Courts: The Front Polisario Case or "The Unintended Awakening of a Giant"' (2017) 2 *European Papers* 907; E Milano, 'Front Polisario and the Exploitation of Natural Resources by the Administrative Power' (2017) 2 *European Papers* 953.

of EU-Morocco relations in its favour.[160] In this regard, Enzo Cannizzaro predicted that despite 'its modest and unassuming tone, *Front Polisario* will probably be regarded as a significant jurisprudential development … and could silently contribute to the development of one of the most controversial doctrines in international law, namely *jus cogens* …'.[161] I am much less sanguine about *Polisario* and its sister cases. There certainly are problems with the General Court's initial decision, such as the treatment of the Front Polisario as a person only under EU law, its vague and unhelpful references to the lack of an 'absolute' prohibition against economic dealings with occupied territories, and its characterisation of the Association Agreement as being objectionable only as an administrative omission rather than a wrong against the Front Polisario and the Sahrawi people. Nevertheless, it gets the question of standing correct as a matter of juridical rationality, if not quite so much as a matter of EU positive law.

The ECJ's decisions in the *Polisario* and *Western Sahara Campaign* cases are far more insidious. They reveal a vision of legality without rights, in that the Court conceded that the Western Sahara and its resources ought not to be disposed of in the way the applicants complained of but denied them the 'entitlement' to make that complaint. The progression from the ECJ Decision in *Polisario* to the *Western Sahara Campaign* Decision, followed by the adoption of the latter in *Polisario II* reveals a creeping over of the habits and attitudes of abstract, constitutional review under Article 267 TFEU into the Article 263 TFEU judicial review function as well, such that Article 263 TFEU applicants are not seen as bearers of rights but merely as convenient dumping grounds for manifesting the abstract norms of the EU legal order. Worse, the ECJ invokes a Kagan-esque exceptionalist vision of the EU as uniquely committed to international law, human rights, democracy and all the other splendid things listed in Article 3(5) TEU[162] to construct an irrebuttable presumption of rectitude; that is, that the EU can do no wrong.[163] On this line of thought, it follows that if

[160] C Ryngaert, 'The Polisario Front Judgment of the EU Court of Justice: A Reset of EU-Morocco Trade Relations in the Offing' (RENFORCE Blog, 15 January 2017), http://blog.renforce.eu/index.php/en/2017/01/15/the-polisario-front-judgment-of-the-eu-court-of-justice-a-reset-of-eu-morocco-trade-relations-in-the-offing-2/.

[161] E Cannizzaro, 'In Defence of *Front Polisario*: The ECJ as a Global *Jus Cogens* Maker' (2018) 55 *CML Rev* 569, 577.

[162] Cannizzaro speaks of a theme of *Völkerrechtsfreundlichkeit*, according to which the jurisprudence of the ECJ is depicted as particularly open to the reception of international law norms. E Cannizzaro, 'The Neo-Monism of the European Legal Order' in E Cannizzaro, P Palchetti and RA Wessel (eds), *International Law as Law of the European Union* (Leiden, Martinus Nijhoff, 2011) 57. For a different view, see J Klabbers, *The European Union in International Law* (Paris, Pedone, 2012) 77. For a useful survey of the literature, see J Odermatt, 'The Court of Justice of the European Union: International or Domestic Court International Organisations and Courts' (2014) 3 *Cambridge Journal of International and Comparative Law* 696, 697–700.

[163] As Van der Loo puts it, 'the reasoning of the Court is based on the remarkable assumption that it is unthinkable that the EU would not act in good faith or contrary to international law'. Van der Loo (n 127) 257.

exploiting a third party by treaty is wrong, then it simply did not happen.[164] The listing of 140 companies in the Western Sahara in the schedules to the Association Agreement, the preferential tariffs accorded them for decades, the multiple visits by the Commission officials to the territory at the invitation of Moroccan authorities, the carving up of Western Saharan waters, etc, are all 'too illegal to be true'[165] and must be disregarded as 'factual anomalies falling outside the scope of'[166] judicial notice.

The ECJ made no mention of Article 3(5) TEU in *Polisario*. In *Western Sahara Campaign*, however, it specifically identified Article 3(5) TEU as the 'lens' facilitating the ECJ's singularly rose-tinted conception of the EU's interactions with the wider world.[167] As such, one is reminded of the famous satirical essay by Rudolf von Jhering on the 'Heaven of Legal Concepts', where, in contrast to Kant's world of embodied beings, all illusions of self and personhood fall away and abstract legal concepts are revealed in all their true splendour. Deserving jurists ascend to this paradise after death, where they bathe in the ether of pure thought, unencumbered by the real world below.[168] From time to time certain candidates come by who are suitable for admission but for an inability wholly to shake off their impressions and attitudes of earthly existence. In von Jhering's telling, these special cases are allowed to drink from a spring whose waters induce the complete and total forgetting of all terrestrial memories.[169] Article 3(5) TEU performs a similar function: it is the Lethean draft that transports EU judges out of the sordid world of *de facto* things into a realm of pure, ineffable normative perfection.

[164] See Hilpold (n 159) 916 (describing the Court's logic as one where 'there could not be what must not be'). See also E Kassoti, 'Between *Sollen* and *Sein*: The CJEU's Reliance on International Law in the Interpretation of Economic Agreements Covering Occupied Territories' (2020) 33 *Leiden Journal of International Law* 371, 381–82.

[165] V Kube, 'The Polisario Case: Do EU Fundamental Rights Matter for EU Trade Policies?' (*EJIL: Talk!*, 3 February 2017), www.ejiltalk.org/the-polisario-case-do-eu-fundamental-rights-matter-for-eu-trade-polices/.

[166] S Hummelbrunner and A-C Prickartz, 'EU-Morocco Trade Relations Do Not Legally Affect Western Sahara – Case C-104/16 P Council v Front Polisario' (*European Law Blog*, 5 January 2017), https://europeanlawblog.eu/2017/01/05/eu-morocco-trade-relations-do-not-legally-affect-western-sahara-case-c-10416-p-council-v-front-polisario/.

[167] Larik (n 145).

[168] R von Jhering, 'Im Juristischen Begriffshimmel: Ein Phantasiebild', in *Scherz und Ernst in der Jurisprudenz*, 3rd edn (Leipzig, Breitkopf & Härtel 1885) 273.

[169] *Ibid* 253.

8

General Conclusion

THIS BOOK AIMED to set out a normative critique of the European Union's legal relations with distant strangers in the light of Kant's philosophy of right. Along the way, we uncovered a number of myths and paradoxes, such as that the current edifice of international environmental law might be built upon an improper commodification of the commons, that the phrase 'public property' is a contradiction in terms, that the article of faith that human beings possess human rights solely by virtue of their humanity is palpably false, and so on, all of which might lead to future research agendas. The remit of this study, however, was expressed in the three simple questions posed at the beginning of chapter one: (1) Are the EU's unilateral assertions of authority over distant strangers defensible? (2) Does the EU owe any obligations towards the distant strangers for whom it makes law? (3) If so, does the EU fulfil them? The short answers to each of these are: (1) 'Yes' in substance but 'No' as regards institutional structure; (2) 'Yes'; and (3) 'No.' I now expand upon each in turn.

I. ARE THE EU'S UNILATERAL ASSERTIONS OF AUTHORITY OVER DISTANT STRANGERS DEFENSIBLE?

In chapter two, I demonstrated that the EU asserts 'jurisdiction' – understood in the sense of *authority* – over distant strangers in numerous policy areas as diverse as competition, environmental, financial and maritime regulation, and that it defends its right to do so on the basis of Article 3(5) of the Treaty on European Union (TEU), and ultimately public international law. In chapter three, I considered certain prominent 'Grotian' approaches to justifying the EU's and similar extraterritorial assertions of authority premised upon ideas of advancing universal values or protecting global interests, as well as a conception of 'global public goods' as things that enhance utility generally and globally, but which individual states have little or no incentive to supply on their own. Upon examination, I argued that these explanations were beset by certain fundamental flaws, such as an inability to distinguish between harms that were actionable from those that were not, as well as the problematic implication that sufficiently powerful political communities had a right, if not an obligation, to offer political authority wherever in the world it was wanting. I also demonstrated that this deeply *imperial* outlook is not entirely absent from the jurisprudence of the European Court of Justice (ECJ).

In chapter four, I began to set out an alternative rationale for such assertions of jurisdiction starting from the Kantian premise that the sole natural right of human beings is not to the satisfaction of interests, needs, values or moral ends generally, but in the simple idea of not being a thing at the mercy of another. On this conception of the organising principle of all law, it follows that force is permissible in interpersonal relations only if it is contained within the bounds of the forms of private law, and that the concept of political authority is simply an extension of the idea of a fiduciary in private law, such that relations of political authority and obedience are governed by principles analogous to those that govern relations between fiduciaries and principals.

Chapter five then argued that as fiduciaries of their subjects, political authorities are obligated to provide them with 'public goods', understood as things which must be provided publicly in order to ensure no member of the community is rendered subject to the arbitrary choice of any other person. It was then argued that the rights of political authorities regarding the provision of public goods may be analogised to rights in personality rather than in property; their actionability does not depend upon harm or loss. Finally, where the provision of such public goods is threatened by distant strangers, political authorities may justifiably assert authority over them, because nothing a political authority does to ensure a rightful condition for its subjects can ever constitute a wrong against any other person, state or non-state. In contrast to the Grotian approach of trying to solve problems of global magnitude by positing expansive duties on the part of sovereigns towards all of humanity, this book instead provided the same starting from the 'republican' premise that a sovereign's rights of jurisdiction and obligations of accountability pertain first and foremost to its own subjects.

Measured against this yardstick, the EU does quite well indeed. Whatever one might think about the EU's effects upon its Member States' capacity to provide domestic public goods, it can be said that the EU is perhaps the pre-eminent, contemporary guardian of many forms of the global commons today, be it in the environment, competitive markets or cyberspace and social media. Using the Emissions Trading Directive as primary example, it was demonstrated that the ECJ's adamant refusal to rely upon the effects doctrine and the technique of territorial extension are both normatively justifiable, as well as possess considerable doctrinal support. As such, the Emissions Trading Directive[1] and similar measures may serve as a model to be emulated by other states and political organisations of jurisdiction.

[1] Parliament and Council Directive 2003/87/EC of 13 October 2003 establishing a scheme for greenhouse gas emission allowance trading within the Community and amending Council Directive 96/61/EC [2003] OJ L275/32.

The thornier issue concerns the institutional frameworks in which such EU extraterritorial measures are enacted. Just as no person can determine by herself the terms by which she interacts with others, no state can declare the legality of its relations with distant strangers unilaterally, but must submit to international adjudication to answer legal challenges. In this regard, the internal constitutional structure of the European Union and the judicial politics of the ECJ pose almost perfect impediments to the rightfulness of the EU's unilateral assertions of jurisdiction over distant strangers. The 'shibboleth' of the EU as a 'new legal order'[2] enables EU institutions – in particular the ECJ – to evade what little international judicial scrutiny exists of political organisations of jurisdiction other than states.

II. DOES THE EU OWE OBLIGATIONS TOWARDS DISTANT STRANGERS OVER WHOM IT CLAIMS AUTHORITY?

If political authority is rightful only if held in fiduciary capacity, then 'human rights' – or at least the legal entitlements that go under that name in contemporary 'European' legal practice – are simply those principles in public law subjects invoke in order to hold their sovereigns to account. In this way, human rights serve as basic legal guarantees against domination and instrumentalisation both by political authorities and other private persons. Contrary to much popular rhetoric, 'human rights' as they appear in this legal practice are neither rights at international law, nor do they inhere in human beings purely by virtue of being human. Instead, they are essentially *constitutional* rights that obtain whenever any political actor purports to assert authority over a person. As such, I depart from the bulk of the scholarship on that topic, which treats human rights jurisdiction as a function of a political actor's factual ability to attain or procure desirable ends for human beings. Instead, it lies in the making of a claim of authority over the individual, regardless of whether that sovereign has the factual ability to make good on its claim in reality.

Chapter six argued that this characterisation also explains the set of practices going under the name of 'human rights' in positive legal practice, in particular the Strasbourg jurisprudence on the concept of 'human rights jurisdiction'. Moreover, I also showed that precedent exists in European Convention on Human Rights (ECHR) jurisprudence, establishing that the technique of territorial extension gives rise to human rights obligations to distant strangers. As such, I conclude that the EU does indeed owe human rights obligations towards distant strangers, even on my austere, Kantian theory of human rights. That said, I also argued that the source of human rights obligations is not the

[2] T Isiksel, 'European Exceptionalism and the EU's Accession to the ECHR' (2016) 27 *European Journal of International Law* 565, 571.

ability of any sovereign to effect factual changes to individuals' material interests, needs or well-being generally, as is urged by most accounts of human rights jurisdiction. If anything, the Strasbourg case law on 'human rights jurisdiction' provides confirmation of Kant's insight that legal rights – as human rights emphatically are – can be achieved only within a context of political institutions entitled to use force.

III. IF SO, DOES THE EU FULFIL THEM?

The final chapter turned to the rules of standing for judicial review of acts of the EU in Article 263 of the Treaty on the Functioning of the European Union (TFEU), and argued that the criteria of 'direct' and 'individual concern' effectively deny most litigants the opportunity to seek vindication of their rights before the courts of the EU. The Article 267 TFEU preliminary reference procedure is no substitute, because it is not designed to vindicate rights, but to ensure the uniform application of EU law in Member State courts. Put differently, an applicant in a preliminary reference is simply not the master of her claim; that designation belongs to the national judge who drafts and makes the reference.

A close examination of the *Polisario* and *Western Sahara Campaign*[3] cases revealed another startling conclusion. Article 3(5) TEU, upon which the ECJ grounds the EU's competence to enact extraterritorial measures asserting authority over distant strangers, is also the very same tool pressed into service to deny those distant strangers even the slightest glimpse of accountability. The Article 3(5) TEU wording that the EU 'shall contribute to … the strict observance and the development of international law, including respect for the principles of the United Nations Charter', is interpreted not as a standard against which claimants may criticise acts of the EU where its acts arguably are not in strict observance of the law, but as a presumption that the EU *always* acts in strict observance of international law. On this logic, the EU can do no wrong to distant strangers, even if it actually has. This goes far beyond the injustice created by the requirements of direct and individual concern, which at least recognise the existence of obligations owed to the claimant, even if they limit that claimant's ability to enforce them. The use the ECJ makes of Article 3(5) TEU, however, is as an unrebuttable presumption of rectitude, effectively allowing for the illegality of an act of the EU to be pled specifically for the purpose of denying applicants the right to complain about them.

****

[3] Case C-104/16 P *Council v Front Polisario* ECLI:EU:C:2016:973 (21 December 2016); Case C-266/16 *Western Sahara Campaign UK, The Queen v Commissioners for Her Majesty's Revenue and Customs, Secretary of State for Environment, Food and Rural Affairs* ECLI:EU:C:2018:118 (27 February 2018).

And so, this critique of the rightful relations between the EU and distant strangers concludes with the finding that the EU has rights against distant strangers that its institutions are quick to recognise and prosecute, but that distant strangers also have rights against the EU, which the same institutions systematically deny or foreclose. This might strike the reader as perfectly unsurprising, for 'Nothing is more banal than a political institution trying to exempt itself from the very checks that it insists on applying to rival institutions'.[4] That said, the critiques I make are subtly but crucially different from that offered by other studies, for instance those finding contradictions or a lack of guiding principle in EU external action with respect to the promotion of human rights, the rule of law and democracy.[5] The concern flagged in this book is not that the EU's relations with the wider world reflect *ethical* confusion or hypocrisy, for neither confusion nor hypocrisy is illegal in and of itself.

Rather, the confusion and/or hypocrisy is deeper, because it is *juridical.* As Kant states in the *Perpetual Peace*,

> Both philanthropy and respect for the *rights* of the human being are duties: but the former is only *conditional* duty whereas the latter is *unconditional* duty, commanding absolutely, and whoever wants to give himself up to the sweet feeling of beneficence must first be completely assured that he has not transgressed this unconditional duty.[6]

There is no point talking about beneficence, values or ethics in foreign policy until the question of rightful relations has first been settled. It is for this reason that a political community 'cannot compromise here and devise something intermediate' such as 'a cross between right and expediency; instead all politics must bend the knee before right …'.[7] As it appears, the current state of affairs entails asserting authority over distant strangers for the purpose of preserving the equal freedom of EU subjects, and then denying that same dignity to distant strangers subjected to EU jurisdiction. This is incompatible with the very idea of rightful relations, because it means that distant strangers are placed under more obligations than they can in turn place upon the EU. As such, it is

[4] Isiksel,(n 2) 578.

[5] See, eg, A Williams, *EU Human Rights Policies: A Study in Irony* (Oxford, Oxford University Press, 2005) 196–97:

> That distinctions exist between the Community's internal and external approaches to human rights has been well documented. However, the state of bifurcation suggests that we are dealing with more than a number of discrete inconsistencies. Rather, the analysis of the whole narrative of human rights in the Community suggests that a systematic and systemic division has been created along the internal/external fault line. Indeed, by adopting a more searching reading of the Community's texts a pervading sense of irony is revealed.

See also U Khaliq, *Ethical Dimensions of the Foreign Policy of the European Union: A Legal Appraisal* (Cambridge, Cambridge University Press, 2008) 455–58.

[6] I Kant, 'Toward Perpetual Peace' in MJ Gregor (ed & tr), *Practical Philosophy: The Cambridge Edition of the Works of Immanuel Kant*, 9th edn (Cambridge, Cambridge University Press, 2006) 8:386, 351.

[7] *Ibid* 8:380, 347.

incompatible with public right, without which all 'subtilizing' about the promotion of rights, democracy, welfare and universal values is merely 'unwisdom and veiled injustice'.[8]

Ultimately, therefore, what is at stake is not a matter of the effective or prudent conduct of EU foreign policy, but of constitutionalism. The question is not whether the EU, its institutions, Member States and peoples are living out 'their' values or otherwise 'doing good' in the wider world. Rather, it is whether the EU possesses the sort of constitutional existence – whether there is even an 'it' – to have values at all.

[8] *Ibid* 8:385, 350.

Bibliography

Alexy, R, 'Kant's Non-Positivistic Concept of Law' (2019) 24 *Kantian Review* 497.

Allott, P, 'Epilogue: Europe and the Dream of Reason' in JHH Weiler and M Wind, *European Constitutionalism Beyond the State* (Cambridge, Cambridge University Press, 2003).

Allum, JR, '"An Outcrop of Hell": History, Environment, and the Politics of the Trail Smelter Dispute' in RM Bratspies and RA Miller (eds), *Transboundary Harm in International Law: Lessons from the Trail Smelter Arbitration* (Cambridge, Cambridge University Press, 2006).

Anghie, A, *Imperialism, Sovereignty and the Making of International Law* (Cambridge, Cambridge University Press, 2005).

Ankersmit, L, Lawrence, J and Davies, G, 'Diverging EU and WTO Perspectives on Extraterritorial Process Regulation' (2012) 21 *Minnesota Journal of International Law* 14.

Arendt, H, *The Origins of Totalitarianism* (Cleveland-New York, Meridian Books, 1958).

——, 'What Is Authority?' in *Between Past and Future: Six Exercises in Political Thought* (New York, Viking Press, 1961)

——, 'Foundation I: Constitutio Libertatis' in *On Revolution* (London, Penguin Press, 1963).

——, *Lectures on Kant's Political Philosophy* (Chicago, University of Chicago Press, 1982).

Arnull, A, 'Private Applicants and the Action for Annulment under Article 173 of the EC Treaty' (1995) 32 *Common Market Law Review* 7.

Attanasio, DL, 'The State Obligation to Protect' (PhD thesis, University of California, Los Angeles 2015).

Augenstein, D, 'To Whom It May Concern: International Human Rights Law and Global Public Goods' (2016) 23 *Indiana Journal of Global Legal Studies* 225.

Augenstein, D and Kinley, D, 'When Human Rights "Responsibilities" Become "Duties": The Extra-Territorial Obligations of States That Bind Corporations' in S Deva and D Bilchitz (eds), *Human Rights Obligations of Business: Beyond the Corporate Responsibility to Respect?* (Cambridge, Cambridge University Press, 2013).

Aust, HP, *Complicity and the Law of State Responsibility* (Cambridge, Cambridge University Press, 2011).

Baiasu, S, 'Right's Complex Relation to Ethics in Kant: The Limits of Independentism' (2016) 107 *Kant-Studien* 2.

Bartels, L, 'Article XX of GATT and the Problem of Extraterritorial Jurisdiction: The Case of Trade Measures for the Protection of Human Rights' (2002) 36 *Journal of World Trade* 353.

——, *Human Rights Conditionality in the EU's International Agreements* (Oxford, Oxford University Press, 2005).

——, 'The WTO Legality of the Application of the EU's Emission Trading System to Aviation' (2012) 23 *European Journal of International Law* 429.

——, 'A Model Human Rights Clause for the EU's International Trade Agreements' (Berlin-Aachen, German Institute for Human Rights & MISEREOR, 2014).

——, 'The EU's Human Rights Obligations in Relation to Policies with Extraterritorial Effects' (2014) 25 *European Journal of International Law* 1071.

——, 'Policy Coherence for Development Under Article 208 of the Treaty on the Functioning of the European Union-Towards a Complaints Mechanism' (2016) *Cambridge Legal Studies Research Paper Series* 1.

Beck, U and Grande, E, *Cosmopolitan Europe* (Cambridge, Polity, 2007).

Beitz, C, 'Human Rights and the Law of Peoples' in DK Chatterjee (ed), *The Ethics of Assistance: Morality and the Distant Needy* (Cambridge, Cambridge University Press, 2004).

Bellamy, R, 'A European Republic of Sovereign States: Sovereignty, Republicanism and the European Union' (2017) 16 *European Journal of Political Theory* 188.

Ben-Naftali, O and Shany, Y, 'Living in Denial: The Application of Human Rights in the Occupied Territories' (2003) 37 *Israel Law Review* 17.

Bennett, M and Harewood, J, *Vanuatu* (Melbourne, Lonely Planet, 2003).

Benvenisti, E, *Sharing Transboundary Resources: International Law and Optimal Resource Use* (Cambridge, Cambridge University Press, 2002).

——, *The International Law of Occupation*, 2nd edn (Oxford, Oxford University Press, 2012).

——, 'Sovereigns as Trustees of Humanity: On the Accountability of States to Foreign Stakeholders' (2013) 107 *American Journal of International Law* 295.

——, 'Legislating for Humanity: May States Compel Foreigners to Promote Global Welfare?' in R Liivoja and J Petman (eds), *International Law-making: Essays in Honour of Jan Klabbers* (Abingdon, Routledge, 2014) 13–14.

——, *The Law of Global Governance* (Leiden, Brill-Nijhoff, 2014).

——, 'Sovereignty and the Politics of Property' (2017) 18 *Theoretical Inquiries in Law* 447.

——, 'Upholding Democracy Amid the Challenges of New Technology: What Role for the Law of Global Governance?' (2018) 29 *European Journal of International Law* 9.

Berman, A, 'Taking Foreign Interests into Account: Rulemaking in the US and EU' (2017) 15 *International Journal of Constitutional Law* 235.

Besson S, 'The Authority of International Law – Lifting the State Veil' (2009) 31 *Sydney Law Review* 343.

——, 'The Right to Have Rights: From Human Rights to Citizens' Rights and Back' in M Goldoni and C McCorkindale (eds), *Hannah Arendt and the Law* (Oxford, Bloomsbury Publishing, 2012).

——, 'The Extraterritoriality of the European Convention on Human Rights: Why Human Rights Depend on Jurisdiction and What Jurisdiction Amounts To' (2012) 25 *Leiden Journal of International Law* 857.

——, 'The Allocation of Anti-Poverty Rights Duties: Our Rights, but Whose Duties?' in K Nadakavukaren-Schefer (ed), *Poverty and the International Economic Legal System* (Cambridge, Cambridge University Press, 2013).

Beyerlin, U and Marauhn, T, *International Environmental Law* (Oxford, Bloomsbury Publishing, 2011).

Bird, C, 'Harm Versus Sovereignty: A Reply to Ripstein' (2007) 35 *Philosophy & Public Affairs* 179.

Birks, P, 'The Roman Law Concept of Dominium and the Idea of Absolute Ownership' (1985) *Acta Juridica* 1.

——, 'Harassment and Hubris the Right to an Equality of Respect Modern Jurisprudence' (1997) 32 *Irish Jurist* 1.

——, 'Definition and Division: A Meditation on *Institutes* 3.13' in P Birks (ed), *The Classification of Obligations* (Oxford, Clarendon Press, 1997).

——, 'The Content of Fiduciary Obligation' (2000) 34 *Israel Law Review* 3.

Birks, P and Descheemaeker, E (ed), *The Roman Law of Obligations: The Collected Papers of Peter Birks* (Oxford, Oxford University Press, 2014).

Bodansky, D, 'What's in a Concept? Global Public Goods, International Law, and Legitimacy' (2012) 23 *European Journal of International Law* 651.

Bossche, A-M, 'EU Competition Law in 3D' in I Govaere et al, *The European Union in the World: Essays in Honour of Marc Maresceau* (Boston-Leiden, Martinus Nijhoff, 2014).

Bradford, A, *The Brussels Effect: How the European Union Rules the World* (New York, Oxford University Press, 2020).

Brent KA, 'The Certain Activities Case: What Implications for the No-Harm Rule?' (2017) 20 *Asia Pacific Journal of Environmental Law* 28.

Brierly, JL and Clapham, A (ed), *Brierly's Law of Nations: An Introduction to the Role of International Law in International Relations*, 7th edn (Oxford, Oxford University Press, 2012).

Broberg, M, 'What Is the Direction for the EU's Development Cooperation after Lisbon? A Legal Examination' (2011) 16 *European Foreign Affairs Review* 539.

——, 'Don't Mess with the Missionary Man! On the Principle of Coherence, the Missionary Principle and the European Union's Development Policy' in PJ Cardwell (ed), *EU External Relations Law and Policy in the Post-Lisbon Era* (The Hague, TMC Asser Press, 2011).

——, 'From Colonial Power to Human Rights Promoter: On the Legal Regulation of the European Union's Relations with the Developing Countries' (2013) 26 *Cambridge Review of International Affairs* 675.

Broberg, M and Fenger, N, *Preliminary References to the European Court of Justice*, 2nd edn (Oxford, Oxford University Press, 2014).

Brown, GW, 'The European Union and Kant's Idea of Cosmopolitan Right: Why the EU Is Not Cosmopolitan' (2014) 20 *European Journal of International Relations* 671.

Brunnée, J, 'Procedure and Substance in International Environmental Law' (2020) 405 *Receuil des cours* 81.

——, 'The Global Climate Regime: Wither Common Concern?' in Anja Seibert-Fohr and others (eds), *Coexistence, Cooperation and Solidarity: Liber Amicorum Rüdiger Wolfrum*, Vol 1 (Leiden, Brill, 2011).

——, 'International Environmental Law and Community Interests: Procedural Aspects' in E Benvenisti and G Nolte (eds), *Community Obligations across International Law* (Oxford, Oxford University Press, 2018).

Buchanan, A, *Human Rights, Legitimacy, and the Use of Force* (Oxford, Oxford University Press, 2010).

Buckland, WW and McNair, AD, *Roman Law and Common Law: A Comparison in Outline*, 2nd edn (Cambridge, Cambridge University Press, 1965).

Burrows, A, *Principles of the English Law of Obligations* (Oxford, Oxford University Press, 2015).

Byrd, BS and Hruschka, J, *Kant's Doctrine of Right: A Commentary* (Cambridge, Cambridge University Press, 2012).

Cafaggi, F, 'Transnational Private Regulation and the Production of Global Public Goods and Private "Bads"' (2012) 23 *European Journal of International Law* 695.

Caney, S, 'Cosmopolitan Justice, Rights and Global Climate Change' (2006) 19 *Canadian Journal of Law & Jurisprudence* 255.

Cannizzaro, E, 'The EU's Human Rights Obligations in Relation to Policies with Extraterritorial Effects: A Reply to Lorand Bartels' (2014) 25 *European Journal of International Law* 1093.

——, 'In Defence of Front Polisario: The ECJ as a Global Jus Cogens Maker' (2018) 55 *Common Market Law Review* 569.

——, 'The Neo-Monism of the European Legal Order' in E Cannizzaro, P Palchetti and RA Wessel (eds), *International Law as Law of the European Union* (Leiden, Martinus Nijhoff, 2011).

——, 'The EU's Human Rights Obligations in Relation to Policies with Extraterritorial Effects: Rejoinder to Enzo Cannizzaro' (*EJIL: Talk!*, 23 January 2015), www.ejiltalk.org/rejoinder-to-enzo-cannizzaro/.

Carey Miller, DL, 'Public Access to Private Land in Scotland' (2012) 15 *Potchefstroom Electronic Law Journal* 119.

Cavallar, G, 'Kantian Perspectives on Democratic Peace: Alternatives to Doyle' (2001) 27 *Review of International Studies* 229.

Chalmers, D, Davies, G and Monti, G, *European Union Law: Text and Materials*, 3rd edn (Cambridge, Cambridge University Press, 2014).

Clapham, A, *Human Rights: A Very Short Introduction*, 2nd edn (Oxford, Oxford University Press, 2015).

Cooreman, B, 'Addressing Environmental Concerns through Trade: A Case for Extraterritoriality?' (2016) 65 *International & Comparative Law Quarterly* 229.

Craig, P, 'Standing, Rights, and the Structure of Legal Argument' (2003) 9 *European Public Law* 493.

Craig, P and de Búrca, G, *EU Law: Text, Cases, and Materials*, 5th edn (Oxford, Oxford University Press, 2015).

Crawford, J, *The International Law Commission's Articles on State Responsibility: Introduction, Text and Commentaries* (Cambridge, Cambridge University Press, 2002).

——, *Brownlie's Principles of Public International Law* (Oxford, Oxford University Press, 2012).

——, *State Responsibility: The General Part* (Cambridge, Cambridge University Press, 2013).

Cremona, M, 'Coherence through Law: What Difference Will the Treaty of Lisbon Make?' (2008) 3 *Hamburg Review of Social Sciences* 11.

——, 'Coherence in European Union Foreign Relations Law' in P Koutrakos (ed), *European Foreign Policy: Legal and Political Perspectives* (Cheltenham, Edward Elgar, 2011).

Criddle, EJ and Fox-Decent, E, *Fiduciaries of Humanity: How International Law Constitutes Authority* (Oxford, Oxford University Press, 2016).

Dashwood, A et al, *Wyatt and Dashwood's European Union Law* (Oxford, Bloomsbury Publishing, 2011).

De Baere G, *Constitutional Principles of EU External Relations* (Oxford, Oxford University Press, 2008).

De Baere, G and Ryngaert, C, 'The ECJ's Judgment in Air Transport Association of America and the International Legal Context of the EU's Climate Change Policy' (2013) 18 *European Foreign Affairs Review* 389.

Delgado Casteleiro, A, *The International Responsibility of the European Union: From Competence to Normative Control* (Cambridge, Cambridge University Press, 2016).

den Heijer M, 'Procedural Aspects of Shared Responsibility in the European Court of Human Rights' (2013) 4 *Journal of International Dispute Settlement* 361.

den Heijer M and Lawson R, 'Extraterritorial Human Rights and the Concept of "Jurisdiction"' in M Langford et al (eds), *Global Justice, State Duties: The Extraterritorial Scope of Economic, Social, and Cultural Rights in International Law* (Cambridge, Cambridge University Press, 2013).

den Hertog, L and Stroß, S, 'Coherence in EU External Relations: Concepts and Legal Rooting of an Ambiguous Term' (2013) 18 *European Foreign Affairs Review* 373.

De Schutter, O, 'UN Special Rapporteur on the Right to Food: Addressing Concentration in Food Supply Chains – The Role of Competition Law in Tackling the Abuse of Buyer Power' (2010) Briefing Note 3, www.srfood.org/images/stories/pdf/otherdocuments/20101201_briefing-note-03_en.pdf.

De Schutter, O et al, 'Commentary to the Maastricht Principles on Extraterritorial Obligations of States in the Area of Economic, Social and Cultural Rights' (2012) 34 *Human Rights Quarterly* 1084.

De Witte, B, 'Too Much Constitutional Law in the European Union's Foreign Relations?' in M Cremona and B De Witte (eds), *EU Foreign Relations Law: Constitutional Fundamentals* (Oxford, Bloomsbury Publishing, 2008).

Dickson, J and Eleftheriadis, P (eds), *Philosophical Foundations of European Union Law* (Oxford, Oxford University Press, 2012).

Dill, J, 'Towards a Moral Division of Labour between IHL and IHRL during the Conduct of Hostilities' in Z Bohrer, J Dill and H Duffy (eds), *The Law Applicable to Armed Conflict* (Cambridge, Cambridge University Press, 2020).

Dobson, NL and Ryngaert, C, 'Provocative Climate Protection: EU "Extraterritorial" Regulation of Maritime Emissions' (2017) 66 *International & Comparative Law Quarterly* 295.

Dorfman, A and Harel, A, 'The Case Against Privatization' (2013) 41 *Philosophy & Public Affairs* 67.

Douglas-Scott, S, *Constitutional Law of the European Union* (London, Longman, 2002).

Doyle, MW, 'Kant, Liberal Legacies, and Foreign Affairs' (1983) 12 *Philosophy & Public Affairs* 205.

——, *Empires* (Ithaca, Cornell University Press, 1986).

Dupuy, P-M and Viñuales, JE, *International Environmental Law* (Cambridge, Cambridge University Press 2015).

Duvic-Paoli, L-A, *The Prevention Principle in International Environmental Law* (Cambridge, Cambridge University Press, 2018).

Dworkin, R, 'The Model of Rules I' in R Dworkin, *Taking Rights Seriously* (Cambridge, Harvard University Press, 1978).

——, *Sovereign Virtue: The Theory and Practice of Equality* (Cambridge, Harvard University Press, 2000).

——, *Justice for Hedgehogs* (Cambridge, Harvard University Press, 2011).

Dyson J, 'Essex Lecture 2014: The Extraterritorial Application of the European Convention on Human Rights' (2014), www.judiciary.gov.uk/wp-content/uploads/JCO/Documents/Speeches/lord-dyson-speech-extraterritorial-reach-echr-300114.pdf.

Eckes, C, 'EU Accession to the ECHR: Between Autonomy and Adaptation' (2013) 76 *Modern Law Review* 254.

Edelman, J, 'Property Rights to Our Bodies and Their Products' (2015) 39 *University of Western Australia Law Review* 47.

Eeckhout, P, *EU External Relations Law* (Oxford, Oxford University Press, 2011).

Eide, A, 'The International Human Rights System' in A Eide and W Barth Eide (eds), *Food as a Human Right* (Tokyo, United Nations University, 1984).

Eleftheriadis, P, 'The Moral Distinctiveness of the European Union' (2011) 9 *International Journal of Constitutional Law* 695.

——, *A Union of Peoples* (Oxford, Oxford University Press, 2020).

Emerson, M et al, *Upgrading the EU's Role as Global Actor* (Brussels, Centre for European Policy Studies, 2011).

Evans, M and Koutrakos, P, *The International Responsibility of the European Union: European and International Perspectives* (Oxford, Bloomsbury Publishing, 2013).

Fahey, E, *The Global Reach of EU Law* (Abingdon, Routledge, 2016).

Felber, C, *Money: The New Rules of the Game* (Cham, Springer, 2017).

Feunteun, T, 'Cartels and the Right to Food: An Analysis of States' Duties and Options' (2015) 18 *Journal of International Economic Law* 341.

Fierro, E, *European Union's Approach to Human Rights Conditionality in Practice* (Leiden-Boston, Martinus Nijhoff, 2003).

Fleury Graff T, 'Accords de Libre-Échange et Territoires Occupés: À Propos de l'arrêt TPIUE, 10 Décembre 2015, *Front Polisario c. Conseil*' (2016) 120 *Revue générale de droit international public* 263.

Flikschuh, K, *Kant and Modern Political Philosophy* (Cambridge, Cambridge University Press, 2000).

Fox-Decent, E, *Sovereignty's Promise: The State as Fiduciary* (Oxford, Oxford University Press, 2011).

——, 'From Fiduciary States to Joint Trusteeship of the Atmosphere: The Right to a Healthy Environment through a Fiduciary Prism' in K Coghill, C Sampford and T Smith (eds), *Fiduciary Duty and the Atmospheric Trust* (Abingdon, Routledge, 2013).

Fox-Decent, E and Criddle, EJ, 'The Fiduciary Constitution of Human Rights' (2009) 15 *Legal Theory* 301.

Franklin, MA, *Injuries and Remedies: Cases and Materials on Tort Law and Alternatives*, 2nd edn (Mineola, Foundation Press, 1979).

Ganesh, A, 'The European Union's Human Rights Obligations Towards Distant Strangers' (2016) 37 *Michigan Journal of International Law* 475.

Gattini, A, 'Between Splendid Isolation and Tentative Imperialism: The EU'S Extension of Its Emission Trading Scheme to International Aviation and the ECJ'S Judgment in the *ATA* Case' (2012) 61 *International and Comparative Law Quarterly* 977.

Gauttier, P, 'Horizontal Coherence and the External Competences of the European Union' (2004) 10 *European Law Journal* 23.

Giglio F, *The Foundations of Restitution for Wrongs* (Oxford, Bloomsbury Publishing, 2007).

Goldsmith, JL and Posner, EA, *The Limits of International Law* (Oxford, Oxford University Press, 2005).

Gondek, M, *The Reach of Human Rights in a Globalising World: Extraterritorial Application of Human Rights Treaties* (Cambridge, Intersentia, 2009).

Greenleaf, G, 'The Influence of European Data Privacy Standards Outside Europe: Implications for Globalization of Convention 108' (2012) 2 *International Data Privacy Law* 68.

Gregor, M, 'Kant's Theory of Property' (1988) 41 *Review of Metaphysics* 757.

Griffin, J, *On Human Rights* (Oxford, Oxford University Press, 2008).

Grotius, H, von Deman Magoffin, R (tr), Brown Scott, J (ed), *Mare Liberum [The Freedom of the Seas]* (1609) (New York, Oxford University Press, 1916).

Grotius, H, Kelsey, FW (tr), Brown Scott, J (ed), *De Jure Belli Ac Pacis [On the Law of War and Peace]* (1625) (Oxford, Oxford University Press, 1925).

Habermas, J, and Rehg, W (tr), *Between Facts and Norms: Contributions to a Discourse Theory of Law and Democracy* (Cambridge, MIT Press, 1996).

——, 'Kant's Idea of Perpetual Peace: With the Benefit of 200 Years' Hindsight' in C Cronin and P De Greiff (eds), J Habermas, *The Inclusion of the Other: Studies in Political Theory* (Cambridge-Malden, Polity Press, 1998).

——, 'The Crisis of the European Union in Light of a Constitutionalization of International Law: An Essay on the Constitution for Europe' in J Habermas and C Cronin (tr), *The Crisis of the European Union: A Response* (Cambridge-Malden, Polity Press, 2012).

Hadjiyianni, I, 'The Court of Justice of the European Union as a Transnational Actor through Judicial Review of the Territorial Scope of EU Environmental Law' (2019) 21 *Cambridge Yearbook of European Legal Studies* 128.

——, *The EU as a Global Regulator for Environmental Protection: A Legitimacy Perspective* (Oxford, Bloomsbury Publishing, 2019).

Harding, M, 'Manifesting Trust' (2009) 29 *Oxford Journal of Legal Studies* 245.

Harel A, *Why Law Matters* (Oxford, Oxford University Press, 2014).

Harris, JW, *Property and Justice* (Oxford, Oxford University Press, 1996).

——, 'Ownership of Land in English Law' in N MacCormick and P Birks (eds), *The Legal Mind: Essays for Tony Honoré* (Oxford, Clarendon Press, 1986).

Harvey, D, *Cosmopolitanism and the Geographies of Freedom* (New York, Columbia University Press, 2009).

Hathaway, OA and Shapiro, SJ, *The Internationalists: How a Radical Plan to Outlaw War Remade the World* (New York, Simon and Schuster, 2017).

Helmore, E, 'Trump Cancels Denmark Trip after PM Says Greenland Is Not for Sale' *The Guardian* (21 August 2019).

Henkin, L, 'That S Word: Sovereignty, and Globalization, and Human Rights, *Et Cetera*' (1999) 68 *Fordham Law Review* 1.

Herlin-Karnell, E, 'EU Values and the Shaping of the International Legal Order' in D Kochenov and F Amtenbrink (eds), *The European Union's Shaping of the International Legal Order* (Cambridge, Cambridge University Press, 2014).

Herlin-Karnell, E and Konstadinides, T, 'The Rise and Expressions of Consistency in EU Law: Legal and Strategic Implications for European Integration' (2012) 15 *Cambridge Yearbook of European Legal Studies* 139.

Hertogen A, 'Letting Lotus Bloom' (2015) 26 *European Journal of International Law* 901.

Higgins, R, *Problems and Process: International Law and How We Use It* (Oxford, Clarendon Press, 1995).

Highet, K and Kahale III, G, 'Certain Phosphate Lands in Nauru' (1993) 87 *American Journal of International Law* 282.

Hillion, C, '*Tous Pour Un, Un Pour Tous*! Coherence in the External Relations of the European Union' in M Cremona, *Developments in EU External Relations Law* (Oxford, Oxford University Press, 2008).

Hilpold, P, 'Self-Determination at the European Courts: The *Front Polisario* Case or "The Unintended Awakening of a Giant"' (2017) 2 *European Papers* 907.

Hobbes, T, and Tuck, R (ed), *Hobbes: Leviathan*, Revised Student Edition (Cambridge, Cambridge University Press, 1996).

Honoré, T, 'The Dependence of Morality on Law' (1993) 13 *Oxford Journal of Legal Studies* 1.

Howe, G, 'Sovereignty and Interdependence: Britain's Place in the World' (1990) 66 *International Affairs* 675.

Huber, J, 'Theorising from the Global Standpoint: Kant and Grotius on Original Common Possession of the Earth' (2017) 25 *European Journal of Philosophy* 231.

Hummelbrunner, S and Prickartz, A-C, 'EU-Morocco Trade Relations Do Not Legally Affect Western Sahara – Case C-104/16 P *Council v Front Polisario*' (*European Law Blog*, 5 January 2017), https://europeanlawblog.eu/2017/01/05/eu-morocco-trade-relations-do-not-legally-affect-western-sahara-case-c-10416-p-council-v-front-polisario/.

Isiksel, T, 'On Europe's Functional Constitutionalism Towards a Constitutional Theory of Specialized International Regimes' (2012) 19 *Constellations* 102.

——, 'European Exceptionalism and the EU's Accession to the ECHR' (2016) 27 *European Journal of International Law* 565.

Jeffrey, L and Vine, D, 'Sorry, Sadness, and Impoverishment: The Lives of Chagossians in Mauritius' in S Evers and M Kooy (eds), *Eviction from the Chagos Islands: Displacement and Struggle for Identity Against Two World Powers* (Leiden, Brill, 2011).

Jennings RY, *The Acquisition of Territory in International Law* (Manchester, Manchester University Press, 1963).

Kagan, R, *Of Paradise and Power: America and Europe in the New World Order* (New York, Alfred A Knopf, 2003).

Kant, I, 'Naturrecht Feyerabend' (1784) (Vinx, L (tr), 2003).

——, *Groundwork of the Metaphysics of Morals* (1785) Gregor, MJ (ed & tr) (Cambridge, Cambridge University Press, 1998).

——, 'Toward Perpetual Peace' (1795) in MJ Gregor (ed), *Practical Philosophy: The Cambridge Edition of the Works of Immanuel Kant*, 9th edn (Cambridge, Cambridge University Press 2006).

——, 'The Doctrine of Right' (1797) in MJ Gregor (ed), *Practical Philosophy: The Cambridge Edition of the Works of Immanuel Kant*, 9th edn (Cambridge, Cambridge University Press 2006).

——, *Anthropology from a Pragmatic Point of View* (1798) Louden, R (ed & tr) (Cambridge, Cambridge University Press, 2006).

Kassoti, E, 'The *Front Polisario v. Council* Case: The General Court, *Völkerrechtsfreundlichkeit* and the External Aspect of European Integration (First Part)' (2017) 2 *European Papers* 339.

——, 'Between *Sollen* and *Sein*: The CJEU's Reliance on International Law in the Interpretation of Economic Agreements Covering Occupied Territories' (2020) 33 *Leiden Journal of International Law* 371.

Kaul, I, 'Global Public Goods: Explaining Their Underprovision' (2012) 15 *Journal of International Economic Law* 729.

Kaul, I, Grunberg, I and Stern, MA (eds), *Global Public Goods: International Cooperation in the 21st Century* (Oxford, Oxford University Press, 1999).

Kaul, I and Mendoza, RU, 'Advancing the Concept of Public Goods' in I Kaul et al (eds), *Providing Global Public Goods: Managing Globalization* (Oxford, Oxford University Press, 2003).

Khaliq, U, *Ethical Dimensions of the Foreign Policy of the European Union: A Legal Appraisal* (Cambridge, Cambridge University Press, 2008).

Kirschenbaum A, *Equity in Jewish Law: Beyond Equity : Halakhic Aspirationism in Jewish Civil Law* (Hoboken, KTAV Publishing, 1991).

Klabbers, J, *An Introduction to International Institutional Law* (Cambridge, Cambridge University Press, 2002).

——, *The European Union in International Law* (Paris, Pedone, 2012).

Koch, C, '*Locus Standi* of Private Applicants under the EU Constitution: Preserving Gaps in the Protection of Individuals Right to an Effective Remedy' (2005) 30 *European Law Review* 511.

Kochenov, D and Amtenbrink, F, *The European Union's Shaping of the International Legal Order* (Cambridge, Cambridge University Press, 2013).

Kontorovich, E, 'Economic Dealings with Occupied Territories' (2015) 53 *Columbia Journal of Transnational Law* 584.

Koskenniemi, M, 'What Use for Sovereignty Today?' (2011) 1 *Asian Journal of International Law* 61.

Krisch, N, 'Europe's Constitutional Monstrosity' (2005) 25 *Oxford Journal of Legal Studies* 321.

——, *Beyond Constitutionalism: The Pluralist Structure of Postnational Law* (Oxford, Oxford University Press, 2010).

——, 'The Decay of Consent: International Law in an Age of Global Public Goods' (2014) 108 *American Journal of International Law* 1.

——, 'Liquid Authority in Global Governance' (2017) 9 *International Theory* 237.

——, 'Authority, Solid and Liquid, in Postnational Governance' in R Cotterell and M Del Mar (eds), *Authority in Transnational Legal Theory: Theorising Across Disciplines* (Cheltenham, Edward Elgar, 2016).

Kube V, 'The Polisario Case: Do EU Fundamental Rights Matter for EU Trade Policies?' (*EJIL: Talk!*, 3 February 2017), www.ejiltalk.org/the-polisario-case-do-eu-fundamental-rights-matter-for-eu-trade-polices/.

——, *EU Human Rights, International Investment Law and Participation: Operationalizing the EU Foreign Policy Objective to Global Human Rights Protection* (Cham, Springer, 2019).

Kumm, M, 'The Cosmopolitan Turn in Constitutionalism: An Integrated Conception of Public Law' (2013) 20 *Indiana Journal of Global Legal Studies* 605.

——, 'Sovereignty and the Right to Be Left Alone: Subsidiarity, Justice-Sensitive Externalities, and the Proper Domain of the Consent Requirement in International Law' (2016) 79 *Law and Contemporary Problems* 239.

Laby, AB, 'The Fiduciary Obligation as the Adoption of Ends' (2008) 56 *Buffalo Law Review* 99.

Larik, J, *Foreign Policy Objectives in European Constitutional Law* (Oxford, Oxford University Press, 2016).

——, 'A Line in the Sand: The "Strict Observance" of International Law in the Western Sahara Case' (*Verfassungsblog*, 2 March 2018), https://verfassungsblog.de/a-line-in-the-sand-the-strict-observance-of-international-law-in-the-western-sahara-case/.

Lauterpacht, H, 'The Grotian Tradition in International Law' (1946) 23 *British Year Book of International Law* 1.

——, 'Property Relations Between States. State Territory' in E Lauterpacht (ed), *International Law: Volume 1, The General Works: Being the Collected Papers of Hersch Lauterpacht* (Cambridge, Cambridge University Press, 1970).

Lawrence, J, *Governmentality in EU External Trade and Environment Policy: Between Rights and Market* (Abingdon, Routledge, 2018).

Le Moli, G, '*President of the Republic et al. v. Ali Ayyoub et al.*' (2019) 113 *American Journal of International Law* 791.

Lenaerts, K, Maselis, I and Gutman, K, *EU Procedural Law* (Oxford, Oxford University Press, 2014).

Libgober, B, 'Can the EU be a Constitutional System without Universal Access to Judicial Review' (2014) 36 *Michigan Journal of International Law* 353.

Locke, J, 'Second Treatise of Government' in P Laslett (ed), *Locke: Two Treatises of Government*, Student Edition (Cambridge, Cambridge University Press, 1988).

Lowe, AV, 'Blocking Extraterritorial Jurisdiction: The British Protection of Trading Interests Act, 1980' (1981) 75 *American Journal of International Law* 257.

Lowenfeld, AF, *Public Law in the International Arena: Conflict of Laws, International Law and Some Suggestions for Their Interaction* (1980) 163 *Recueil des cours* 311.

Ludwig, B, '"The Right of a State" in Immanuel Kant's Doctrine of Right' (1990) 28 *Journal of the History of Philosophy* 403.

Maljean-Dubois S and Richard, V, 'The International Court of Justice's Judgement of 20 April 2010 in the *Pulp Mills on the River Uruguay (Argentina v. Uruguay)* Case' in P Almeida and J-M Sorel (eds), *Latin America and the International Court of Justice: Contributions to International Law* (Abingdon, Routledge, 2016).

Mann, FA, *The Doctrine of Jurisdiction in International Law* (The Hague, AW Sijthoff, 1964).

Manners, I, 'Normative Power Europe: A Contradiction in Terms?' (2002) 40 *Journal of Common Market Studies* 235.

——, 'The Constitutive Nature of Values, Images and Principles in the European Union' in S Lucarelli and I Manners (eds), *Values and Principles in European Union Foreign Policy* (Abingdon, Routledge, 2006).

Mavroidis, PC, 'Free Lunches? WTO as Public Good, and the WTO's View of Public Goods' (2012) 23 *European Journal of International Law* 731.

Mayer, B, 'The Relevance of the No-Harm Principle to Climate Change Law and Politics' (2016) 19 *Asia Pacific Journal of Environmental Law* 79.

Merrill, TW, 'Is Public Nuisance a Tort?' (2011) 4 *Journal of Tort Law* 1.

Michaels, R, 'Two Paradigms of Jurisdiction' (2005–06) 27 *Michigan Journal of International Law* 1003.

Milano, E, 'Front Polisario and the Exploitation of Natural Resources by the Administrative Power' (2017) 2 *European Papers* 953.

Milanovic, M, *Extraterritorial Application of Human Rights Treaties: Law, Principles, and Policy* (Oxford, Oxford University Press, 2011).

——, '*Al-Skeini* and *Al-Jedda* in Strasbourg' (2012) 23 *European Journal of International Law* 121.

——, 'The Drowning Child' (*EJIL: Talk!*, 3 September 2015), www.ejiltalk.org/the-drowning-child/.

——, 'Jurisdiction and Responsibility: Trends in the Jurisprudence of the Strasbourg Court' in A van Aaken and I Motoc (eds), *European Convention on Human Rights and General International Law* (Oxford, Oxford University Press, 2018).

Milanović, M and Papić, T, 'As Bad as It Gets: The European Court of Human Rights's *Behrami and Saramati* Decision and General International Law' (2009) 58 *International & Comparative Law Quarterly* 267.

Mill, JS, *Considerations on Representative Government* (London, Parker, son, and Bourn 1861).

——, *Utilitarianism*, 7th edn (London, Longmans, Green, and Co, 1863).

Miller, PB, 'A Theory of Fiduciary Liability' (2010) 56 *McGill Law Journal* 235.

——, 'Justifying Fiduciary Duties' (2013) 58 *McGill Law Journal* 969.

Modirzadeh, N, 'The Dark Sides of Convergence: A Pro-Civilian Critique of the Extraterritorial Application of Human Rights Law in Armed Conflict' (2010) 86 *International Law Studies (US Naval War College)* 349.

Mommsen, T, *Römisches Staatsrecht*, Vol 3 (Berlin, S Hirzel, 1888).

Moreno-Lax, V and Costello, C, 'The Extraterritorial Application of the EU Charter of Fundamental Rights: From Territoriality to Facticity, the Effectiveness Model' in S Peers et al, *The EU Charter of Fundamental Rights* (Oxford, Bloomsbury Publishing, 2014).

Morgera, E, 'Bilateralism at the Service of Community Interests? Non-Judicial Enforcement of Global Public Goods in the Context of Global Environmental Law' (2012) 23 *European Journal of International Law* 743.

Moyn, S, *The Last Utopia* (Cambridge, Harvard University Press, 2012).

Münkler, H, 'Das Prinzip Empire' in U Speck and N Sznaider (eds), *Empire Amerika: Perspektiven einer neuen Weltordnung* (Munich, Deutsche Verlags-Anstalt, 2003).

Nagle, A, *Kill All Normies: Online Culture Wars From 4Chan And Tumblr To Trump And The Alt-Right* (Alresford, Zero Books, 2017).

Newark, F, 'The Boundaries of Nuisance' (1949) 65 *Law Quarterly Report* 480.

Neyers, JW, 'Reconceptualizing the Tort of Public Nuisance' (2017) 76 *Cambridge Law Journal* 87.

Neyers, JW and Botterell, A, 'Tate & Lyle: Pure Economic Loss and the Modern Tort of Public Nuisance' (2015) 53 *Alberta Law Review* 1031.

Niesen, P, 'The West Divided? Bentham and Kant on Law and Ethics in Foreign Policy' in D Chandler and V Heins (eds), *Rethinking Ethical Foreign Policy: Pitfalls, Paradoxes, and Possibilities* (Abingdon-New York, Routledge, 2007).

——, 'Restorative Justice in International and Cosmopolitan Law' in K Flikschuh and L Ypi (eds), *Kant and Colonialism: Historical and Critical Perspectives* (Oxford, Oxford University Press, 2014).

Nolan, A, 'Holding Non-State Actors to Account for Constitutional Economic and Social Rights Violations: Experiences and Lessons from South Africa and Ireland' (2014) 12 *International Journal of Constitutional Law* 61.

Odermatt, J, 'A Giant Step Backwards: *Opinion 2/13* on the EU's Accession to the European Convention on Human Rights' (2014) 47 *New York University Journal of International Law and Politics* 783.

——, 'The Court of Justice of the European Union: International or Domestic Court International Organisations and Courts' (2014) 3 *Cambridge Journal of International and Comparative Law* 696.

Ohlin, JD, *The Assault on International Law* (Oxford, Oxford University Press, 2015).

O'Keefe, R, 'Legal Title versus *Effectivités*: Prescription and the Promise and Problems of Private Law Analogies' (2011) 13 *International Community Law Review* 147.

Olson, M, *Logic of Collective Action Public Goods and the Theory of Groups*, 2nd edn (Cambridge, Harvard University Press, 1965).

Özsu, U, 'De-Territorializing and Re-Territorializing *Lotus*: Sovereignty and Systematicity as Dialectical Nation-Building in Early Republican Turkey' (2009) 22 *Leiden Journal of International Law* 29.

——, 'The Ottoman Empire, the Origins of Extraterritoriality, and International Legal Theory' in A Orford and F Hoffmann (eds), *The Oxford Handbook of the Theory of International Law* (Oxford, Oxford University Press, 2016).

Paasivirta E, 'The European Union and the United Nations Convention on the Law of the Sea' (2015) 38 *Fordham International Law Journal* 1045.

Pallikkathayil, J, 'Persons and Bodies' in S Kisilevsky and MJ Stone (eds), *Freedom and Force: Essays on Kant's Legal Philosophy* (Oxford, Hart Publishing, 2017).

Pengelly M, 'Trump Confirms He Is Considering Attempt to Buy Greenland' *The Guardian* (18 August 2019), www.theguardian.com/world/2019/aug/18/trump-considering-buying-greenland.

Penner J, 'On the Very Idea of Transmissible Rights' in James Penner and Henry Smith (eds), *Philosophical Foundations of Property Law* (Oxford, Oxford University Press, 2013).

Peters A, 'Humanity as the A and Ω of Sovereignty' (2009) 20 *European Journal of International Law* 513.

Pettit, P, *Republicanism: A Theory of Freedom and Government* (Oxford, Oxford University Press, 1997).

Pinheiro Walla, A, 'Global Government or Global Governance? Realism and Idealism in Kant's Legal Theory' (2017) 13 *Journal of Global Ethics* 312.

Pinker, S, 'This Week's Big Questions: The End of Men, Vegetarianism and Is Felix Baumgartner a Showoff?' *The Independent* (19 October 2012), www.independent.co.uk/voices/comment/this-weeks-big-questions-the-end-of-men-vegetarianism-and-is-baumgartner-a-show-off-8218849.html.

Pippin RB, 'Mine and Thine? The Kantian State' in P Guyer (ed), *The Cambridge Companion to Kant and Modern Philosophy* (Cambridge, Cambridge University Press, 2006).

Pogge, TW, 'Is Kant's *Rechtslehre* a Comprehensive Liberalism?' in M Timmons (ed), *Kant's Metaphysics of Morals: Interpretative Essays* (Oxford, Oxford University Press, 2002).

Poiares Maduro, M, 'Interpreting European Law: Judicial Adjudication in a Context of Constitutional Pluralism' (2007) 1 *European Journal of Legal Studies* 137.

Raible, L, 'Title to Territory and Jurisdiction in International Human Rights Law: Three Models for a Fraught Relationship' (2018) 31 *Leiden Journal of International Law* 315.
Rao, N, 'Three Concepts of Dignity in Constitutional Law' (2011) 86 *Notre Dame Law Review* 183.
Rasi, A, 'Front Polisario: A Step Forward in Judicial Review of International Agreements by the Court of Justice?' (2017) 2 *European Papers* 967.
Rawls, J, 'Kantian Constructivism in Moral Theory' (1980) 77 *The Journal of Philosophy* 515.
Raz, J, 'Legal Positivism and the Sources of Law' in *The Authority of Law* (Oxford, Oxford University Press, 1979).
——, *The Morality of Freedom* (Oxford, Clarendon Press, 1986).
——, 'Authority and Justification' in *Authority* (New York, New York University Press, 1990).
——, 'The Problem of Authority: Revisiting the Service Conception' (2006) 90 *Minnesota Law Review* 1003.
——, 'Legitimate Authority' in *The Authority of Law: Essays on Law and Morality*, 2nd edn (Oxford, Oxford University Press, 2009).
Rechtschaffen, C and Antolini, DE, 'Common Law Remedies: A Refresher' in C Rechtschaffen and DE Antolini (eds), *Creative Common Law Strategies for Protecting the Environment* (Washington, Environmental Law Institute, 2007).
Rhimes, M, 'The EU Courts Stand Their Ground: Why Are the Standing Rules for Direct Actions Still So Restrictive' (2016) 9 *European Journal of Legal Studies* 103.
Ripstein, A, 'Authority and Coercion' (2004) 32 *Philosophy & Public Affairs* 2.
——, *Force and Freedom: Kant's Legal and Political Philosophy* (Cambridge, Harvard University Press, 2009).
——, 'Just War, Regular War, and Perpetual Peace' (2016) 107 *Kant-Studien* 179.
——, *Private Wrongs* (Cambridge, Harvard University Press, 2016).
——, 'Property and Sovereignty: How to Tell the Difference' (2017) 18 *Theoretical Inquiries in Law* 243.
——, 'Kant and the Law of War' (Manuscript on File with Author) (28 June 2018).
Roberts, A, 'What is a Military Occupation?' (1985) 55 *British Yearbook of International Law* 249.
Robertson, RE, 'The Right to Food – Canada's Broken Covenant' [1989] *Canadian Human Rights Yearbook* 185.
Rossi, E and Sleat, M, 'Realism in Normative Political Theory' (2014) 9 *Philosophy Compass* 698.
Roughan, N, *Authorities: Conflicts, Cooperation, and Transnational Legal Theory* (Oxford, Oxford University Press, 2013).
Ruiz Fabri, H, 'Human Rights and State Sovereignty : Have the Boundaries Been Significantly Redrawn?' in P Alston and E MacDonald (eds), *Human Rights, Intervention, and the Use of Force* (Oxford, Oxford University Press, 2008).
Ryngaert, C, *Jurisdiction in International Law*, 2nd edn (Oxford, Oxford University Press, 2015).
——, *Unilateral Jurisdiction and Global Values* (The Hague, Eleven International Publishing, 2015).
——, 'EU Trade Agreements and Human Rights: From Extraterritorial to Territorial Obligations' (2018) 20 *International Community Law Review* 374.
——, 'The *Polisario Front* Judgment of the EU Court of Justice: A Reset of EU-Morocco Trade Relations in the Offing' (*RENFORCE Blog*, 15 January 2017), http://blog.renforce.eu/index.php/en/2017/01/15/the-polisario-front-judgment-of-the-eu-court-of-justice-a-reset-of-eu-morocco-trade-relations-in-the-offing-2/.
——, *Selfless Intervention: The Exercise of Jurisdiction in the Common Interest* (Oxford, Oxford University Press, 2020).
Samuelson, PA, 'The Pure Theory of Public Expenditure' (1954) 36 *Review of Economics and Statistics* 387.
Sand, PH, 'Principle 27: Cooperation in a Spirit of Global Partnership' in JE Viñuales (ed), *The Rio Declaration on Environment and Development: A Commentary* (Oxford, Oxford University Press, 2015).

Sands, P and Peel, J, *Principles of International Environmental Law*, 4th edn (Cambridge, Cambridge University Press 2018).
Sax JL, 'The Public Trust Doctrine in Natural Resource Law: Effective Judicial Intervention' (1970) 68 *Michigan Law Review* 471.
Scheinin, M, 'Just Another Word? Jurisdiction in the Roadmaps of State Responsibility and Human Rights' in M Langford et al (eds), *Global Justice, State Duties: The Extraterritorial Scope of Economic, Social, and Cultural Rights in International Law* (Cambridge, Cambridge University Press, 2012).
Schwartz, T and Skinner, KK, 'The Myth of the Democratic Peace' (2002) 46 *Orbis* 159.
Scott, J, 'Extraterritoriality and Territorial Extension in EU Law' (2014) 62 *American Journal of Comparative Law* 87.
Scott, J and Rajamani, L, 'EU Climate Change Unilateralism' (2012) 23 *European Journal of International Law* 469.
Seeley, JR, *The Expansion of England: Two Courses of Lectures* (1883) (Cambridge, Cambridge University Press, 2010).
Sen A, *Development as Freedom* (New York, Knopf Doubleday, 2011).
Seneca, Griffin, M, and Inwood, B (trs), *On Benefits* (Chicago, University of Chicago Press, 2011).
Shackelford, SJ, 'The Tragedy of the Common Heritage of Mankind' (2009) 28 *Stanford Environmental Law Journal* 109.
Shaffer, G, 'International Law and Global Public Goods in a Legal Pluralist World' (2012) 23 *European Journal of International Law* 669.
Shany, Y, 'Taking Universality Seriously: A Functional Approach to Extraterritoriality in International Human Rights Law' (2013) 7 *Law and Ethics of Human Rights* 49.
Shapiro SJ, 'Authority' in J Coleman and SJ Shapiro, *The Oxford Handbook of Jurisprudence and Philosophy of Law* (Oxford, Oxford University Press, 2004).
Shaw MN, *International Law*, 8th edn (Cambridge, Cambridge University Press, 2017).
Shue, H, 'Mediating Duties' (1988) 98 *Ethics* 687.
——, *Basic Rights: Subsistence, Affluence, and U.S. Foreign Policy*, 2nd edn (Princeton, Princeton University Press, 1996).
Simmons, AJ, *Justification and Legitimacy: Essays on Rights and Obligations* (Cambridge, Cambridge University Press, 2001).
Simon, D and Rigaux, A, 'Le Tribunal et Le Droit International Des Traités : Un Arrêt Déconcertant (Trib. UE, 10 Déc. 2015, Aff. T 512/12, Front Polisario c Conseil)' (2016) n° 2 *Europe: actualité du doit de l'union européenne* 5.
Skinner, Q, *Liberty Before Liberalism* (Cambridge, Cambridge University Press, 1998).
——, 'Freedom as the Absence of Arbitrary Power' in C Laborde and J Maynor (eds), *Republicanism and Political Theory* (Malden-Oxford, Blackwell, 2009).
Slobodian, Q, *Globalists: The End of Empire and the Birth of Neoliberalism* (Cambridge, Harvard University Press, 2018).
Spaventa, E, 'A Very Fearful Court? The Protection of Fundamental Rights in the European Union after Opinion 2/13' (2015) 22 *Maastricht Journal of European and Comparative Law* 35.
Spielmann, D, 'Speech to Gray's Inn: The European Court of Human Rights as Guarantor of a Peaceful Public Order in Europe' (2014), http://echr.coe.int/Documents/Speech_20141107_Spielmann_GraysInn.pdf.
Sprankling, JG, *The International Law of Property* (Oxford, Oxford University Press, 2014).
Stone, MJ, 'Kant's Apparent Positivism' in S Kisilevsky and MJ Stone (eds), *Freedom and Force: Essays on Kant's Legal Philosophy* (Oxford, Hart Publishing, 2017).
Stone Sweet, A, 'Why Europe Rejected American Judicial Review – And Why It May Not Matter' (2002) 101 *Michigan Law Review* 2744.
Stucke, ME, 'Looking at the Monopsony in the Mirror' (2012) 62 *Emory Law Journal* 1509.
Sunstein, CR, 'Beyond the Precautionary Principle' (2003) 151 *University of Pennsylvania Law Review* 1003.

Talmon, S, 'The Security Council as World Legislature' (2005) 99 *American Journal of International Law* 175.
Tasioulas, J, 'Towards a Philosophy of Human Rights' (2012) 65 *Current Legal Problems* 1.
——, 'Minimum Core Obligations: Human Rights in the Here and Now' (Washington, World Bank, 2017).
——, 'Working on the Core: A Response to Commentators' (15 June 2018), http://jamesgstewart.com/working-on-the-core-a-response-to-commentators/.
——, 'Saving Human Rights from Human Rights Law' (2019) 52 *Vanderbilt Journal of Transnational Law* 1167.
——, 'Human Dignity and the Foundations of Human Rights' in JC McCrudden (ed), *Understanding Human Dignity* (Oxford, Oxford University Press, 2013).
Tesón, FR, 'The Kantian Theory of International Law' (1992) 92 *Columbia Law Review* 53.
Tietje, C, 'The Concept of Coherence in the Treaty on European Union and the Common Foreign and Security Policy' (1997) 2 *European Foreign Affairs Review* 211.
Tomaševski, K, 'Human Rights Indicators: The Right to Food as a Test Case' in K Tomaševski and P Alston (eds), *The Right to Food* (Dorderecht, Martinus Nijhoff, 1984).
Tzeng, P, 'The State's Right to Property Under International Law' (2016) 125 *Yale Law Journal* 1805.
Tzevelekos, V, 'Reconstructing the Effective Control Criterion in Extraterritorial Human Rights Breaches: Direct Attribution of Wrongfulness, Due Diligence, and Concurrent Responsibility' (2014) 36 *Michigan Journal of International Law* 129.
Vaidhyanathan S, *Antisocial Media: How Facebook Disconnects Us and Undermines Democracy* (Oxford, Oxford University Press, 2018).
van Alebeek, R and Nollkaemper, A, 'The Legal Status of Decisions by Human Rights Treaty Bodies in National Law' in G Ulfstein and H Keller (eds), *UN Human Rights Treaty Bodies: Law and Legitimacy* (Cambridge, Cambridge University Press, 2012).
van Dam, C, *European Tort Law* (Oxford, Oxford University Press, 2013).
van der Loo G, 'Law and Practice of the EU's Trade Agreements with "Disputed" Territories: A Consistent Approach?' in I Govaere and S Garben (eds), *The Interface Between EU and International Law: Contemporary Reflections* (Oxford, Hart Publishing, 2019).
van Elsuwege P, 'EU External Action after the Collapse of the Pillar Structure: In Search of a New Balance between Delimitation and Consistency' (2010) 47 *Common Market Law Review* 987.
van Vooren, B, Blockmans, S and Wouters, J, *The EU's Role in Global Governance: The Legal Dimension* (Oxford, Oxford University Press, 2013).
Varuhas, JN, 'The Concept of "Vindication" in the Law of Torts: Rights, Interests and Damages' (2014) 34 *Oxford Journal of Legal Studies* 253.
——, *Damages and Human Rights* (Oxford, Bloomsbury Publishing, 2016).
von Feuerbach, PJA, *Kritik des natürlichen Rechts als Propädeutik zu einer Wissenschaft der natürlichen Recht* (Altona, Verlagsgesellschaft, 1796).
von Glahn, G and Taulbee, JL, *Law Among Nations: An Introduction to Public International Law* (Abingdon, Routledge 2015).
von Jhering, R, 'Im Juristischen Begriffshimmel: Ein Phantasiebild', *Scherz und Ernst in der Jurisprudenz*, 3rd edn (Leipzig, Breitkopf & Härtel, 1885).
von Verdross A, 'Forbidden Treaties in International Law' (1937) 31 *American Journal of International Law* 571.
Virgin Islands History.Org, 'A Historic Referendum' (*The Danish West-Indies*), www.virgin-islands-history.org/en/history/sale-of-the-danish-west-indian-islands-to-the-usa/a-historic-referendum/.
Waldron, J, 'Enough and as Good Left for Others' (1979) 29 *Philosophical Quarterly* 319.
——, 'Two Worries About Mixing One's Labour' (1983) 33 *Philosophical Quarterly* 37.
——, 'Kant's Legal Positivism' (1996) 109 *Harvard Law Review* 1535.
Warren, S, 'Cleaning Fairy', Allegedly Breaks into Random Home, Tidies Up' (*The Huffington Post*, 31 May 2012).

Weiler, JHH, 'The Transformation of Europe' (1991) 100 *Yale Law Journal* 2403.
——, 'The Political and Legal Culture of European Integration: An Exploratory Essay' (2011) 9 *International Journal of Constitutional Law* 678.
Weinrib, EJ, 'Poverty and Property in Kant's System of Rights' (2002) 78 *Notre Dame Law Review* 795.
——, 'Private Law and Public Right' (2011) 61 *University of Toronto Law Journal* 191.
——, *Corrective Justice* (Oxford, Oxford University Press, 2012).
Welwod, W, 'Of the Community and Propriety of the Seas (1613)' in D Armitage (ed), R Hakluyt (tr), Hugo Grotius, *The Free Sea* (Indianapolis, Liberty Fund, 2004).
Werner W, 'Mankind's Territory and the Limits of International Law-Making' in R Liivoja and J Petman (eds), *International Law-making: Essays in Honour of Jan Klabbers* (Abingdon, Routledge, 2014).
Wilde, R, 'Human Rights Beyond Borders at the World Court: The Significance of the International Court of Justice's Jurisprudence on the Extraterritorial Application of International Human Rights Law Treaties' (2013) 12 *Chinese Journal of International Law* 639.
Willaschek, M, 'Why the *Doctrine of Right* Does Not Belong in the *Metaphysics of Morals*: On Some Basic Distinctions in Kant's Moral Philosophy' (1997) 5 *Jahrbuch für Recht und Ethik* 205.
——, 'Right and Coercion: Can Kant's Conception of Right Be Derived from His Moral Theory?' (2009) 17 *International Journal of Philosophical Studies* 49.
Williams, A, *EU Human Rights Policies: A Study in Irony* (Oxford, Oxford University Press, 2005).
Wood, A, 'The Supreme Principle of Morality' in P Guyer (ed), *The Cambridge Companion to Kant and Modern Philosophy* (Cambridge, Cambridge University Press, 2006).
Woolman, S, 'The Amazing, Vanishing Bill of Rights' (2007) 124 *South African Law Journal* 762.
World Bank, *World Development Report 2008: Agriculture for Development* (Washington, World Bank, 2007).
Zielonka, J, *Europe as Empire: The Nature of the Enlarged European Union* (Oxford, Oxford University Press, 2007).
——, 'America and Europe: Two Contrasting or Parallel Empires?' (2011) 4 *Journal of Political Power* 337.
Zimmermann, R, *The Law of Obligations: Roman Foundations of the Civilian Tradition* (Oxford, Oxford University Press, 1996).
——, 'Innkeepers' Liability – Die Entwicklung Der Gastwirtshaftung in England' in A Heldrich, J Prölss and I Koller (eds), *Festschrift für Claus-Wilhelm Canaris zum 70. Geburtstag*, Vol 2 (Munich, Beck, 2007) 1435.
Zylberman, A, 'Why Human Rights? Because of You' (2016) 24 *Journal of Political Philosophy* 321.
——, 'Human Rights and the Rights of States: A Relational Account' (2016) 46 *Canadian Journal of Philosophy* 291.

Index

accountability 149, 154, 182, 190, 225, 227
of states to foreign stakeholders 56–63
of EU to distant strangers 20, 190, 202–3
evasion of external 149
fiduciary 20, 201
human rights as principles of 'public' fiduciary 19, 100–3, 154, 173, 182
EU's democratic and accountability deficit 118–19
action
of EU institutions, review of in cases of manifest error 37
external dimensions 8, 9, 25, 30
internal dimensions 8
adscriptus glebae 129, 147
aircraft emissions
and harm 140
imposition of charges upon foreign aeroplanes 37
offsetting requirements 37–8, 48, 53, 68
positive obligations in case of 130–1
territorial extension 27, 28
see also pollution
alienation 90, 97
social fragmentation and 147
American Declaration of Independence 3
animal welfare regulation 40, 147
antitrust law, effects doctrine 19, 47
Arendt, Hannah 5, 158–9, 168, 184
loophole of 182–5
authority
and control 66
de jure and *de facto* 173
defining 44
in context of EU–Morocco agreements 198–206
fiduciary power as form of 85
and freedom 95–6
and human rights jurisdiction 167–88
Arendt's loophole 182–5
attribution of conduct 178
capability 169–75
control 175–82
legitimate expectation 172–3
occupation cases 174
special legal relationship 171–3
Kantian conception 168
personality and property rights 96–7
versus 'soft power' 45–6
in a State versus an Empire 76
see also power and authority in the wider world

Bartels, Lorand 17, 22–3, 190, 200, 202
compliance interpretation 28–36, 43
legal effects and spatial scope of EU law 36–9
see also compliance interpretation
Beck, Ulrich 76–7
Benvenisti, Eyal 17, 18, 38, 41, 42, 47, 148, 152, 204
global condominium metaphor 57
harmless interests, obligation to accommodate 61, 62, 63
normative bases (moral intuitions) 58
restricted Pareto optimality condition 62, 63, 137
sovereign trusteeship 55, 56–63, 64–5, 68, 78, 85, 92, 137
on UDHR 58, 65
Besson, Samantha 20, 158–9, 162, 167, 168, 183, 184
***Bosphorus* presumption** 151
Byrd, Sharon 5

capability, authority and human rights jurisdiction 169–75
Categorical Imperative (Kant) 6–10
climate change 25, 41, 52, 134
global public goods 140, 144, 147
see also Emissions Trading Directive (2008/101); Emissions Trading Scheme; pollution
coercion 46, 49
in Kant's philosophy of right 8, 10–11, 15, 18, 83
equality of action and reaction 12

limitations upon right to provide public goods 131–2
public purpose and necessity 145
and right to regulate global public goods 133
torts, division of 87
see also force
colonialism 117, 215
and territory 108
Kant's anti-colonialism 107–9, 144–5
Commentary to the Maastricht Principles 33
Committee on Economic, Social and Cultural Rights (CESCR), General Comments 30–1
Common Agricultural Policy (CAP) 2
Common Commercial Policy 25
Common Foreign and Security Policy (CFSP) 29, 71–2, 149
Decision 198
erroneous rule in 50
fact pattern 201
General Court interpretation 50, 199
and human rights 167
legal effects 201
and *Polisaro* Decision 200, 201
power and authority 49, 50
reasoning 36–7
relevance 200
rule in 50, 187–8
sovereign equality principle 36
standing 36
see also EU–Morocco agreements
compensation
expropriation 124
for third states for unilateral measures affecting them 63
as the remedy for violations of property rights 86–91
requirement of tangible economic injury 129–30
tort law 88–9, 91
vulnerable people 134n56
wrongful damage 91
compliance interpretation 17, 22–3, 44
Bartels on 28–36, 43
general international law, jurisdiction under 34–5
human rights jurisdiction 31–4
and legal effects 37
standing 36
conferral of powers principle 70
constitutional objectives, policy consistency/coherence 69–72
constitutional review, compared with judicial review 195
constitutionalism 16, 57, 229
constructive trust, theory of 203
see also negotiorum gestio
control 55, 69, 75, 76, 84, 123
alien 179
authority and human rights jurisdiction 175–82, 177n115, 178, 184n153
factual 179
over social media platforms 147, 148
personal 183
physical 33, 172, 178, 179, 182
territorial 34, 66, 167, 169, 175, 179, 181
control orders (UK) 101, 102
Corell Memorandum 204
see also Western Sahara
corrective justice, 'rational billiard board' model of 13, 87–8
cosmopolitan rights 132, 133
Court of Justice of the European Union (CJEU)
invocation of *Lotus* judgment (1927) 41–4
justification of extraterritorial legislation 22
rejection of 'effects' doctrine 19, 37–8, 49–50, 69, 122, 146, 225
Crawford, James 113–14

damage and injury 86–91
damnum iniuria datum **(wrongful deprivation)** 86, 89
democratic participation, and sovereign trusteeship 62
dignitas **(status, honour or worth)** 86, 89
dignity
as freedom 18
and global public goods 123
as independence 77–81, 200–1
and well-being 159
dispute resolution 104–5, 146
inter-state disputes 150–1
distant strangers
authority over 19–20
see also authority
as 'constructive' subjects 187
entitlement to alter legal rights and obligations of 20
EU asserting power over 154
exclusion from benefits of government, Benvenisti's argument from the need to justify 59

factual effects of extraterritorial measures over 22, 36
human rights of 14
legal effects of extraterritorial measures over 22
secret nocturnal visitor problem 78–9, 89
self-determination 172
trusteeship obligations to 60
unilateral assertions of authority over, whether defensible 18, 224–6
whether EU fulfils obligations 20, 227–9
whether EU owes obligations towards 27, 226–7

dual illegality 62, 68
see also public law taboo

Dworkin, Ronald 10–11, 12, 13, 71, 99–100

effects doctrine 19, 33, 35, 49, 121
cross-border effects 136
harms and wrongs 69
in US antitrust law 47
partial adoption by General Court of 49
rejection by ECJ of 19, 37–8, 49–50, 69, 122, 146, 225
see also factual effects of extraterritorial measures; legal effects of extraterritorial measures

Emissions Trading Scheme (EU) 27–8, 52, 53–4
coercive nature of 49
legislation for humanity 60
non-exclusionary logic of 48–9

environmental law
harm prevention principle 139, 140–1
international public trusteeship 127n25
'no-harm' principle 19, 122, 139, 140
public good, regulation as 129
state obligation to provide regulation 130–1
United States 126

equity
equity-based theory of unilateral measures 61–2
in Kant's philosophy of right 85

equivalence/non-duplication of measures 61–3

***espace juridique* doctrine** 169, 188

ethics 6–7
relationship between law and 6, 8–9, 11–3, 85, 166
in foreign policy 14, 159, 166, 228–9

EU courts
access to 20, 190–8
EU-Morocco agreements 191–2, 198–206
standing for judicial review before EU courts 192–8
direct and individual concern under Article 263 TFEU 195–8, 206
legal effects requirement 193–5

EU-Morocco agreements 198–206
de facto application 212–15
law on international responsibility of states 201–2

European Convention on Human Rights (ECHR) 20, 30, 66
jurisprudence on human rights obligations to distant strangers 155
state jurisdiction under Article 1 167, 168n1, 169, 170, 184, 186

European Court of Human Rights (ECtHR) 65–6

European Union (EU)
critique of integration 117–18
imperialism, suggestions of 52, 73–7, 146, 188, 225
Kantian themes 4
supranationalism of 116–18, 151
evangelism, and multilateralism 25–8
external action 8, 9, 25, 30

extraterritorial jurisdiction 1, 14, 17, 22, 121–53
competition 49–50
global public goods, provision of 120, 121–53
see also global public goods
harm, irrelevance of 139–44
harm-based justifications 19
human rights, and 154–89
as 'philanthropy' 166–7
'imperial,' described as 72–3
public goods, provision of
global 132–46
limitations upon right to provide 131–2
other than roads and waterways 128–31
theory 122–32
public purpose and necessity 144–6
versus territorial extension technique 40–1, 47, 50–1
unilateralism 120
see also factual effects of extraterritorial measures; legal effects of extraterritorial measures

factual effects of extraterritorial measures, versus legal effects 22, 36, 52, 193
'Brussels Effect' in corporate regulation 46
fiduciary obligations 85, 86, 127–8, 152, 194
inseverably compound 101
of occupying forces 204
of trustees *de son tort* 201, 203, 205
fiduciary relationships 85, 86, 167, 204, 205, 215
'a right to a person akin to a right to a thing' 84, 85, 97, 100
arising in wrongful conditions 173–4, 203–5
fiduciary relationships involving only 'factual' effects 86, 194
fiduciary state
control orders, suspected terrorists 101–2
environmental regulation 130–1
fiduciary purpose 102–3
and human rights 100–3
sovereigns as fiduciaries 100–1
force 7, 10–12, 14
see also coercion
Frederiksen, Mette (Danish Prime Minister) 108–9
freedom
and authority 95–6
'external' 9
and force 10
'innate' right to 83
liberal concept 9
philosophy of right (Kant) 7, 9–12, 80, 83, 95–6
and sovereignty 103
sui juris, free man as 83
Front Polisario (Sahrawi national liberation movement), Western Sahara 190, 191, 206–7
agreement with Mauritania 207
individual concern requirement 207
see also Sahrawi liberation movement, Western Sahara

General Court
disputed territory terminology 212
Rules of Procedure 208
global commons 140, 142, 147, 225
global justice 3, 13–14, 57, 68
global public goods 1, 17, 52, 132–46
concept 54
extraterritorial jurisdiction to provide 120, 121–53
harm, irrelevance of 139–44
multilateralism 53
non-rivalrous/non-excludable 17, 63, 64
public purpose and necessity 144–6
right to regulate 132–9
sovereign trusteeship 63, 64–5
state's right of jurisdiction 132
territorial extension 22, 23, 39–40
unilateralism 115
see also extraterritorial jurisdiction; public goods
greenhouse gas emissions 53
Grotius, Hugo 17, 55, 63, 79, 94, 104, 133
on defence of the freedom of the high seas 61, 63
regular war tradition 103
Gulf War (second) 4

Habermas, Jürgen 4, 7, 7n25
harm
attempts to abolish distinction between harms and wrongs 67
attenuation of concept 140
harm-based theories of jurisdiction 144
harmlessness 78–9
harmless interests, obligation to accommodate 61, 62, 63
irrelevance of 139–44
'no-harm' or harm prevention principle, in environmental law 19, 122, 139, 140
and public nuisance 125
substantive and procedural harm prevention 140–3
wrongs and harms 18, 63–9, 144
compensation 88
distinction between 67, 77, 113, 144
moral damage 114, 142
public actors and human rights jurisdiction 65–7
torts, division of 86–91
well-being, argument from 67–9
see also torts
Harris, Jim 93, 94n62, 110n150, 110n151
hegemonic states 77, 78, 144
High Representative of the Union for Foreign Affairs and Security Policy 118
high seas
and emissions 28, 37, 46, 47
fishing regulation 39

freedom of 37, 61, 74, 133
and *Lotus* judgment 41
non-rivalrous/non-excludable global public goods 63, 133
piracy, combating 149
and *Shrimp/Turtle* 49
see also waters, navigable
highways 126
Hobbes, Thomas 4, 10n42, 57n19
homelessness 128
human rights
and allocation of human rights obligations 158–9, 163
as background ethical objectives 159
as 'basic' rights 163
clauses in treaties 166–7
compliance interpretation 17, 31–4
dignity as independence 77–81
of distant strangers 14
effects doctrine, rejection in *Banković* 33
and equal moral worth 58
extraterritorial obligations 154–89
and fiduciary state 100–3
interests and needs 164
international human rights law (IHRL) 156
international norms, turning into binding EU law 28
jurisdiction *see* human rights jurisdiction (state jurisdiction)
Kantian philosophy 156, 162, 163, 165
as legal and directed 160–5
legal claims for breach of public fiduciary obligations by political authorities 19
little historical continuity in term 154
'moral theories of law 156–60
''negative' obligations to respect and refrain from violation 20, 28–9, 160
new legal order, guardianship of fundamental rights 150
normative theory 154, 155
'positive' obligations to protect, fulfil and prevent violation 17, 20, 28–9, 36
public fiduciary 156–67
relational rights and obligations 163
residual or subsidiary duties relating to poverty 162
as rights and as a philanthropy 166–7
'status-based' theories 164
violations of 17, 20, 28–9, 36, 99, 163
see also European Convention on Human Rights (ECHR); European Court of Human Rights (ECtHR); Universal Declaration of Human Rights (UDHR), 1948
Human Rights Committee (HRC) 169, 170
human rights jurisdiction (state jurisdiction) 31, 38, 66
and authority 167–88
Arendt's loophole 182–5
attribution of conduct 178
capability 169–75
control 175–82
legitimate expectation 172–3
occupation cases 174
special legal relationship 171–3
CESCR General Comments 31–2
conflation with general rules of jurisdiction in international law 167
Strasbourg Court, study choice 155
and territorial extension 31–44, 185–8

immanent critique 13–16
imperialism 72–3, 77
independence
dignity as 77–81, 200–1
innate right of states to 103
and private law 91
indeterminacy, state of nature, defects in 92
***iniuria* (wrongful use)** 86, 89
International Civil Aviation Organization 27
International Court of Justice (ICJ) 109
on presumed consent 138–9
international law
general international law, jurisdiction under 34–5
and international relations 15
of occupation 204
positivist conceptions 56
property and personality rights in 103–14
territory, as property or body 105–9
property relations in 109, 111
International Law Commission (ILC), Drafting Committee 113
international legal order, Kantian
building blocks of general theory of law 83–97
legislating on property and personality 96–7
state of nature, defects in 91–6
torts, division of 86–91

dispute resolution 104–5
fiduciary state 97–103
and human rights 100–3
separate, public person of the state 97–100
foedus pacificum (congress of democratic republics) 115–16
legislatures, lacking of 104, 105
permanent congress of states 104
and private law 82–130
property and personality 103–14
and effective administration 107
no property, only personality 109–14
problems with property model of territory 107–8, 109
territory, as property or body 105–9
theory of republican international order 12, 18, 19, 115–16, 146–7
International Tribunal for the Law of the Sea (ITLOS) 148
interpretation, legal
dynamic, purposive or teleological 136
revisionist 136
see also compliance interpretation

judicial review procedure
direct and individual concern under 195–8, 206
Polisaro litigation 190, 191
jurisdiction
conflation of human rights and general rules of jurisdiction 167
extraterritorial 121–53
under general international law 34–5
harm-based theories 144
human rights *see* human rights jurisdiction (state jurisdiction)
illegal excess of 37, 40–1
jurisdictional reasonableness 68
objective territorial 35
ordinary rules 23
prescriptive 23, 39, 51, 136, 179
territorial principle 78
treaty provisions 160
unilateral jurisdiction theory 68–9, 146

Kagan, Robert 4
Kant, Immanuel 1, 3, 6, 9, 15, 55n14, 91, 135, 144, 168
Categorical Imperative 6–8
on choice 7, 9, 10, 84n8, 84n10
citations to 21
on coercion 8, 10–11, 15, 18, 83
on colonialism 117, 144
definition of a person and of a thing 83
on freedom 7, 9–12, 80, 83, 95–6
on human rights 156, 162, 163, 165
Innate Right of Humanity 83
Lauterpacht compared 107–8
on law of market overt 124n9
Locke compared 93
on money 129
philosophy of right *see* personality rights; philosophy of right (Kant); property rights
on property rights 84n5, 85, 86, 90, 92–4, 96–7
on public law 12, 85
'rational billiard ball' model of corrective justice 13, 87–8
rediscovery of *Doctrine of Right* 5–6
republican democracy of *see* republican theory of international order
on state of nature 91–6, 103
original contract 91–6
postulate of public right 95n71
on serfs 123
on sexual intercourse, legality of 96
on the state of nature 105
on territory 105–6
Universal Principle of Right 7
Kellogg-Briand Pact 103
Kissinger, Henry 118
Kompetenz-Kompetenz 118

Lauterpacht, Hersch 97–8, 106–7, 108
legal effects of extraterritorial measures
authority and human rights jurisdiction 179
and factual effects 36, 52, 193
and spatial scope of EU law 36–44
standing 193–5
territorial extension technique 50–1, 187
legal personality 71
legal positivism 6
Lex Aquilia 89n37
Lisbon Treaty ***see*** **Treaty of Lisbon**
Locke, John 17, 55, 59, 92–3, 94
Lotus **judgment (1927)** 52, 56
and *Air Transport* 41, 42, 52
CJEU jurisprudence 41–4
independence rationale compared 136
PCIJ, Turkey's submission before 41, 136n62

positivist conception of international law 56
revisionist interpretation 136
loyalty, duty of (EU) 70

Mann, FA 37, 42
Milanovic, Marko 20, 31n38, 34, 65, 66n83, 159–60
authority and human rights jurisdiction 175–6, 178, 179, 184
Mill, John Stuart 17, 55, 58
missionary principle 53–81
Air Transport (Case C-366/10) 55, 68–9
blurred frontiers 69–77
borders versus frontiers 76
constitutional objectives, police consistency/coherence 69–72
dignity as independence 77–81
harms and wrongs 63–9
and political messianism 77
sovereign trusteeship of humanity 56–63
and territorial extension 72–7
monadic concepts 163, 164–5
moral damage 114, 142
Morocco
fishing zones 192
presence in the Western Sahara 206, 207, 211
waters under jurisdiction 192
see also EU–Morocco agreements; Western Sahara
multilateralism
and emission trading obligations 61
and evangelism 25–8
and global public goods 53

nationality principle
general international law 35
spatial scope and legal effects 37
necessity, and public purpose 144–6
'negative' obligations to respect and refrain from human rights violations 20, 160
negotiorum gestio 203
see also constructive trust
Neo-Kantianism 7
Newtonian physics 11
'no-harm' or harm prevention principle
environmental law 19, 122, 139, 140
see also harm
non-intervention 67
non-reciprocity, state of nature, defects in 92
normative power 45, 76n134, 83, 168
nuisance, public and private 122, 124–5

obedience 46
Ombudsman, EU 159
other-regardingness 57
original contract 91–6
interlocking operation of legislature, executive and judiciary 95
see also Kant, Immanuel

Pareto optimality condition, restricted, Eyal Benvenisti's 62, 63, 137
peremptory obligations 94
personality rights 96–7
authority 96
inalienability 91, 96, 97
international law 103–14
legislating on personality 96–7
with property 103–14
property rights distinguished 93–4
'state personality' 97
torts 86, 89
without property 105–9
see also property rights
Philadelphia Constitutional Convention (1787) 25–6
Pinker, Steven 4
***Plaumann v Commission* (Case 25/62), and standing** 196, 198, 209, 210
policy consistency/coherence, values and constitutional objectives 69–72
political messianism 77
pollution
air/aviation 53, 147
climate change-inducing 134
haze, in Singapore 53, 144n98
transboundary environmental 139, 140
victims 130
see also aircraft emissions; Emissions Trading Scheme
'positive' obligations to protect, fulfil and prevent human rights violations 17, 20, 36
postnational constitutionalism 16
power and authority 22–52
deference 46
distinction between 44–51
obedience 46
post-Lisbon Articles 23–8
'soft power' and authority 45–6
precautionary principle 142–4, 146

preliminary reference procedure 192, 193, 216–23
prescriptive jurisdiction 23, 39, 51, 136, 179
private law
damage and injury 86–91
forms 82–130
immanent critique and private law analogies 16
private right 83–97
property and personality, legislating on 96–7
Roman 18, 82, 83, 86, 89–90, 126
state of nature, defects in 91–6
private nuisance 18, 89n34, 122, 125, 129–30
Process and Production Methods (PPM) 47, 87
property rights
original acquisition of 92–5
authority 96
contracts for service 93
damnum iniuria datum (wrongful deprivation) 89
immovable property, Roman law 106
and international law 103–14
international law 103–14
ius disponendi de rea sua (right to dispose of a thing at will) 110
Kantian philosophy 84n5, 85, 86, 90, 92–4, 96–7
legislating on property 96–7
mixing of labour 93
personality rights distinguished 93–4
personality without property 109–14
and private law 96–7
self-ownership 90
state of nature, defects in 92–3
states as bearers 127
territory as property 105–9
transmissibility of property 96, 97
see also personality rights
proportionality principle 131–2
protected interests 79
protective principle
general international law 35
spatial scope and legal effects 37
public fiduciary rights, human rights as 156–67, 181
human rights as legal and directed 160–5
human rights as rights and as philanthropy 166–7
'moral' theories of human rights law 156–60
public goods
alternative conception 121–2
concept 54
distribution problem 55
environmental regulation 129
global *see* global public goods
inherently public goods 126
limitations upon right to provide 131–2
money 129
other than roads and waterways 128–31
Ripstein's theory 122–32, 147
compared with 'conventional' approach 126
and environmental approaches 126
limitations upon right to provide 131
precursors 126–7
social welfare systems 128–9
state obligation to provide 122–5
theory of 122–32
public law, and private law 12, 85
public law taboo 68
see also dual illegality concept
public nuisance 122, 124–5
common law 125
forms 125
global public nuisance 133
interference with 125
and special damage 125n15, 125n16
wrongfulness of 126
public right
human rights and fiduciary state 100–3
interference with 125
and international legal order 97–103
separate, public person of the state 97–100
Shue on 98
public trust doctrine 126, 127
Pufendorf, Samuel Freiherr von 104

Raible, Lea 20, 180–1
Rawls, John 6, 7, 9n41
Raz, Joseph 168, 173
reasonableness 35, 62, 68
regulation
animal welfare 40
'Brussels Effect' in corporate regulation 46
environmental 129
as a public good 129
right to regulate global public goods 132–9
state obligation to provide 130–1
relational rights and obligations 163, 164–5

republican theory of international order 12, 18, 115–16, 184
appraising the EU 146–7
extraterritorial jurisdiction 19, 147
reputation 91, 143n96
res publica 126
restitution 88, 89, 91
'Thomistic' or 'scholastic' theories of 88, 113
rights
acquired 83, 93–4, 96
to compensation *see* compensation
cosmopolitan 132, 133
innate 93–4, 96
Kant on
right to a person akin to a right to a thing 84
innate and acquired rights 83, 93–4, 96
personality rights *see* personality rights
property rights *see* property rights
right against a person 84
right to a 'thing' 83–4
rights and virtues 13
Universal Principle of Right 7, 80
legal 85, 154
moral 158
see also Doctrine of Right (Kant); human rights; philosophy of right (Kant)
Ripstein, Arthur 5–6, 84n5, 84n7, 121–2
kidnap of child example 173–4
on roads 124–32
theory of public goods 122–32, 147
compared with 'conventional' approach 126
and environmental approaches 126
limitations upon right to provide 131
precursors 126–7
on torts 87
see also global public goods; public goods
roads 124–6
rule-utilitarianism 78–9
Ryngaert, Cedric 39–40, 41, 42, 47, 54n4, 55n12, 67–8, 78
dual illegality concept 62, 68
list of maxims 62–3
unilateral jurisdiction theory 68–9

Sahrawi liberation movement, Western Sahara 20, 192, 198, 201, 220–1, 222
claim to self-determination 206
and Front Polisario 210, 215
Sax, Joseph 127
Scott, Joanne 27n17, 28n22, 40–1, 47, 50–1
Shany, Yuval 20, 169–72, 174n103, 184
***Shrimp/Turtle case* (1998)**
and nature of territorial extension 46, 47, 50
possible violation of a bargain between states 51
slavery 9–10, 80
alieni juris, slaves as 83
contracts for 95
Slobodian, Quinn 117–18
social contract theories 59
sovereignty
and freedom 103
fundamental characteristics 181–2
interdependence of individual sovereigns 59
necessity for sovereign states 58
'patrimonial' sovereign 108
pooling of 117
and self-determination 58
sovereign trusteeship theory 56–63, 64–5, 68, 78, 85, 92, 135–6
standing of distant strangers
EU law and courts 190–223
legal effects requirement 193–5
Plaumann Decision 196, 198, 209, 210
privileged applicants 36
procedural question of 36
required by Article 263 TFEU 198
sovereign equality principle 36
state of nature
defects in 91–6, 103
see also Kant, Immanuel
states
bearers of property rights 127
Benvenisti on role of 57
conceived as aggregations of private persons 98–9
fiduciary *see* fiduciary state
hegemonic 77, 78, 144
jurisdiction *see* human rights jurisdiction (state jurisdiction)
law of state responsibility 112–13, 201–2
permanent congress of 104
as public fiduciaries of subjects 18
public goods, obligation to provide 122–5
separate, public person of the state 97–100
state jurisdiction *see under* human rights
state personhood 98

status as public authorities 127
and territory 135
see also personality rights; property rights; sovereignty
substantive and procedural harm prevention 140–3
Sunstein, Cass 142, 143

Tasioulas, John 156–61, 162, 164, 165
taxation, extraterritorial 43–4
territorial extension 17, 20
extraterritorial jurisdiction compared 40–1, 47, 50–1
extraterritorial measures with legal effects 168, 188, 200
human rights jurisdiction 31–4, 185–8, 226
and missionary principle 72–7
nature of territorial extension 46–51
Shrimp/Turtle compared 46, 47, 50
see also extraterritorial jurisdiction; power and authority in the wider world
territory
as property or body 105–9
territoriality principle 35, 78
legal effects of extraterritorial measures 37, 43
see also territorial extension
terrorism 101–2
third countries
bilateral agreements with the EU 25
equivalent measures 61
investment treaties with the EU 159, 166
partnerships with 24, 27
torts
compensation, right to 88
damnum iniuria datum (wrongful deprivation) 86, 89
deprivation of means, characterised as 87
division of 85, 86–91
gain-based remedies 88
iniuria (wrongful use) 86, 89
restitution 88, 89, 91
torture 163, 164
***Trail Smelter Arbitration* (1941)**
human rights jurisdiction 33
'no-harm' principle 139, 140
and public goods 54
treaties
between EU and third countries 159, 166, 190
investment 159, 166
ordinary language, read in 217
illegal treaties 217
forbidden because prohibiting a state from protecting its citizens abroad 181n143
relative effects of (*pacta tertiis nec nocent nec prosunt* principle) 199, 201, 212, 214, 215, 218
violating *erga omnes* norms 217
Treaty of Lisbon
pillar structure of the EU, abolition 71
reforms 118, 197–8
Treaty on European Union (TEU) 18, 22
basic objectives, obligatory force 69
Common Foreign and Security Policy (CFSP) 149
concepts of policy consistency and coherence 69
external and internal matters in Article 21 24–5, 29
global public goods and extraterritorial rights 23–4
and human rights as ethical objectives 159
human rights as rights and as philanthropy 166
and legal accountability 119
on legal personality of the EU 116
on values 27, 55
Treaty on the Functioning of the European Union (TFEU)
direct and individual concern under Article 263 195–8, 206
trespass 18, 64, 79
physical invasion requirement 129

unilateralism
equity-based theory of unilateral measures 62
in extraterritorial jurisdiction 120
global public goods 115
as power to create new trespassory obligations 94
problems of 67–8
state of nature, defects in 92
unilateral assertions of authority over distant strangers, whether defensible 18, 224–6
unilateral jurisdiction theory 68–9, 146
United States
antitrust law 47
Endangered Species Act 46
environmental law 126

purchase of Danish West Indies (1917) 107, 108
withdrawal from Paris Climate Accord 53
Universal Principle of Right (Kant) 7, 80
utilitarianism 160

Vaidhyanathan, Siva 147–8
values
challenging measures incompatible with 72
and constitutional objectives 69–77
and philosophy of right (Kant) 14
plurality of 157, 159–60
Treaty on European Union (TEU) 27, 55
Vattel, Emer 104
Von Jhering, Rudolf 223

waters, navigable 125, 126
Weiler, Joseph 77, 117, 118
well-being
and dignity 159
plurality of values 159–60
wrongs and harms 67–9
Western Sahara
Corell Memorandum 204
legal and political struggle over 190
litigation over 20
mislabelling as disputed territory 207–9
Morocco's presence in 206, 207, 211
Sahrawi liberation movement 20, 72, 191, 192
World Trade Organization (WTO) 46–7, 118
see also Shrimp/Turtle case (1998)
wrongs and harms 18, 63–9, 144
see also harm

Zielonka, Jan 73

www.ingramcontent.com/pod-product-compliance
Lightning Source LLC
Chambersburg PA
CBHW071352220926
51613CB00008B/94